ALSO BY JOHN MOSIER

Grant: A Biography

Cross of Iron:
The Rise and Fall of the German War Machine,
1918–1945

The Blitzkrieg Myth:
How Hitler and the Allies Misread the Strategic
Realities of World War II

The Myth of the Great War:
A New Military History of World War I

HITLER VS. STALIN

THE EASTERN FRONT, 1941–1945

JOHN MOSIER

Simon & Schuster Paperbacks

New York   London   Toronto   Sydney

Simon & Schuster Paperbacks
1230 Avenue of the Americas
New York, NY 10020

Previously published as *Deathride*

First Simon & Schuster paperback edition June 2011

SIMON & SCHUSTER PAPERBACKS and colophon are
registered trademarks of Simon & Schuster, Inc.

For information about special discounts for bulk purchases,
please contact Simon & Schuster Special Sales at
1-866-506-1949 or business@simonandschuster.com.

The Simon & Schuster Speakers Bureau can bring authors
to your live event. For more information or to book an event,
contact the Simon & Schuster Speakers Bureau at
1-866-248-3049 or visit our website at www.simonspeakers.com.

Designed by Renata Di Biase
Maps by Paul Pugliese

Manufactured in the United States of America

10 9 8 7 6 5

Library of Congress Cataloging-in-Publication Data
Mosier, John, date.
    Deathride : Hitler vs. Stalin : The Eastern Front, 1941–1945 / John Mosier.—
1st Simon & Schuster hardcover ed.
        p.   cm.
    Includes bibliographical references and index.
    1. World War, 1939–1945—Campaigns—Eastern Front.   2. World War,
1939–1945—Germany.   3. World War, 1939–1945—Soviet Union.   4. Hitler, Adolf,
1889–1945—Military leadership.   5. Stalin, Joseph, 1879–1953—Military leadership.
I. Title.   II. Title: Deathride.
    D764.M736 2010
    940.54'217—dc22   2010003334
ISBN 978-1-4165-7348-7
ISBN 978-1-4165-7350-0 (pbk)
ISBN 978-1-4165-7702-7 (ebook)

CONTENTS

Military history is nothing but a tissue of fictions and legends, only a form of literary invention; reality counts for very little in such an affair.

Gaston de Pawlowski, Dans les rides du front

HITLER VS. STALIN

I

INTRODUCTION:
PSEUDO-REALITY AND THE SOVIET UNION

In appearance everything happens in Russia as elsewhere.
There is no difference except at the bottom of things.

Marquis de Custine, *Letters from Russia* (1839)[1]

T he war between Joseph Stalin and Adolf Hitler was a savage
conflict that raged over an enormous battlefront stretching
from the Baltic to the Black Sea. In less than a year and a
half, German, Hungarian, and Romanian armies penetrated into
the depths of the Russian heartland, reaching historic towns on
the Volga and the Don whose last experience of invasion had
been centuries before. During the course of the next two and a
half years the Red Army retraced that journey in the opposite direction, all the way to the Oder and the Danube, reaching cities
whose last experience of Russian soldiery had been almost precisely 140 years earlier, during the Napoleonic Wars.

The enormous geographic scale of the conflict was more than
matched by the savagery of the fighting, the casualties sustained
by the combatants, and the appalling level of suffering inflicted
on the hapless civilians of European Russia and central Europe,
whose peoples had not experienced such a series of calamities
since the Thirty Years War. The scale of suffering and ruin was
so vast as to be unimaginable. Hitler's wicked and ghastly geno-
cidal campaign against European Jewry is almost submerged in

this litany of horror and depravity, even though that genocide was one of his two main goals.

Hitler's other aim was the destruction of Bolshevism. Our loathing and consternation regarding the Holocaust tends to make us see these two aims as entirely separate. But before the outbreak of the war on September 1, 1939, Hitler's great public relations coup with his fellow Germans and Austrians was to meld the two. Indeed from his public speeches in the 1930s, one could draw the not unreasonable inference that his antipathy toward the Jewish people was largely restricted to those who had espoused Bolshevism.[2]

A consideration of that complex notion lies outside the aims of this book, as does the Holocaust itself. Suffice it to say that to accomplish those two tasks Hitler was willing to see the Third Reich, that mighty state that he had spent decades creating, destroyed. But today the prosperous, peaceful, and culturally rich Jewish communities of Germany, Austria, central Europe, and the Baltic can hardly be said to exist. But neither does the USSR.

That by the first week of May 1945, Hitler was already dead, his armies destroyed, the cities of what he had intended to be a great imperial realm shattered by American and British bombers, should not lull us into forgetting the astonishing extent to which Hitler's evil empire nearly triumphed.

Stalin, who planned his own holocaust in secret while basking in the world's admiration as the man who beat Hitler, survived his former ally by barely eight years. By that time, the allegedly victorious citizens of the USSR, no less than those of their client states, were beginning to envy the defeated Germans and Austrians. Hitler had boasted that the empire he created would last a thousand years. The one Stalin had forged collapsed before the millennium. The only enduring legacy of both men is our memory of the mountains of corpses they left behind.

Given the extent to which Hitler persuaded or tempted the citizens of Austria and Germany, two of the world's most culturally and intellectually advanced nations, into carrying out his nefarious schemes, his infamy, and theirs, naturally preoccupies us. We sometimes forget that Hitler's chief adversary for the greater part of the Second World War was in no way less wicked. When the historical record is examined fairly, the difference between the depravity of the two men is difficult to discern. Most of the perceived differences are a function of Stalin's one unquestionable triumph: the image of himself and of the state he largely created.

In the decades since his death, the world has slowly come to an understanding of his remarkable success in that endeavor, together with an awareness of his innumerable crimes. There are still die-hard apologists to be found for the man and his system, and not only in Russia, but by and large they are in pretty much the same global circus as Holocaust deniers.

The sorry history of Stalin's propagandistic triumphs, and its slow unraveling, also lies outside the scope of this book. However, such an understanding is necessary in order to comprehend the reality of the war between the two evil empires. Stalin's great trick was to convince the world that the Red Army had beaten Hitler outright; at that task he succeeded brilliantly. That the state he presided over was, in the words of one economic historian, a "victorious loser," is realized either imperfectly or not at all; one frequently has the impression that the collapse of the Soviet state and its main satellites is seen as a natural event, like a tsunami or an earthquake.[3] There is a vague realization of general causes and effects, but a rather imperfect understanding of the particulars.

One very particular cause of the collapse of the Soviet Union was the Second World War. Looking at the wreckage of Berlin in May 1945, comparing it with Moscow, it was easy to believe that Stalin was victorious. Sixty years later, the architecture tells a different story. Both dictators sought out a war that ended in their mutual destruction. Germany's was apparent in May 1945; the Soviet Union's implosion came four and a half decades later.

That the war destroyed both empires is still poorly understood, masked by the remarkable abilities of Stalin to fool the world into believing that his fantasies were real. He not only built castles in the air, he persuaded people to live in them. Hitler came very close to winning that war, and on the Eastern Front, his soldiers came within an ace of winning outright. In the long retreat back to Berlin and Vienna, they exacted a terrible price on their adversaries. If the astonishing advance of the German army into Ukraine and the Caucasus was, as many of them realized, a deathride, the same must be said about the bloody advance of their opponent. The outcome of the war between the two dictators was a battle to the death for both.

The aim of this book is to provide the educated general reader with a succinct account of this important conflict, one that places the war within the broader context of the rise and fall of the Soviet Union. There are excellent scholarly accounts of almost every aspect of this war. But in addition to being lengthy and technically complex narratives, they lack this broader perspective. The result was described by the classical historian Polybius over 2,000 years ago:

> It has always seemed to me that those who believe they can obtain a just and well-proportioned view of history as a whole by reading separate and specialized reports of events, are behaving like a man who, when he has examined the dissected parts of a body which was once alive and beautiful, imagines that he has beheld the living animal in all its grace and movement.[4]

The scope of the war and the legends that have surrounded it, when coupled with the unfamiliarity of most readers with the history and geography of central Europe, place a burden on even the most avid reader. But Stalin's war with Hitler presents us with an additional difficulty, one perhaps not contemplated by Polybius:

the extent to which one side's account of itself is an elaborate and complex set of falsehoods.

Indeed, the rise and fall of the USSR is a complex and difficult subject itself, justly deserving of a name (Sovietology). From the very first, the Bolsheviks exerted a polarizing effect on Russians and foreigners alike, producing generations of fierce critics, fanatical apologists, and somewhat bemused analysts who, despite their expertise, seem in retrospect to have been more wrong than right.

Looking back on their forecasts and predictions in the light of the collapse of the Soviet Union in 1989–1990, one informed analyst noted that the "most unlikely scenario had been the one closest to the truth, however unlikely and even absurd it appeared at the time."[5]

Considered in the light of what we now know about both the USSR and the war itself, the evidence suggests not only that Hitler came much closer to an outright victory than is often supposed, but that much of what we think is true about this conflict is, if not completely false, very nearly so.

Russia has always presented foreigners with difficulties of language and customs as well as geography. Few people could dispute the exactitude of the widely read account of Astolphe-Louis-Léonor, Marquis de Custine, who visited that country in the 1830s, and certainly not the Russians themselves, as the book was banned there for over fifty years.

A century later, Bolshevik Russia was an even more hermetically sealed and impenetrable state than the Russia of the czars. In most respects people knew less about Russia in 1939 than they did a century earlier, and the situation hardly changed after the end of the Second World War. "After forty years in the West, I am still amazed at how little general understanding there is of Soviet reality," the famous concert pianist and conductor Vladimir Ashkenazy observed in 2005.[6]

The marquis was relatively free to move about, which was

hardly the case for foreigners after the revolution. He was different in another way as well: "I went to Russia to seek arguments for repressive government, I return a partisan of constitutions," he wrote in his Preface.[7] The same could not be said of most later visitors. They came not as sharp-eyed observers, but as pilgrims reaching the Promised Land. With few exceptions, they believed anything they were told: "We used to run a little contest among ourselves to see who could produce the most striking example of credulity among this fine flower of our western intelligentsia," is how the Moscow reporter for the *Manchester Guardian* put it. The reporter, a youthful and idealistic Malcolm Muggeridge, was himself a pilgrim, but one of the small number whose eyes had been opened by the actual experience.[8]

Few foreigners were allowed outside Moscow and Petrograd (the capital had been downgraded, renamed Leningrad), regardless of how enthusiastic their socialism, how credulous they were. Even the most cynical and skeptical of observers were forced to rely almost totally on what the new state chose to reveal about its aims, its progress, and the lives of its people. Governments naturally wish to present their best face both to their citizenry and to the world at large. The Bolsheviks had taken to this idea with enthusiasm from the very first, and as Stalin gradually assumed total control over the new state in the decade before the start of the Second World War, the techniques were carefully refined.

True, there was a certain level of awareness among outsiders that things were not as they seemed. It was a state in which there were, for instance, no airline accidents, no missing persons, and no crime.[9] When, in the decade before the collapse, curious foreigners were allowed to experience Soviet reality with somewhat more freedom, the shock was considerable. David Remnick's summation is apt: "It was Oz, the world's longest running and most colossal mistake."[10]

Metaphors and analogies are powerful descriptors, but historians require facts. In the case of the Soviet Union, the organs of the state were more than happy to oblige, providing reams of statistics backing up whatever assertion they wished to make, remaining grimly and often threateningly silent when asked for facts that might prove less convenient. The Soviet Union was Oz with numbers, reality hidden somewhere in a constantly shifting maze. Winston Churchill summarized the situation with his usual flamboyance when he observed that

> the Bolsheviks have discovered that truth does not matter so long as there is reiteration. They have no difficulty whatever in countering a fact by a lie which, if repeated often enough and loudly enough, becomes accepted by the people.[11]

By the time of the Second World War, Stalin had a great deal of practice in his craft. Although he had inherited the technique from Vladimir Lenin and Lenin's inner circle, he had refined it to an exquisite degree. He thus was able to fashion a simple and compelling account of what he decided would be called the Great Patriotic War, delivering it over the radio (and in public speeches) in installments. After 1945 these addresses were collected and disseminated all over the world in a small volume with the same title.[12]

His version of the war was perfectly pitched. After recoiling from the treacherous and unprovoked Hitlerite attack, the Red Army managed to prevent the invaders from reaching Moscow. The great battle before the gates of Moscow was the first in a series of staggering defeats, in which the Hitlerites were driven out of the homeland and Hitler defeated. They were driven out by the roused patriotic fury of the Russian people, whose strength was reinforced by the goals of socialism and inspired by the example of Stalin himself, who personally took control of the Red Army and was thus the architect of the victory over Hitler.

After May 1940, Hitler had few supporters in the West, and

after 1945, the world justly recoiled from his savagery. There was no limit to what he was capable of doing, and as Germany had been finally defeated, Stalin's account seemed plausible enough. As one of France's greatest modern historians observed, the goodwill that Stalin had squandered in the years before the war he managed to recoup once the Soviet Union was invaded; indeed the Soviet victory, due to the power of the Red Army, became one of the regime's most important achievements.[13] In the decades after the war, as the system's failures became more and more obvious (at least to its citizens), the sufferings and victories of the Great Patriotic War became even more important: they explained both why things were not any better than they were, and why Russia was a great power. Whatever the facts of the case, they were rapidly submerged in the legends.

There is nothing particularly unusual in that. The French, the British, and the Germans all came out of the First World War with their own legends. The brilliant, and brilliantly sarcastic, French writer Jean Dutourd's comments about that process describes the inevitable aftermath of any great war: "While our soil was being littered with statues of dying soldiers in cheap stone, Gallic cocks in brass, and weeping angels cast in concrete, the war veterans were reducing their epic to the level of street-corner gossip."[14]

The idea that governments are known to lie, particularly during a war, is hardly novel, but there is an additional complication for historians who come along later trying to divine the truth. Once the process of weaving deceptions begins, the deceptions are not limited to the public at large. As David Lloyd George, British prime minister after 1916, observed in his memoirs:

> The reports passed on to the ministers were, as we all realized much later, grossly misleading. Victories were much overstated. Virtual defeats were represented as

victories, however limited their scope. Our casualties were understated. Enemy losses became pyramidal. That was the way the military authorities presented the situation to Ministers, that was their active propaganda in the Press. All disconcerting and discouraging facts were suppressed.[15]

So historians trying to piece together the true state of affairs by examining documents and the accounts of eyewitnesses perforce must operate more like lawyers in criminal cases than traditional researchers.

The Soviet case is much more difficult than the British, and not simply because it involves Russia. Stalin, a keen student of the First World War, not only systematically did all the things that Lloyd George accused officials in his own government of doing, but he murdered, imprisoned, or made complicit in his crimes those who said anything to the contrary of his ideas. When Nikita Sergeyevich Khrushchev delivered his denunciation of Stalin in February 1956, he revealed the extent to which there were real crimes:

> Of the 139 members and candidates of the Central Committee who were elected at the 17th Congress, 98 persons, i.e., 70 per cent, were arrested and shot (mostly in 1937–1938). . . . Of 1,966 delegates with either voting or advisory rights, 1,108 persons were arrested on charges of anti-revolutionary crimes.[16]

In his speech Khrushchev also remarked that "When we look at many of our novels, films and historical-scientific studies, the role of Stalin in the Patriotic War appears to be entirely improbable." Indeed, Stalin's role *was* entirely improbable, but it was also of a piece with the legend Stalin had created. Moreover, like the other fabrications about the Soviet state, the Stalinist account of the war has proven to be remarkably durable, despite its improbability.

There are four reasons for the sturdiness of the Stalinist legends. The first two, while unexceptionable, account for their power. Stalin's narrative offers a clear and compelling account of this complex struggle. His account resonates with the idealism of socialism that people naturally find attractive.

But Stalin's version of the war has not been received as a myth, a legend, or a folktale; rather it is treated as though it is history, which leads us to the other two reasons for its success. His account of the war was the latest installment in a series of successful fictions that were almost universally accepted in the West as being facts. Finally, the facts themselves, the very stuff of history, were controlled and manipulated to fit the story. Unraveling the close connection between the creation of fiction and the manipulation of fact is a complex process.

The fictions were so artfully woven, so interconnected, that the word "lie" is hardly an adequate characterization of them: taken together they formed an alternative universe, a world in which, to use a phrase of the great Austrian novelist Robert Musil, "Pseudo-reality prevailed."[17] In order to understand the war between Stalin and Hitler, it is necessary first to understand that pseudo-reality. The existing narratives of the war are part of that alternative Bolshevik universe. The world according to Stalin is a world in which not only does the "improbable" become the sober truth, but in which virtually every fact is often in some way backward.

Consider: in the first decade after the end of the Second World War, the slogan "Socialism Triumphant over Nature" appeared inside the USSR and its satellites. The phrase was not simply intended as a rhetorical flourish. In Hungary, for instance, it meant that the state decided that properly socialist farms could grow oranges, despite what one might think were the obvious difficulties, and this bizarre experiment was attempted.[18] But in the context of the history of the USSR, there was nothing bizarre about it. On the contrary, the notion had a respectable scientific pedigree.

In the 1930s, a Russian agronomist and dedicated member of the party, Trofim Denisovich Lysenko, had argued that the Mendelian concept of heredity was a capitalist fiction, that Mendel had it backward.[19] This eccentric idea was perfectly consistent with Marxism, a self-described scientific philosophy, and indeed was derived from it. Moreover, Lysenko campaigned tirelessly for his ideas. As a result, Lysenkoism became an accepted scientific principle inside the USSR, with appalling consequences for agriculture. In 1913, Russia had been the world's largest exporter of grain; by 1987 it was the world's largest importer.[20]

To say that Lysenko's pseudo-science was the sole culprit, or even the chief reason, for the problems of Soviet agriculture would be overly simplistic. For one thing, during the 1930s Stalin's agricultural policies resulted in the deaths of millions of people from starvation, most of them Ukrainian, to the extent that in Ukraine the Holodomor (to give the famine its Ukrainian name) is seen, not without good reason, as a form of genocide.

The number of victims during the Holodomor staggers the imagination. In 1998 Soviet general Dmitri Antonovich Volkogonov estimated that over nine million people died as a result of Stalin's campaign to collectivize agriculture, a figure that is more or less accepted today as a reasonable estimate.[21]

It was indeed a holocaust. But in the alternative Soviet universe, it never happened. Nor was this denial confined to the organs of the state. In the 1930s, sources regarded as respectable and responsible, from the Moscow correspondent of the *New York Times* to celebrities like George Bernard Shaw, assured us that there was no food shortage in the Soviet Union, and there were certainly no deaths from starvation; that tragic fate only befell the victims of Western capitalist oppression.[22]

Meanwhile, as the decades passed by, Western intellectuals not infrequently assumed that "the Soviet standard of living would far surpass the West's. . . . Bread would soon be distributed free in the people's democracies. . . . The Iron Curtain would soon be reversed . . . by defectors 'escaping from penury.' "[23] That the rulers of the communist states were unable to produce enough food for their own people, that indeed there were acute shortages at every level well into the 1970s, that the situation was better than in the past only because the past had been so frightful—all of these glaring flaws were airily dismissed. The result was a complicated lie of such complexity that the only characterization is the one usually attributed to the physicist Wolfgang Pauli, "So wrong it isn't even wrong."[24]

A state that can manage its public relations so brilliantly can represent itself in any way it wishes, and in the case of the war, it did far more than what Lloyd George characterized his generals as doing, creating an account that reverses reality in stupefying ways. In 1940 the Soviet security services marched some 15,000 captive Polish officers into the woods and murdered them. In 1943, after the Germans had occupied Stalin's recently acquired Polish territory, a wolf uncovered some of the graves. The Germans then found most of the remains of the murdered officers and promptly publicized to the world the evidence of Stalinist atrocities, even calling in representatives of the Red Cross to authenticate the evidence.

The Katyn Woods Massacre, as it came to be known, is one of those rare instances in which, as of 1991, all the facts have become known. We know the names of the vast majority of the victims, we have eyewitnesses who confirmed that the killings were carried out by the Soviets. Perhaps most important of all for many in the West, we have the results of an investigation carried out by the Russians themselves, as well as a formal recognition by the government that there really was a massacre and that it was carried out by the Soviet security services exactly as the Germans had claimed.[25]

Stalin, however, did more than deny the evidence and produce a convincing alternative story. At the Nuremberg trials, the Soviet prosecutor insisted that the Germans be tried for the Katyn Massacre. When the main trial began, he also demanded that the Germans be prosecuted for killing Soviet military personnel taken as prisoners of war, going to great lengths to prove that this was not merely the "action of individual guards. . . . It was the result of systematic plans to murder."[26] German directives to this effect, particularly the one that began with the sentence "The Bolshevist soldier has therefore lost all claims to be treated as an honorable opponent in accordance with the Geneva Convention," are prominent in that section of the indictment.

Stalin stood the truth on its head, and the Allied leaders, who knew perfectly well who had killed the Polish officers, let him do it. The Soviet Union had never signed the relevant conventions, nor had the Red Army of the Bolsheviks ever paid the slightest attention to them: what would generally be called atrocities and war crimes were in fact a deliberate instrument of state policy.

Bolshevik atrocities in no way justify the behavior of the Wehrmacht, whose personnel were involved in a series of crimes of a similar nature; the only difference being that the Soviets murdered and mistreated prisoners of war on a larger scale, as though a serial killer who murders seventy innocent people is in some way worse than one who kills fifty.[27]

Katyn Woods was more than a horrible atrocity in a war rife with atrocities. Just as Lysenkoism illustrates the extent to which a pseudo-reality prevailed, Katyn Woods helps us to understand both why it prevailed and why we should care.

The murder of a few tens of thousands may seem insignificant when compared to the even more horrible deaths of what turned out to be countless millions, but Stalin essentially destroyed the leadership that Poland needed as a nation if it was to survive the war with any semblance of independence. "The Polish government never recovered from the wound he inflicted, and the memory of it has been etched deeply in the collective memory of the Polish people," is the judgment of the author of the definitive study of the massacre, and even for people who suffered as the Poles did, Katyn was a ghastly crime: "Looking back I see nothing but ruins, only mountains of corpses," is how Dmitri Shostakovich, himself of Polish extraction, puts it.[28]

This massacre was not an isolated instance. At the same time as the Katyn Woods Massacre, Stalin directed his own ethnic cleansing: some 275,000 Poles, members of classes the Bolsheviks judged undesirable, were deported into the distant interior of the USSR in the first six months of 1940. The forced movements were stopped only by the German invasion in June 1941, at which time a little over 300,000 people had been banished to the periphery of the country: "Polish administration, the Polish Army, and Polish intellectuals ceased to exist"; or, to quote Stalin himself, "We must smash them into oblivion."[29]

Although the dimensions of the Polish catastrophe have always been known, the vast majority of analysts and historians have ignored it. In their accounts they "choose to pass over it in silence. Silence is a widespread practice," to quote the authors of one of the few books to deal with this morbidly fascinating subject.[30] In cases where it was impossible to remain silent, one sees phrases such as "several thousand missing Polish army officers, supposedly interned by the Soviets," or that "evidence . . . has been used convincingly to prove the culpability of both sides . . . motives for which are equally persuasive."[31]

Stalin ensured that his version of history would prove a sturdy construct because he made the evidence support him. He eliminated most of the witnesses to the contrary, and in various ways he incriminated the survivors, pulling them into his own peculiar universe so that they hardly knew what the truth was.

In so doing, Stalin raised grave difficulties for future historians, who understandably prefer documentary evidence to hearsay, archives to stray anecdotes, and statistics to eyewitnesses whose testimonies are largely unverifiable. Unfortunately, one of the few givens in the history of the Soviet state is the unreliability of those traditionally important sources.

Given a situation in which every industrial accident was treated as an act of deliberate sabotage by foreign agents and their stooges, the man who wrote a report pinpointing design defects or shoddy quality control could easily find himself in dire trouble. We all know that subordinates often tell their superiors what they think they want to hear. In the case of the USSR, telling the boss what he didn't want to hear had fatal consequences. When Pavel Vasilievich Rychakov, chief of the air force in 1941, defended the horrific safety record of his pilots by pointing, correctly, to the abysmal quality control and design of Soviet aircraft, he was arrested, accused of being part of a conspiracy that included others, and shot.[32]

As is often the case with Stalin, the story rapidly escalated into a complex tale of improbabilities. Among those that Rychakov implicated under torture was the brother of Lazar Moiseyevich Kaganovich, who was responsible for the aircraft factories (Lazar Moiseyevich himself was a senior member of the Central Committee). Stalin made the improbable claim that Mikhail Moiseyevich, a Russian Jew, had been "designated head of Hitler's puppet government," adding that "I have the testimonies."[33]

So documentary evidence of any kind thus has to be regarded with suspicion. Nor do the recollections of witnesses carry the same weight as they would elsewhere. Men and women who had been adults in 1941 and were still alive in 1956 had become habituated to internal censorship. They not only refused to say out loud what they thought; oftentimes they didn't even know what they should think. As the Polish philosopher Leszek Kolakowski observed, "This is the great triumph of socialism in the sphere of knowledge: to the extent that it succeeds in demolishing the notion of truth, it cannot be accused of lying"; or as a wry Soviet era proverb has it, "He lies like an eyewitness."[34]

Given the depth and breadth of these deceptions, and the extent to which the refracted reality that resulted from them affected the survivors, the notion that any Soviet claim about an event as important as the Great Patriotic War, or any particular event in that war, can be taken as true is highly dubious.

These examples of Soviet duplicity and deceit are not presented as an exercise in Stalin bashing. Rather they are intended to help the reader understand the broader context of a highly distorted Soviet reality that is the warrant for the approach taken in this history of the war on the Eastern front. In almost every other field of study propaganda is generally recognized for what it is, and discounted: no reputable historian gives the slightest credence to the North Korean and Chinese communist claims as to Allied air losses, war crimes, and involvement in bacteriological warfare during the Korean War.[35] But as we shall see in this account of the war between Stalin and Hitler, almost every Soviet claim is either accepted as the sober truth or nearly so.[36] That being the case, a brief account of the extent to which we now know how skillfully and systematically every significant piece of data was manipulated by the Soviets is a useful corrective as well as an indispensable prelude to this account of the conflict.

That account begins with an appreciation of one of the basic parameters used to evaluate military success in warfare, the loss figures for the combatants. As General Volkogonov observed, in warfare there is a "fundamental principle of the military art, namely, that the objective should be gained at minimal cost in human life."[37] By that rather basic standard, Stalin was, as the general points out, "ignorant."

Loss figures for the Wehrmacht for both world wars have always been available, based on the reports generated by the medical services every ten days. Those records show that 1,419,728 German soldiers were killed on the Eastern Front and 997,056 were missing as of December 31, 1944, for a total of 2,416,784 officers and men.[38]

Although many of those listed as missing were taken prisoner and should have survived the war, the men who survived Soviet prison camps were in a distinct minority, perhaps as few as 10 percent.[39] So the higher figure is a more accurate reflection of German losses against the Soviet Union. The total number of German soldiers killed in action in all other campaigns comes to roughly 735,000 men, roughly one third of the total war dead: two out of three German soldiers killed in action died on the Eastern Front.

On the Soviet side, even such a basic figure as the number of war dead proves to be slippery. In the decades after 1945, Soviet calculations of losses underwent substantial revision, the result being to raise the numbers considerably. Initially, the number given out was 7.5 million dead, and in the immediate postwar era that figure was provisionally accepted, when mentioned at all. Soviet writers were reluctant to state any hard numbers as to their losses.[40] That number, however improbable, was duly confirmed. After the fall of the USSR, and the consequent opening of some of the archives, the official figures that emerged showed slightly under seven million dead.[41]

As we shall see in the pages that follow, Soviet figures have very little credibility, are in fact simply another instance of how Stalin created facts to substantiate the pseudo-reality of his state. But even putting that reservation aside and accepting the official Soviet data, the Germans clearly had an enormous advantage in the casualty exchange rate, the advantage being about 3.5:1, a calculation that suggests the reasoning behind General Volkogonov's characterization of Stalin.

The skeptical reader might well retort that given the relative sizes of the two combatants, Stalin could afford such losses; a rather precarious moral point but one that is often implicit in what is written about the war. Stalin himself created this particular myth when he said in 1941, "Our reserves in manpower are inexhaustible."[42] The population data suggests otherwise. In 1939 the population of the USSR was between 167 and 170 million people. But the population of Hitler's Reich was at least 86 million.[43] A simple calculation therefore shows that the Soviet manpower base could not sustain the casualty exchange rate deduced from even the most favorable Soviet figures. Eventually, had the war continued, Stalin would have discovered that his manpower was not inexhaustible.

The key question, however, is how to interpret the ratio as an indicator of combat effectiveness. The first obvious comparison is with how the Allies fared in Europe when they fought the Germans. By a conventional and unexceptionable American army reckoning, the Allies had slightly under 200,000 soldiers killed, and in turn killed over 250,000 Germans, for a ratio of 5:4.[44] In other words, the exchange ratio was reversed, although not much, suggesting that the combatants were evenly matched.

So the Germans did much better against the Red Army than they did against the Allies. The narrative of the war in the following chapters explains why, and relates the course of the war accordingly.

Of course Stalin provided a convenient explanation for the imbalance: the German successes of the first days of the war, owing to Hitler's treacherous surprise attack, disguise the resilience and success of his army.

The problem with Stalin's tale is that as the facts about Soviet losses gradually began to emerge, the relatively low losses and the surprise attack, two central features of the legend, become more and more difficult to sustain. During Stalin's lifetime, not only were statistics invented and manipulated to agree with his commands, but when the data failed to meet his expectations, the men who created it were murdered. Stalin's successors knew very well that the official data was highly dubious.

In the 1960s, Mikhail Andreyevich Suslov, one of the senior figures of the regime after Stalin's death, estimated the death toll at twenty million, and the first careful estimate of Soviet war dead, done by an émigré historian, calculated the death toll at about 27 million. More recent studies done after the collapse of the USSR raise the total, so that a highly respectable reference book gives an estimate of between 28 and 30 million, with the authors stipulating that the death toll could be as high as 35 million, a figure that includes civilian deaths as well, another complex issue that will be discussed in the final chapters.[45]

Although at some point the raw numbers become meaningless, the most recent data reveals an important trend. In Stalin's version of the war the heaviest losses occurred initially, owing to the treacherous surprise attack, and the official loss figures dutifully reflected steadily declining losses and a steadily growing Red Army. More recent data paints a contrary picture. The number of dead Soviet troops was actually higher in each successive year of the war. In the seven months of 1941, 4.3 million men were killed, a staggering death toll given that the usual estimate of the Red Army's combat strength in June 1941 was only 5.5 million men.

As bad as 1941 was, the next three years were hardly better. In 1942, the death toll was seven million; in 1943, the year of the great victories of Stalingrad and Kursk, it was nearly 7.5 million men. In 1944, it was, for the first time, significantly down, only 6.5 million deaths, but in the final months of the war, the Red Army lost nearly three million men. The Germans continued to win the casualty exchange right up until the end of the war. The claim routinely made by sympathetic scholars that as the war continued, and particularly toward the end, the Red Army "decimated" the Wehrmacht, is simply wishful thinking.[46]

Just as the complex web of fabrications that characterized the

USSR provides the rationale for skepticism about the Stalinist legend of the Great Patriotic War, the dramatic imbalance of the casualty exchange implies that Germany maintained a constant tactical superiority on the battlefield. That imbalance suggests that Lloyd George's pithy description of the situation he confronted in the First World War is an accurate representation of the war on the Eastern Front: "Victories were much overstated. Virtual defeats were represented as victories, however limited their scope. Our casualties were understated. Enemy losses became pyramidal."

The view of the war from the top of the mountains of dead Russian corpses reveals a considerably different landscape from the traditional one celebrated by historians. This conflict really was a war that Hitler came very close to winning. That idea requires an adjustment of the mind which is quite difficult. After half a century in which the achievements of the Red Army have become firmly embedded in our consciousness, the notion that its triumphs were mostly smoke and mirrors is difficult to accept.

That Stalin left the world with a mythology of the state he built that seems impervious to reason is his one unquestionable triumph. For most people, its very imperviousness suggests that it must have some basis in reality. Here, perfectly summed up, is the basis, the final words from Aleksandr Solzhenitsyn's *The First Circle*, in which the hapless prisoners are being transferred to another circle of Stalinist hell:

> Tossing about the cargo of crowded bodies, the gay orange and blue van moved through the city streets, passed a railroad station, and stopped at an intersection. A shiny maroon automobile was waiting for the same red light to change. In it rode the correspondent of the progressive French paper *Libération*, who was on his way to a hockey match at the Dynamo stadium.

The correspondent noted the legend on the side of the van:

MYASO VIANDES FLEISCH MEAT

He remembered that he'd already seen more than one such today, in various places in Moscow. And he took out his notebook and wrote in red ink:

"On the streets of Moscow one often sees vans filled with foodstuffs, very neat and hygienically impeccable. One can only conclude that the provisioning of the capital is excellent."[47]

II

UNDERSTANDING THE EVIL EMPIRES:
TWO CASE HISTORIES

We must consider how very little history there is; I mean real authentic history. That certain Kings reigned, and certain battles were fought, we can depend upon as true; but all the coloring, all the philosophy of history is conjecture.

Samuel Johnson[1]

When we think about the titanic struggle between Hitler's Germany and Stalin's Russia, the names of Walter Wever and Mikhail Nikolayevich Tukhachevsky hardly leap into mind. Both men were already dead when the Second World War began, quickly forgotten, their contributions to the German and Russian armies remembered by only a handful of specialists. But their meteoric rises and tragic ends afford us the very best window into the two dictatorships they served.

The careers of these two men give us an admittedly partial but still valuable explanation of why the war between Hitler and Stalin was such a bloody and prolonged affair. Although hardly famous, each man had his followers who claimed, with some justification, that history would have been different had he lived. There is no doubt that each man had an enormous impact on the system he served, and that the system had an enormous impact on him, leading to his early death.

Walter Wever, the first chief of staff of the German air force, was killed in a plane crash in 1936. Andreas Nielsen, the German general commissioned by the United States Air Force to write a study of the command structure of the Luftwaffe, summed up his achievements simply: with Wever's death the "Luftwaffe lost the first, and perhaps the most decisive, battle of World War II."[2]

Strong words, but understanding the grounds for this judgment is a crucial first step toward appreciating both the enormous successes of the German offensives of 1939–1941, and the largely disappointing results in the subsequent years.

A number of historians and biographers have made the argument that had Stalin listened to his pleas and supported his plans, the Red Army that Tukhachevsky championed through the 1920s and 1930s would have been the well-armed and well-trained military that its admirers imagined actually existed; that if he had lived, if his reforms had prevailed, Hitler would not have dared to attack the USSR.[3] Given the secrecy with which almost every facet of Soviet life under Stalin was hidden or distorted, tracing the consequences of Tukhachevsky's failure and ultimate fate is not easy. But the evidence suggests that the Russians paid a heavy price for Stalin's decisions regarding Tukhachevsky.

Early on, Walter Wever was recognized as one of the German military's outstanding officers. Born in 1887 in West Prussia, he entered the army as an officer trainee at seventeen. Eighteen months later he was commissioned as a *leutnant*, the lowest of the German officer ranks. By 1909 he was one of the three battalion adjutants of the 10th Grenadier Regiment; by 1912 he was regimental adjutant.

Wever, promoted to *oberleutnant* on the eve of the Great War, was a *hauptmann*, or captain, by 1915, serving both as a brigade adjutant and a battalion commander. By 1916 he was with the staff of the 8th Reserve Corps; by 1917 he was in the operations division of the great general staff itself, the department that Erich Ludendorff had directed before 1914. Wever was one of the 4,000 officers selected for the postwar army under the draconian reductions dictated by the victorious Allies at Versailles.

From the first, his superiors regarded him as the outstanding officer of his generation. A remarkable judgment, given that the generation included Erwin Rommel (born 1891), Heinz Guderian (1888), and Erich von Manstein (1887), generally credited with devising the plan for the May 1940 attack in the west, and the driving spirit behind some of the most impressive German victories in the east.

Wever's postwar promotions support the idea of his talent. After being included in the tiny officer corps of the new postwar army, Wever was promoted to major in 1926 (Manstein: 1927), lieutenant colonel in 1930 (Guderian: 1931), and full colonel in 1933 (Rommel: 1938), having been shuttled back and forth between command and staff positions.

By the early 1930s, when his subsequently more famous colleagues were being considered for divisional commands, Wever was slated to be the next chief of staff. And then, abruptly, after a distinguished career in the army, he transferred to the air force, where he was an outsider, a newcomer, an infantryman in a service dominated by fighter pilots.

Wever had always been fascinated by airplanes, but that hardly explains such a dramatic career move. The air force, or Luftwaffe, was presided over by Hermann Göring, one of Hitler's most trusted confidants and supporters: transferring into that service automatically put a cap on Wever's career. No matter how brilliant he was, he would never be *the* commander of the air force in the way he was slated to be had he stayed in the army.

Although retrospectively we think of the SS as being the distinctively National Socialist branch of the German military, in 1933, it was still, as the name Schutzstaffel indicates, simply an armed bodyguard. The Luftwaffe was explicitly to be the most National Socialist of the three branches of the military, its officers included. And indeed this was the case with Wever.

Wever fit in another way. Although the air forces of the world were new services, there had been plenty of airmen in the First World War, and that was where the next generation of senior air officers came from. But in Germany, matters were different, and it is fascinating to consider whether it was this infusion of talent from other areas, both military and civilian, that was one of the bases of German military success.

When Göring had looked around for the de facto leader of the air force, his choice was Erhard Milch, managing director of Deutsche Luft Hansa, a civilian. The other luminary of the Luftwaffe, Ernst Udet, was also a civilian. Although Udet had been a crack fighter pilot during the war, his air force experiences ended in 1918. Until Wever came along, the air force high command had few professional officers.

Despite his infantry background, Wever's progress in the Luftwaffe was dizzying. In September 1933, he joined the Luftwaffe. In October he was promoted to major general and effectively became chief of staff of the air force. He was thus in a position to dictate air force doctrine, to determine how a future war would be fought. Although overshadowed by Göring and Udet, Wever was the professional staff officer who determined how the air force would conduct operations in a future war. It is no accident that the leading historian of the German air force during this period refers to this as the "Wever era" of the German air force.[4]

For most students of history, the problem in appreciating Wever is that his ideas have been so thoroughly integrated into military operations that today they seem truisms. But when Wever assumed command, a deeply confused state of affairs prevailed in military aviation. The leaders of the major air forces subscribed to the notion, usually and with some justification ascribed to the Italian aviation theorist Giulio Douhet, that the decisive weapon was the strategic bomber. Fleets of bombers would destroy the enemy's cities and factories, forcing him to surrender. In contemporary usage, this is called strategic airpower, as opposed to tactical airpower, the use of airplanes to support the operations of ground forces.

The idea of strategic airpower was particularly interesting to the British and Americans, and by the time Wever became chief of staff, the Royal Air Force was dominated by strategic airpower advocates. For the Allies, tactical airpower was the poor relation, and would remain so throughout the war.[5]

One of the most significant implications of this doctrine was that it meant that air force commanders would conduct a war largely independent of the naval and ground forces, targeting cities and factories located far behind the front lines. It is difficult to overestimate the implications of this segregation of objectives and plans, and the consequences for ground commanders. Henry Pownall, chief of staff for the British Expeditionary Force in France 1939, remarked in exasperation that "I am just as puzzled as the French . . . at our [air] arrangements."[6]

In striking contrast, the Luftwaffe was charged with carrying out operations in support of army objectives; that is, its primary mission was tactical, not strategic. This decision had been made before Wever, but he was the officer who took the various isolated bits and pieces and fitted them together in one comprehensive and unified theory of operations, and this doctrine was the basis of the Luftwaffe's amazing successes both in May 1940 and in spring 1941. "Air warfare is based upon cooperation," Wever insisted. "The antiaircraft artillery, the air reporting organizations, and all the measures which we are forming for civil air defense offer just as great a contribution to the command of the air as the air force itself."[7] Making allowances for organizational differences, Wever's emphasis on cooperation and balance and his insistence on absolute mastery of the airspace over the battlefield have now become well nigh universal.

But at the start of the war only the Germans had a comprehensive and integrated concept of how to use the tactical air arm. So Wever's doctrine gave the Germans a major advantage. With complete dominance of the skies above the battlefield, the Germans were able to advance without being disrupted or in many cases even being observed. Their specially developed ground attack aircraft, the infamous Stuka, was able to operate with impunity, delivering precision air strikes on strongpoints and troop concentrations; and their vulnerable transport planes were able to land airborne troops and secure key positions in Belgium and the Netherlands.

The Stuka was the perfect example of how the tactical air doctrine determined the equipment needed. Emphasizing tactical air, the Germans had realized that the traditional ideas of bombing, in which the plane flew over the target and unloaded its bombs on it, were flawed. Low-flying bombers were reasonably accurate, but they were vulnerable to fighter attacks from above and ground fire from below. If they flew at higher altitudes, the probability of hitting a target smaller than a city block was low. As there were no precision-guided bombs or missiles, the only reliable way to hit a small target from the air was to dive directly into it, releasing the bomb at the last moment and then pulling up. Although the French, American, and Japanese naval air forces were all developing dive-bombers, in May 1940 the Luftwaffe was the only land-based air force that had both the planes and the coordination systems to make use of them.

There are numerous reasons why the Allies lost so quickly in May 1940. But the most recent evidence suggests that the German mastery of the concept of tactical airpower is actually the only serious advantage they possessed.[8] That is particularly the case in light of a technological deficiency on the Allied side— French and British troops had no antiaircraft systems to accompany them into battle, while German units had an entire air defense system deployed with their combat units. The integration of ground-to-air defenses into the ground units is a telling example of how comprehensive the Wever doctrine was. Air defense was too important to be left exclusively to fighter aircraft.

In consequence, when the Allied air forces tried their hand at tactical bombing missions, their pilots were subjected to intensive ground fire from below and fighter planes from on high. Although one of the basic assumptions of the airpower theorists was that the bombers would always get through, actual combat revealed this idea to be mistaken. On May 14, 1940, when the French and British air forces tried to halt the German advance over the Meuse River by bombing the advancing columns, there was an unprecedented slaughter: the RAF alone lost nearly fifty planes. That total was roughly half of its bomber force in France; it was, as one sympathetic historian has observed, "one of the blackest days in RAF bomber operations."[9]

It took time for this unpleasant reality to sink in, mainly because the impact of the strategic bombing enthusiasts on public opinion was enormous. By the early 1930s, eerily coinciding with Hitler's ascent, the general public was already being bombarded by horrifying scenarios of an aerial apocalypse, in which civilization would be destroyed from the air. The major cities of Europe would be laid to waste in a matter of hours, or at most a few days.[10] Wever's insistence on air defense systems ensured that the cost of this destruction to anyone attacking Germany would be extremely high.

But at the same time, he pushed for the construction of exactly the sort of long-range heavy bombers that would bring about the destruction that everyone assumed would occur in any future war.

To understand the importance of this initiative, it is necessary to understand a curious and surprisingly obscure fact about the whole notion of strategic bombing that was terrorizing the world in the 1930s. Although the general public was alarmed by this new concept, in 1933 no air force in the world actually had any bombers capable of carrying out the sort of attacks that everyone feared. The air forces of the world consisted of planes with short ranges capable only of carrying light payloads of explosives, what were tactical as opposed to strategic bombers.[11] Building a plane that could travel at high speeds for long distances while carrying a heavy bomb load was a considerable technical challenge that was not solved until well into the war.

For the inhabitants of many European cities, and for the world in general, the distinction was academic: if a city was close enough to their airfield, short-range bombers, although designed to destroy troop concentrations, railheads, and bridges, could wreak unprecedented havoc on civilians. So the civilians being targeted, and the historians writing about their sufferings, may be pardoned for not paying attention to the issue of tactical versus strategic bombing or for seeing Guernica, Barcelona, Warsaw, Rotterdam, and London as examples of the terrors of strategic bombing, preludes to the destruction of Hamburg, Dresden, and Tokyo. But the British and Americans were able to destroy those German and Japanese cities precisely because they had strategic bombers, aircraft capable of flying long distances, carrying heavy payloads of explosives. The Allies were simply more successful at this new and horrifying form of war than their adversaries.

But the chronology of heavy bomber development reveals a complex reality that allows us to appreciate how far-sighted Wever was. The American Army Air Corps did not call for a long-range bomber until 1934. The first B-17 bomber did not enter service until July 1937, and went through years of modifications before it became a true long-range strategic bomber. Specifications for the British equivalent, the Lancaster, were drawn up only in 1936, and the plane didn't enter service until 1942.

By contrast, Wever had demanded that work begin on a strategic bomber in 1933. So the Germans were well positioned to win the race to build a true long-range heavy bomber. After 1945, the surviving German generals offered various justifications for why the Luftwaffe had failed to develop such a plane. As was the case with many of their postwar rationalizations, the arguments were not subjected to any critical scrutiny, but accepted at face value, the more so since the issues involved were both technical and complex.[12] Although the challenges were formidable, it is difficult to imagine that the German aircraft industry was so greatly inferior to the British and Americans that it was incapable of solving them.

The issue of guidance and oversight in German weapons procurement and design is a highly technical one that lies outside the scope of this book, but the general principle is easily understood. Absent someone at the top able to keep the basic objectives clearly in focus, what gets produced may be technically fascinating but if it fails to get the job done, the designers have lost sight of the goal. The problem was leadership: Wever combined managerial competence and a breadth of vision that enabled him to see the new aspect of warfare holistically.

Fortunately for Germany's future adversaries, that unique quality of leadership was absent in the Third Reich, Wever excepted. The Wehrmacht entered the war with obsolete tanks that were unsuitable for modern warfare and with antitank weapons so feeble that their shells bounced off enemy armor.[13] Such statements certainly sound like wild exaggerations, but, as is the case in many areas where Hitler and Stalin are concerned, they are true. One of Hitler's accurate complaints about his generals was they understood nothing about "the economic aspects of warfare"; the generalization could be extended into areas outside of economics.[14]

So not only did Wever's tactical air doctrine anticipate what would become the standard for air forces after 1945, but his ideas encompassed the fashionable prewar thinking of the Anglo-American strategic bomber enthusiasts as well. He understood that it was necessary to have both a strong tactical air component and a powerful strategic component, and the few of his writings that have survived make the point:

> The objective of any war is to destroy the morale of the enemy. The morale of a leader and of a nation is reflected, to a great extent, in the armed forces of that

nation. Thus, in a war of the future, the destruction
of the armed forces will be of primary importance. . . .
This can mean the destruction of the enemy air force,
army, and navy, and the source of supply of the enemy's
forces, the armament industry. . . . The point at which
the concentrated use will be made of the air force at any
given time will be decided by the situation as a whole.[15]

Insofar as a future war with France was concerned, the war games
Wever directed convinced him that there was no need for a strategic bombing campaign. Almost all of France's heavy industry
was in the northeastern part of the country, easily within reach of
Germany's short-range tactical bombers and ground troops. Nor
was the transportation system leading to the frontiers particularly
vulnerable. There was too much redundancy, with the various
strongpoints connected by multiple lines of track, roads, and waterways. So although in theory transportation systems were ideal
candidates for bombers, in the French case, the redundancy of
the system, taken in conjunction with the difficulty of destroying
a bridge or rail line from the air, reduced the chances of success
considerably.

Moreover, northeastern France was densely populated. Plaster-
ing the targets with tons of high explosive would undoubtedly kill
large numbers of civilians. The airpower enthusiasts were all dis-
turbingly enthusiastic about leveling major cities to the ground.
Their notion of war involved civilian deaths on a large scale; indeed to an alarming extent they saw strategic airpower as winning wars on its own precisely because it would wreak havoc on
the civilian population, destroying enemy morale at the source,
as it were. But as the passage just quoted above suggests, Wever
was flatly opposed to the idea: "Attacks against cities made for the
purposes of inducing terror into the civilian population are to be
avoided on principle."[16] Wever felt such attacks would be coun-
terproductive unless in retaliation for enemy attacks on German

cities. In a war with France, therefore, tactical airpower directed against strictly military targets would be sufficient.

But Wever was not under the impression that Hitler's attentions were fixed on France. Rather Hitler, like a good many of his senior generals, saw Germany's destiny, its proper place, in the east. And that meant a war at some point with Russia.

In terms of airpower, Wever realized that a war with Russia was most likely unwinnable without a strategic bomber force. The European capitals of Germany's likely enemies in a future war, Belgrade, Brussels, The Hague, London, Paris, Prague, and Warsaw, could all be bombed by tactical aircraft flying out of airfields near the German borders. The most distant, Warsaw, was hardly more than ninety minutes away.

But Moscow and Leningrad, each almost 1,700 kilometers from Berlin, and the industrial centers of Stalingrad and Kharkov (over 2,000 kilometers) were out of reach. Given the Luftwaffe's inventory of planes in 1933, Soviet factories behind the Ural Mountains might as well have been in Iowa, and this was true for every air force in the world.[17]

So at the same time as Wever was determining the Luftwaffe's tactical objectives in a future war and how it would achieve them, he demanded that German aircraft designers come up with the long-range strategic bomber that would enable the air force to carry the war into the Soviet heartland. The project's code name made its mission clear: the Ural bomber, that is, a heavy bomber that could depart Germany and hit targets behind the Ural Mountains, thus depriving the USSR of its otherwise unreachable strategic and industrial base.

If a war with the Soviet Union broke out, the Ural bomber would be a decisive weapon. While the tactical air arm gave the army command of the battlefield, the strategic bombers would deprive the Soviets of the ability to produce weapons and get them, together with reinforcements, to the front. The strategic bomber, in other words, would give the Germans the same advantage over their enemy that the British and the American air forces would enjoy over the Germans in summer 1944.

There were key differences, however, and these were all to the advantage of the Germans. The Soviet air defense system was, by comparison with both the German and the British systems, rudimentary. In the enormous open spaces of the Soviet heartland, population centers were spread out: there was little chance of confused aircrews unloading their bombs on the wrong target, as was frequently the case in Great Britain and western Europe. If a section of track was hit, a bridge destroyed, rail traffic would come to a halt until it could be repaired. There were no alternative routes available. The rail lines frequently skirted population centers, so could be pounded from the air without the risk of murdering thousands of civilians.

By 1933, thanks to the secret cooperative efforts between Germany and Russia, enough German officers had been in the USSR to provide details about the transportation and industrial infrastructure. The quality and quantity of military goods could be concealed, and the USSR led the world in concealment. However, the road and rail system couldn't be, particularly when the issue was as simple as looking out the window and noticing whether the rail line was single- or double-tracked, whether there was a highway running alongside and what its condition was.

One can imagine Wever sitting in his office, rubbing his hands in delight. The Soviet air force was housed in bases close to the frontier. A massive air assault would not only give the Luftwaffe command of the air, it would destroy the fighters that could stop the strategic bombers, allowing them to penetrate deeply into the heartland, destroying troop concentrations, munitions depots, railheads, and factories. The USSR was the one country in Europe where the theories of the airpower enthusiasts would probably work. But the challenges of developing a strategic bomber were immense. That the Germans could surmount them is by no means a foregone conclusion. But there is also no reason to assume that Heinkel, Junkers, Arado, and Messerschmitt were less capable than their British or American counterparts, or less advanced.

By June 1936, Walter Wever was at the peak of his career. He had defined how the air force would fight, was dictating what weapons it needed, and, perhaps even more importantly, had proven he could mediate among the inflated egos of the air force leadership. He was affable and charismatic; there seemed no limit to what he could accomplish. The Ural bomber would be the jewel in his crown. In conjunction with Germany's highly developed tactical airpower, the bomber would give them an overwhelming superiority in the air.

On June 3, 1936, Wever took off from Dresden, headed for Berlin. He had already learned to fly his own plane, and as one of the Luftwaffe's top commanders, he had commandeered a Heinkel 70, an extremely fast light bomber that had come into military service only in 1935.

Piloting high-speed aircraft is a young man's game. At Wever's age, the reflexes are too slow. A pilot with decades of experience can compensate, but Wever had been flying for only a few years, was still an enthusiastic amateur. He had no business piloting a plane that had racked up over half a dozen world speed records.

At Dresden he made the classic amateur's mistake, neglecting to go through his preflight checklist. He simply climbed in, started the engine, and took off. He had forgotten to unlock the aileron controls: the plane couldn't gain altitude, and crashed at the end of the runway. As the Heinkel was largely made of a magnesium alloy, it was highly flammable, and it burst into flames before Wever could get out.[18]

Wever learned to fly, insisted on flying, for the same reason that Hitler would sit down and produce a sketch of some building project he wanted, whether it was for his residence at Berchtesgaden or the design for concrete bunkers on the Franco-German border. In National Socialism the leadership imperative, the

Führerprinzip, demanded practical demonstrations of heroic prowess. The great man's morale, his will, enabled him to brush aside the handicaps suffered by ordinary mortals. That was why he was capable of great deeds. It was National Socialism that led Wever to the air force, it was National Socialism that led him to fly, and it was National Socialism that prevented the air force from telling him he was too valuable to be risking his life by tearing around the country in high-speed machines.

In a system that placed so much emphasis on the personal, that centered around a series of concentric rings of power, each based on one man, that man's death made the system wildly unstable. Absent Wever, the strategic bomber program never got going, one reason being that it conflicted with Ernst Udet's dive-bomber fixation.

The extent of this disaster was masked for a long time, mainly because of the confusion that prevailed in the world about the nature of strategic bombing. That confusion was not restricted to ordinary people walking the streets of Paris or Munich. Göring once observed, jokingly, that Hitler didn't care what kind of bombers the air force had, only how many. The same could be said of many other world leaders at the time, who behaved as though bombers were magic carpets, not finicky and complicated machines whose designers still, in 1936, had numerous major problems to overcome.

The horrors of aerial bombardment were compounded and popularized by the Spanish Civil War, with the world press enthusiastically embracing the confusion. An air raid by short-range light bombers on a tactical target was promptly turned into the devastation of an entire city full of innocent civilians: Guernica (and wild reports about Barcelona) became the model for what would happen to every other city in the event of a war. Allied jitters and Spanish Republican propaganda combined with apocalyptic scares to convince everyone that Armageddon was at hand if a war began.

When the fighting started, the examples multiplied, and the Battle of Britain, the air war of fall 1940 in which the Luftwaffe mounted bombing raids against British cities, ascended into the mythosphere, following initial and highly misleading reports of the aerial destruction of Warsaw and Rotterdam. So it is forgotten that in 1940 Germany had no strategic air force: the bombers that were sent across the Channel were the same tactical aircraft that had been used to support conventional infantry objectives lying close behind enemy lines.

Those planes couldn't reach the northern airfields of Great Britain, where the fighter planes were based; they were too slow and too lightly armed to evade their interceptors; and they didn't carry enough bombs to inflict the level of destruction required. In the war with the Soviet Union, those weaknesses would be repeated, only on a larger scale, because after Wever's death, the Luftwaffe never developed the strategic bomber force that he realized would be a vital component in such a war.

Mikhail Tukhachevsky, the USSR's great general, whose status was almost mythical by the time Wever died, wasn't killed in a freak accident. He was arrested, tried, and shot on Stalin's orders, the result of a deliberate and concerted program to destroy the leadership of the Red Army. Nothing could point up the difference between these two systems so neatly as the lives and deaths of Tukhachevsky and Wever.

Tukhachevsky's early career illustrates the paradoxes of Russia, its revolution, and the bitter aftermath.[19] Born in 1893, he came from a family of aristocratic landowners, graduated from the famous Aleksandrovskoye military academy at or near the top of his class, and was commissioned as a junior officer in the prestigious Semyenovsky Guards Regiment stationed in Petrograd.

After World War I, the notion passed into history that the army of the czar was in shambles, unprepared for modern warfare and presided over by fools and incompetents. But the Russians were as prepared for this new war as any of their allies, which is to say they were not prepared at all.[20] Their elite regiments, like those of the British and French armies, were thrown headlong into combat in a series of poorly coordinated frontal attacks, and were annihilated within six months.

Tukhachevsky was lucky. He survived the Masurian disasters of August 1914, when the two Russian armies invading Prussia were destroyed by the German defenders in what was misleadingly named the Battle of Tannenberg. In February 1915, he was captured by the Germans in their attack on Łomża, a town in what is now northeastern Poland, about 150 kilometers north of Warsaw. Russian folklore has the young officer repeatedly trying to escape, and that may well be true. He ended up at Ingolstadt in Bavaria, where difficult officer prisoners were sent.

The young prisoner of war was thus spared the next two years of combat and collapse. Compared to the prison camps of the Second World War, Ingolstadt was a luxury hotel, so when Tukhachevsky showed up back in his homeland he was ready to fight. In most accounts, he escaped in late 1917, made his way to Petrograd, and promptly joined with the Bolsheviks. As the only solid information on his activities we have dates from spring 1918, when he surfaces in Moscow, it is more probable that he simply wandered off: the Germans stopped worrying about their Russian officer prisoners in late 1917, and let them all go when armistice negotiations began in December.

When the young ex–prisoner of war returned to Russia and threw in his lot with Lenin, the Bolsheviks were in a precarious situation. After his arrival in Petrograd in 1917, Lenin had shrewdly capitalized on the growing war weariness. He succeeded in getting people to see him as a man who wanted peace. Heady with the surprising success of the October Revolution, he had assumed that the revolution would spread into western Europe. When that revolution failed to materialize, he was forced to reconsider his options.

So the Bolsheviks agreed to an armistice in December 1917, and Leon Davidovich Trotsky, who was commissar for foreign affairs, began negotiating with the Germans, the Austrians, and the Turks. At first glance Trotsky's position seems unrealistic: the Russian armies were dissolving, and their adversaries had occupied an enormous swath of European Russia, almost all of present-day Estonia, Lithuania, Poland, Belarus, Moldova, and Ukraine. Fighting had already broken out in the adjacent areas, as nationalists and Bolsheviks began the first act of the Civil War. Nonetheless, the Bolsheviks demanded that the Germans hand all the seized territory back to them and go home.

When that idea was hooted down, Trotsky hit on a bizarre scheme: proclaiming there was neither war nor peace, he packed his bags, left Brest-Litovsk, and went back home. The Germans then resumed their advance into Russia. So the Bolshevik scheme collapsed, and by March they had capitulated completely. By signing the Treaty of Brest-Litovsk, the new government renounced its claims on all the occupied territories, including the areas seized from Turkey in the Turkish War of 1874, and agreed to pay war reparations to the tune of six billion marks. In return the Central Powers agreed not to seize any more Russian territory, hardly much of a bargain.

Lenin had no use for scraps of paper, and in any event he had more pressing issues on his mind. At the end of January he authorized the creation of what was formally known as the Army of Workers and Peasants, and Trotsky, fresh from his foreign policy experience, was made commissar of war, a shift that speaks volumes as to the Bolshevik attitude toward foreign affairs. Given that Trotsky had no military background, Lenin's appointment was curious, best explained by the fact that the actual (or rather nominal) military commander was a career officer, Sergei Sergeyevich Kamenev, a regimental commander in the war who had become an ardent Bolshevik.[21]

Very few officers had joined the Bolsheviks, so Trotsky greeted the young Tukhachevsky with open arms. True, he was a junior officer with only a few months of combat experience, but the Bolsheviks needed men with Tukhachevsky's qualities. At Brest-Litovsk, Trotsky and Lenin had been exclusively concerned with stopping the German juggernaut; in their desperation, they had been willing to sign anything that Max Hoffmann, the de facto chief negotiator, had put in front of them. Only belatedly had they realized that ending the war freed the senior commanders of the Russian army to contest their seizure of the country. And these commanders all promptly started trying to reclaim the country. The bloodless October Revolution turned into a bloody civil war.

For Trotsky, Tukhachevsky was the perfect exemplar of what the Bolsheviks were advocating, the poster boy for the inexorable success of the October Revolution. If the young guards officer hadn't existed, he would have been invented, as indeed would be the case later on, when the regime manufactured countless Soviet heroes in every walk of life.[22] Luckily for Lenin and Trotsky, the young officer was the real item. Educated, intelligent, devoted to the cause, he also possessed that rare quality necessary for all great generals, the willingness to take risks.

In the year and a half after his arrival in Moscow, Tukhachevsky commanded the 1st, 5th, 8th, and 13th Armies, was shuttled from one critical area to another. In the overheated mythmaking of the early years of the Soviet Union, he was dubbed the Red Bonaparte, the most important military figure the regime had. There's no doubt this was true. Nor is there any doubt that he was head and shoulders above the other Bolshevik commanders. What's questionable is the extent to which that evaluation says very much about his actual abilities.

Generals become famous and respected for winning battles that determine the course of wars. But the Russian Civil War has neither an Edgehill nor a Worcester (the battles that marked the beginning and end of the English Civil War). Nor, despite the enormous size of the Red Army by summer 1918, is there a Gettysburg or even a Pea Ridge. Even the minor skirmishes are elusive, and the surprisingly low casualty figures for the Whites, as the anti-Bolshevik forces came to be known, suggest there were very few pitched battles: most of the devastation was wreaked on the hapless civilian populations caught in the proximity to the two armies. But even the Soviet figures (the only ones we have) reveal a casualty ratio of about 7:1 in favor of the Whites, an exchange rate that suggests serious deficiencies in the Bolshevik forces.[23]

The Whites, scattered around the periphery of European Russia, were never able to coordinate their operations, were always outnumbered, and had little in the way of logistical support. Given the choice between a battle of annihilation that they might lose, or at best a Pyrrhic victory, they would disengage. And since the Whites had most of the officers from the czarist army, they were better able to manage this than their opponents: where professionalism really shows in an army is in how well it is able to disengage and retreat. Only one White senior commander was killed in action: Lavr Georgievich Kornilov, hit by an artillery shell during the attempt to take Ekaterinodar in April 1918. Indeed, there were so many surviving White generals that Stalin's henchmen were busily murdering them all through the 1930s.

So the notion of the Red Bonaparte was a fiction, albeit a claim that was widely believed. After all, Lenin had presented himself as an apostle of peace: the Bolsheviks wanted to end the war, and in this claim at least they were truthful. The idea that once ordinary soldiers and civilians perceived the essential rightness of the Bolshevik cause they would join it en masse was a sincere belief, not a cynical ploy.

"Old Europe is facing toward the proletarian revolution," Grigory Yevseevich Zinoviev, the president of the newly formed Comintern wrote in spring 1919, listing "three Soviet republics: in Russia, in Hungary, and in Bavaria." Zinoviev, one of Lenin's closest collaborators and the dominant Bolshevik intellectual of the time, then went on to say that "no one will be surprised if, when these lines are actually published, we already have not three but six or even more soviet republics."[24] Given that rhetoric, it was natural that a former czarist guards officer would become one of the revolution's leading generals: if not in reality then in the fantasy world painted by the Bolsheviks.[25]

Like almost every other Soviet claim made both then and afterward, Zinoviev's was not only false, it predicted the obverse of reality. By the time his confident assertion of the establishment of soviet republics hit the newsstands, the leaders of the Bavarian Soviet Republic were dead, along with their short-lived state. The Hungarian government of Béla Kun lasted only a little longer. The lives of both soviet republics were measured in days.

The Bolshevik leaders had badly miscalculated: Lenin believed the revolution would spread like wildfire, and Tukhachevsky was of the opinion that once the Army of Workers and Peasants entered a country, its workers and peasants would spring to the red flag, creating a growing and irresistible force.

Although it's easy to dismiss their error as being the product of idealism and inexperience, the root causes of the failure were more fundamental. As good Marxists (or Marxist-Leninists) they ignored the power of nationalism, which they believed was an insignificant force compared to the real conflict between classes. They believed that the disasters of the war had shown the workers and peasants the folly of nationalism, and had opened their eyes to international solidarity based on class interests.

Exactly the contrary was going on. The collapse of the three central European empires was the signal for every ethnic group of any size to agitate for its own state. Regardless of how they felt about the Bolsheviks or any other political group, the Finns, Estonians, Lithuanians, Latvians, Moldovans, Belorussians, Ukrainians, and Poles, to name only the chief groups of European Russia, wanted their own states.

Nationalism wasn't the only problem the Bolsheviks failed to manage. By January 1918, with Lenin's explicit encouragement, the systematic use of terror had already begun, with its attendant executions, forced labor under harsh conditions, and arbitrary arrests.[26] War crimes, such as the taking of hostages and executions of prisoners of war, were in full swing by the summer of 1918, as were the first labor camps.

The terror both intensified resistance and generated a backlash, first in the Baltic, as German and Baltic troops drove the Bolsheviks back, but further south as well. As Lenin's mandated revolts spread into Germany and Hungary, so did the terror. By the end of 1919 the new Soviet state was still enclosed, still under siege, and a new and formidable opponent had emerged: Poland.

The kingdom of Poland had existed as a large and powerful state well into the eighteenth century. After its decline, it was partitioned among its neighbors in the 1790s, and the Russians, who took over the largest part, regarded Poland as emphatically theirs. But the historic kingdom of Poland was enormous, including much of present day Belarus, Lithuania, and Ukraine. In 1918 the Poles were determined to assert their sovereignty over those areas as well as the historically German lands of Posen and Silesia.

Moreover, unlike the other successor states, the Poles came onto the arena with a large and experienced army, since they had fought on both sides in the Great War. But now, as compelling proof of the power of nationalism, the former adversaries made common cause, determined to re-create the ancient Polish nation regardless of the consequences, the attitudes of Great Britain and France, or the claims of others to their historic kingdom.

It was at this point, early 1920, that Lenin, two years away from his first crippling stroke, made yet another mistake. Although the Bolsheviks were still living precariously on the edge of chaos and defeat, he decided to go to war with Poland.[27]

Trotsky, a realist, was appalled. In 1920 the Red Army was little more than a motley collection of wild-eyed revolutionaries, forcibly drafted civilians, and czarist veterans with dubious loyalties. Given their superior numbers, and the logistical and strategic difficulties of the Whites, the Reds were steadily prevailing in the Civil War. But an armed horde is not an army, and in the Soviet case there was another complication. Although Trotsky presided over an army of six million men, he couldn't bring that overwhelming mass to bear on Poland: when the war began, Tukhachevsky's four armies altogether came to 85,000 men.[28] The Red Army would outnumber its adversaries, but not with anything approaching an overwhelming force. So Trotsky was right to object.

But Lenin was still convinced that the Polish people would embrace Bolshevism and rise up to throw off the oppression they had suffered at the hands of the ruling classes and the Roman Catholic Church. So in April 1920, Trotsky got his orders, Tukhachevsky was given the command, and the war began in earnest.

At first the Red Army did well enough. The Poles, trying to expand into what they saw as their historical territory, were grossly overextended, their armies strung out over a front of some 700 kilometers, all the way from Vilna in the northwest to Kiev in the southeast. To make matters worse, at the extreme left and right wings of this front, Polish armies were in contact with hostile forces (ethnic Germans and Lithuanians in the north, Ukrainians in the south, the surviving Whites at both ends), who were no more interested in seeing eighteenth-century Poland reconstituted than were the Bolsheviks.

Although ever active and imaginative Soviet analysts would subsequently argue that the Poles were simply imperialist tools, lavishly supplied, trained, and armed by the French and British, and in league with the Whites, the exact contrary was the case. Poland lacked the resources to fight a major war, and the British and the French, wary of Poland's attitude toward the Allied decisions about the frontiers of that state, weren't about to supply them.[29]

Poland's other problem was the size of its army. The core consisted of a 50,000-man force trained and equipped by the French to fight on the Western Front: a military more than adequate to defend the country, but far too small to invade anyone else's. Once the Red Army threw its weight into the struggle, the only option for the Poles, like the Whites, was to retreat. As the Polish forces pulled back from relatively unfriendly areas like Belorussia and Ukraine, they not only benefited from greatly reduced interior lines of communications, but as the front shrank, their forces became more concentrated, retreating toward Warsaw. Regardless of intentions, the result was highly predictable: a large-scale battle of annihilation between the two armies.

By August 1920, the outlines of this battle were clear. In the earlier months there had been very little serious fighting, so both sides were largely intact. As Tukhachevsky saw the problem, all he had to do was concentrate his superior numbers, and close in on the Poles from three sides. So his plan, which Kamenev, the nominal supreme commander, had already approved, required the Bolshevik armies operating out of western Ukraine to move on Warsaw, catch the Poles in a giant pincer movement, and crush them.

But the commanders in Ukraine, particularly Semyon Mikhailovich Budyonny, a former cavalry sergeant who was now in charge of the 1st Cavalry Army (the famous Konarmiya), saw matters differently. They had never much cared for the former guards officer, and were disposed not to cooperate simply because he had been given command of the main force. Aside from that, they felt that the most profitable plan was to continue their successful advance toward the fortress city of Lvov, rather than engaging in a great battle at the gates of Warsaw.

That was particularly the view of Stalin. Although technically only a political officer, he was emerging as the dominant personality among Lenin's disciples, and had forged a close relationship with Budyonny, to whom he was superior in every way except equestrian skills. Moreover, given what we now know of Lenin's orders to Stalin in February 1920, it seems that his hanging back was also in obedience to Lenin's directive regarding the seizure of Galicia.[30] As a result, Tukhachevsky's plan was never implemented: the Poles smashed Tukhachevsky's armies outside Warsaw, then turned east and south. In the Battle of Komarów (August 31, 1920), the Poles surrounded Budyonny's Konarmiya and came close to annihilating it.

The Bolshevik retreat became a rout, with Russian losses approaching those suffered in August–September 1914, when a similar lack of cooperation had given the Germans a great victory. The usual casualty estimate for the 1920 war is 150,000 men; once again, Lenin had no alternative but to negotiate with a victorious opponent, and the Treaty of Riga, which the Bolsheviks signed on March 18, 1921, was even more humiliating than the Treaty of Brest-Litovsk in March 1918.[31]

Although the primary reason for the Red Army's defeat was strictly military, namely, the failure of senior commanders to work together, the primary cause was Lenin. He was oblivious to the string of revolutionary failures, convinced that the world would shortly go red, that all the Red Army had to do was put in an appearance and the Poles would join up. In order to provide them with incentives he insisted that "we shall go forward for ten-twenty versts [kilometers] and hang the kulaks, priests, and landowners. Bounty: 100,000 rubles for each man hanged."[32]

Such orders had predictable consequences. By the end, when the army had become a panic-stricken mob, wounded Bolsheviks were pleading with their comrades to kill them on the spot so they would be spared the torture inflicted on them by vengeful Polish soldiers.

In the aftermath of the Polish War, the area of the Soviet

Union that lay along the new Polish frontier was plunged into anarchy, despite the best efforts of the security services, who employed methods that were already, in 1920–1921, becoming habitual. A new and horrible phase of the Civil War was about to begin, and Trotsky chose the former czarist lieutenant turned Bolshevik general to direct it.

Fresh from the disasters of the Polish War, Tukhachevsky now entered a new phase of his career and directed two violent internal repressions. The most infamous of these, whose memory survived inside the Soviet Union even after the Stalinist memory hole engulfed all else, was the Kronstadt Rebellion.

When sailors from Kronstadt, the traditional naval base of Russia's Baltic Fleet, who had initially been enthusiastic supporters of the October Revolution, rebelled against Lenin's regime, his response was to crush them. Trotsky, who enthusiastically endorsed the idea, chose Tukhachevsky to eliminate the sailors as quickly as possible.

The Kronstadt naval base was located on Kotlin Island, a sliver of land in the Gulf of Finland. There was a deep water channel cut through the gulf that allowed steamships access to Petrograd, but by January of most years, nearly half the Baltic was frozen over. In most winters it was possible to walk to Kotlin Island from either side of the gulf, so the attack was a matter for ground troops, not ships.

On the other hand, an infantry attack across kilometers of open ice would only replicate the slaughters of the First World War. Although the Red Army had access to enough artillery to solve the problem of the mutiny by shelling the base until the survivors surrendered, Tukhachevsky, under pressure to dispatch the problem quickly, mounted direct infantry assaults across the ice. He had been given an amazingly large force, by most accounts, over 50,000 men, to subdue a garrison that had never numbered much over 10,000. But a massed infantry attack across the ice, directed at a fortified position, was bound to be a costly affair. The sailors managed to hold out for ten days, and the Red Army suffered appalling casualties, with perhaps 10,000 men killed in action. One former Red Army officer argues that casualties were worse than anything experienced during the Civil War.[33]

From Lenin's point of view, the operation was a great success, and Tukhachevsky was handed another counterinsurgency role. Unlike the Kronstadt affair, the Tambov Revolt, sometimes referred to as the Antonovschina, after one of its leaders, Aleksandr Stepanovich Antonov, has largely been passed over, probably because it was out in the provinces, while Kotlin Island was at the front door to Petrograd.

But the forces engaged were larger, and the fighting, which had begun on a small scale in 1920, went on for much longer. By 1921, the rebels had roughly 50,000 men under arms. Tukhachevsky had all the resources of the Red Army at his disposal, with over 100,000 men in the field, together with armored trains and artillery. Given the imbalance in force, one would think that the revolt would have been easily crushed. Instead, it dragged on for months, and by June 1921, Tukhachevsky authorized the use of chemical weapons to clear the forests in which the insurgents were based, just as he had earlier authorized taking hostages and executing suspected rebels without trial.

In the early 1920s, the Bolsheviks not only had no compunctions about engaging in war crimes, but openly discussed them.[34] The concerted and highly effective campaign of bland denial of atrocities, coupled with vicious attacks on anyone who espoused a differing view, began later, with Stalin, who realized that to brag about gassing civilians might upset his many well-wishers in the West.

Enough information survives for us to have an idea of the scale of the operation Tukhachevsky directed, its methods, and its consequences. Tens of thousands of civilians, mostly women and children, were incarcerated in camps, tens of thousands more were killed, with the death toll estimated at nearly a quarter of a million.[35] These facts should not be forgotten when we consider Tukhachevsky's subsequent fate.

By 1922 the revolts had been subdued, the Whites were in exile, and Lenin had suffered a major stroke. The result was a dozen or more years of confusion, as Stalin consolidated his power and eliminated his opponents.

The first of those was Trotsky, who had been sidelined by 1925, the same year that Tukhachevsky became de facto chief of staff, a position he held through the next years of bitter party infighting, during which Trotsky and his supporters were removed from positions of authority, expelled from the party, and then, in 1929, deported.

Nonetheless, it was in those years that Tukhachevsky began trying to turn the Red Army into a professional military. He realized the superiority of the German army lay in its emphasis on education, training, and logistics. Education meant that the leadership cadre was more attuned to change, quicker to grasp the impact of technology on warfare, and more aware of the need for training. Men like Walter Wever embodied those principles perfectly.

The mastery of logistics meant that the army would have the capacity to carry out the operations it was ordered to execute, that, for example, soldiers would not only have modern weapons, but enough ammunition for those weapons. The combat units would have the proper means of transport, and a steady flow of supplies to support their actions.

Modernizing the Russian army, or anything Russian for that matter, had been an ongoing struggle since the time of Peter the Great, and the October Revolution had not changed that fact. But Tukhachevsky had an even greater obstacle to overcome. Creating a modern army requires resources. Behind the facade of revolutionary optimism, the USSR was destitute. Everything was from half to a third of what it had been in 1913: the population of the cities, the number of industrial workers, the quantity of agricultural products and agricultural goods.[36] The Soviet Union did not have the industrial base to equip a modern army, nor was it anywhere near developing one.

So Tukhachevsky was on dangerous ground. Whether he realized it or not, his desire to turn the undisciplined mobs of the Civil War into an actual army automatically subjected him to suspicion. The older commanders, men of limited abilities to begin with, who already disliked him for his czarist past, were aghast at his demands for an army that relied on tanks and trucks and modern artillery. In their rather selective memories, cavalry had won the wars against the Whites and the Poles, its value thus proven in the post-1918 world. Like Sir Douglas Haig, the commander of the British forces in France during the First World War, they were firmly convinced that armies should be built around horses and rifles, not tanks and machine guns.

As the former were substantially cheaper than the latter, and as there was no war looming in the near future, these retrograde notions of horses and foot soldiers converged nicely with the desire of most governments to reduce military expenditures. The Soviet Union, ravaged both by the Civil War and the loss of some of the most prosperous parts of European Russia, could not afford to modernize its military.

So during the 1920s and early 1930s, Tukhachevsky operated under conditions of benign neglect. The state refused to give him the resources required, but it largely left the army alone when it came to doctrine, training, and organization.

It is from this period, the 1920s, that Tukhachevsky's considerable reputation was developed. His admirers painted him as a military genius. Not only was he a victorious general of the Civil War, a great trainer and planner, but he was also a brilliant military thinker. As we have seen, the great general part hardly holds water. His only successful campaigns were against his fellow Russians, marked by atrocities, war crimes, and heavy casualties among his own forces.

The notion that he was an important military thinker has survived to this very day, with Tukhachevsky being credited with arguing for a new form of offensive operations, usually translated as "deep battle," seen as an antidote to the broad front offensives that characterized the First World War. Such broad frontal attacks would ultimately fail, owing to the violation of a classical principle in warfare, which can be easily understood as the necessity for the concentration of force.

Tukhachevsky's solution, deep battle, was a massive blow delivered on a narrow front, a blow so powerful that it would break through the enemy's lines, strike deep behind them, and then encircle the enemy's adjacent positions: penetration leads to envelopment, and then to annihilation.[37] This was the solution to the stalemates of the First World War, akin to the one proposed by J. F. C. Fuller in Great Britain and Charles de Gaulle in France. At bottom, the notion anticipated how the Wehrmacht would conduct offensive operations. The success of the deep battle concept depended on successful breakthrough operations, and those operations required tanks and mechanized forces, which tied in perfectly with Tukhachevsky's insistence on developing a modern army built around the internal combustion engine.

The idea of deep battle was not Tukhachevsky's; it was developed by Viktor Alexeivich Triandafilov, a talented young officer who became deputy chief of staff in 1930, only to be killed in an airplane crash the following year.[38] But Tukhachevsky was in a position to promulgate this new doctrine through manuals, to organize the army into armored and mechanized units capable of carrying it out, and to lobby the leadership for funds to develop the weapons needed. Whether he was a great military thinker or simply a competent staff officer, he worked energetically to turn the Army of Workers and Peasants into a professional military equivalent to the best European armies.

Whether Tukhachevsky's theories would have worked in combat situations, they were analogous to what Wever was establishing for the Luftwaffe, in that both men understood what was required to fight and win a modern war. Tukhachevsky was on the right track; perhaps more importantly, he was overseeing the emergence of a new professional officer class, technicians rather than party hacks, men who were of the same mind, who wanted a modernized and professional army.

Although Tukhachevsky's tenure as de facto chief of staff ended in 1928, as assistant commissar for defense he exerted an enormous influence on the military, attracting a cadre of younger officers who wanted the USSR to have a professional army. And in 1931, Stalin, who had hitherto resisted his arguments for pouring resources into the armaments industry, reversed course. Soviet industry was able to begin designing and producing the equipment a modern army needed.

It appeared that Tukhachevsky's efforts were beginning to bear fruit, albeit with some personal cost, since after 1928 he was essentially cut off from the chain of command inside the military. Given the complex bureaucracy of the party, its complicated relationship to the government itself, and Stalin's assiduous promotion of the myth of collective leadership, it was difficult for outside observers to decipher exactly who was in charge of what. The realization that the country's most brilliant and accomplished senior general had essentially been sidelined came in retrospect, and was seen either as an instance of Stalin's jealousy or, by the sheeplike party faithful, as proof that he had been plotting against the all-wise leader.

On a personal level, Stalin was unquestionably jealous. As a professional Bolshevik, he had good reason to be wary of his fellows. He had never been seen as Lenin's successor, certainly not by Lenin, who probably did believe in the idea of a collective leadership. Stalin's slow and cautious ascent to absolute power was not the result of any formal process. Technically, he was simply one of the members of the Central Committee, and for a long time Western leaders behaved as though the committee actually ran the country, that Stalin was by no means an absolute ruler.

Having essentially schemed his way into power, Stalin knew how that worked, how you established coteries of loyalists and used them as your base. In a democracy, that meant establishing political parties, going out and campaigning in elections, which was what Hitler was doing. In the USSR the process was subterranean, so Stalin was vigilant. A man like Tukhachevsky, intelligent and charismatic, was a threat. So Stalin took care to separate the young general from the officers whose respect he had won.

However, there was more than personal and professional jealousy at work. Socialist intellectuals in Europe had never been able to decide what to do with the military. Their first instinct was suspicion: soldiers could be used to repress the workers, and had been. France's bitter experiences in 1871, suitably reshaped and propagandized, were kept fresh. Right up until August 1914 a good many dedicated socialists believed that the solidarity of the working class would trump national chauvinism and wars would never be fought. If that was the case, armies no longer had any purpose except as instruments of repression to keep the people from power.

The First World War dimmed that idealism but did not destroy it. Indeed, it was the intellectual foundation for the beliefs of men like Lenin and Tukhachevsky that the masses would rise up and support the invading Red Army (in Poland) and join in with the professional revolutionaries in Germany. Stalin, having firsthand experience both in the Civil War and the Polish debacle, realized this view was exceedingly naive.

Jean Jaurès, the French socialist leader who had been murdered in July 1914, had advanced a more practical idea, that when the state was threatened, it could be protected by a general mobilization of the male population, a citizen army whose revolutionary zeal would make them more than a match for their adversaries.

So Jaurès favored conscription, which would give everyone the basic skills required, but opposed a professional military, which would either try to take over the state (as Napoleon had done) or let itself be used as a repressive instrument (as had happened in 1871).

In France before 1914, and in Germany afterward, the socialists tried to manage this problem in two ways. They demanded political allegiance from the senior officers. In France before 1914 that had meant that only socialists could be promoted to senior positions, a decision that had disastrous consequences when the war began. At the same time, ever suspicious, the socialists tried to limit the military budget in every way possible. In the minds of most socialist intellectuals then, there was an inherent contradiction between the idea of professional military and the ideal of a socialist state, and even when in power, they were wary. After the war started, socialist politicians in France were as much concerned about some successful general seizing control of the government as they were about the Germans taking Paris.[39]

The Bolsheviks had thus inherited a thorny issue, and they knew it. So Stalin replaced Tukhachevsky with Boris Mikhailovich Shaposhnikov, who had distinguished himself not as an officer of any competence but by his advocacy of a close alignment of the party and the military. This position was in perfect accord both with traditional socialist aims, as well as traditional socialist fears of the military.[40]

So Tukhachevsky was shunted off to command of the Leningrad Military District. This was an important command, but clearly a lateral move. But at the same time, Stalin handled the situation carefully: if a man felt he was truly cast out of favor, he might then be tempted to foment serious discord, either in revenge or self-protection.

Stalin had developed a fascinating technique. He would put a man through the labyrinth of the Bolshevik bureaucracy like some mad scientist running a rat through a maze, subjecting him to alternating doses of rewards and punishments. The result was that no one could say for sure exactly what their situation was. Having effectively demoted Tukhachevsky to a minor post, in 1933 Stalin arranged for him to be decorated with the Order of Lenin for his work in strengthening the Red Army, and then turned around and had him elevated to the supreme military rank, Marshal of the Soviet Union.

Although by now he had essentially been removed from any position of direct authority over the military, in 1936, as assistant commissar for defense, Tukhachevsky was selected to deliver the report on the military preparedness of the Red Army to the Central Committee. Soothingly titled *Sentinel of Peace*, the widely disseminated report, while making all the necessary genuflections to the party and to Stalin, emphasized the importance of training, education, and better living conditions; it also clearly laid out the need for even greater sums of money to be devoted to military needs. The explicit goal: "the military training of the Red Army will reach a level unattainable by any other state."[41] By implication, this meant an army like Germany's, where Tukhachevsky had recently been. Stalin could hardly have been pleased.

Despite these honors, the new marshal knew things were not going well. That same year (1936) Dmitri Shostakovich came seeking his advice. The two men were friends, despite the difference in age and profession, but the young composer was in serious trouble with Stalin, ostensibly because of the opera he had written that was based on a short novel by Nikolai Leskov, *Lady Macbeth of the Mtsensk District*:

> Tukhachevsky agreed to see me. We locked ourselves in his office. He turned off his phones. We sat in silence. And then we started talking very softly. I spoke softly because my grief and despair wouldn't allow me to speak in my normal voice. Tukhachevsky spoke softly because he feared prying ears.[42]

He was right. In May 1937 he was arrested and tortured until he confessed to being a German spy. The original of Tukhachevsky's confession has blood on it.[43] He was promptly tried, found guilty, and then shot (on June 12, 1937). Stalin had Tukhachevsky's wife, his two brothers, and one of his sisters shot; the other sisters were sent to the camps. There was a special organization of internment for small children; Tukhachevsky's daughter, Svetlana, eleven when he was murdered, was imprisoned until she was seventeen, then sentenced to five years in the camps.[44]

Whatever his weaknesses, there is no doubt that Tukhachevsky was a dedicated communist who worked tirelessly to professionalize the Red Army. He was not single-handedly responsible for that effort, any more than Wever was single-handedly responsible for the development of the Luftwaffe. But both men were highly influential, and their untimely deaths encourage a series of speculations: How would the war have gone had the long-range bombers Wever wanted been available for the Battle of Britain in 1940? Would Hitler have dared to attack the USSR had Tukhachevsky succeeded in modernizing the Red Army?

After Wever's death the Luftwaffe failed to develop a strategic air arm of long-range heavy bombers. After the Russian marshal's murder, whatever progress had been made in training and doctrine, in the ideas of deep battle, and even in modern weaponry, was systematically overturned, dismantled, and cast aside. The armored units Tukhachevsky had demanded, that he and his followers had lobbied for, that had actually been created, were disbanded: henceforth tanks would be used only to support infantry operations.

In retrospect it is striking how the life and death of each man epitomized the strengths and weaknesses of the two totalitarian states, revealing the fatal weakness inherent in each system that would ultimately result in its collapse. The deathride had begun.

III

THE DICTATORS' GAMBLE

> During the war and after the war, Stalin advanced the thesis
> that the tragedy our nation experienced in the first part of the
> war was the result of an "unexpected" attack by the Germans
> against the Soviet Union. But, comrades, this is completely
> untrue.
>
> Nikita Khrushchev, Secret Speech[1]

Tukhachevsky's arrest in June 1937, and his subsequent torture, trial, and execution for spying, was certainly not the
first such case in the USSR. People had been disappearing
in the Soviet Union since 1918. When Malcolm Muggeridge was
set to leave for the USSR as correspondent for the *Manchester
Guardian*, the influential socialist intellectual and Bolshevik enthusiast Beatrice Webb had brought the matter up:

> "It's true," she said suddenly, apropos of nothing, "that
> in the USSR people disappear." She accented the word,
> showing her teeth as she did so. Clearly she would have
> been self-content to promote the disappearance of cer-
> tain tiresome people in the same expeditious way.[2]

Mikhail Bulgakov had treated the same subject in the seventh
chapter of his great novel *The Master and Margarita*: "Odd things
happened in that apartment, people started to vanish from it
without a trace."[3]

Both were speaking well before the onset of what is now generally referred to as the Great Terror: that only began in 1936, with
arrest and trial of Sergei Kamenev, Grigory Zinoviev, and fourteen other prominent old Bolsheviks. They confessed to a bizarre
series of fantastic and improbable crimes, and were sentenced to
death. In January 1937 there was a second round of trials, this one
of seventeen lesser figures. Selected foreign observers were invited
to attend the trial, with the overwhelming majority impressed by
the workings of Soviet justice; since the defendants confessed,
surely they must have been guilty. "Everything is true, except for
the facts," as A. T. Cholerton, the talented British journalist covering the USSR, observed.[4]

So Tukhachevsky was not the first major figure to perish. On
the contrary, by the end of 1938, so many prominent people had
disappeared that he was simply another name. Stalin had about
three quarters of the senior officers of the Red Army and the
senior party cadres murdered. A million people were killed outright, another five million sent to labor camps, where the survival
rate was one in ten.[5]

Nor was the Bolshevik Bonaparte the only high-ranking military man to disappear. Only two of the five marshals survived,
along with two of the fifteen army commanders, seven of the
fifty-seven corps commanders, and thirty-two of the 186 divisional commanders. All eleven of the assistant commissars and
ninety-eight out of the 108 men on the military soviet were gone.[6]

But those figures, horrific as they are, were submerged in the
general reign of terror. Khrushchev told Churchill that about ten
million people had already perished before 1937, most of them in
the Holodomor, the hunger famine. Today Russian and Western
researchers more or less agree with his estimate, but at the time,
and for many decades afterward, the reality of those millions of
deaths simply failed to register on the outside world; when mentioned at all, it was either in the manner of Beatrice Webb, or,
more crudely, expressed contemptuously, as by the correspon-

dent for the *New York Times:* "You can't make an omelet without breaking a few eggs."[7]

That Stalin's purge had, in Khrushchev's words, been responsible for the "annihilation of many military commanders and political workers during 1937–1941 because of his suspiciousness," simply failed to register in the West. After 1945, right up until the collapse of the Soviet state, the extent of the "annihilation" was questioned, blandly minimized, or even denied. Since Stalin had been victorious in his war, whatever damage he had inflicted on Russia must not have had any great effect. The men who replaced the dead officers were the victors of the Second World War, the new party members able to rebuild a country ravaged by Hitler's treacherous surprise attack. So even though Sovietologists and military historians noted the Great Terror, dutifully listed the figures, the data remained a minor footnote to Stalin's account of the conflict, despite what Khrushchev remarked as the inherent "improbability" of his narrative.[8]

But the Great Terror was a catastrophe for the Red Army that went far beyond the loss of almost every field grade officer. Khrushchev remarked that the purge went all the way down to the level of company commanders: when the new chief of staff of the 30th Rifle Division arrived at his new post in Dnieperopetrovsk, the senior officer commanding was a major. Everyone else had been arrested.[9]

But the purges also played havoc with the industrial infrastructure that was slowly being developed. No one even today knows the fate of many of the Soviet Union's best armaments experts. Even their full names have disappeared into the memory hole. Khalepsky, the army's tank expert, was shot in 1938, along with Zaslavsky, who had designed the first Soviet armored vehicle. The heads of the major design shops were killed, along with the heads of the tank factories.

Most of the engineers at the Kharkov Locomotive Factory, the men who had designed the highly successful BT series of tanks that had so impressed the Germans in Spain, were arrested. The same fate befell most of the senior aircraft designers. It is true that some of these men were later released, as was the case with Andrei Nikolaevich Tupolev, one of the founders of Soviet aviation. But as far as the Second World War was concerned, the damage had been done. The dry figures regarding release and rehabilitation ignore the reality of flesh and blood: a man who is hauled off in the middle of the night, beaten, made to confess to an imaginary crime, and then hustled off to a forced labor camp, even if he is set free, is never the same person. After 1939 the primary characteristics of Soviet society are paralysis and fear, and this situation would continue throughout the war. Engineers, technicians, and scientists disappeared into the camps, along with lowly but still vital railway workers and mechanics.[10]

Stalin was careful to conceal his actions in directing the purge, just as he was an expert in sending conflicting signals to his subordinates. Having personally orchestrated all the killings, he then, at the end of 1938, arranged for a decree forbidding any further mass arrests. The decree—and again this was typical Stalin behavior—was initially signed by Stalin (as first secretary) and Vyacheslav Mikhailovich Molotov (as the prime minister), and then promptly released as a joint declaration of the Central Committee and the All-Union Council of People's Commissars. Not only did the decree ending the terror (more or less) carry the mask of collegiality, but it gave the credulous the illusion that the senior leadership was finally taking action to correct the excesses of zealous party officials at the local level, and this in turn gave many otherwise intelligent Russians the idea that Stalin did not know what was going on.[11]

The unmasking of conspiracies of spies and traitors, with the inevitable arrests, tortures, confessions, and executions, did not however abruptly stop in December 1938, as the dates given for the Great Terror (1936–1938) often seem to suggest. Pavel Rychakov, air force chief of staff, was shot in spring 1941 for telling Stalin the truth about the poor design and quality control of his aircraft; at about the same time, Boris Lvovich Vannikov, commissar for armaments, was arrested and tortured as the result of a disagreement with one of Stalin's newly appointed replacement marshals. These were hardly isolated examples.[12] The survivors of the Great Terror were beginning to understand the cost of disagreeing with Stalin or one of his cronies, or giving him news he was not disposed to hear.

For the army, the cost of the Terror included more than tens of thousands of innocent officers and their families. It was not just Tukhachevsky who perished: his ideas about the need for modernization and professionalism died as well. At his trial, Semyon Budyonny, one of Stalin's military stooges, accused Tukhachevsky of "wrecking" the army by pushing for tanks and mechanized units. A telling comment, and one that signaled a major shift. The surviving senior officers were all men of exceedingly modest abilities. Some, like Budyonny and Kliment Yefremovich Voroshilov, were marooned in the past, preferring horses to tanks. Voroshilov had even been bitterly opposed to the formation of mechanized units.[13]

Others, like Grigory Ivanovich Kulik, who now became the head of the Red Army's artillery, were simply meddlers, but their meddling would have serious consequences. Kulik demanded that production of the modern (and excellent) 76.2 millimeter gun be stopped in favor of the 107 millimeter howitzer, a gun that had been in service with the czar's armies and was designed to be pulled by horses. Kulik's reasoning was simple: he had heard that the Germans were increasing the armor on their tanks, so that a bigger gun would be needed. The argument over the two guns went all the way to Stalin, who observed that he was familiar with the older gun from his Civil War days, and that it was an excellent weapon.

The debate is a perfect example of the Oz-like nature of the highest echelons of the government. The 76.2 millimeter gun, which fired an armor-piercing shell at a very high velocity, was a formidable antitank weapon. After the German invasion of the USSR, the Germans made extensive use of captured stocks of this weapon: mounted on an obsolete tank chassis and called Marder (Marten), it was the first successful self-propelled anti-tank weapon the Wehrmacht put into service.

If, as Kulik claimed, the Germans were increasing the thickness of the armor on their tanks (they weren't), the correct technical decision would have been to increase the hitting power of the existing weapon by increasing the length of the barrel and modifying the ammunition. During the war German engineers relied on both techniques to effect dramatic improvements in the hitting power of their guns. Since the supposedly more powerful 107 millimeter weapon Stalin remembered so fondly was a howitzer, it was designed to lob high-explosive shells down on enemy troops, not to disable armored vehicles. But apparently the only person in this debate who understood the difference between a gun and a howitzer was Vannikov, who ended up being arrested and tortured for "sabotage."[14] Instead of the modern army run by professionals that Tukhachevsky was trying to create, the Red Army was becoming the exact opposite.

The result of Kulik's meddling, Stalin's ignorance, and the fate of those with intelligence who opposed them had serious consequences. Although the 76.2 millimeter gun was eventually mass-produced, Kulik's opposition, taken with Stalin's apparent concurrence, and Vannikov's arrest, limited not only the number of the initial version that the Kirov factory in Leningrad produced, but drastically curtailed the production of ammunition as well.

These shifts help to explain an otherwise paradoxical situation. In the mid-1930s, foreign military observers recorded the modernization championed by Tukhachevsky and his followers, and gave the Red Army very high marks.[15] Their observations were confirmed by what was known about Soviet doctrine. Like the French and the Germans, the Red Army's leadership saw a successful offensive as requiring the coordination of all arms of service: "the isolated use of different arms would give the advantage to the enemy: it would give him the opportunity to strike our troops piecemeal, cause futile losses, and in due course bring defeat during a given stage of battle." [16]

So the combat capabilities of the Red Army in the two years immediately preceding the German attack were judged according to what had arguably been true in 1937. But these capabilities were destroyed in the years that followed. This erroneous estimate of the Red Army's strength was dramatically reinforced by the time lag between the formulation of ideas of military modernization, and the production of the actual equipment to accomplish that end.

Tukhachevsky's fall coincided with the emergence of the first examples of the modern weapons he had championed. Those weapons, such as the T-34/76 medium tank, were by and large excellent designs. Although hamstrung by the purges, the first prototypes of the new tank were built in January 1940, and production was scheduled to begin in June with the modest goal of 500 machines the first year. But Kulik, who in the words of the leading expert on Soviet armor "developed a strong dislike" for the vehicle, managed to hobble initial production. Still, nearly 1,000 of these vehicles were in service by June 1941. [17]

Although dwarfed by the reputation of the T-34, the Soviet heavy tank produced exclusively at Leningrad, the KV-1, was also a first-class design, and the 1940 reorganization of Soviet armor called for each division to have sixty-three of these, 210 T-34 tanks, and 102 of the older light tanks, of which the USSR had an enormous supply on hand. But by June 1941 the Red Army had just over 500 of the heavy tanks in service, roughly enough of both of the new types to equip four armored divisions to full strength.

Had these new tanks been concentrated into two armored

corps (each of two divisions), in theory the Red Army would have possessed a potent and modern strike force. Instead, the new vehicles were scattered throughout the army. Not only did this drastically dilute the power of the new vehicles, but it greatly increased tactical problems: the armored commanders, all of whom were new and inexperienced as a result of the purges, had to deal with a mix of obsolete and new vehicles.

The variety of types assigned also greatly complicated routine maintenance and supply. By contrast, the Germans and the French limited the types of vehicles assigned to their units; insofar as was possible, the bulk of the tanks assigned to an armored unit were all of one type. This practice not only simplified logistics and training, but meant that armored commanders were deploying groups of vehicles with the same characteristics and limitations. When the vehicles were themselves new to the service, this practice was particularly important as it centralized the process of maintenance and the inevitable discovery of weaknesses and peculiarities inherent in complex machinery.

Adding to this muddle were two other problems. The T-34/76, for example, was designed to carry eighty rounds of 76.2 millimeter ammunition, but Kulik's opposition to the main tank gun, described above, had dramatically limited the number of shells produced. When the war began, the amount available for each tank was between six and twelve rounds. But at least the medium tank crews actually had armor-piercing shells; the KV-1 crews had to use ordinary artillery shells that were of little use against enemy tanks.[18]

The other grave difficulty is a curious one that throws an intriguing light on the realities of Soviet data. On paper, according to the official figures, each year after 1936 Soviet tank factories produced on average as many new tanks as the total number of vehicles the Wehrmacht had in service, a staggering disproportion.[19] By June 1941 the Red Army should therefore have had nearly 28,000 tanks, enough to equip the sixty-one armored divisions that the 1940 plan demanded, each with its complement of 375 vehicles.[20]

But the situation on the ground reveals a dramatically different story. One of the best equipped units in the Red Army was the 3rd Mechanized Corps, based in Lithuania. It had 460 tanks, including 109 of the new medium and heavy vehicles. But as a mechanized corps was supposed to have two armored divisions, it should have deployed 750 tanks, of which only 204 should have been light tanks. In other words, the corps was operating at only about three fifths of its authorized strength in absolute numbers, and at only one fifth of its supposed hitting power in medium and heavy vehicles. At the other end of the front, the 19th Mechanized Corps had only 280 vehicles, almost all of them light tanks. The most powerful unit in the Red Army, the 6th Mechanized Corps (based around Minsk), had only half of the complement of T-34 tanks called for.[21]

Factories were supposed to produce a certain number of tanks to meet production quotas set in Moscow, so they dutifully reported that those quotas had been met, reckoning that Stalin or one of his minions would not actually stand at the end of the assembly line counting vehicles, an assumption fortified by the growing realization that complaints generally tended to have unfortunate results for the person doing the complaining. The factory managers were right, because the scheme to equip sixty-one armored divisions made sense only if Moscow believed it had enough tanks to equip them.

The falsification of production statistics is only part of the story. From the very first, the emphasis in Soviet production was on turning out large numbers of the finished products, often without any regard for quality. For example, in the 1920s the USSR had begun intensive production of tracked agricultural vehicles, beginning with reverse-engineered foreign models obtained abroad, such as the Kommunar series of tractors, of which over 3,000 were produced by 1930.

The Kommunar tractors were built at the Kharkov Locomotive Factory, which, along with the factories in Leningrad, also produced most of the Soviet tanks of the 1930s, including some 8,000 of the Soviet BT series tanks that were the mainstay of Red Army tank units. The estimate of the foreign engineers who visited the Kommunar part of the factory was that the vehicles, if they ran at all, had a service life of only a few hours, while the BT series tanks had a highly theoretical working life of only 100 hours.[22]

The short life expectancy had two consequences. On the one hand, it precluded much serious training. Simply by learning how to drive the vehicle, tankers would shorten its operational life dramatically: "Most commanders felt lucky to have T-34 drivers with three to five hours of instruction."[23] If a war began, the cross-country speed of even a very fast tank, a working life of 100 hours, the abysmal level of training of tank crews, all meant that grandiose notions of deep battle, of lightning thrusts, were hardly sustainable if the vehicle had to be scrapped after being driven for less than a week.

Like training and proficiency, the state of repair and maintenance is difficult to quantify, and the subject is often simply ignored: the complex mechanisms of modern warfare are treated like the muzzle-loading cast iron guns of the eighteenth century. The first armored theorists, notably J. F. C. Fuller, had written about tanks as though they were perpetual motion machines. In a memorable passage, Fuller cited several famous battles, arguing by analogy that "weapons form ninety-nine percent of every victory," and that the use of tanks would therefore guarantee success.[24]

True enough, if we assume the weapons are actually working. In order to keep a tank running, it is necessary to have spare parts, repair facilities with specialized equipment, and vehicles capable of towing the disabled tank to the facility. Given the unreliability of Soviet industrial goods, the existence of a developed logistical infrastructure was extremely important. At bottom, this was the practical implication of Tukhachevsky's desire to modernize the army, one far more important than an actual doctrine. But when the marshal and his apostles perished, so did their emphasis. There is no evidence that the new leadership of the Red Army paid any attention to those needs. On the contrary: in 1941 "the huge Soviet tank park of 22,000–24,000 vehicles was largely immobile: 44 percent of the tanks required rebuilding, and 29 percent required replacement of a major component such as an engine or transmission."[25]

As the disproportion in tanks, so too with manpower. A traditional problem: in the Polish War of 1920, the Bolsheviks could put only half a million men in the field, which was barely 10 percent of their military strength.[26] Two decades later, although on paper an infantry division counted 14,483 men, the estimate of the researcher who has gone over the actual strengths is that "the Red Army was woefully understrength, with most divisions numbering 8,000 or less, even before the German onslaught."[27]

As a statistical construct, the Red Army was every bit as formidable as the Bolsheviks claimed and as their admirers (and enemies) in the West believed. But in June 1941 it was simply the military variant of the tableau that Custine summoned to mind so vividly in 1839: "the facades of villages, made of planks and painted canvas, and set up, in the distance, at every quarter league of the route, in order to make the triumphant sovereign believe that the desert had become people during her reign."[28]

By contrast, the leaders of the Wehrmacht, whatever their numerous moral deficiencies, had learned from their experiences, beginning with the invasion of Austria in 1938. They discovered that running motor vehicles on a paved road can result in mechanical failures entirely independent of combat. Those failures created a new set of logistical problems: when a tracked vehicle weighing twenty tons or more breaks down, it can hardly be pushed off the road like a car or truck.

So the Germans had been forced to develop a whole military infrastructure of support for the mechanized units modern armies depended on. Their tanks and trucks were supported by wheeled transporters (as well as railroad cars), tanker trucks carrying fuel, special towing vehicles, mobile repair shops stocked with spare parts, and trained mechanics. They also were forced to develop a communications system that enabled feedback from the users to the producers, so that weaknesses could be remedied, and vehicles retrofitted and improved. Twenty-first-century motorists take such matters for granted, but in the 1930s they were still being worked out.

The Germans had learned that tracked vehicles capable of removing disabled tanks were an indispensable part of any armored division, but the Soviets never built any, so the removal of disabled vehicles was highly problematic, as was the all-important matter of replacement parts: Soviet factories turned out tanks, not spare parts.[29] There was thus no comparison between the logistical support systems of the two military establishments.

But there was one curious way in which the armies of the two dictators were alike. In both cases the incessant barrage of propaganda emitted by both states concealed serious structural weaknesses in their armies. Symbolically if not literally, the death of Tukhachevsky was the death of any serious peacetime efforts to create a modern and professional Soviet army in which training and logistics would be emphasized. Absent the guiding hand of Walter Wever, the German air force, supposedly the key arm of the National Socialist regime, failed to meet the challenges of a rapidly evolving aircraft industry; it failed not only to develop the strategic bomber Germany needed, but to maintain a steady stream of modern replacements for its aging air fleet.

But then for a mad dictator bent on world conquest, Hitler hardly exerted himself to crank up Germany's industrial capacity in support of his efforts. Because the Second World War would see the emergence of the tank, which dominated the European battlefields, the figures for German tank production are revealing.

In December 1940, when planning for the June 1941 offensive went into high gear, the German tank inventory was hardly larger than it had been in August 1939. At that point the Wehrmacht possessed 3,437 tanks; in May 1940, it had 3,223; and at the end of December it had 3,799 vehicles.[30] This was hardly much of an increase, particularly when it is considered that in May 1940 the Allied tank force was at least as large as the German one, and probably larger.

But the modest increase in the size of the tank park, quite revealing in itself, is misleading. In August 1939 the vast majority of Germany's armor consisted of light tanks that combat soon proved hopelessly obsolete, highly unsuitable for modern warfare. These vehicles constituted 82 percent of the tank force. The army knew they needed to be withdrawn from service and replaced with newer and better models. But by the end of 1940, light tanks still constituted slightly over 70 percent of the inventory. The tank production figures, typical for the manufacture of other armaments as well, do not suggest that Hitler was arming himself to the teeth.

In fact, by the end of 1940, in Germany the basic tools of warfare a modern army needed—tanks, planes, and guns—were either obsolete or had been found not suitable. Some, although excellent designs, were reaching the end of their effective service life. The famous fighter plane designed by Messerschmitt (the Bf 109) had entered service in 1936. For the Luftwaffe to maintain the air superiority over the battlefield German tactics mandated, a newer design was desperately needed. The same was true for the other two aircraft vital to the new German way of waging war, the infamous Stuka ground attack plane and the Junkers transport required by the airborne units.

The air force needed more than a strategic bomber: by 1941 it needed a whole new set of airplanes. But none was forthcoming, and, as with the tanks, there seemed to be no particular sense of urgency either in developing new vehicles or in producing suitably modified and improved versions of what was already in service. By June 1940, German tank commanders were aware that even their best tank designs were hopelessly outgunned by their French opponents, and no wonder: the Mark 3 tank was equipped with a truly wretched 3.7 centimeter weapon: the ammunition issued to hapless tankers and antitank gun crews bounced off the armor of the French and British vehicles. The 8.8 centimeter towed gun that would so impress the Allies (particularly in Africa in 1941–1942) was actually an antiaircraft gun hastily pressed into service by army commanders desperate for something to stop Allied tanks.

So production of the Mark 3 tank with the popgun stopped in July 1940, and the new vehicles were equipped with a marginally better 5 centimeter gun. The Mark 3, thus equipped, had originally been intended to be the main battle tank of German armored units, but by the start of the Russian campaign there were only a few hundred of the newer vehicles on hand, hardly sufficient to equip four armored divisions in the prewar table of organization. The heavily armored and armed tanks, the potent antitank guns the Allies encountered from 1943 on, all were new designs produced as a result of the Wehrmacht's needs in Russia.

After the occupation of Czechoslovakia, the Germans had begun equipping their woefully understrength armored units with Czech tanks, as about 200 of these fell into their hands. This was a decent prewar vehicle, although already obsolete in 1939, and was replaced by a new and improved model. The newly acquired Czech production system was actually considerably more efficient than its German counterpart and managed to produce more examples of the new design (called the 38t) than the Germans managed to produce of their improved Mark 3 equipped with the 5 centimeter gun. But even so, there were fewer than 500 of these newer Czech tanks in service even as late as May 1941— equipped with a gun that everyone knew had been hopelessly outclassed two years earlier.[31]

There was no corresponding push to design new weapons or to produce more of the existing ones. It was not until spring 1941 that there was any appreciable acceleration in the production of armaments, well after Hitler had reached his decision to attack, and Soviet production had increased as well.

When these crippling weaknesses on both sides are noted, they are used either as proof of Stalin's inherently peaceful intentions or of Hitler's manic grandiosity. But either view contradicts the basic classical principle enunciated by Publius Flavius Vegetius Renatus in the late Roman Empire:

> He who wishes for peace, prepares for war. He who wants victory must instruct his soldiers diligently. He who hopes for a favorable outcome leaves nothing to chance. No one will provoke, no one gives offense, to a superior he knows will fight.[32]

In other words, it was precisely their weaknesses, when coupled with their boundless self-confidence, that made Hitler and Stalin so dangerous. They either lacked the true certainty that comes from superior wisdom (sometimes expressed as a healthy skepticism), or they simply felt themselves beyond that standard.

Stalin's ambivalence manifested itself early on. In public, he did nothing to prevent party spokesmen from attacking the rising tide of fascism. With the outbreak of the Spanish Civil War in 1936, the USSR became the acknowledged international leader of the antifascist camp. The Soviets poured arms and military experts into the fledgling republic to support it in the bitter struggle that was being waged, just as Hitler and Mussolini did for the Nationalists.

Behind the scenes Stalin behaved differently. After Hitler's ascent in 1933, Stalin had begun very cautious overtures to Berlin and even to Rome.[33] At the same time as he was allowing arms and experts to be sent to Spain, he was playing Chiang Kai-shek off against Mao in the Chinese struggle.[34] Although the idea of Stalin supporting Chiang as opposed to Mao seems at first glance peculiar, it is consistent with how the wily Georgian operated. He was not willing to see another Bolshevik emerge with enough of a power base to challenge him as sole leader of world communism any more than he was willing to let the socialists and anarchists dominate the Spanish Republic: his agents in Spain were as interested in getting rid of their fraternal enemies as in fighting off the fascist menace.[35]

As the Spanish Civil War slowly wound down, an event that conveniently coincided with Stalin's elimination of the military and party cadres, he began to send out more public signals of interest in coming to an agreement with Hitler. The first such signal was his address to the 18th Party Congress on March 10, 1939, but as we now know, his remarks on that day were only the first open acknowledgment of what had been going on sporadically since 1934, and had been steadily intensifying as the Spanish Civil War came to an end.[36]

In any event, by the end of August 1939, the two dictators were in agreement. To the consternation of almost everyone, including many devout Bolsheviks, the two signed a treaty: when the Second World War began on September 1, 1939, Stalin was Hitler's ally. The consternation was understandable, but in retrospect the alliance was logical. Regardless of their ideological difference (sometimes overemphasized), Hitler and Stalin had two points of agreement: they both wanted to eliminate Poland from the map, and they both despised the Western democracies.

Whether or not they perceived their respective military limitations, both men had a shrewd understanding of how economic forces had shaped the course of the First World War, a war that both countries had lost. Wilhelmine Germany was an industrial power of the first order. It had no difficulty in producing all the armaments it needed. By contrast, the Russia of the Romanovs lacked the manufacturing base necessary to match the German and Austro-Hungarian armies it confronted.

Germany's weakness, both in 1914 and 1939, was its dependence on imports, both to keep its population fed adequately and to supply its factories with raw materials. Although Bolshevik policies had a disastrous impact on agriculture, the Soviet leadership was perfectly willing to starve its citizens in order to export foodstuffs abroad in return for what it saw as more pressing needs.

Stalin and Hitler regarded themselves as the leaders of countries with complementary needs and in analogous positions. They wanted to restore their respective states to their pre-1914 greatness and remediate the fatal weakness that the war had laid bare. For both men the shadow of that disastrous conflict loomed large. It shaped their thinking, and gave them concrete objectives whose achievement could be used to increase their stature both at home and abroad.

Publicly, the treaty they signed was what it claimed to be, a nonaggression pact. But the treaty was a foreign policy iceberg: the most important parts were beneath the surface. As with every other aspect of the Soviet Union, the matter is still clouded in propagandistic justifications: two decades after the collapse Stalin's rapprochement with Hitler is still being justified and obfuscated, a salutary reminder of the persistence of Bolshevik fictions when they coincide with ordinary chauvinistic impulses.[37] That its implications are therefore poorly grasped is not surprising.

The economic arrangements of reciprocal imports remediated the strategic weaknesses of both countries. At the same time, the territorial arrangements contained in the secret part of the pact allowed the two dictators free hands in reshaping their states, in returning them to their prewar size. Hitler gave Stalin a free hand in all the newly independent Baltic lands that had been Romanov provinces: Finland, Estonia, Latvia, Lithuania. He recognized the historical Russian interest in that part of southeastern Europe known as Bessarabia, which after 1919 had been incorporated into Romania.

The pact mentioned neither Poland nor trade, but both signatories knew exactly what they were about. The division of central Europe into two spheres of influence meant there would be no Poland; that nation would now be folded into Germany and Russia. So at one stroke, Stalin regained all the areas lost in 1917–1920, and Hitler would fulfill the aspirations of the Austrian pan-Germans of 1900, melding the Habsburg and Hohenzollern empires into one vast and powerful state.

The division into two spheres of influence would ensure that the nominally neutral states on the extreme ends of the demarcation line, Sweden, Hungary, and Romania, would now engage in desperate balancing acts, thus providing Hitler even more economic security. He could now afford to thumb his nose at the blockade conducted by the Royal Navy as in 1914–1919, which was believed to have ultimately brought that great power to its knees. But with Swedish iron ore, Russian chrome and manganese, Romanian oil, and the agricultural bounties of the east, a blockade would have little impact on fortress Germany.

Stalin had equally cogent reasons: he had succeeded where Lenin and his circle had failed, had regained all the lost provinces with one stroke of the pen. The Wehrmacht would dispose of Poland for him, and he may certainly be forgiven for assuming that the Red Army could smash whatever puny resistance anyone else was capable of mounting. The resulting triumph would do more than elevate his status: the lost provinces were the wealthiest part of the Romanov empire, the core of European Russia. It required no particular sagacity to see the advantages to both men and their states, and in fall 1939 and spring 1940, the two dictators systematically implemented their plans.

As is often the case, their acts had unintended consequences.

On the one hand, Hitler's invasion of Poland, although a military success that exposed the moral weakness and military impotence of Great Britain and France, plunged him into a war with both powers. Stalin was hardly the only person to reckon that such a war would be a repetition of the last one, a bloody struggle that would go on for years, exhausting both sides. In that quite plausible scenario, the Bolshevik state would emerge as the dominant power, if not in the world, certainly in Europe.

However, Stalin's approach to Hitler was no short-term tactical move. We know this because on August 27, 1939, two prominent European communists wrote Stalin to confirm that "the position of the Party should always remain the same: to resist the aggression of Fascist Germany."[38] Stalin's response was swift and unequivocal. Georgi Mikhailovich Dimitrov, the more famous of the two letter writers, was summoned to Moscow. On September 7, 1939, Stalin lectured him on the error of his ways:

> The division of the capitalist countries into fascist and democratic countries has lost its meaning . . . [he declared, and he] proposed a renunciation of the slogan of a unified popular front. Communists in capitalist countries ought to rise up resolutely against their own governments, against the war.[39]

In other words, in the near future Stalin was not only serious about the pact, but he was serious about the alliance. He was willing to drain the reservoir of foreign goodwill he had filled up by assuming the moral leadership of the antifascist front if by doing so he strengthened the USSR. By now he was in a position to dictate to the surviving party cadres with absolute freedom: whatever he said was Holy Writ, and one reads through accounts of the tortuous rationalization of foreign communists as they sought to reconcile this abrupt shift, the apologia of sympathetic chroniclers, with a certain horrified fascination.[40]

After the signing of the pact, events moved swiftly over the next ten months, from the attack on Poland (September 1, 1939) to the capitulation of France (June 22, 1940). Although a comprehensive account of those months lies outside our purpose here, certain events deserve mention, as they have a bearing not only on the uneasy relationship that developed after the August pact, but explain the hesitations of both men.

Insofar as Hitler believed that he could devour Poland with impunity, he was mistaken, although neither his calculations or the consequences were as disastrous as is sometimes claimed: whatever chance the Poles had to fight off the Germans until Allied military action took effect disappeared when the Red Army moved into Poland on September 17. By the end of the first week of October, the country had once again ceased to exist. At first glance, it would appear that Stalin was the winner. Hitler was now at war with both Great Britain and France. The Soviet dictator could sit on the sidelines and plan his next move, secure in the belief that his gamble had paid off: it would be a long war.

Close scrutiny suggests a slightly different perspective. The Anglo-French military response revealed not only a fundamental lack of will, but a certain military incapacity. The best the Allies could manage was to lay plans for a naval blockade, thus confirming Hitler's prudence in securing his supplies of raw materials. Nor was the acquisition of half of Poland a prize to be scorned. Between the two world wars, German imports from Poland had been substantial, about what was anticipated by Stalin and Hitler in August 1939 for subsequent years. As we shall see below, the Second World War was very much a war whose objectives were primarily economic, as the Allied plans developed during fall 1939 make clear.

Those plans were hatched largely in response to Stalin's next move. Now that Poland was no more, Stalin turned his attention further north. Fabricating a provocation, and making demands on the Finnish government that it was not about to accept, Stalin engineered a war with Finland.

On November 30, 1939, the Red Army attacked. Four armies, totaling nearly half a million men, supported by an estimated 2,000 tanks and 2,000 artillery pieces, stormed across the two stretches of accessible border. Kirill Afanasievich Meretskov, Stalin's chief of staff, was one of the few Soviet generals with recent combat experience (he had fought with the Republicans in the Spanish Civil War). He estimated that the entire operation would take less than two weeks. Given the forces opposing him, this was by no means a naive estimate. Finland had a regular army of 156,000 men, fifty-six fighter planes, twenty-five tanks, and 422 artillery pieces. Most of the equipment was obsolete.

Helsinki, the capital, was within easy bombing distance of short-range aircraft, and the Soviet air force began bombing it on the first day of the war. But despite the enormous Soviet advantages in equipment and manpower, for the next two and a half months, although Finland was ultimately forced to give in to the Soviet demands, the Finns fought the Red Army to a standstill.[41]

Clearly Stalin had miscalculated badly, and on several different levels. Over the course of the fighting, the Soviets appear to have lost about 1,600 tanks, to an enemy with no armor and no anti-tank weaponry of note.[42] Initially, the Soviets claimed to have lost "only" 48,745 dead and 149,000 wounded, but, like all other data released during Stalinist times, this figure is a fiction. The current estimate accepted by most Finnish historians is for a death toll in excess of a quarter of a million Russian soldiers, with another quarter of a million wounded. Khrushchev, in a famous passage in his memoirs, claimed that Soviet losses came to a staggering total: "I'd say we lost as many as a million lives."[43] As Stalin never tired of pointing out, Khrushchev was an uneducated peasant who "doesn't understand statistics," so perhaps he was speaking figuratively.[44] But there's nothing absurd about his estimate: no one really knows how many soldiers went missing, how many perished from cold and hunger, and how many were murdered as a result of Stalin's fury at the initial failures.

The failure of the air campaign was surprising. Over the course of the Finnish War, the Soviet air force claimed to have flown over 40,000 sorties. The Finns recorded 2,075 separate strategic bombing attacks, which killed and wounded about 2,600 civilians.[45] Somewhere between 300 and 400 Soviet planes were shot down by Finnish antiaircraft defenses, and Finland's handful of pilots claim to have shot down another 200. Although pilots and ground crews tended to exaggerate the number of planes downed, given that Finland had no air force and no antiaircraft defenses, the figures suggest a low level of military effectiveness on the part of the Soviet air force, as well as provide an assessment of the relatively insignificant results of strategic bombing, given the aircraft of the period.

In addition to demoralizing his sympathizers in the West, the military debacle revealed the price the Red Army paid in blood for its losses during the Terror. Historically the German military had had close ties with the Finns; German military intelligence, the Abwehr, was hardly unaware of just how badly the Red Army performed in combat, just as they had some notion of the disorganization and chaos that accompanied its earlier offensive into a hapless Poland.

The surprisingly poor performance of the Red Army against Finland meant that instead of two weeks, the conflict dragged on for three months: time enough for the Allies to plan their next move. Although the twists and turns of that plan need not detain us here, the result essentially put the seal on the Second World War as a conflict whose objectives would be economic rather than political or military. The Allied plan was to interdict the shipments of iron ore flowing from Scandinavia into Germany, the idea being that if the Allies could shut off those shipments, the Germans would be unable to manufacture the tanks and planes they needed.

Stalin and Hitler had their own riposte: on February 11, 1940, they signed a commercial agreement that greatly expanded the trade provisions agreed on in August 1939, increasing the value of goods transferred by approximately 400 percent. Hitler received grain, oil, and valuable metals that his armaments industry needed.[46] In return, Stalin received machinery and equipment that he could then reverse-engineer and manufacture locally. As a result, the dictators could thumb their noses at the Allies, and promptly did so.

They were greatly aided by the next Allied fiasco: the Anglo-French naval expedition to seize Norway. By the time the ships sailed, the Finns had come to terms with Stalin, so the always thin pretext for intervention had disappeared. The German navy's plan to preempt the Allied invasion was a brilliant tactical and strategic success. The Allies had been first to plan and first to set sail, serene in the belief that they controlled the high seas with their vastly superior navies. In the event, the Germans slipped past them and got to Norway first, and overran Denmark as well. Strategically, the German counter not only ensured that the iron ore would continue to flow into German factories, but it made London and Paris focus on Norway to the exclusion of the theater in the south. When, on May 10, 1940, the Germans struck France, Belgium, and the Netherlands simultaneously, they therefore achieved a considerable tactical surprise.

Nor were they alone. Stalin had assumed this new war of the capitalist powers would be a repeat of the previous one, at least in the west. Although he had already assessed the leadership of Great Britain and France as being feeble and incapable, he was as astonished as the rest of the world at the rapid German successes of May 1940. In less than three months, the Germans had seized

Norway, Denmark, Belgium, Luxembourg, and the Netherlands, forced France to sue for terms, and driven the British back to their island, and in less time than the Red Army had required to subdue Finland.

Hitler was now master of Europe, so Stalin could congratulate himself on his sagacity in reversing what the world, and most communists, perceived as a steadfast Bolshevik opposition to fascism. He had guessed correctly. On the other hand, by the end of June 1940, Hitler was vastly more powerful than he had been at the end of the previous August.

The most perplexing and mysterious period of the Second World War was about to begin.

Historians and biographers often write as though the motivations of Stalin and Hitler are easy to divine, provided one has access to the proper documents. But the two dictators may very well be the most secretive individuals in history. Hitler openly boasted about his penchant for secrecy. When he appointed Franz Halder army chief of staff on September 1, 1938, Hitler referred to this explicitly: "You will never be able to discover my thoughts and intentions until I give them out as orders. . . . You will never learn what is going on in my head." [47]

By comparison with Stalin, however, Hitler's thoughts and intentions are pellucidly clear. Stalin used the Bolshevik fiction of collective leadership to mask his actions as well as his motives, taking particular pains to create the impression that he was removed from the daily repressions, blunders, and tragedies that were rampant in Soviet life. At every stage there appears to have been a conscious effort on his part not only to keep his fellow Bolsheviks guessing what he wanted and what he meant, but to mislead them on key issues.

Partly in desperation, then, there has been a tendency to view Hitler's decision to attack Stalin, and Stalin's refusal to believe that he would be attacked, as instances of psychological derangement. The idea of Hitler as madman is a subtext throughout much that has been written about him, and particularly when it comes to the war.[48] Bolshevik propaganda, antifascism, and barely disguised sympathies have precluded the same treatment of Stalin. But his biographers, no more than his critics, have been unable to provide a convincing explanation for the problem that Khrushchev posed and that has since been confirmed by a variety of sources: Stalin was given ample warning of the attack and brushed it aside. He absolutely refused to believe it was happening.

There is no need to resort to the mystical or the psychological to explain the behavior of both dictators in the months preceding June 1941. Hitler's behavior is the easier to explain. On the one side, he became increasingly alarmed by Stalin's territorial grabs and his crude diplomacy. Stalin now proceeded to claim his share of what was left of the Baltic, annexing Estonia, Latvia, and Lithuania outright. The pact had carved up the area into German and Soviet spheres of influence, but that phrase suggested a relationship on the order of the one the Germans enjoyed with Hungary, Slovakia, Romania, and Bulgaria, not outright possession.

There was a disturbing clumsiness about Stalin's moves, and that clumsiness was brought to a head by the abrupt Soviet invasion of Bessarabia and Bukovina that began on June 28, 1940. The August 1939 pact had explicitly recognized a Soviet interest in Bessarabia, but the recognition of interest was hardly the same as ceding the region outright to the Bolsheviks. But the pact had said nothing about the adjacent region, Bukovina; it had been part of the Habsburg empire, never a Russian possession, but Stalin moved into there as well.

Stalin's moves in the southeast posed a potential threat to the flow of oil from southern Romanian fields, and Hitler's response came quickly. In July he ordered the army to begin work on a plan for a Soviet invasion. Six months later, after a visit to Berlin from the rudely bumbling Molotov, Hitler gave the order for a greatly expanded plan of attack that would take place in May 1941, while his minions continued to negotiate with Stalin's emissaries about the trade agreements.

Hitler's moves, generally presented in isolation, as though Stalin's were either entirely reasonable or totally unrelated, are well known, Stalin's considerably less so. However, the most recent evidence confirms what German interrogations of captured Soviet officers revealed in 1941, that Stalin was in fact planning to attack Hitler at the first opportune moment.[49] For approximately fifty years this idea has been either dismissed as beneath contempt or savagely attacked, despite the fact that it conforms to the pattern of Soviet behavior both before 1939 and after 1945.

So the recent evidence contradicts a long established Stalinist legend, and certainly explains Hitler's motivation: his attack on the Soviet Union was a preemptive strike.

What the information about Stalin's intentions does not do, however, is explain why Stalin remained so convinced that Hitler would not attack. He had an extensive network of spies operating all over the world and thus had access to much information that subsequent historians did not have (and in some cases still lack), but there's no doubt that he was receiving a steady flow of reports from a wide variety of sources pointing to the eventual June attack.

His determination created a paralysis in the Red Army that had been widely noted. As we shall see in the following chapter, that paralysis is exaggerated. However, it seems true that Stalin discounted the information he was receiving, and that he was convinced the news was either a provocation or a ruse, right up until the shooting actually began (and then some).

Given that Stalin was dead wrong, the idea that he had already elevated himself, lived in splendid arrogance and isolation, is certainly a tempting explanation. He may well have been in that state of mind; however, when we consider the pattern of his decision making, a much simpler and more rational idea emerges, one that stands in sharp contradiction to Hitler's.

As this brief account of Hitler's actions has suggested, his foreign policy and military decisions were astonishingly correct. He may well have miscalculated the Allied response to the Polish invasion, but by June 1940, it can hardly be said that France and Great Britain had made him pay for his error; nor would they. The Allied coalition that defeated Hitler was the almost exclusive creature of the United States and the Soviet Union. The former had been neutral in 1939–1940, the latter Hitler's ally.

Hitler was a supremely wicked man; unfortunately, his wickedness was matched by his evil genius. Thus far, his boldest strokes had been wildly successful. In March 1940, no one had the slightest inkling of the astonishing events of the next three months. His penchant for seemingly wild gambles, beginning with the notion that he could remilitarize the Rhineland and get away with it, had paid spectacular dividends.

He definitely overreached himself as the months went by, but his judgments of the military situation were more correct than incorrect, as they had been consistently since his ascent to power. Moreover, a penchant for bold moves, the attempt to deliver the master stroke that will reverse the situation as if by magic, while a high-risk strategy, is also the hallmark of strategic genius.

By contrast, Stalin, who was no gambler, was cautious and careful, continually guessed wrong. He had reckoned that the collectivization of agriculture would eventually result in greater productivity. It signally failed to do so: by the start of the war, years after the conclusion of the collectivization campaign, production of grain was substantially below the 1913 figure, even relying on Soviet data that was highly inflated.[50]

By diverting all the available resources to industrialization, he believed he could propel the Soviet Union into the ranks of the great industrial powers. Instead, the only serious progress was in the numbers being generated by obedient party hacks. He had imagined that he could eliminate the experienced commanders of the Red Army, replace them with inexperienced and inept trainees: the debacle of the Finnish War, which he had allowed his generals to estimate would be short and conclusive, demonstrated how wrong he was in matters military.

In reaching an agreement with Hitler, he had supposed that a future war would be long and exhausting, that he would be the real winner. Instead, by July 1940, Hitler was astride Europe, having vanquished his adversaries on the continent.

Stalin had imagined that his abrupt reversal of Bolshevik opposition to the fascists would be but a ripple on the pond; instead, it destroyed the ideals of many of the cause's most enthusiastic adherents in the West.

Surrounded by sycophants and lackeys, few of whom possessed more than a grade school education, he continued on, serene in his estimate of himself, punishing those who were blamed for his mistakes, and creating a well nigh total paralysis of the state at every level.

He now continued to blunder in his dealings with Hitler: the abrupt annexation of Bessarabia and Bukovina set off alarm bells in Bucharest, ensured that the ramshackle Romanian government would now have no choice but to throw in that country's lot with Hitler. Molotov's behavior in Berlin, where he acted with the Germans the way he was accustomed to dealing with his subordinates, hardly helped the situation, and again, it is impossible to believe that Molotov was a loose cannon. He had been chosen for the role by Stalin because he was the perfect instrument of the great dictator's aims.

No one knows what was going on in Stalin's mind, and for each mistake, a charitable explanation can be found. However, when considered as a whole, it is difficult to escape the conclusion that his decisions were usually wrong and his judgment faulty. Given the pattern, it is no surprise that he refused to believe what he was being told: his entire career had been based on a refusal to listen to what anyone was telling him. The only real difference in this case was that he was unable to have the messengers with the bad news murdered, as in most instances he couldn't lay his hands on them.

So now, in the first six months of 1941, he was poised to make the greatest mistake of his life, to continue on the course he had set, confident that Hitler would not attack in 1941.

Curiously, although no one disputes either the error or the magnitude of it, this is the one mistake Stalin made for which there is a great deal more justification than any of the others.

It is tempting to note that since in July 1940 Hitler started the planning process for a Russian invasion, one that actually happened within twelve months, his intentions were therefore obvious. But the situation is not so simple. On the one hand, Hitler ordered plans for operations that never took place (an attack on Gibraltar, an invasion of Great Britain, an offensive operation against Malta). That he told the army to start planning meant only that he had told them to start planning.

Massive troop concentrations hardly constituted evidence that an attack was imminent. Thus far, even when a planned operation actually occurred, it rarely did so within the prescribed time frame. Hitler ordered the start of the offensive against France six times between October 1939 and May 1940, but only the last order actually resulted in an attack.

Nor did the operation against the USSR bear all that much resemblance to what had been planned when it was finally executed. In March 1939, Hitler directed the army to begin planning an attack on Poland. That plan, called Weiss, was the first and last time the Wehrmacht was allowed to plan an operation on its own and execute it pretty much within the projected time frame. From then on Hitler recast, rejected, and interfered with each plan, often getting advice from officers outside the normal chain of command. Gelb, the plan for May 1940, was typical of the new process. It went through major revisions, revisions instigated by relatively junior officers who had access to Hitler. The operation was delayed over and over again, and the final version was substantially different from what was originally envisioned.

Actually, the situation was even more chaotic than an analysis of any one operation indicates. Not only was Gelb modified and delayed, but in March 1940, Hitler essentially moved it to the back of the line, so that the preemptive Scandinavian strike could be carried out. The situation inside the German high command after September 1939 was a sort of controlled chaos, given Hitler's demands, his increasing interference, his abrupt changes of priorities, and his penchant for listening to officers who in the normal course of things had no business being involved in planning military operations (not according to the high command in Berlin, at any rate).

By early May 1941 there was another wrinkle. In trying to read Hitler's intentions, there was one factor that constrained any army: the need to stage major military operations at certain times of the year. In northern Europe, the most suitable start date was early May, when the summer months of fair weather lay ahead and there would be plenty of daylight. This was particularly the case given that the most logical invasion route into Russia from western Europe ran roughly parallel to the Baltic Sea. That window of opportunity was particularly relevant in northwestern Russia, as it typically started raining in September, turning the landscape into a soggy mass that stabilized only when the ground froze. And indeed the start date for Barbarossa, the Wehrmacht's plan for the invasion, assumed the offensive would begin in May 1941.

However, in February, Hitler, responding to the British move into Greece, and the wavering Yugoslavian government, worried about the vulnerability of the Romanian oilfields. He responded to the perceived threat by ordering the Wehrmacht to mount a major offensive to secure Greece. That operation, Marita, assumed that the Germans would be able to transit Yugoslavia and Bulgaria. When the situation in Yugoslavia made that unlikely,

Hitler added that country to the list. In fact, the operation was thrown together so hastily that it never even got a name, only a number (25). When Stalin gave his May speech, the Balkan operations were still going on, with the airborne attack on Crete. His assumption that Barbarossa, the new code name for the invasion, although it had definitely been planned for 1941, would probably be delayed until the following May was hardly irrational.

Nor was Stalin's recurrent worry about a provocation irrational. Both Stalin and Hitler staged provocations that enabled them to declare war on one of their neighbors. Hitler had done it in 1939 against Poland, and Stalin did it in November against Finland (and quite possibly in July 1941 against Hungary).[51] By Stalin's standards, the senior German generals were dangerously out of control; who knew what they might do?

At the same time, Stalin, who paid little attention to British and French propaganda, certainly saw the extent to which Hitler's moves paralleled his own: both men were determined to regain the lands and peoples amputated from their countries after 1918, and in that sense, Hitler's territorial acquisitions were simply attempts to redraw the maps just as Stalin's were. Indeed, that was the whole point of the diplomatic arrangements of the August 1939 pact and its subsequent revision. From Stalin's vantage point in the Kremlin, Hitler's moves in 1934–1939 were justifiable, and the Soviet dictator did the same thing in the months following the signing of the pact.

Technically, it was the British and the French who had declared war on Hitler, not the other way around. It was the Allies who had decided to invade a neutral country (Norway), only to have been forestalled by the Germans. Hitler's moves, therefore, were primarily defensive responses. If Stalin continued to feed him millions of tons of oil, grain, and metals, there would be no reason for Hitler to attack him.

The increasing evidence of troop concentrations could likewise be dismissed: most of the movement was in the southeast, centered on the projected offensives in the Balkans. And since Stalin planned his own attack to seize the Romanian oil fields, was husbanding his strength, his habitual reluctance to make bold moves counseled prudence. Since Soviet troops would be driving south into Romania, and not north; they could wait until August or September to begin.

We now know that as the days of June 1941 wore on Stalin was increasingly nervous, that he did make certain decisions to ward off a possible attack, that he was hardly insouciant and blithe. All these actions indicate the behavior of a man who has made a conscious decision to gamble. So Stalin held back, waiting for the right moment, and Hitler seized it. Both men gambled, and lost.

Into the Maelstrom:
The First Seventeen Days

The modern tendency is to avoid taking decisions, and to pro-
crastinate in the hope that things will come out all right in the
wash. The only policy for the military leader is decision in action
and calmness in the crisis.

Field Marshal Montgomery[1]

Although the weather is invariably brought up in any discussion of the Eastern Front, the basic strategic problem con-
fronting the German planners had little to do with rain and
temperature: an offensive that began in May would have 120 days
of good weather. In northwestern Russia and the Baltic, September and early October are typically wet, but then, as the nighttime
temperatures drop, the ground begins to freeze, and mud is no
longer a constraint. We envision western Russia on the latitude of
Moscow as being extremely frigid in the winter, but in December
the average lows in Moscow, while below freezing, are only six degrees Centigrade colder than in Prague.

The coldest nights are in February. In partial compensation, the
fall is surprisingly dry: at any one point in the year, precipitation
in New York City is half again greater than in Moscow. The Germans had reckoned that the conflict would probably be over by
the end of September, but the weather gave them a comfortable
margin of error. Their main problem would be dealing with the

SWEDEN

FINLAND

Helsinki

Gulf of
Finland

Tallinn

Lake
Ladoga

Leningrad

ESTONIA

Novgorod

Pskov

Dmyansk

Kalinn

Riga

LATVIA

Velikiye Luki

Rzhev

Klin

Moscow

Baltic
Sea

Dvinsk

Mozhaisk

Kolomna

LITHUANIA

Polotsk

Vitebsk

Vyazma

Kaunas

Smolensk

Tula

Danzig

Vilna

Orsha

EAST
PRUSSIA

NORTH

BELORUSSIA

Roslavl

CENTER

Grodno

Minsk

Bryansk

Bialystock

Orel
Livny

Warsaw

Brest

Gomel

Kursk

Voronezh

POLAND

Konotop

Don

Belgorod

Kiev

Kharkov

GALICIA

Lvov

Lubny

Tarnopol

UKRAINE

Izyum

SLOVAKIA

SOUTH

Dniester

Donets

Uman

Dnepropetrovsk

Balta

Zaporozhye

Budapest

Rostov

HUNGARY

Dnipro

Danube

Odessa

Perekop

Sea of
Azov

Kuban

Belgrade

ROMANIANS

Kerch

CRIMEA

Novorossiysk

YUGOSLAVIA

ROMANIA

Sevastopol

Yalta

Black Sea

BULGARIA

GREECE

TURKEY

0   100 miles
0   150 kilometers

SOVIET
UNION

German Gains, 1941

· · · · · · ·	June 21, 1941
·—·—·—	July 16, 1941
— — —	August 25, 1941
·—·—·—	October 1, 1941
————	December 5, 1941

mud of September, as, despite Moscow's claims about modernization, very few roads in European Russia were paved.

The problem was the same as in 1914–1918, particularly so since the Soviet frontier was now where it had been in August 1914. The terrain along this lengthy irregular border was bisected by an enormous tract of riverine swamp, the Pripet Marshes, 100,000 square kilometers of boggy ground that stretches from southwestern Belorussia into northeastern Ukraine. The main area of the swamp is some 150 kilometers east to west and roughly 450 kilometers south to north. The area was sparsely inhabited (the only city of any size was Pinsk, on the western fringe), and the marshes were essentially impossible to cross.

Given the depth and breadth of the area, any offensive operation had to be divided into two almost entirely independent efforts. As in the First World War, on the Eastern Front geography dictated strategy. In terms of major operations both at the start and end, the Eastern Front was actually two distinct regions, separated by the enormous area of the marshes. There was a continuous front only after the German advance flowed around them.

Napoleon had evaded this problem by staying to the north. In his offensive, which began on June 24, 1812, the Grande Armée crossed the Niemen River moving toward Kovno (now Kaunus in Lithuania), then began to veer further inland, following a path that led from Kovno to Vilna (Vilnius), then to Smolensk, and finally to Moscow. The famous Battle of Borodino was given that name because it was fought near the village of Borodino, about twelve kilometers southeast of Moscow (which is why the French have persisted in calling it the Battle of Moscow).

Napoleon was therefore taking the shortest route to what he correctly considered the twin cities that were the core of the Russian empire, Moscow and Petrograd (Leningrad). But if Moscow fell, Petrograd, the capital, was then cut off from the rest of the country. In 1940, the two cities were still the heart of the country, so General Erich Marcks, whom Franz Halder, the German chief of staff, had charged with developing the plan for Russian operations, opted for the same route. "Moscow," opined Marcks, an experienced artillery officer with a degree in philosophy and a fondness for the great cities of Europe, "contains the economic, political, and spiritual center of the USSR. Its capture would destroy the coordination of the Russian state."[2]

Moscow, in other words, was like London, or the Paris Marcks so admired. Thus from the onset of planning, German officers were making an assumption that was almost entirely erroneous. True, Moscow had always been the religious center, the historic capital, but by the twentieth century, Russia was more like Germany than France or Austria or Hungary. One could hardly say that Berlin, the capital of the First Reich after 1871, was the spiritual center of Germany, and certainly not its economic hub. Nor is there any evidence that Hitler felt he was abandoning the government when he was in Berchtesgaden, 750 kilometers distant from the capital.

Until the October Revolution, the political and cultural center of Russia was Petrograd, which had been the capital since 1725, when Peter the Great built his palace there. Russian industry, such as it was, was concentrated around the former capital, in the southeast, or hundreds of kilometers to the east. A list of the cities with Soviet tank, locomotive, and diesel engine factories (a reliable guide to where Soviet industries were located) suggests just how wrong Marcks was: Leningrad, Kharkov, Stalingrad, Kirov, Chelyabinsk, Nizhni Tagil, Gorki, Vyksa, Kolomna, and Mitishchi; only one was actually in Moscow's environs, and only Mitishchi was close to the city.[3] All the important industrial centers were somewhere else, as was the case with Germany.

Leaving aside the fact that Marcks was wrong in every particular, this plan was simply a recapitulation of Napoleonic strategy, the same tired thinking that had characterized the original Gelb. The initial plan ignored the offensive threat to the most vulnerable part of the Reich posed by the concentration of forces Stalin had demanded as part of his own offensive scheme. The only novelty in the plan presented to Hitler on August 5, 1940, was tactical: it incorporated the lessons learned in France and the Balkans, relying on speed and airpower to achieve deep penetrations of Soviet space. Marcks and his staff also envisioned the campaign as taking the same amount of time, between nine and seventeen weeks.[4]

Hitler demanded a vast expansion. For him, the war was not about symbols, it was about resources. He saw, correctly, that although the Moscow–Leningrad axis was arguably the brain and the heart of the USSR, those organs were dependent on the resources at the other end of European Russia, in Ukraine, the Caucasus, and the fertile lands lying along the lower reaches of the Don and Volga Rivers, historically known as "Black Earth" Russia. Those resources, spread over a vast area, formed a whole series of separate objectives. Since the death of Walter Wever had resulted in the stalling of the development of the Luftwaffe's long-range heavy bomber, the only way to seize them was by taking them on the ground.

Hitler's insistence on giving the economic objectives priority over the Napoleonic one was sensible in another way. On the northern attack route, the Germans would have to contend with a terrain that was hardly ideal for the deployment of armored thrusts. Russia to the north of the marshes was a continuation of the lightly forested landscape that began to the north of Berlin and Dresden, and stretched all the way across the Baltic up to Novgorod and Kazan. To the southeast, however, the terrain was more promising. There was a vast swath of prairie land stretching from Hungary north of the Danube to Kiev up to Samara in east-central Russia. Merging into that plain along the southern flank was an equally enormous swath of dry grasslands that skirted the Black Sea and ran all the way to the Volga. The rolling plains and relatively temperate climate of the region made it excellent tank country, certainly far better than what the German armored units had encountered in France and the Balkans. The terrain to a certain extent compensated for the vast distances and the virtually nonexistent road and rail network.

But even in the swampier northwest, there were compensations. Towns and villages were extremely sparse compared to western Europe. European Russia lacked the dense network of small stone villages and fortified towns that characterized northern France, Belgium, the Netherlands, and Italy. Tactically speaking, those towns, together with the monasteries and castles that dotted the rural landscape, gave defending armies a series of fortified anchor points from which to mount defensive operations; despite their age, they were resistant to high explosives, and generally dominated the surrounding landscape.

The relative sparseness of settlements, and the use of wood as opposed to stone, was a common feature of the region. In the nineteenth century, both the Russians and the Austrians, realizing the military implications of this characteristic, had built extensive fortifications in the parts of Poland they had occupied. However, the engineers of the two empires had concentrated their resources on fortresses, not on defensive lines, the idea being that from the protection of a great fortification such as Pryzemysl or Lvov, troops could successfully contest any invasion; if surrounded they could hold out indefinitely, remain a threat to the enemy's rear.

In the 1920s the Bolsheviks had pursued a more modern approach, attempting to create a defensive line in the true sense of the word, analogous to the one the Germans built both in the east and the west in the 1920s. Although primitive compared to the state-of-the-art system the French built after 1918, the combination of simple concrete blockhouses, underground bunkers, and antitank obstacles had proven extremely effective on the Western Front in September 1939, and in Finland several months later.

However, as a result of Stalin's territorial conquests in 1939 and 1940, the frontier had moved considerably beyond these defensive positions. They were now useless, had largely been abandoned, and no plan existed to create a new defensive shield further west. In consequence, Friedrich Paulus, the staff officer who had been studying the Soviet Union in light of the projected invasion plan, emphasized the need for deep advances through gaps in the Soviet deployment, and the consequent encirclement of the forces that a rapid advance would presumably cut off from the rest of the country. Tactically, it was important to prevent the Red Army from retreating into the interior, and any successful campaign had to be concluded by October, so the Germans had a window of five months, assuming the May start date.

But Paulus, no more than his colleague Marcks, was still fixated on Moscow as the main objective. Nor did he have any concrete suggestions about how the army should deal with the vast distances involved, absent a heavy bomber force that could destroy troop concentrations far behind the front lines as well as the vital railroad junctions, factories, and supply depots.

So the resulting December 18, 1940, plan, Barbarossa, as modified by Hitler, thus envisioned three massive pincer movements that would reach deep into Soviet territory. One army group was allotted to each, and identified by its position in the line. Army Group North, commanded by Wilhelm Ritter von Leeb, was to drive through the Baltic toward Leningrad.[5] As it had the smallest section of the projected front, it was allotted only twenty-six divisions.

Von Leeb was probably the most vociferous anti-Hitlerite of the senior generals. But he was an exceptionally able officer who had distinguished himself as commander of Army Group C in May 1940 during the attack on France. His two subordinate commanders were outstanding. Erich Höpner, who would lead the 4th Armored Group, was a Bavarian cavalry officer who, like George Patton, had made the switch to tanks early on, and risen to command of an armored corps before the war began. Von Leeb's other main force was the 18th Army, under Georg von Küchler. Unlike Höpner, von Küchler was that relative rarity among the senior generals, a Hitler supporter. He was a seasoned general who had directed army groups in 1939 against Poland and in 1940 when he led the invasion of the Netherlands.

At the same time, Army Group Center, commanded by Fedor von Bock and composed of the 4th and 9th Armies, would strike out to the north of the marshes, one side of the pincers aiming for Smolensk, the other traversing an arc pointing to Vilna. As it reached Smolensk, Army Group Center would form a continuous front with Army Group North. By the time the German forces crossed the Daugava River (which flows to the northwest toward Riga on the Baltic coast), it was anticipated that the northwestern front would have been consolidated, all the way down to Minsk.

Such a deep thrust required the expert use of mechanization and armor, but von Bock, despite a certain unfortunate streak of Prussian chauvinism, was familiar with complex operations. He had been in charge of the occupation of Austria, had commanded Army Group North in the Polish invasion, and then Army Group B in May 1940. His two armored groups were commanded by two outstanding exponents of armored warfare: Heinz Guderian and the vastly underrated Hermann Hoth.

Army Group South, given the most ambitious goals, was under the direction of the Wehrmacht's senior general, Gerd von Rundstedt. His three armies (6th, 11th, and 17th) and the 1st Armored Group under Ewald von Kleist, would sweep out of Galician Poland, in a huge arc aimed at Kiev, taking advantage of the good terrain, its left flank shielded by the Pripet Marshes. The main axis of this advance would be to the south of Kiev, and the left, or exposed flank of the German forces would be shielded by the Dnieper River, which, after leaving Kiev flows in a southeasterly direction toward the Black Sea, then makes an abrupt southwesterly turn, emerging outside Odessa. Once the bend of the river was reached, the next target would be Rostov, a key city located at the mouth of the Don River, where it flows into the Black Sea.

At the same time, two Romanian armies, the 3rd and 4th,

would attack across their frontier, thus fixing the Red Army units in place, so the Russians would be attacked from the flank. This enormous envelopment, pinning the Russians against the seacoast, was possible because the bulk of the Soviet troops assigned to the Kiev Military District (the Southwestern Front) were deployed right along the frontier.

So the first phase of Barbarossa would consist of three giant pincer movements that, penetrating deep into Soviet territory, would outflank the Red Army completely. Once the Germans reached the Daugava in the north, and the Don in the south, the second phase would begin: a movement on Leningrad and Moscow at one end, and on Rostov and points further east on the south.

The force available for this immense task was tested by combat, and in two ways that were even more significant than having been under fire. The crucial mechanized units had learned from experience the importance of logistical support to keep the thousands of motorized vehicles required in running condition, and supplied with fuel and ammunition. "In modern mobile warfare, tactics are not the main thing, the decisive factor is the organization of one's resources," Wilhelm Josef Ritter von Thoma observed.[6]

Von Thoma, who had directed the German tankers in the Spanish Civil War, was in a position to know, and the Wehrmacht's experiences in 1939–1941 had amply confirmed his judgment. In 1941 no army in the world had this level of experience in mechanized warfare. Nor did any army have the crucial doctrine that demanded close cooperation between the air force and the army that was the distinctive signature of German offensive operations. Although both factors are difficult to measure, they are clearly of crucial importance in determining success on the battlefield.

At the same time, the resources available for Barbarossa had been weakened by the operations that had taken place in the preceding months. The casualties incurred during the successful attack on Crete (May 20, 1941), which had involved some of Germany's best troops, and a third of the air force's transports, meant that the attacks by airborne troops that had so rattled the Dutch and Belgians in May 1940 would not be repeated in Barbarossa.

Hitler's Balkan adventure had required nearly thirty divisions, a third of them armored or mechanized, the best forces the army had. Casualties had been minimal, but moving those divisions from Greece to the north was difficult, and the wear and tear on equipment had been considerable.[7] Nor had the losses sustained in the Battle of Britain in fall 1940 been made good. By November 1940 trained aircrews were at only three quarters of the June 1940 strength.[8] But the May 1940 offensive plan had also stretched the military to the utmost: the only thing novel about the projected offensive of June 1941 was the scale.

Regardless of the relative strength of the Red Army and the Wehrmacht, the defense of the Soviet Union was problematic. As the Germans had learned in previous campaigns, the terrain lacked the natural and man-made features that favored the defenders over the attackers, offering instead vast open stretches in which to maneuver the large mechanized units that now dominated warfare, a factor often ignored in assessments of the campaign.[9] On balance, the size of the area the Red Army had to defend more than compensated for whatever deficiencies the Germans had in 1941.

A coherent and effective national defense plan required two closely related transportation systems: a truly national one consisting primarily of multi-tracked rail lines that would enable men and equipment to move from the interior to the front, and a system of all-weather roads running roughly in parallel to the front, enabling the defenders to shuttle reinforcements to choke off breakthroughs. The second of these, whether it ever existed at all (which is highly doubtful), was, like the fortresses of the older frontier, now useless. Despite the emphasis on modernization and industrialization, the Soviet rail network was essentially the same as it had been under the czars, and in considerably worse shape: railroad personnel had been particularly hard hit by Stalin's belief that all accidents were the results of sabotage.[10] So the German plan capitalized on the difficulty the Russians would have both in getting reinforcements from inside the country to the front, and the basic impossibility of shuttling units in parallel to the front and shutting down German breakthroughs.

There were two final features that heavily favored the attacking Germans. After October 1939, when the frontier moved westward some hundreds of kilometers, the original defensive positions (much of which dated from czarist times) were now deep into the interior. When Kirill Meretskov became chief of staff of the Red Army in spring 1940, he worsened the situation considerably. Meretskov ordered that all the defensive positions be decommissioned and the army moved up right behind the new frontier. As a result, not only were there no real defensive positions behind the frontier, but when the troops deployed up to it the Red Air Force moved its planes up as well. The greater part of the Soviet air fleet was now located in new airfields immediately behind the frontier.

Soviet officers were taken aback. As Colonel Ilya Starinov recorded later:

> When I learnt that preparations were being made to dismantle the defense obstacles in the frontier zone I was simply stunned. Even everything we had succeeded in setting up in the years 1926–1933 was in fact eliminated. There were no longer any stores with prepared charges.... The Ul'yanovsk School of Special Engineering, which was the only training institution which turned out ... commanders for ... radio-controlled mines, was made into a communications school.[11]

At the same time, Meretskov ordered the start of a major construction program: new roads were built, existing roads were widened, and bridges reinforced to support the new heavy tanks, particularly in Ukraine.

Generally speaking, armies establishing defensive positions want a transportation system that runs in parallel to the frontier: that enables them to shuttle supplies and reinforcements to whatever area is the most heavily attacked. But the new Soviet construction projects were all directed toward the enemy, just as, in spring 1941, was the German construction work on the other side of the frontier. After the poor showing of the January 1941 war games, Meretskov was sacked and replaced by Georgi Konstantinovich Zhukov. But under Zhukov, efforts at building up an attack infrastructure, particularly in Ukraine, only intensified.

So an observer looking at the Soviet positions as they developed in autumn 1939, and particularly by summer 1940, would deduce that these units were stationed not for defense, but for an impending attack, which is probably why the senior surviving officers of the German high command insisted that their attack was a preemptive one, a deduction that could be made simply by looking at the way the Red Army was deployed.[12]

Their deployment is the second factor that greatly improved the odds in favor of the Germans. Red Army units, instead of being held back from the frontier so as to counter any German attack, were almost all massed along the border, grouped into four military districts: Baltic, West, Kiev, and Odessa.[13] The Kiev headquarters controlled no fewer than four separate armies (5th, 6th, 12th, 26th), built around sixteen armored and eight motorized divisions. To the south, the Odessa District had only one army, the 9th, but that army was the most powerful, with four armored and two motorized divisions, the same number as the Baltic District, even though it had three separate armies (8th, 11th, and 27th). In the middle of the line was the Western District, consisting of four armies (3rd, 4th, 5th, and 10th), built around twelve armored and four motorized divisions.

The largest and most powerful army, the 9th, was opposite Romania, where it could strike directly at Bucharest and the oilfields, as the land on the east of the Carpathian Mountains was the same rich cultivated landscape as in Ukraine. Two separate armies, the 12th and the 18th, were in position to move across the Carpathians, preventing any German riposte to their offensive. But the bulk of the Kiev District's armored formations would strike directly into the Hungarian plain. To that end the majority of the new T-34 medium tanks had been distributed to the units there.[14]

All in all, this was a force of some 2.7 million men, almost all of them massed along the frontiers. It was a most curious disposition of force. Apocryphally, when Napoleon had looked over the defensive dispositions of the French army at the start of the One Hundred Days, he had snorted that this was all very well if the only aim was to stop smugglers, a remark that was perfectly descriptive of the Red Army almost a century and a half later.

The key to any counterattack is the speed with which the defenders react, move to the threatened point, and choke down the thrust before it penetrates very far. Conversely, an army is thus at its most vulnerable either when it is reeling back from a failed attack, or when it is poised to deliver the attack. At that moment, its troops are massed so as to move forward, ammunition and fuel have been moved up close to the front, and all roads (such as they were) packed with men and equipment aimed in one direction, toward the enemy.

Although mechanization vastly increased the speed with which armies could move, in one key aspect it made matters worse. A column of infantry could always be turned around by giving a simple command, its constituent units then moving off in the opposite direction (or even swapping places if they were marching along roads or across open fields). With a column of tanks, however, the maneuver is vastly more difficult, and the difficulty is compounded by the length of the column itself.

The Germans had already discovered that their initial ideas of armored divisions of 400 tanks were unworkable, particularly as the size and firepower of the individual vehicle increased. Larger tanks needed more room, and combat effectiveness dictated more motorized infantry be added to each armored unit. The Germans had learned firsthand in Poland and then in France how vulnerable tank units were without infantry support alongside. But these mixed columns of armored and unarmored vehicles posed all kinds of logistical problems, not least of which was they required enormous areas in which to maneuver, as well as control of the airspace. Redeployment of mechanized and armored divisions to meet a new and unexpected threat, one that came from a different direction, was a complex affair even without being under fire.

For the Red Army the problem was complicated by the lack of any coherent defensive doctrine. Successful rules covering behavior in emergencies have to be simple and unambiguous, and the German rule set (no need to wait for orders, move over to the attack as fast as possible, we're right behind you) was exactly that.

By contrast, the Red Army, which had been from the very first built around the principle of offensive action, had no defensive doctrine, nor had any serious attention been given to developing one. The most basic preparations for defense, such as the establishment of a central headquarters responsible for coordinating the deployment of reinforcements in the event of an attack, had not been taken, as the official idea was that in the event of any attack, the Red Army would move forward and engage the enemy on enemy soil.[15]

Given the rigid chain of command Stalin had imposed on it, there was scarcely any movement toward giving local commanders, even at the highest levels, any discretion. All this was potentially fatal, even without accounting for the effects of the violent removal of all the senior officers, right down to very low command levels.

So on June 21, 1941, the Red Army, despite its imposing size and a decent complement of modern equipment, essentially consisted of 2.6 million individual human targets. No one was authorized to fire back if attacked, no one was authorized to move an inch without an order, and everyone was in the wrong place at the wrong time.

Of course the amateurishness of the deployments made perfect sense if your armies were poised to attack: at that point you wanted them massed on the frontier, bunched up so they could exploit the breakthroughs. By 1939 everyone knew that: the Germans had attacked Poland from all three sides, overwhelming the defenders. In May 1940 they had attacked all across the front, from the Netherlands down to Strasbourg. So as an offensive plan, Stalin's deployments were logical, particularly since this was the one thing the Red Army was trained and equipped to do, and had some experience in doing.

Any catastrophe has complex causes. Although the ultimate cause of the disaster that began to unfold on June 22 was Stalin, it must be said that once the evidence of an impending attack became manifest, there was really not much that he or anyone in the Kremlin could do to remedy the situation. It was far too late to move the troops back, and although much is made about his refusal to authorize the defenders to shoot back in the first hours of the offensive, it is highly doubtful that this would have done much good. In 1941, surprise tactical air-to-ground attacks were essentially unstoppable.

In May 1940, the Dutch defenders had been expecting the German attack, were in good defensive positions, and fought back vigorously: they were nonetheless overwhelmed by the assault. In December 1941, the Americans certainly fought back quickly enough at Pearl Harbor, but the Japanese still managed to inflict heavy damage on the fleet. And in both cases, the defenders were not only accustomed to operating independently, but were manning good defensive positions.

In the chaos and confusion of any offensive, communications with the rear generally are the first casualties, one reason why the Germans had moved decision making further down the chain of command whenever possible. But the Soviet system was dependent on an unbroken communications link going all the way back to the Kremlin. Nothing could be done without authorization from Stalin himself.

From Stalin's actions on the night before the start of the war, as more information began flooding in about the impending attack, it would seem that he was beginning to realize that an attack might well occur, that he was not in the state of complete denial that is often supposed. Georgi Zhukov, who was at that time chief of staff, had received news of the impending attack from a deserter and had asked to be allowed to see Stalin. He went to the Kremlin with Semyon Konstantinovich Timoshenko, the commissar for military affairs, and as close to a seasoned officer as Moscow had left. The two men hoped to persuade Stalin to put the Red Army on full alert. Stalin had already ordered the movement of reinforcements: the 19th, 20th, 22nd, and 23rd Armies were to deploy on a line stretching across Belorussia down to Ukraine, and his old crony from the Civil War, the aging and inept Semyon Budyonny, had been dispatched to Briansk to command them; another army, the 16th, would move in place behind the forces in the far south.

But these actions, like his refusal to put his armies on full alert, suggest that Stalin was thinking not in terms of September 1939 and May 1940, but as though the situation was a repeat of August 1914, when weeks had passed before there were any critical battles. Logically speaking then, Stalin was not so much in denial as he was fighting the previous war, thinking in terms of a conflict whose initial phases would extend over some weeks, not days.

There is a second way in which Stalin's actions suggest he was still thinking in terms of August 1914. Looking back after 1918, many people believed that the war could have been avoided had the leaders of the combatants (Germany and Austria in particular) been more able to control events in the field. The general belief was that the mobilization of armies had a domino effect. Once the troops were sent to the front, facing enemy troops also on full alert, it was practically inevitable that there would be incidents. The leaders of both sides would promptly lose control of the situation. This notion was the same one that Tolstoy had advanced in *War and Peace*: events unfolded on their own, and the leaders were powerless to control them.

Armies are often accused of being prepared to fight the previous war. Whether this is true or not, Stalin's actions, both before June 22 and afterward, were perfectly consistent with the behavior of a man whose military ideas were firmly rooted in the past.

The one fact that seems indisputable is that right up until the bombs and shells started raining down on the USSR, the main concern of everyone in authority was to make sure that no one would "yield to enemy provocations," as Timoshenko told General Dimitri Grigorevich Pavlov, commander of the important Western Military District, at one in the morning of June 22.[16]

The all-important order to start shooting back was not issued until 7:15 in the morning. It called for the Red Army to destroy the invaders, but not to cross the border. By signaling his restraint, Stalin was hoping for what in retrospect seems to be the height of folly: "Yet despite everything, Stalin persisted ... he hoped to settle things diplomatically."[17] In retrospect this notion seems delusional, but it was consistent with the idea of a slowly developing conflict that could be controlled from Moscow, and with the response of the British and French in September 1939. Besides, at the time the order was issued, no one in Moscow had any idea of how much damage had already been done, or even the scope of the attack.

One of the main reasons for this was that the Red Army's

chain of command was firmly anchored to telephone lines. It made sense for Timoshenko, in Moscow, to use the telephone to talk to army commanders hundreds of miles distant, but the reliance on wired communications extended all the way down to the company level. Given the obsession in the USSR with sabotage, the collapse of the telephone system was naturally blamed on commandos and secret agents operating behind Soviet lines; the more likely explanation is that shock waves from explosions toppled the telephone poles, while the bombing of local headquarters destroyed the switchboards.

In any event, on June 22, the Red Army was not using radios but was totally committed to telephones, the result being that no one really knew exactly what was going on, so each layer of command had to send officers down to the next level to ascertain the true state of affairs. The same problem bedeviled the air force: the only way for a pilot to report what he had seen on the ground below was to fly back to his base.

Not that there was much aerial reconnaissance possible. As Colonel Boris Vanyushkin, commander of the 23rd Soviet Air Army, later admitted to his German captors, "Our airfields lay far too close to the frontier, and their positions were perfectly well known to the Germans . . . both old and new types stood all about in uncamouflaged rows."[18]

This was a practical lesson in the dangers of massing your forces too close to the projected battlefield. Germany's tactical aircraft had very short operating ranges, so its airfields had to be close to the target areas. The trick for the defenders was to keep their airfields back far enough so as to be out of range, as the RAF had done in the Battle of Britain. But as we have seen, the Red Air Force had obligingly located its enormous air armada right behind the border, where the planes would be in perfect position to support a Soviet attack, but were vulnerable to a surprise raid.

Once the Luftwaffe had control of the airspace over the battle zones, the close proximity of the German airstrips to the border was an advantage in another way: aircraft could spend more time over the battlefield, as the time and fuel it took them to reach it was substantially less. Since round-trips were shorter, they could be mounted more frequently. In May 1940 that led to the widespread belief that the Allied air forces were grossly outnumbered by the Germans. In reality the Germans had fewer planes in service, but managed the process of landing, refueling, and rearming more efficiently, thus creating the impression that they had more airplanes. Theoretically, the Allies had just as many planes as the Germans, but for the beleaguered French infantry, that hardly seemed the case.

By the time the orders to fight back began to trickle down, the ground targets had already shifted from airfields and communications centers to direct support of the objectives of the ground forces. By eleven in the morning, when Molotov made a radio broadcast admitting that the country was at war, the Germans were already over the frontier and most of the advanced Soviet forces were overrun. By the late afternoon, most German units had advanced on the average about fifty kilometers, which meant that the armies of the Western and Baltic Military Districts had already been enveloped, destroyed, or cut off. Only in the south was the advance proceeding more slowly, as von Rundstedt's vast flanking movement unfolded.

Although the Soviet response was considerably muddled by Stalin's command decisions, by midday the Red Army, and particularly the Red Air Force, was fighting back. German airfields were just as close to the border on one side as the Soviet air force bases were on the other, and given the relative sizes of the two air forces, there was no way that the Luftwaffe could achieve mastery of the air in a few hours.

In accordance with Stalin's unshakable determination to attack, Soviet bombers were attacking the German airfields by midday, the result being the same sort of slaughter in the air that the Allies had experienced in May 1940, when their bombers had been massacred by the German air defense system.[19] What the initial aerial assault had not destroyed on the ground, faulty doctrine now finished off, as Soviet bomber crews made the same mistake British and French pilots had made thirteen months earlier:

> The Russian bombers came in, held to their course, and made no attempt to evade either flak or fighters. Their losses were frightful. When ten had already been shot down, another fifteen would appear on the scene. They went on coming the whole afternoon . . . we saw twenty-one crash, and not one got away.[20]

By the end of that first day, the Germans had complete mastery of Soviet airspace. Some 1,500 Soviet aircraft had been destroyed on the ground, and another 300 had been shot down, while the Germans had lost thirty-five planes. In May the Germans had roughly 1,300 operational aircraft, and they believed that the Russians had twice that many. Like all German estimates this one had a fatal flaw, in that it assumed that Russian aircraft were maintained to the same standard as their own, while in reality the Red Air Force was, as its hapless commander had tried to tell Stalin, hobbled by shoddy manufacturing processes and ignorant mechanics.

But within twenty-four hours, it was a moot point: the Germans had command of the air over the projected battle space, so their air-to-ground attack aircraft, the Stukas, were able to operate with impunity in support of the fast-moving mechanized columns. Unlike the level flight bombers in other air forces, the German dive-bombers were, by the standards of the war, highly accurate: as the fighting developed over the next month, the core of the Soviet tank force was destroyed, not by German tanks and antitank guns but from the air.

That same afternoon, Stalin decided that what was needed was a shake-up at the military district level. He dispatched Zhukov to

Kiev. Boris Shaposhnikov, one of the few surviving Soviet officers with any formal military training, went with the moronic Grigory Kulik to the Western District, effectively replacing Pavlov (who was subsequently arrested and shot), and Kirill Meretskov, the man who had presided over the disasters of the Finnish War, was sent to the Baltic District. Stalin had not yet grasped the dimensions of the catastrophe that was engulfing the armies of the western border: by the time the new commanders reached their destinations, located their colleagues, were properly briefed, the forces under them no longer existed as effective combat units, nor was there any way to communicate with them even if they had.

When Stalin dispatched Zhukov south, he in effect assumed direct command of the Red Army. That same afternoon, he made, finally, one practical and sensible decision: he ordered the relocation of Soviet industry from the western provinces into the interior, thus obliquely confirming Hitler's ideas about the importance of the southeast and establishing how wrong General Marcks and his colleagues in Berlin were about the importance of Moscow. Stalin was determined to continue the fight.

Although reports from the front were incoherent, fragmentary, and in some cases nonexistent, Stalin was rapidly becoming aware of the dimensions of the catastrophe that was unfolding. Within hours of the start of the attack, his air force was almost completely destroyed on the ground. The hapless Pavlov had already lost over 700 planes in his district alone, and by the time Stalin was shaking up command, the district's air commander, Igor Alexeivich Kopets, had already shot himself.[21]

Stalin was receiving intelligence, but his mind had not processed the implications, because he now issued a directive that signed the death warrant of the armies in the west. That evening he sent out a detailed order:

Directive Number 3 ordered the Northwestern and Western Fronts to "encircle and destroy" the enemy and to take Suwalki by the evening of June 24. The Southwestern Front received a similar order to "encircle and destroy" the Germans at Vladimir Volynsky and to take the Polish city of Lublin within forty-eight hours.[22]

Stalin was thus recapitulating the French experience of the First World War to the extent that clearly he was conscious of how that war had been fought. Marshal Joffre had issued similarly fantastic orders, demanding attacks in which the French infantry were slaughtered without ever reaching their objective. But there was a key difference. As the French historian and combat veteran Jean-Norton Cru remarks, "had orders been followed to the letter the French Army would have all been dead by August 1915."[23] French commanders at every level balked, stalled, temporized, unwilling to see their men murdered for nothing. When caught out, they were retired, relieved of command, or transferred.

But in the Red Army, the penalty for failure, as for the passive-aggressive behavior to which Norton Cru alludes, was death. The only real choice was whether the victim was killed trying to fight the enemy or shot by his own side. Understandably, many men chose the former option. But already it was beginning to dawn on a few that there was a third option: surrender. As generals vanished in the maelstrom, even temporarily, Stalin was justifiably nervous.

The Soviet ruler was right to be worried. At the end of the first week, enough was known of the German advance for the dimensions of the catastrophe to emerge. In Soviet-occupied Galicia, the Germans had broken through the old fortified line stretching roughly between Przemysl and Rawa-Russka within forty-eight hours, and Lvov (the historic fortress town of Lemberg) had fallen by June 30. In the Baltic the situation was even worse: Riga fell on June 29, and the advancing Germans had penetrated past Bialystok and Minsk, which they occupied on July 1. By July 3, von Bock's Army Group Center recorded 324,000 Soviet soldiers taken prisoner and 3,332 tanks destroyed.[24]

By the time Stalin finally made his first radio address, on July 3, most of the northwestern part of the USSR was in German hands. The fall of the city of Pskov, on July 9, cemented the loss. Although far inland, Pskov connected to the Baltic through the lakes of Pskov and Peipus. It was a natural anchor point for the advanced defense of Leningrad, serving as a hinge for a line that ran south by southeast, through Ostrov, and along the River Niemen, which lay to the southeast. There had been a desperate attempt to stop the German advance, as once the Germans got across the river they would be closing in on Smolensk, and were in fact approaching Moscow to the northeast and Leningrad to the north. But as Pskov fell, at the end of the 9th, the Germans were also astride the Niemen. Of the major towns north of the Pripet Marshes, only the ancient city of Polotsk, on the River Dvina, remained, the tip of a minor salient, as the German advance had surged past Vitebsk to the south. This was breakthrough on a grand scale. When the German armored columns reached Vitebsk, they had gone some 520 kilometers from their advanced positions on the frontier opposite the Soviet occupied city of Brest.

The annihilation of the Soviet armies defending this vast area was bad enough, but strategically the situation was even worse than those losses suggest. The German advance had flowed around the marshes of the Pripet, and although technically there was a large salient almost 100 kilometers across, with only a slender German bridgehead on the southern side of the extension, there was no way the Red Army could take advantage of this gap, even had there been the resources to mount an offensive to the north of Kiev: they would have been driving directly into an impassable swamp.

Only in the south were the Germans having problems. In order to execute the vast sweeping movement that would eventually pivot on Kiev and sweep to the southeast, von Rundstedt's divisions had to traverse central and eastern Galicia, either moving due east or wheeling up from Hungary and executing a turn. The historic border between Hungary and Galicia was determined by the northern Carpathians, so the German offensive had to spread out in enemy territory before it could move forward effectively. That took time, and Galicia was one of the few parts of the USSR where the terrain gave the defenders any sort of advantage. The countryside was irregular, chopped up by rivers, and dotted with defensive positions the Habsburg rulers had built to fend off a Russian invasion.

It was also the military district with the best-equipped Soviet units and more than its fair share of the few surviving competent commanders, since Stalin had aimed for this to be the decisive front in his projected offensive. Zhukov and Khrushchev, whom Stalin had sent to Kiev once the fighting began, made up in energy what they lacked in ability: both were determined party apparatchiks; whatever they thought, initially they followed Stalin's directives without hesitation. This theater was the one front where Stalin's third directive was followed in timely fashion. Generally speaking, in Belorussia and the Baltic, by the time local commanders received the order to attack, or to mount an aggressive defense of a position, the Germans were already there, the headquarters itself under attack.

Complicating von Rundstedt's task was the coalition he depended on to anchor his right flank while his mechanized columns debouched into Galicia and began the turn. The Romanian armies that constituted the bulk of his right flank were by Wehrmacht standards badly equipped for modern warfare, their commanders understandably cautious, accustomed to the slow tempo of the Great War. For the Romanians, whose army had never distinguished itself in combat, there was an additional disincentive. Their troops had been badly mauled in the Red Army's June 1940 offensive into Bessarabia and Bukovina.

The glacial progress on the right gave the Russians a greater opportunity to try to stop the German advance in Galicia. That this was so was not lost on Russian commanders, both back in Kiev and in Galicia itself. On June 26, the armored units of the Kiev District that were still intact launched a major attack against units of the 11th and 16th German Armored Divisions around Brody in one of the largest armored engagements of the war to date.

The problem for the Russians was that even with the new medium and heavy tanks that they possessed, they were still vulnerable to air-to-ground attacks. Although German tankers and antitank gunners were horrified to find their shells simply bouncing off the new Soviet vehicles, their reliance on tactical air support meant that the Russian tanks were mostly destroyed from the air, or by the air defense units accompanying the ground troops, whose 8.8 centimeter guns were effective against even the heaviest Soviet tanks. In consequence, Russian tankers rarely were able to do serious damage of the sort that one would assume would be the case, given the numbers of vehicles and their technical specifications.[25]

In that regard, the record of one of these Soviet armored divisions is eloquent testimony. The 32nd Division was perhaps the most lavishly equipped armored unit in the Red Army, with 173 of the new T-34 tanks, and forty-nine of the heavy KV vehicles. In position outside Lvov, the unit was in action for a month, at which point it had only forty-five tanks left. But casualties had been light: most of the losses were due to basic maintenance problems and the lack of mechanics and spare parts. "A striking feature of the division was the disparity between its assets and results . . . its combat record was hugely disappointing."[26] So were the defensive efforts of the other Kiev units, their firepower wasted in a series of uncoordinated partial attacks whose only concrete achievement was the loss of most of their tank force. By July 2, Tarnopol, the last major town in eastern Galicia, fell.

Two rivers along the eastern side of Galicia formed a natural barrier separating it from Ukraine and Russia proper, as they ran almost due south, in parallel. Both were crossed by major railroad lines, one going east out of Tarnopol (on the Sereth, the more westerly of the two rivers), the other crossing at Husiatyn, further south. Once the Germans crossed those two rivers, a task greatly facilitated by the railroad bridges, they would be in open country, and there were precious few Soviet troops and tanks standing between them and the riches of the Don basin. Stalin's mania for attacking had destroyed the armies of the Kiev Military District almost completely: it had lost some 2,300 tanks and 160,000 men killed, the 5th, 6th, and 26th Armies virtually annihilated.[27]

Once the Germans crossed the rivers, the rate of advance in the south picked up considerably. By July 7, the northwestern Ukrainian town of Berdichev had fallen, and on the 10th the Germans entered Zhitomir, just to the north. The only other important towns, Mogilev and Kamenetz were in German hands as well. Zhitomir was less than 100 kilometers from Kiev. In the south, the Romanians were poised to take Richenau, about the same distance north of Odessa.[28]

The war was less than three weeks old, and officers in the German high command were already beginning to think that it had been won. "It is thus probably no overstatement to say that the Russian campaign has been won in the space of two weeks," Franz Halder, the mediocre and excitable chief of the German general staff wrote.[29]

By the most conservative calculation possible, the Red Army had lost at least a quarter of its army already, well over 600,000 men, while the Wehrmacht had losses of 22,000 dead.[30] True, only some 2.68 million men had been in the district commands on June 21, so there was still an enormous force to be deployed, another 2.7 million soldiers. But with some minor exceptions, the best troops and the most modern equipment (including all of the new tanks that were operational) had been in the armies strung out along the frontier. Their replacements would be inferior.

Nor was manpower alone sufficient to win a modern war. That required tanks and guns and planes, the vast majority of which were now smoking hulks or hastily abandoned derelicts, constituting losses of perhaps as many as 7,000 armored vehicles and 6,000 aircraft.[31]

By comparison, the German tank force was actually larger at the end of June than it had been at the end of May: it had lost 179 vehicles, less than the monthly production, so it had 4,824 tanks in service at the end of June, whereas at the end of May there had only been 4,538. Losses in other categories had been light as well. It would be another month before losses exceeded production.

Since Halder was clearly wrong, his words are usually held against him, but they suggest that at bottom the German officer corps, with its emphasis on professionalism and its close study of history, had not quite grasped what they were up against. From their perspective, professional officers knew when it was time to quit fighting, even if their leaders didn't. Thus far in the war, governments had surrendered with far fewer losses: the French, whose army in 1940 was not that much smaller than the Russian forces in the west, had sued for an armistice after losing 100,000 dead. Given the losses in the first seventeen days of the war, to assume that the breaking point had been reached was quite logical—but only if one made the dubious assumption that in the Soviet Union things were the same as elsewhere. The Marquis de Custine was right.

DEEP BATTLE: FROM THE
BREAKTHROUGH TO THE FALL OF KIEV

All wars have their routs. Let us look at the map and see what
can be done.

General Doumenc[1]

The whole notion of a breakthrough is predicated on the
idea that your enemy's defenses are like a dike holding out
the ocean: small leaks can be plugged, but if the storm surge
is powerful enough, it will rupture the barrier completely. And
when that happens, there is nothing left to contain the flood. The
task of the defenders, then, to extend this imperfect analogy, is to
build a new dike to contain the surging advance in front of the key
objectives before the attackers can flood the interior completely.

Speed is thus all-important, whether one is attacking or defending: the attackers have to reach their objectives before the defenders can organize and fight them off. That was the essence of
Tukhachevsky's idea of deep battle, and thus far into the Second
World War, the Germans had realized (or rather Hitler had realized) that the swiftness with which a successful blow was delivered was all important. In May 1940 the Germans had moved so
quickly that the French had never been able to create a watertight
second containment line.

Rapid movement also had a powerful psychological effect: in
terms of the resources available, there was no reason why the Allies could not have kept on fighting to the bitter end in May 1940,

just as the Poles did in 1939. But each of the four Allied combatants in the west was unwilling to face the consequences of that step. Although each situation was different, they weren't willing to risk paying the price of further resistance, either in the deaths of their soldiery or the suffering inflicted on the civilian population of their countries.

In early July the odds were that by September the Germans would be in Moscow, and that the war would be over; by July 14, the high command back in Berlin was already pondering "the strength and organization of the units that would be left behind in the East as occupation troops . . . after the conclusion of Operation *Barbarossa*."[2]

So the Germans pushed on, and in Ukraine, where von Rundstedt's armored columns had by now destroyed the defending Soviet forces, the gains were truly spectacular. Having crossed the Sereth River and escaped the confines of historic Galicia, the Germans were now moving to the southeast. Traveling in parallel to the two main rivers of Ukraine (the Dniester and the Dnieper), they were pushing the front forward so the debris of the opposing Soviet armies would either flee or be swept into the Sea of Azov.

As this advance continued through July and into August, the pressure on von Rundstedt's right wing eased, and the Romanians began to advance along the coast, approaching the important Soviet naval enclaves of Odessa and Sevastopol.

Thus far the Germans had been destroying the confused and isolated Red Army units piecemeal. It was not that the Soviet commanders weren't trying to stop the advance: Soviet units were dutifully following Stalin's order to attack and destroy the invaders. But Stalin's orders to keep on attacking prevented local commanders from establishing a defensive position against which the German advance would, eventually, exhaust itself. At the same time, the lack of communications meant that the constant Soviet attacks were uncoordinated and easily beaten off. So the attacks, delivered piecemeal, slowed the Germans down, but had no effect on their progress.

So it was in Ukraine, where General Mikhail Petrovich Kirponos, in charge of the Kiev Military District, was trying to block the German swing toward Kiev. Kirponos was one of the few Soviet generals, perhaps the only one, who had emerged from the Finnish War with his reputation unscathed. But in that war he had been merely a division commander. He did his best, but the attacks Stalin demanded of his poorly trained units hardly got off the ground before they fell to pieces.[3] Although there's no denying that the surviving Russian troops were doing their best to stave off the German advance, their efforts were feeble: already, on July 7, Berdichev had fallen, and Zhitomir would be overrun a few days later (July 10).

Historic Russian cities like Zhitomir were important military objectives in very concrete senses. Favorably situated on navigable waterways, they were built around a fortified central core, squarely athwart whatever transportation infrastructure had been developed over the centuries. In the case of Zhitomir, sitting on the banks of the River Teteriv, the city was a major transportation hub, dominating the main route from Kiev to the west. The traditional importance of such towns and cities meant that their urban centers had a higher proportion of stone and masonry buildings.

Despite the advances in armor and airpower, dense urban clusters could prove formidable obstacles, and it was often difficult if not impossible for mechanized units to bypass them. This was particularly the case in Russia, where such cities often were the only places affording easy crossing of rivers during the spring and summer (the Teteriv, like most Russian rivers, was frozen over from November to March). But the Russian railroad right of way, significantly wider than the one that was standard in the west, provided excellent roadways in such situations. The easiest and most practicable way to get to Kiev was to follow the road and rail line once it crossed the river.

Stalin's insistence on attack also meant that his armies, already disorganized by the ferocity of the German offensive, were required to conduct a war of maneuver. This is difficult under any circumstances, particularly given the absence of radio communications, adequate intelligence, and tactical air support. His directive also meant that the Russians were essentially playing to the strengths of their adversaries, whose superior training and mastery of the logistics of mechanized warfare only increased the natural and understandable inclination of their soldiers to try to avoid combat in urban areas.

Indeed, after 1945, it appears that Soviet officers, who were taught that the Blitzkrieg had failed in the Soviet Union, were given as the main reason that it couldn't deliver cities. Whether this was true or not, following Stalin's demands meant that not only were the defenders trying to fight the enemy on the enemy's own terms, but key strongpoints for any defense were essentially abandoned.[4]

The Teteriv, a tributary of the Dnieper, joins it some fifty kilometers north of Kiev. At Zhitomir it is about fifty meters across, no mean obstacle, since it was essentially lying across the axis of the German advance and formed a natural barrier. The problem for the hapless Kiev Military District command was that all the other rivers in Ukraine would be roughly in parallel to the German columns and form no barriers at all to their advance. Having failed completely to hold any sort of line to the west and northwest of the Teteriv, the hapless Russians now had to contend with their own rivers as obstacles to any counterattack they could deliver.

It was in the north, however, that the most unsettling defeat occurred. As they jumped off on June 22 from German-occupied Poland, the German line of advance had essentially been along a line from Brest to Moscow, mainly because that was the historic main rail line leading to Moscow. At Brest the line diverged, one to the northwest, connecting to Warsaw, where there was a main line going to Leningrad, the other going to Smolensk, as well as to the southeast, where it eventually connected with the Lvov–Odessa railway. Most foreigners traveling to Moscow by land took the western, or Baltic, line, but for the Russians themselves, the more inland route was one of the country's major land transportation corridors.

The major city on the route to Moscow was Smolensk, one of the most ancient towns in Russia. The relative ages of Russian cities is a good indicator of their traditional importance to the economy, as is their size: Smolensk was the third largest city in Russia. Located 360 kilometers southwest of Moscow, it was an important objective in its own right, a Zhitomir writ large, as it were. Over the centuries (the city dated from 863 or earlier) possession of the city had been a key determinant in the long struggle for national formation, first in the wars between Lithuania and Muscovy, and then between Russia and Poland.

Practically speaking, Smolensk was the last obstacle of any importance before Moscow, and the only militarily sound place to defend the capital was along a line that stretched from Smolensk northwest through Vitebsk, Polotsk, and Dvinsk, this last town sitting athwart the Warsaw to Leningrad rail line. From this position the defenders would be able to use a whole series of rivers as anchor points, forcing the attackers to mount a series of separate operations, each one channelized by the rivers. At Vitebsk, the Dvina River makes a sharp northwesterly turn, having connected all three cities before it flows to the sea.

There was a relatively narrow gap between the Dvina at Vitebsk and the Dnieper at Smolensk, while to the southeast of the ancient Russian city there was a complicated network of rivers. The 100-kilometer gap between the two cities was where any attacking force would be forced to make its main effort, and even if the line were penetrated, the rivers would make the classical breakthrough operation, in which the attacking armies spread out and cut off the beleaguered defenders, difficult.

Three weeks into the war, Moscow was deploying reinforcements to the northern front that were, at least on paper, significant: no fewer than four separate armies (16th, 19th, 20th, and 28th), in addition to the forces still battling to the west. If there was one place where the Red Army could throw up a defensive line and stop the German advance, this was it. Moreover, in addition to the natural defenses, there was, at least in theory, a fortified line that had been built long before the war to guard the approach to Moscow, what was now called the Stalin Line.

It is interesting to speculate the extent to which this line was sufficient to anchor a successful Soviet defense, but it would be pure speculation because, in what was by now becoming a familiar pattern, even though it was only three weeks into the war, the Soviet 20th Army launched a major attack against the advancing German troops, throwing almost all of the Soviet armor in the area into action.

This attack, launched on July 6, was the first organized Soviet response to the German offensive. There had been abortive attempts in the preceding days, but by the standards of July 1941, the Soviet moves around Smolensk were planned and coordinated. The 5th and 7th Mechanized Corps of the Red Army were, at this point, as close to reasonably intact formations as the Red Army possessed, with 700 tanks.

Unfortunately, the only result of the three-day engagement was the nearly complete destruction of the Soviet forces. The two German commanders operating in this section of the German offensive were Guderian, regarded by British military historians as the father of the Blitzkrieg, and the even more talented Hoth. They finessed the Soviet jabs, moving around them (and through the debris of the two Soviet mechanized corps), executing the sort of operation German officers had always admired the most, a double envelopment, in which the attackers formed a giant pincers, sealed off their enemies, and left them in the rear. A week later (July 16), Smolensk fell to the Germans, who were now in position not only to separate the two main cities of Leningrad and Moscow, but to envelop them both.

The German commanders had the considerable luxury of air-to-ground supremacy, but given the distances involved, that the Luftwaffe could control the airspace over a battlefield the Red Army had deliberately chosen, a battlefield that was hardly more than one hour of air time from Moscow, was frightening.

In many respects what has generally been called the Battle of Smolensk was one of the most deftly executed German operations of the entire war, made all the more impressive by the fact that Hoth and Guderian were seriously overstretched, their men exhausted, their vehicles wearing out. The complex double envelopment, in which the Soviet forces would be caught in a vast pincers as they moved to the attack, would be repeated over and over again in the east, so Smolensk proved to be a signpost pointing to future operations, both those that occurred and those that were planned.

Smolensk was also indicative of two other features of the war as its shape was beginning to emerge. Traditionally, battles had not only a specific geographical location, a battlefield, but a definite time frame, a point at which the participants, whether they won or lost, were conscious that the battle had ended. But even though the Germans had crossed the Dnieper, had secured the objectives, defeated the Russian attack, the fighting continued on without pause. Although Guderian, one of the victors, visited Smolensk on the 17th, recording that it was largely undamaged, there is nothing in his dry-as-dust record of those days to indicate any sort of self-consciousness as to his victory, or for that matter, that a battle had even been fought. Smolensk was simply another leap forward.

If the German commanders on the ground were too preoccupied with the next set of objectives, while their Soviet counterparts were struggling to prevent them from being reached, in Moscow there was now, perhaps for the first time, an appreciation of what was happening. The loss of Smolensk, and the resulting pocket formed by the pincers, in which somewhere in the neighborhood of a quarter of a million Soviet soldiers were cut off, was a deeply ominous forecast for the direction the war would take. Given the absolute control over the news, hardly anyone outside the Kremlin realized the extent to which the front was collapsing. But by now, nearly a month after the start of the attack, Stalin and the leadership were beginning to get a reasonable grasp on the shape of the front, the size of their resources, and where the main German efforts were likely to be.

In the Secret Speech, Khrushchev made what was perhaps the most astonishing revelation of the day when he characterized Stalin's conduct in these first few days of the war:

> It would be wrong to forget that, after [our] severe initial disaster[s] and defeat[s] at the front, Stalin thought that it was the end. In one of his [declarations] in those days he said: "Lenin left us a great legacy and we've lost it forever." After this Stalin for a long time actually did not direct military operations and ceased to do anything whatsoever. He returned to active leadership only when a Politburo delegation visited him and told him that steps needed to be taken immediately so as to improve the situation at the front.[5]

The idea of Stalin collapsing in a funk resonated with the anti-Stalinist myth that the surviving party cadres gradually embraced after Khrushchev's speech, and understandably so: the alternative to blaming Stalin was to in some measure realize that the entire project was, to quote David Remnick again, "the world's longest running and most colossal mistake."[6]

Recent evidence suggests a more complex picture. It was only in the early morning hours of June 29 that Stalin erupted, and in a rage, not a funk. By all accounts he said pretty much what

Khrushchev reported (suitably sanitized so as not to offend the ears of the party faithful), and then, shouting out that he was resigning, he stormed off to his dacha and refused to do anything more until a panic-stricken delegation came to him and pleaded for him to return.[7]

That Stalin was severely shaken is unquestionable; those who heard the July 3 radio address can still recall the halting strange new tone of voice. However, his rage and retreat was as much an act as an authentic display, mostly aimed at distancing himself from the ongoing disaster; he may well have imagined that by the time he returned (on July 1), the situation would have stabilized.

There's no doubt however that he was now firmly in charge, and, after his fashion, directing the war. Antoine Rivarol once famously observed that "To do nothing is a terrible advantage, but it must not be abused."[8] Stalin's actions on his return show the wisdom of the aphorism. As supreme commander and self-appointed generalissimo, Stalin had two ideas. The first was to emulate Marshal Joffre, to demand offensive operations, regardless of their cost, their chances of success, and the realism of their objectives. That had been true from the very first directives he had sent out on the afternoon of June 22, demanding, for instance, that the Western Front armies move on Lublin (well inside German-occupied Poland), while they were in the process of losing Lvov, 200 kilometers to the southeast.

Whether or not the French generalissimo had been right in his demands, the conditions of the new warfare, the combat experience of the Germans, and the untrained nature of the Soviet forces negated any chance this strategy had for success. The situation on the front was changing so dramatically, the front was shifting eastward so rapidly, that Stalin's demands were impossible to meet: the poorly trained and completely inexperienced Soviet units who received them were already disintegrating around their commanders.

But the real slaughter of the Red Army began not on June 22, but during those terrible weeks in July, as entire armies, blindly following the orders to attack, vanished in the forests of the north or were lost in the folds of the rolling prairie land of Ukraine. No fewer than ten Soviet army groups were bypassed, encircled, cut off, and most destroyed (or taken prisoner) that horrific summer. In the center, between Vilna and Minsk, the 3rd, 10th, and 13th Armies; at Smolensk, the 16th, 19th, 20th, and 28th; in west-central Ukraine, the 6th, 12th, and 18th. And that was in addition to the forces of the Northwest Front (the Baltic District) that were overrun in the opening days and disappeared in the initial surge.

Losses on such a scale were an ominous portent for the future. Soldiers who survive combat learn from their experiences, especially if their experiences were defeats. That had been the case with the Allies in the Great War, the Poles in 1939, and the French (again) in 1940. The surviving units of French and Polish veterans of those defeats, re-formed and given American equipment, subsequently gave a good account of themselves on the battlefields of Africa, Italy, and France.

There was a certain ghastly calculus at work: the fewer casualties, the more veterans to teach the lessons required for success and survival. Conversely, when smaller units (companies or even regiments) were wiped out in combat, there was no one left to transmit the all-important lessons. The next cohort had to learn everything on its own, start from the beginning.

So the high level of loss in the Red Army in the first months of combat had serious implications. The officers who had experienced the mobile and combined arms operations of their opponents were either dead or prisoners of war. Their successors would have to learn the hard way.

As Stalin took control, he ensured this problem would get worse, and in several bewildering and highly destructive ways. In addition to demanding nothing but offensive operations, his other idea, perhaps no more than the reflexive instinct of a Bolshevik apparatchik, asserted itself. What was needed was a thorough reorganization of the structure of the army. As is often the case when bureaucrats respond to crises, the results were mixed. Stalin decided, quite sensibly, that the existing formations were far too large to be controlled, particularly given the inexperience of the staffs involved. Henceforth what in Soviet parlance were known as armies would be dramatically smaller, forces of only five or six divisions. This was a significant shift: the four armies of the Kiev District, for example, consisted of no fewer than sixty-eight divisions. The result was to create a wildly misleading table of organization. As we have seen, even before the war, Soviet divisions had never had their official levels of men and equipment. Stalin's reorganization froze this shrunken state: from now on, although the Soviet high command would dispose of dozens of "armies" of various descriptions, and thus deploy hundreds of "divisions," the reality on the ground was that a Soviet division was little more than anyone else's regiment, a Soviet army little more than anyone else's army corps.

At the same time, the mechanized corps concept would be done away with entirely. Even though General Pavlov, who had concluded from his experiences in the Spanish Civil War that independent armored formations were worthless, had by now been arrested and executed for his failures, his spirit, as personified by the surviving cronies of the Russian Civil War, lived on. Considered in isolation, the decision to downsize armored units was not entirely unreasonable, given the shortage of officers and vehicles. But at the same time, however, Stalin ordered the formation of thirty new combat units, each at corps strength. These new units would consist of horsemen. Essentially the motorized units were being disbanded and cavalry units were being created, as the motorized infantry divisions were also downgraded to being simple infantry divisions.[9] This was going back to the days of the Civil War and the Red Cavalry with a vengeance.

Once the shooting started, Stalin turned his attention to his other obsession, one that the Great Terror was only the most dramatic or visible aspect. Just as every industrial accident was the result of "wrecking," a deliberate act of sabotage instigated by foreign spies (but carried out by outwardly loyal Soviet citizens), every military setback was the result of treason. Stalin had already applied this approach to military discipline in 1940, as news of the disasters of the Finnish War began to reach him. Although little remarked, there was a round of terror in spring 1940, as the officers associated with the failures were tried and executed.[10]

But now, in July 1940, the Stalinist meat grinder went into full gear. As we noted earlier, in early July, the hapless General Pavlov, commander of the Western Military District, had been arrested, tried, and then shot. Under torture, he implicated Meretskov, who was arrested as well. In late July, enraged by the loss of Smolensk, as part of his reorganization scheme for the army Stalin had the commanding officers of all four fronts shot, thus ensuring that the survivors of the early disasters would not be around to provide the newcomers with the benefits of their experiences.

However, he was hardly content with a few summary executions to set an example for the survivors. As the situation continued to worsen, he wrote and signed Order 270, the relevant portion of which is worth quoting in full:

> I order that (1) anyone who ... surrenders should be regarded as a malicious deserter whose family is to be arrested as a family of the breaker of the oath and betrayer—of the Motherland. Such deserters are to be shot on the spot. (2) Those falling into encirclement are to fight to the last ... [otherwise] are to be destroyed by all available means while their families are to be deprived of all assistance.[11]

Leaving aside the stupefying immorality of this concept, its crippling effect on the Soviet war effort is notable. Nearly three million soldiers were missing at the end of 1941, a force larger than the entire army in European Russia that June. By early August, most of the mass encirclements had already occurred as the Germans surged forward. Indeed the sheer numbers of Red Army units wandering around, technically behind the German lines, would provoke yet another disagreement in the German high command, between those who felt that the time had come to consolidate the immense territories already conquered, that the enemy was defeated, and those who wanted to press on to the end.

But the point here is that there were enormous numbers of Russian soldiers who had been cut off, and those who had surrendered were now dead men walking: condemned to a slow and agonizing death in the German camp system, their families would meet the same fate back home.

Stalin's Order 270 was a gross error from a purely military point of view. It created a body of men with nothing to gain by their continuing allegiance to the USSR, either as their homeland or as the personification of the ideals of communism. This was manpower that Stalin doubly lost, as the Germans used Soviet prisoners on the Eastern Front to do work that otherwise would have had to have been done by their own men, an issue entirely separate from the formation of combat and police units from the ranks of these prisoners.

In practice, what Stalin's order meant was that soldiers who escaped and made their way back into Soviet territory were incarcerated and shipped off to prison camps; in the parlance of the time, they were called "stragglers," which of course was precisely what they were not. Stalin's order thus not only deprived the Red Army of experienced manpower, but it tied up the beleaguered transportation system as well as keeping large numbers of able-bodied men in the security services so as to be able to transport, guard, and investigate these unlucky soldiers.

All this on top of the obvious problem that ensues from executing officers for failures: not only does it prevent anyone learning from mistakes, but it produces risk-averse behavior at every level, one obvious consequence being the tendency to misrepresent the true state of affairs in every way possible so as to escape responsibility; thus Zhukov, on July 29, telling Stalin that "on the strategic axis of Moscow the Germans are unable to mount a major offensive operation in the near future owing to their heavy losses."[12]

In fairness to Zhukov, this was the briefing when he was relieved of his job as chief of staff and replaced by Shaposhnikov, allegedly because he recommended evacuating Kiev and trying to hold a defensive line on the north (or rather east) bank of the Dnieper. Although Zhukov was right, Stalin now abruptly changed course, insisting that Kiev be held.

Although Stalin's tenacity may perhaps be seen as commendable fortitude in the face of adversity, he failed to insist that the Red Army do the most logical and necessary task: reorganize a defensive position that it had a reasonable chance of holding and force the Germans to mount a frontal attack to get them out of it. The difficulties of mounting counterattacks went far past lacking the command and control capabilities necessary for such attacks to succeed. By definition they opened up gaps in the line that the enemy could easily exploit. In the abortive fight for western Ukraine, as in the Battle of Smolensk, that was precisely what had happened: the Germans were able to move between the Soviet armies and cut them off in the rear. This was classic military practice—any eighteenth-century general could have grasped it—and given the situation, the only practical defensive strategy was to form a line and devote all one's efforts to holding it. But that was the very last thing that Stalin was willing to do.

By a curious coincidence, at the same time that Stalin was

composing Order 270 (it was officially signed on August 28), Hitler was convening his generals to give them their orders for the next phase of the war. In the original planning debates, despite the disagreements between Hitler and the army, there had been a general agreement that once a continuous forward line had been established somewhere south of Leningrad, it would be necessary to discuss the order in which further objectives would be achieved. However, Hitler had already made up his mind what the next step would be: his generals were there to receive their marching orders, not to engage in a discussion or choose a new set of objectives.

The army commanders from the very first had envisioned the objectives of a war with Russia in a traditional way: destruction of the armies and occupation of the old and new capitals, especially Moscow. After the fall of Smolensk, and the steady advances of Army Groups North and Center, that view hardened: they believed they could take Moscow in short order.

So it was then, at the end of August, that the simmering disagreement between Hitler on the one hand and his generals on the other came to a boil. The most articulate spokesman for the army's point of view was Guderian, flush from his unbroken string of victories in the first weeks of the war, and frustrated by what he had been told of Hitler's intention. The difference between his relations with Hitler and the relations of Stalin's generals to the Soviet dictator is instructive.

> Hitler let me speak to the end without once interrupting me. He then began to talk and described in detail the considerations which had led him to make a different decision. He said that the raw materials and agriculture of Ukraine were vitally necessary for the future prosecution of the war. He spoke once again of the need of neutralizing the Crimea, "the Soviet aircraft carrier for attacking the Romanian oilfields." For the first time

I heard him use the phrase: "My generals know nothing about the economic aspects of war." [13]

Guderian understandably felt he was right and Hitler was wrong, and he was distressed to find that the other generals, who he was sure agreed with him, simply nodded their heads.

Given Guderian's reputation, most historians have essentially agreed with Samuel Mitcham's blunt assessment that Hitler's decision "was one of the greatest mistakes of the war." [14] However, the judgment seems highly debatable. As we shall see, Stalin apparently did not decide to defend Moscow until some point in mid- to late October. The decision to relocate both the heavy industries and Lenin's remains, made within the first few days after the invasion, suggests that he was always at some level contemplating having to abandon Moscow.

To a great extent the objectives of both sides during the Second World War were concerned with economics rather than military strategy, the Allied decision to invade Norway in 1940 being only the first instance. If Hitler's assessment of waging war for economic objectives was in error, it was a mistake shared with Winston Churchill, the British navy, and (subsequently) with the American and British strategic bomber commands.

Hitler's determination, coming as it did at the end of August, meant that the war would continue into December, if for no other reason than the distances involved. It will be recalled that after Wever's death, the Luftwaffe had failed to develop a heavy bomber with the range and payload required to strike deep behind the enemy lines. It thus lacked the means to destroy objectives located far behind the enemy lines, to degrade the flow of materials into them, and to prevent the movement of reinforcements from deep in the interior. Germany's only recourse was physical conquest and occupation. Thus was the wisdom of Wever's plan for a long-range bomber first confirmed, years before the advent of the Allied strategic bombing campaign and the air war over Germany.

So the problem Hitler's generals now faced was as simple as it was daunting. Although by the end of August the Germans had advanced enormous distances into the Soviet Union, the economic objectives in the southeast that Hitler had set were as far distant from their present positions as the 1941 frontier was from where their soldiers stood as Hitler spoke. Regardless of the successes in the south, victories that by the end of August were simply assumed, the diversion of resources there would guarantee that the war would be prolonged. That this was so was a result not of Soviet resistance but of Hitler's decision to destroy the USSR's means of waging war: the generals of Army Groups North and Center were convinced that they could be in Moscow within weeks if they would be allowed to continue. But now their forces would be drained off to support the advance into Ukraine and the Caucasus.

Given what had happened thus far, there's no reason to doubt the generals' estimate. That there was a steady stream of Russian troops moving into the theater is generally used as proof that resistance was stiffening and that the German advance had either stalled or would shortly. But two things are overlooked in that appreciation.

First, the Germans were moving in a steady stream of reinforcements as well. In June 1941, the Wehrmacht had an appreciable portion of its strength spread out over Europe: seven divisions in the Balkans, eight in Norway, thirty-eight in the west (mostly in France and Belgium), one in Denmark, and two still in Germany, a good one fourth of the total army strength.[15]

Taken all together, these divisions were substantial, particularly when compared to the Soviet divisions, which, as we have seen, were already drastically understrength and underequipped. Some of the German units, notably two of the armored divisions, had been intended for use in the initial attack, but now this sizable force essentially became the German reserve, and the high command began feeding them into the advancing front.

For example, the 1st Army Corps commanded by General Georg Lindemann, which had been deployed in the Balkans in April 1941, did not reach the Eastern Front until August, when it was sent to Smolensk. This was hardly a negligible force, as it consisted of no fewer than three full German infantry divisions. In July, the 2nd Armored Division, which had also been in the Balkans, arrived, and shortly after that a Spanish unit, the famous Blue Division, along with the three motorized divisions comprising the Corpo di Spedizione Italiano in Russia, the first deployment of what would eventually (by July 1942), become a force of ten divisions.[16]

Although the reorganization and redeployment of German (and other Allied) forces make an exact accounting extremely difficult, there was a steady stream of new divisions arriving through the fall and into the spring of 1942, by which point at least four more armored divisions had arrived.

At the same time, entirely new units were being created and sent to the front. In July 1941, the 189th and 190th Sturmgeschütze Abteilungen were followed by the 202nd in September and the 177th in October.[17] The Sturmgeschütze, or assault gun, was a tank with a fixed superstructure as opposed to rotating turret. It was therefore able to mount a considerably more powerful main gun, and had a lower profile. German tank experts were opposed to the whole principle to the point of refusing to let the crews wear the same black uniforms as the tankers. But these vehicles, whose design rapidly evolved over the next months of the war, proved themselves formidable weapons in combat. They gave the infantry highly mobile heavy artillery with which to destroy strongpoints that would otherwise have held them up. In addition, they were effective tank killers, the first wave of what gradually became a large family of tracked turretless vehicles.

The Abteilungen present unique difficulties in evaluating the strength and hitting power of the Wehrmacht, but some understanding of them is vital to appreciating the true state of affairs on the ground. Confusingly, the Germans used the word "Abteilung" both to denote units formally attached to a division as well as to a unit that was entirely independent of the traditional division and corps structure. Consequently, these units floated outside the existing tables of organization. They were of varying sizes, but as we shall see, as the Germans deployed successive generations of new tanks, tank destroyers, and assault guns, the tendency was to deploy them as independent units.

In a war in which the Bolsheviks boasted of hurling entire armies and groups of armies (the fronts) into battle, the deployment of smaller units is easily ignored. But the hitting power of such units, as indicated by their action reports, reveals them to be an extremely potent part of the Wehrmacht. From the very first days of the struggle, the assault guns, working in close cooperation with the infantry, gave the Germans an overwhelming advantage in those places where the Red Army was able to go into action. The importance of these independent units in combat was out of all proportion to their numbers.

So contrary to a widespread assumption among historians, there was a steady stream of men and equipment on the German side during summer and fall 1941. Moreover, German casualties were not increasing appreciably as the war went on. By the time Hitler and his generals were squabbling, German losses had in fact started to decline. On July 20, 11,071 German soldiers had been killed in action during the preceding ten days, while on July 30, the previous ten-day death toll had risen to 16,433. But it then began to decline: on August 10, it was 15,201; on August 20, 13,534; by August 31 it was down to 10,721.[18]

On the other side, not only had the bulk of the Red Army's first line armor and air been destroyed by the time Hitler made his decision, but the technologically superior core of it, such as the impressive T-34 tanks, had essentially been wiped out. Certainly the tanks and planes could be replaced, new crews found (whose level of training, realistically speaking, was no worse than the training of those who had perished), but replacing the thousands of vehicles lost was no easy task given the dislocation of the factories that Stalin had ordered. Production of the T-34 tank in the last three months of 1941 was only half of what it had been in the previous three months: in July, Timoshenko had complained that he was out of tanks, and the situation only got worse after that.[19]

By the end of August, the Germans had consolidated their advances in the Baltic and were gearing up for the next surge, one that would take them to Leningrad and Moscow. In the south, von Rundstedt had all of Ukraine south of the Dnieper, up to Dnepropetrovsk; from there the limit of the advance went back to the southwest: Odessa was under siege, but the Crimea and southeastern Ukraine was still in Soviet hands.

Although Talinn had fallen on August 28, no other city of any size had come under German control. In the north, Talinn and Smolensk were the last major cities before Leningrad and Moscow respectively, while in the south, the Germans had bypassed Kiev in their drive to the Black Sea. Although subsequently much would be made of Hitler's alleged failure (the Germans had not captured Moscow or Leningrad, nor would they do so), this was simply a species of boasting, akin to a man claiming he was in good shape because his head was still on his shoulders while his arms and legs had been cut off.[20]

Anyone who looked at the map could see that the main threat to the German advance was in the middle of the line, where there was already a bulge developing, a Russian salient into territory the Germans had already conquered. As the weeks of August passed, this salient became larger and larger as the German advance occupied all of western Ukraine.

By the end of the month the substantial Russian salient

stretched roughly from northwest of Kiev almost to where the River Pripet turns to the west, then made a turn and ran along the River Sozh for nearly 400 kilometers, a roughly triangular blob with a base, the side opposite Kiev, stretching for nearly 600 kilometers, all the way down to the south of Dnepropetrovsk.

Although Zhukov had argued that the Germans were too exhausted by the end of July to advance further, this was either wishful thinking or the result of faulty intelligence. The German pause was occasioned by the need to shift the forces in the north through Belorussia so they could attack into the salient, wipe it out, and prepare the German line for the next great surge.

Zhukov had already told Stalin that Kiev must be evacuated, and now, as the Germans began to close around the city, even the mediocre generals and party leaders Stalin had surrounded himself with could see the picture. There's an interesting and revealing contrast between Guderian and Hitler debating how to deal with success, and Stalin's minions trying to give him bad news. Budyonny "knew he might be dismissed or even arrested," but on September 12 he told Stalin that Kiev must be evacuated to spare further losses, this when the end was clearly nigh. He was then sacked, and when he tried to get Timoshenko to back him up, his colleague replied that "I don't want to put my head in the noose."[21]

Stalin's obsessions coupled with the justified fears of his subordinates for their lives (and the lives of their families and relatives) meant that the Soviet opportunities for a successful defense were squandered. As the Ukrainian salient was slowly emerging during August, it presented the Russians with an excellent opportunity either to build up a defensive line, abandoning everything on the European side of the Dnieper (including Kiev), which was what Zhukov had suggested, or to regroup their forces to try to strike at the vulnerable left flank of the German forces as they moved into the salient.

So although Khrushchev was technically wrong in his assertion that Stalin did nothing to direct military operations, his rather crude wording was actually not far off the mark: through a combination of meddling and indecision, Stalin came close to losing the war outright in those first months. Or, to remove this assessment from the level of personalities, the problem was that Stalin's metronome was set at too slow a speed. He was still fighting the Whites.

The result was sadly predictable. The Germans swept through the salient in a little over a week; by September 11, it was clear that the Germans were on the verge of sealing off the entire area around Kiev. Two days later the two lead German armored groups linked up over 100 kilometers east of the city.

Kiev was surrounded by September 14. Belatedly, a withdrawal was authorized, but by then it was too late. The city, abandoned, was occupied on September 19, and by then the armies of the Southwestern Front had ceased to exist.[22] The German gains were not without a certain cost: up to the end of August, the Wehrmacht had 74,371 men killed in action, and had armor losses of 1,412 vehicles; but the tank park, at 4,376 vehicles, was, in terms of firepower, stronger than it had been at the start of the fighting: almost 80 percent of the tanks lost were Mark 1 and Mark 2 vehicles that the Germans already had discovered were unsuitable for the battlefield.[23] If the Soviet figures for their own losses are in any way remotely true, in the next phase of the fighting the Red Army would, for the first time, be grossly outnumbered in this important category. For the time being, its air force was for all practical purposes out of action.

But the victorious Germans, their basic fighting machine hardly scratched, were becoming increasingly nervous. Their victories against Poland and France had been won on the cheap, and certainly with a minimal loss of German soldiers. Although the easterners in the senior ranks, the officers who had fought on the

Eastern Front in the last war and then in the immediate aftermath, had a healthy respect for the fighting qualities of the Russian soldier, their successes against the French and the British had understandably led them to believe that they could win this war in a few months. The realization that they were still a good distance from victory was sobering.

Moreover, German military intelligence was having great difficulty in estimating the actual size of the Red Army. In this sense Stalin's reorganization schemes, when coupled with the Bolshevik mania for secrecy, had misled the analysts. Even before June 22, Soviet divisions had never been anywhere near full strength. Instead of the 12,000 men the organizational chart called for, the average was about half that. So the Germans had initially overestimated the size of the forces opposing them. But as new units were formed, the basic building blocks became smaller still.

As the summer of 1941 drew to a close, as the Germans counted the number of new formations being deployed and the number of prisoners they had, and they came to the understandable conclusion that there were a great many more Russians out there than they had originally estimated.

The number of prisoners alone was staggering. On July 10, the total had been 600,738. By the end of July it was 813,830, by the end of August, 1,412,410; by the time Kiev fell, it had increased to 1,950,652: essentially there were two Soviet prisoners of war for every three German soldiers going into battle, and no one had any idea how many Russians had been killed.[24]

Then too, in the fast-moving and fluid situation on the battlefield, it was difficult to tell how many Russian soldiers were still out there somewhere, lurking behind the front lines and capable of causing horrendous damage to the already overstretched logistical network, or how many would filter back to their own side and be re-formed. In other words, at the operational level the Germans were still proceeding as though they were facing an opponent who did pretty much what they themselves did, just not as well.[25]

Thus far victorious, but nervous and frustrated, they gathered their resources for what they hoped would be the third and final turn of the screw: the twin cities of the north and the riches of eastern Ukraine and beyond.

The Campaign of Compromises:
October–December 1941

Depression gripped Zotov. It stemmed from the need to complain to someone about the course of the war, which was wildly inconceivable to him. From the reports of the Information Bureau he couldn't make out where the front lines were. One could argue about who had taken Kharkhov or who held Kaluga, but among the railroad men it was well known that no trains were being sent through from the Uzlov railroad junction at Tula, and at Eletz they were backed up as far as Berhova. Bombers had penetrated to the Ryazan-Voronezh line, dropping a few bombs here and there, and sometimes hitting even Krechetovka. Ten days ago, from out of nowhere two stray Germans on motorcycles came through Krechetovka, shooting wildly with their machine guns. One of them was killed and the other one got away, and at the station everything was in confusion and disorder.[1]

Aleksandr Solzhenitsyn

Given the enormous expanse of the Russian front, the differential in minimum winter temperatures between the south and the north, like the differences between the Baltic lowlands and the southern prairies, inevitably began to divide the behaviors of both armies, creating a situation in which although the front lines were a continuous front that at its maximum extent was over 3,000 kilometers, militarily speaking the combat there began to approach a state of affairs in which there were essentially three different campaigns being fought in parallel.

This situation, or tendency, initially dictated by the terrain (the wedge of the Pripet Marshes), was considerably exacerbated by two additional factors. The rift between Hitler and his senior commanders as to their objectives, laid bare in his August decision to concentrate on the southeast, remained. If anything, the gap widened, as the Germans continued to advance deeper into the interior. Moscow and Leningrad, the twin cities that had been from the very first the traditional goals of the professional military planners, were now much closer than they had been at the end of August.

The other factor that increasingly came into play was the traditional tendency of senior German field commands to operate almost independently of one another, and of the high command itself. The men who were now in control of the three German armies in the USSR thus by background and inclination were each convinced that given enough resources they could succeed in their task and bring the war to an end.

For von Leeb, at Army Group North, the prize was Leningrad. For von Bock, at Army Group Center, it was Moscow, while for von Rundstedt at Army Group South, it was the resources of eastern Ukraine. Sorting out the priority to be given to each objective was complicated and led to compromise after compromise. In fall 1940, as we have seen, the army had been focused on the two cities, to the exclusion of all else. Hitler's insistence on the drive to the south was based on a theory of the importance of resources to waging war that was outside the generals' purview.

But as all three objectives had been in the original plan, each man could with justification point to his goal as the primary one after the startling pace and depth of the initial advances. To make matters worse, each man could with even more justification point to his success. With the fall of Smolensk, von Bock felt his armor was poised to take Moscow. All he needed was more divisions.

At the end of August, von Leeb was in the same position with respect to Leningrad, as was von Rundstedt with respect to Kiev and the Crimea.

Whether he consciously understood the extent of the confusion inside the German high command for the first half of the First World War or whether it was simply in his nature, Hitler was determined to be the supreme commander, as his decision about the expansion of the planned offensive against the USSR in December 1940 and his subsequent decisions of late August 1941 made clear.

As the situation changed and more information was available, Hitler began making decisions sequentially. In late August he shifted resources to von Rundstedt to enable him to complete the conquest of Ukraine. In the same time frame (late August–early September) he shut down von Leeb and Army Group North, deciding that now (that is, the first week of September), as the city was encircled, it could essentially be left alone.

The siege of Leningrad, the famous Nine Hundred Days, caused the hapless citizenry a misery that can scarcely be imagined. Conditions inside the city were so frightful that the police had a special unit that investigated cannibalism. The fact that the city remained in Soviet hands is invariably pointed out as yet another German defeat, one of the war's best historians going so far as to call Hitler's decision to have von Leeb settle down to siege warfare "strategically ridiculous . . . one of the greatest mistakes of the war."[2]

The broader context suggests otherwise. With Finland in the war on the German side, and the loss of Estonia to the Germans, Leningrad's importance as a naval base was reduced to insignificance. The gulf was so narrow that ships were never out of range of even the most short-range land-based aircraft, and the water was too shallow to allow much evasive maneuvering to dodge aerial attacks.

Although the city remained the cultural and intellectual center of Russia, its only strategic importance was the same as that of Stalingrad, Kharkov, Gorki, Vyksa, Nizhni Tagil, or Chelyabinsk: its tank factories were one of the Red Army's main sources of armor, particularly of the powerful KV heavy tanks. Although the city's value as the main industrial center had declined since the revolution, the generally accepted estimate that the industries there accounted for over one tenth of all Soviet industrial output is probably true.[3]

But although a city besieged could become an important symbol of the Soviet people's will to resist, and became so, as well as a chilling monument to human suffering, once the city's factories were sealed off from the rest of the country, Leningrad's importance to the war effort was essentially zero.

There is another factor that makes Hitler's decision sound. When Shostakovich made his bitter quip about his native city, to the effect that Hitler merely finished off a city that Stalin had already destroyed, he was reflecting a widespread view among Leningraders about Stalin's attitude toward what they regarded as the center of Russian cultural and intellectual life. They felt that they were in Stalin's eyes pretty much in the same position as the Kulaks of the southern and eastern rural areas, a class to be eradicated. In the complex and ultimately unknowable rivalries that preceded the Great Terror, Sergei Mironovich Kirov, the Leningrad party boss and effective ruler of the queen city, was seen as a dangerous rival to Stalin: it was his assassination that triggered the Terror, the circumstances being such as to give rise to a widespread belief that Stalin was behind it.[4]

It is true that in the bitter months that followed the beginning of the siege, the Russians managed to get supplies into the city during the winter, with convoys of trucks traveling across the icy crust of Lake Ladoga. That ice would support trucks, although the trip was risky, but it would hardly bear the weight of the massive heavy tanks that Leningrad had been famous for making. Not that it made much difference: the Izhorskiy steel factory at Kolpino had been in German hands even before the city was sealed off, and on September 27, von Leeb's soldiers secured the main tank factory, located in the southern suburb of Pulkovo. Had Hitler been collecting famous European cities, Petrograd would have been a worthy addition, but the idea that it had any strategic value seems dubious.

There would also have been a considerable cost involved. Leningrad, owing to its proximity to Finland and Estonia, which after 1917 were independent countries, had always presented the Soviets with defensive problems. Although everyone saw that when Stalin sent Tukhachevsky to command the Leningrad Military District he was in effect sending him into exile, building up the city defenses was important. Whatever the cause for his relocation, Tukhachevsky had at least laid the groundwork for the city's defenses, which were already favored by the terrain. The city was built on a swamp, and indeed there was a great swath of bog to the southeast, from Lake Ilmen past Lake Ladoga. On the southern or Estonian side the ground gradually became higher and firmer, relative both to the city proper and the areas to the east.

In consequence, von Leeb's armored and mechanized units were hardly of much use in breaching these defenses. But over the next few weeks, the German infantry systematically secured the most important objectives for control of the southern approaches to the city, whose defenders, in addition to lacking resources, had to contend with the threat of a Finnish attack from the north.

Initially von Leeb, using troops borrowed from von Bock, was able to mount a concerted attack both on the defensive positions of the southern suburbs and the area north of the main rail line to Moscow, their objective being the historic village (now a suburb) of Schlüsselburg, right on Lake Ladoga.

Although the fighting is generally, and accurately, described as desperate, within three days the Germans had seized all the objectives of real tactical importance, such as Hill 167 and Schlüsselburg (by September 11). At some point during that week, the city became cut off from the rest of the USSR, as the link via Lake Ladoga became an operational possibility only in late November when the lake froze over. The Red Army was well aware of the importance of the oddly named town on the lake. As its name suggests (Schlüssel means key), the small town was the key to the great Russian city to the south, and for the next three weeks there were continuous Soviet attempts to retake it.

As can be imagined, von Leeb was a sorely frustrated general. By now his troops had surrounded the city, they had almost all the most important strong points, could literally look over and down into the place, but all he could do was sit there, while the action shifted further south. Sensibly, von Leeb settled down to strengthen his defenses at Schlüsselburg, the area that was not only the most important for maintaining the encirclement, but also the part of his front that was the most exposed to Soviet attacks.

But there too he was frustrated. Hitler directed the army group to mount an offensive out of its northern positions, subsequently known as the Volkhov bridgehead, after the minor railroad town on the river of that name, some 120 kilometers east of Leningrad. The Germans would move due east in the direction of what at first glance is an insignificant or anyway obscure Russian town, Tikhvin, some 200 kilometers east of Leningrad.

As was often the case with Hitler's objectives, Tikhvin was more important than it appeared at first. An important trading center in the middle ages (it was a stage in the connections from the Baltic to the Volga), it guarded the approaches to the historic kingdom of Muscovy. In Stalinist times it was being turned into an industrial city. It formed the only real base from which to conduct operations in this part of the USSR, and to isolate Moscow from the northwest.[5]

Having seized the area, von Leeb's troops would then turn

north, where the Finnish army had positions on the other side of the River Svir, which ran from Lake Onega into Lake Ladoga, another several hundred kilometers.

So on October 15, von Leeb obediently dispatched the 23rd Armored Corps under General Rudolf Schmidt to take Tikhvin. That was accomplished on November 8, destroying the Soviet 4th Army, which had been in reserve to the east of Leningrad since September. By then Stalin's reserve divisions had arrived from the Far East, and so Hans von Arnim (Schmidt had been sent to Army Group Center, where he took command of the 2nd Army), whose troops were spread out from Volkhov to Tikhvin, now found himself under attack from elements of four Soviet armies.

The fighting continued on through November and early December, with the salient becoming increasingly vulnerable once von Bock's offensive operations on the right flank of Army Group North failed to hold all the crucial areas to the east and southeast of Tikhvin. When von Bock withdrew (during the first week in December), von Arnim was in a precarious position, and finally pulled back into his original positions along the Volkhov River. Von Leeb wanted to pull back even further toward Leningrad, but Hitler refused.

Von Leeb was becoming increasingly frustrated and unhappy, and by mid-November his irritation with Hitler was hardly a secret. He considered the Tikhvin expedition ridiculous, a sign that Hitler was a rank amateur. Curiously and revealingly, however, von Leeb soldiered on as the commander of the army group, and as we shall see, he would be the only one of the three group commanders still in command at the start of 1942.

In the greater scheme of things, the Tikhvin foray was a relatively insignificant chapter in the campaign. Even at the time it was dwarfed by what was going on to the south. However, it establishes a typical pattern of German offensive actions that, while poorly understood, clarify the much more confused situations in the south. The chronology as well as the motivations on the German side are even more important than the actual events; an examination of them is instructive.

Whatever the importance of Tikhvin, von Leeb was either unable or (more likely) unwilling to grasp it. Frustrated in his understandable desire to achieve a traditional military goal, the capture of Leningrad outright, his next objective was the welfare of the men under his command. When he realized that the main drive on Moscow was stalling, and saw that von Arnim was fighting off a vastly larger Soviet force, his first instinct was the commendable one of wanting his troops pulled back into the relative safety around Leningrad, and he lobbied aggressively with Hitler to that end. The dictator, for his part, although he was in general adamantly opposed to tactical withdrawals, was eventually persuaded, and the miserable German soldiery that had taken Tikhvin and held it for over a month withdrew to the northwest.

Aside from more dead Russian and German soldiers, the military result of the whole affair was practically nil. The German withdrawal into what was subsequently called the Volkhov bridgehead, taken in conjunction with the withdrawals further south, encouraged Stalin in the not unreasonable belief that he could throw the Germans back, and it fanned the flames of discontent among senior German officers, who increasingly took refuge in feelings of professional superiority: Hitler was a meddling amateur who failed to understand strategy.

In a campaign of compromises, both Hitler and his generals were becoming increasingly testy about the extent to which their side, whatever it happened to be at the time, was having to compromise.

The most important feature of this unhappy affair, however, is the difference between the reality of it and the appearance. Von Leeb's assumption that his battered 23rd Armored Corps could execute one of the most difficult and demoralizing of military operations, an orderly retreat under fire, reflected his confidence as well as his professional training. Although sometimes the whole notion of military professionalism is mystified, and in some cases certainly difficult to understand, the idea that you backed away from a battle you had no interest in fighting where a victory would accomplish nothing that was worth the risk is simply common sense.

Common sense that in this case reflected a preference that had been institutionalized in the German officer corps even before the First World War, and subsequently sharpened there in over four years of continuous warfare. From the level of company commander all the way up, German commanders had no difficulty in breaking off engagements, if they felt the human cost was unacceptable, and in withdrawing from the field of battle. Defensively, this was the automatic response, the corollary to the notion of the double envelopment that characterized their offensive notions, and that Hoth and Guderian had effected so impressively at Smolensk.

In strictly tactical terms, these decisions, particularly the withdrawal, were unimpeachable. The weakness lay in how they were perceived by the outside world, including the soldiers on the other side. The tactical disengagements German officers instinctively preferred could easily be turned around and represented as defeats. Whether he believed he had won a great victory or not, Stalin promptly represented von Arnim's withdrawal as such, and the world, which desperately wanted to clutch at any straw that suggested that Hitler could be stopped, believed him.

After the Soviet defeat at Smolensk, von Bock, at Army Group Center, had become just as frustrated as von Leeb. He too felt he was poised to break through all the way to Moscow, but had to sit and watch as Hitler switched armored and air force units to von Rundstedt in the south.

But Hitler was in September seriously considering shutting down the three offensive operations entirely. There was still plenty of time for the Germans to create defensive positions anchored on the major cities and towns they now controlled, and the next six to eight weeks, say from the end of September to the middle of November, were the worst part of the year for military operations in northern Europe, particularly in Russia.

Modern armies were dependent on massive amounts of logistical support, and that meant a steady flow of trucks between the railheads and the front lines to reinforce and resupply the steady movement of tanks and soft-skinned vehicles at the front. Given the deplorable roads of Russia, mud was a greater problem than snow and ice.

Generally speaking, it began to rain steadily in September, and the ground gradually turned to mud. Although in western European Russia, it generally began to rain steadily in September, the three rainiest months were June, July, and August; by September, rainfall was less than half of what it would be in, say, New York City. Given the lack of paved roads in the Soviet Union, and the scrub forest lands of the Baltic regions, the worst period for campaigning was the weeks of the fall before low temperatures froze the top layer of soil, roughly from late September all the way through October. October was arguably the worst month, as typically the average low temperatures were erratic enough to make the hardening of the ground a slow process. In 1941, as in most years, by the middle of November the ground, whatever its condition, was frozen, as were most streams and rivers, whether snow had actually begun to fall or not.

Fifteen degrees of latitude separate Sevastopol from Leningrad, which are thus roughly the same distance apart as Houston and Chicago, or Nice and Stockholm. However, despite the fact that Kiev is almost 1,000 kilometers due south of Moscow, the average temperatures in fall and winter are almost identical in both cities. Truly temperate conditions are limited to the coastal areas of the Black Sea and the Sea of Azov: although the Ukraine and the Don basin were much further south, their location inland compensated to a marked extent: it was only in the extremes (the daytime highs and nighttime lows) that the regions differed appreciably.

As von Leeb had closed around Leningrad, he had begun to feel the effects of the climate. Compared to Ukraine, the Baltic was boggier and there was less natural drainage. When the Germans had sealed the city off in early September, they found their positions on the southeastern quadrant of the city considerably hindered by boggy ground that extended for several hundred kilometers, an irregular area running all the way from Lake Ilmen to Lake Ladoga on the far northern perimeter of the city.

So although in mechanized warfare severe cold weather posed special problems, winter was not necessarily going to force an end to campaigning. Rivers, the surface water frozen to a considerable thickness, were no longer serious obstacles for infantry. Roads, their ruts packed with layers of snow and ice, offered far easier transit for off-road vehicles than in the summer and especially than in the fall.

It is often said that the Germans had not anticipated campaigning in the winter. True enough, but they had not anticipated the state of the roads, either. The road problem went far beyond their condition. A soldier with Army Group North stated the situation perfectly:

> In our advance northward, we began to be increasingly hindered by both the worsening roads and intensifying resistance from Soviet rearguards. Our advance was complicated by maps showing main roads and highways that simply did not exist.[6]

And this observation was made in late July, long before the climate became a factor. The problem, in other words, was not simply the condition of roads but the fact that many of them did not even exist. In Stalin's world, all that counted was what was shown on the maps drawn from reports claiming progress in every aspect of Soviet life.

Lower temperatures caused problems both for men and equipment. However, in general, it was only in January that it became significantly colder in Russia than in the Reich and that the nighttime lows began to plummet to temperatures far below anything seen in France or Ukraine. The ancient Russian saying "As the days grow longer, the cold grows stronger" is an apt summary.

Although the frozen ground simplified mobility dramatically, it posed two major problems. Even in relatively moderate cold weather of only a few degrees below freezing, it is difficult to construct trenches, foxholes, or shelters in frozen ground, a problem made worse by the impossibility of pouring concrete when the temperature is below freezing. As temperatures approach zero Fahrenheit, diesel fuel and motor oil thicken considerably. Sudden temperature drops of the sort that are not infrequent in northwestern Russia even in December could wreak havoc on engines. Without shelters or garages, which were among the many shortages of Stalinist Russia, the only way to keep engines working in such temperatures was to keep them running, which of course decreases engine life and increases fuel consumption.

Taken altogether, then, the climate suggested that if the offensives were going to be shut down, mid-September was the time to make the decision, as that would give German engineers almost two months to build shelters and garages, lay out defensive positions, and pour concrete for blockhouses.

Von Bock himself was of two minds, as he felt that the positions he was holding were not practicable for a successful defense, that he either needed to go forward or backward. Meanwhile, back in Berlin, Hitler was being lobbied not only by von Bock, but by Walter von Brauchitsch, technically commander in chief of the army, and also by Albert Kesselring, commander of Luft-flotte 2, von Bock's air arm in the Russian campaign. Despite his subsequent demurrals about the German offensive, Franz Halder, the nominal chief of army staff, felt the same way.[7]

So Hitler acceded to their enthusiasm and authorized a final push to take the capital, an objective that continued to draw the senior German generals, who remained convinced that the seizure of Moscow would bring the war to an abrupt conclusion. As we shall see in the next chapter, Hitler's instincts were right, and his senior commanders were wrong. However, Hitler was persuaded, and so now it was von Rundstedt's turn to be picked clean. Von Bock got the 4th Armored Group (now upgraded or anyway renamed the 4th Armored Army), a supporting air force unit (the 8th Air Army), and nine more divisions. The 2nd Army, and the 2nd Armored Group, although not technically under his command, would attack from the vicinity of Smolensk, in coordination with the great offensive that was to begin.

Hitler was able to shift all these resources around without shutting down the military operations of the affected army group because he was getting a steady stream of reinforcements in addition to the new Wehrmacht units arriving from other parts of Europe. By November there were two Hungarian army groups as well as two divisions from Slovakia operating in conjunction with Army Group South.

The contribution of Hitler's allies, whether reluctant or enthusiastic, is little remarked and usually ignored. In a war of millions, the impact of a stray division here and there seems insignificant, but this is to confuse manpower with firepower. The Spanish Blue Division, for instance, rapidly proved itself on the battlefield, as would the units the SS raised in Belgium, France, and the Netherlands. The three German commanders would naturally have preferred to avoid the headaches of having someone else's army to worry about, but the cumulative effect of the contributions of Hitler's partners was hardly insignificant: it explains why Army Group South was still pressing eastward despite losing so much of its mobile striking force.

Now that Smolensk had fallen and von Leeb was established to the southeast of Leningrad, the main Soviet forces of the Central Front were grouped inside a rough triangle comprised by a line stretching from the east of Smolensk to the southeast, running some 200 kilometers through Bryansk, and then to Orel in the southeast (another 100 kilometers). The troop dispositions, far from forming a continuous line, or front, were clustered behind this line, all the way back to Vyazma. Broadly speaking, the 120-odd kilometers from Smolensk to Vyazma were the base of the triangle, the distance between Smolensk and Bryansk was the hypotenuse, and the 200 kilometers from Vyazma to Bryansk were the adjacent side.

Von Bock's intelligence gave him the idea that since the Soviet armies were dispersed, with one group clustered between the two northern points of the triangle and the other group clustered around Bryansk, there was a golden opportunity for an elaborate and complex offensive operation. He aimed for nothing less than a double envelopment, twin pincers that would capitalize on the Soviet commander's inability to form a cohesive and continuous front.

Generals often have ambitious plans that founder on tactical realities, but in this particular instance, the German forces were successful beyond any reasonable expectation. Operations began on September 30, and the spearhead of Guderian's 2nd Armored Group sailed through the Russian front between Bryansk and Orel, the latter being another historic Russian town, 360 kilometers to the south of Moscow. Together with Smolensk, Orel was the main fortified defense of the capital. German armored columns covered well over 100 kilometers the first day of operations. Orel fell into German hands on October 3, Bryansk on the 6th. Vyazma itself had fallen by the 8th, along with over 600,000 Soviet soldiers taken prisoner and 1,200 tanks abandoned or destroyed.

So far so good, as far as the German commanders were concerned. But the mud was beginning to create serious problems. Nor did it help matters that the first snowfall occurred the day the Germans moved into Vyazma. This early in the year, it promptly melted, but it was a discouraging sign that winter was on the way. Even so, there was very little organized resistance at that time between the German columns and Moscow, although fighting continued through the month.

As the fall days shortened and the weather got nastier, Stalin himself was clutching at straws. On October 3, he was informed that all three fronts had collapsed, this unpleasant news being occasioned by the fall of Orel to Guderian.

Both Orel and Smolensk sat astride the main rail lines into Moscow from Europe, which meant that the advancing Germans had a relatively clear path to the capital. Even this close, not many roads were all-weather; most were still unpaved. The railroad rights of way, consistently the only routes that had been laid down according to civil engineering principles, were thus far more important than they would have been elsewhere. And, as the case with Smolensk, it was a feature of Russian geography that there were no real defensive positions between the cities and the capital. Nor was there the urban density that had slowed von Leeb's advancing forces as they approached Leningrad.

The only city remaining in the fan-shaped area of the German advance was Tula, 193 kilometers due south, an important rail and road junction that linked Smolensk on the west with Ryazin to the east. In traditional military terms, Tula was not part of a good defensive position, as its status under the czars as a minor fortress and comparatively recent settlement suggests (recent by Russian standards: the cathedral was not built until the middle of the eighteenth century).

The fall of Orel was a rude reality check as well as the starting point for a certain amount of panic. Lavrenty Pavlovich Beria, Stalin's security chief, promptly began murdering all the high-ranking prisoners in Moscow, among them the hapless air force general Rychakov, who had been imprisoned for telling Stalin about the true condition of the Red Air Force in 1940.[8]

A few days later, as the German advance continued, showing no signs of stopping, Stalin for the first time began to consider the possibility of quitting the war entirely. He told Beria, who as security chief could be presumed to have contacts with foreign governments and enemy powers, to make use of them. In the words of Zhukov, who was there at the time, Stalin instructed Beria "to sound out the possibilities of making a separate peace with Germany, given the critical situation."[9] When Zhukov was dispatched to talk to Ivan Stepanovich Konev, commander of the Central Front, to see for himself how bad the situation was, he learned that all the avenues leading to Moscow were open. The armies of the front no longer existed, nor did the front. Konev's reserves had been encircled.

Most Muscovites were in the same shape as Solzhenitsyn's fictional railroad officer Zotov: they couldn't understand how the debacle had occurred, nor were they being told its dimensions: they could only guess, given the odd bits and pieces of information that filtered back from the fronts. Zotov was luckier than most of them, since his position on the railroad at least made it possible for him to divine the general outlines of the situation that terrible October. As Nikolai Ivanovich Obryn'ba, an educated young man who was drafted and hastily sent into battle, later recalled:

> In truth I had been astounded: for we had been led, not so much to battle, as to slaughter. The wireless and the newspapers had clamored before the war: "Our borders are unassailable! We will destroy the enemy on his own territory!" And yet the Germans advanced, and we poor, untrained Opolchenie [militia] had been used as a shield against the enemy's armada. It was then that I understood there had been no plan for the

war, no leadership. . . . Stalin was a fictitious supreme commander.[10]

After the fall of Orel, the astonishment of the urban Muscovites turned to panic. A week after Stalin told Beria to see what could be done to come to terms with Hitler, the streets of Moscow exploded in a series of riots that gripped the city for days as terrified citizens, including officials and party members, tried to seize whatever they could and then flee. Stores closed, the transportation system came to a halt, the British embassy was sacked, and the metropolitan police lost control.[11]

For the next few days (or weeks, depending on whether one counts from the news about Orel on the 3rd or Zhukov's dismal report of the 7th), Stalin hesitated between surrender and resistance, as well as the immediate and more practical decision whether to abandon Moscow outright. Most of his entourage was packing up, making plans to leave, and encouraging their subordinates to flee.

As far as the collapse of the fronts went, the bad news continued, with Dnepropetrovsk, the major city of central Ukraine, falling to the Germans on October 12. A few days later came news of the loss of the all-important Black Sea port of Odessa, which fell to the Romanian 4th Army on October 16, after a siege of nearly two months and some desperate fighting.[12] Sevastopol and the remainder of the coast were surrounded and under siege; Ewald von Kleist's 1st Armored Army had already broken through to Osipenko on the Sea of Azov by the 5th. More alarming was news that his tanks had reached Taganrog by the 12th, and thus controlled the approach to Rostov from the sea, since Taganrog dominated the bay of the same name (Rostov was at the head of the bay and the mouth of the Don as it flowed into the Sea of Azov).

Von Rundstedt, presiding over this series of successes, wanted to quit while he was ahead. His logistical problems were not as severe as those of his colleagues to the north, and by the end of October his two armored commanders, von Kleist and von Manstein, had cleaned out the eastern Ukraine. Between them they had over 200,000 prisoners, what was left of the troops in the old Odessa Military District. The only part of the Crimea of any significance that was still in Soviet hands was Sevastopol. Then too, von Rundstedt was the oldest of the senior German commanders. He had been in German service for nearly half a century; he had never been enthusiastic about the Russian campaign, and he was exhausted.

When his troops had reached Taganrog, they had passed over a natural defensive line made by the Kalmius and Mius Rivers, which wandered down from the upper Don basin and emerged to the west of Taganrog. Although still advancing, the Germans were not slow to notice the advantages of this position. Subsequently known as the Mius Line, it became the anchor point of German defenses in the southeast. By the end of October the Germans had taken Kharkov (October 30) and Kursk fell a few days later (November 3). Von Rundstedt's forces had good defensive positions along the riverine network of eastern Ukraine.

But a move on Rostov would create a salient sticking out into hostile territory, the left flank vulnerable to Soviet attack. Moreover, the Sea of Azov was shallow, an enormous saltwater lake. It froze early, in theory exposing the attacking Germans on the section of coast from Taganrog to Rostov to attacks from the south as well. Given that, and the city's position astride the Don, there was no way it could be surrounded. So von Rundstedt was, for once, ready to support Hitler, who, as we have seen, was by the last half of October leaning toward going into winter quarters.

Whatever Stalin's frame of mind during those traumatic weeks, on the 19th, he made a decision: the government would stay in Moscow and fight on. He still had a sizable army in the Far East, defending against the Japanese threat, perhaps as many as half a million men. Assured by his spies that Japan would not attack him, he ordered these divisions west. As they were the only ones in the Red Army to have seen combat in recent years, they formed a powerful and by Soviet standards well-trained force.[13]

In traditional accounts, Stalin's determination was as fixed and unwavering as the steadfast will of the Russian people to resist and the Russian soldiers to fight to the last man. We now know that none of those myths was true. For the moment, the interesting question is why Stalin changed his mind, since clearly he was at least considering the idea of surrender.

Like most of the significant decisions the two dictators made during the war (Hitler's decision to attack, Stalin's refusal to believe he would), the reasoning is unknown. Stalin presented himself later as a man of steel, unmoved by the German onslaught. During his lifetime, the few people who knew the truth understandably remained silent. When Khrushchev denounced Stalin in his famous Secret Speech, he perhaps inadvertently shifted attention away from the horrible fall of 1941 to the catastrophe of the summer.

Just as Stalin was creating his own narrative of the war, Khrushchev created a counternarrative. Although much closer to the truth, Khrushchev's version of events had the result of confirming the idea that whatever Stalin's weaknesses were in June 1941, by July, or maybe August, he was back in charge, and from then on his determination to fight to the last Bolshevik was unwavering. Stalin's uncertainties about victory, like his earlier overtures to Hitler and his decision to attack Germany in the near future, vanished in the Orwellian memory hole.

Although no one will ever know what was going on in Stalin's mind at this point, one clue as to what motivated him may be found in the two public speeches he made in early November on the occasion of the anniversary of the October Revolution. In the first, on November 6, Stalin admitted some Red Army losses, but spoke in stirring terms of

The defense of Leningrad and Moscow, where our divisions recently annihilated some three dozen professional German divisions.... The enemy lost over 4,500,000 killed, wounded and prisoners. There can be no doubt that as a result of the war, Germany, whose manpower reserves are already becoming exhausted, has been considerably more weakened by the war than the Soviet Union, whose reserves are only just now unfolding.[14]

As the casualty analyses make clear, Stalin was wildly mistaken. The only truth contained in this paragraph is in the last phrase. The troops from the Far East were arriving and going into action.

Stalin decided to hold the annual military parade of November 7, despite the military situation. The exact timing of the parade was a closely guarded secret, and at least some of the troops marched directly off toward the front, except for some inexperienced tank drivers who lurched off in an entirely different direction.[15] In the speech he gave that day at Red Square, Stalin repeated some of the figures from his earlier speech, and included two even more astonishing claims:

Our reserves in manpower are inexhaustible.... Hunger and poverty reign in Germany. In four and a half months of war Germany has lost four and a half million soldiers. Germany is bleeding white.[16]

Stalin was certainly not the first wartime commander to take refuge in the fantasy that his opponents were losing many more men than he was. He may well have believed that he was telling the truth: the leaders of governments often believe their own propaganda, and decades of massaging every piece of information so as to put the best possible face on the state of affairs hardly prepared his minions for the sort of blunt honesty that the situation demanded. But the fall of the key cities of European Russia and Ukraine could no more be concealed than the implications of those losses.

Given the rapid mythologizing of the war, it is easy to see why the notion that Stalin was willing to come to terms with Hitler has never been seriously considered. The accounts of Stalin's attempts to negotiate with Hitler in the years before the war are fascinating examples of obfuscation, distortion, and rationalization, by Westerners as well as Russians. So the notion that Stalin seriously entertained giving up has hardly been credited.

That he was in fact willing to come to terms and Hitler spurned his offers is so much at odds with the Stalinist legend, not to mention with the sympathies of his historians and biographers, as to be thought a fantasy. Nonetheless, the evidence exists, both that the overtures were made and that Hitler rejected them.[17] The most convincing explanation for Stalin's decision to fight on regardless is certainly inferential, but it has the virtue of simplicity: by the end of October he realized that Hitler had no interest in negotiating a peace, so Stalin realized that he had no choice but to keep on fighting.

At the same time, as the days of October shortened, the months of the great armored maneuvers with their resultant clashes of tanks, were temporarily over. It would be nearly a year and a half before they resumed. There were two reasons for this. On the one side, there was the weather. Tracked vehicles are better able to handle soft earth and mud than wheeled vehicles, but their advantage is relative: they can get bogged down in mud, they can slide off of the road into a ditch or hole, and they can tip over. As the temperatures dropped, those problems were replaced by others. And even though the German army excelled both at on-site repairs and surprisingly quick rebuilds of their vehicles, after nearly six months normal wear and tear was taking its toll.

At the same time, there was less and less need for the deployment of large armored units on the German side, because the bulk of the Soviet tank force had been destroyed. By the time he gave his two speeches, Stalin was, at least in the short term, out of tanks. To be precise, at one point in October 1941, he was personally handing them out to his commanders in small parcels of a dozen or more. By the middle of November he was frantically trying to find 200 tanks for the defense of Moscow.[18]

The Germans had their own problems, but they also had their own plans. Hitler was willing to shut down his offensive operations for the winter, but the army high command in Berlin now proposed an even more grandiose scheme, a double envelopment of Moscow and of the remaining Soviet armies grouped between the capital and Leningrad. Not surprisingly, this offensive bogged down almost immediately. In this case the verb is quite accurate. The trucks in von Bock's supply, sliding along the rivers of mud that Russian roads had become, were averaging less than ten kilometers a day. Moreover, as part of this ambitious plan, significant German forces were shifted to the wings of von Bock's already overextended sector of the front (at one point it was nearly 650 kilometers across), with Guderian's armored group being diverted to the east, toward Tula, about 200 kilometers southeast of Moscow and an equal distance to the northeast of Orel.

At the same time, another, even more substantial force was sent off to the northeast, away from Moscow, the left wing of the encircling movement. Although what was left of the Red Army was fighting desperately, von Bock's main problem was the intractable terrain. On October 30, he called for a halt. He had decided to wait for the ground to freeze.

His colleagues to the north and south also decided to bring their offensives to a halt. Deprived of the manpower he felt he needed to take Leningrad and sweep on around Moscow, von Leeb chose to dig in.

But von Bock was convinced that one more push would bring him to Moscow. He had support in the German high command, so Hitler acquiesced: the last turn of the screw, called Typhoon, was scheduled to begin on November 15. But this was another compromise: von Leeb had already been told to sally forth toward Tikhvin and the Svir River, and von Rundstedt was now ordered to send von Kleist to take Rostov.

Neither general was enthusiastic. As we have seen, von Leeb's men took Tikhvin but then retreated before a determined Soviet offensive. Von Rundstedt had calculated that he could take Rostov but not hold it, and he was right. Von Kleist fought his way into the city, but his extended force was now vulnerable to the developing Soviet counterattack, and so von Rundstedt ordered a general retreat to his preferred position along the Kalmius River.

This was a compromise Hitler was unwilling to tolerate. He ordered von Rundstedt to hold his ground at all costs. The commander of Army Group South thereupon lost his temper and told Hitler his order was insane, either take it back or he, von Rundstedt, would resign.

The result was, predictably, another compromise. Von Rundstedt was sacked, replaced by Walter von Reichenau, a tough-minded professional officer who was also an enthusiastic supporter of Hitler. Despite that, von Reichenau promptly ordered a retreat to the Kalmius, with Hitler's tacit approval. Three months later von Rundstedt was appointed commander in chief of the armies in the west, so his disagreement with Hitler, far from dooming him as it would have with Stalin, only condemned him to a couple of years in France.

By a curious coincidence, on December 1, while von Rundstedt was arguing with Hitler about withdrawal, von Bock finally threw in the towel. His beleaguered infantry was on the outskirts of Moscow, but its right flank was wide open, the troops were exhausted, and the German offensive had finally ground to a halt. So he gave the order to disengage, and the Germans began to move back from their advanced positions, their withdrawal made considerably more difficult by the massive counterattack Stalin launched on December 6.

So Hitler issued his second order to stand fast, which the local commanders essentially interpreted as meaning that they had to cover their retreat as best they could, since in the next week the front lines shifted westward and the Red Army moved forward.

Of the three commanders, von Bock had been the only one who had lobbied Hitler for continuing the offensive, an offensive that he himself had been forced to call off. Insofar as he believed he could take Moscow, he had failed. But Hitler refused to hold him responsible. Instead, it was suggested that he take an extended leave for health reasons (which were valid; von Bock was at the end of his tether, as he had told Hitler's adjutant on December 16). He was replaced by Günther von Kluge. But a month later, von Reichenau, having taken over from von Rundstedt, collapsed and died, so von Bock's vacation lasted barely a month: on January 18, 1942, he was named commander of Army Group South.

Every account of the fighting in fall 1941 paints a highly convincing portrait of a stiffening and desperate Soviet defense centering on Moscow. By December 5, 1941, the German offensive to seize Moscow, Typhoon, had ground to a halt in the face of fresh new Soviet reinforcements, the feared Siberians. Strengthened by these reinforcements, Stalin ordered a counterattack, which then drove the battered Germans back from the city, recovering hundreds of square kilometers of lost territory and saving Moscow. As Stalin put it in his February 17, 1942, speech on the occasion of the twenty-fourth anniversary of the founding of the Red Army:

> In the violent battles at Moscow, it defeated the German fascist troops which threatened to encircle the Soviet capital. The Red Army threw the enemy back from Moscow and continues to push him westward. Now the Germans no longer possess the military ad-

vantage which they had in the first months of the war by virtue of their sudden and treacherous attack.[19]

The bitter fighting around the capital between the end of October 1941 and the end of January 1942, generally known as the Battle of Moscow, is usually considered one of the decisive battles of the war, and one of the most lethal. Moscow was the first serious German defeat, the end of Hitler's grand schemes.

As this chronological account of the German actions has made clear, seen from the German side, the picture looked rather different. As the casualty analysis at the end of the previous chapter made clear, the idea of desperate battles in November and December is more the stuff of Stalinist legend than sober military history.

The chronology of the destruction of the Soviet armored divisions tells the story. The worst month was not June or July, but September 1941, in which no fewer than seventeen armored divisions were destroyed, four more than in August and five more than in July. A month and a half after the onset of Barbarossa, Stalin still had most of his tank force intact. But as a result of his orders, the incessant counterattacks of August and September resulted in the loss of half of the Soviet tank force. In the following months the numbers dwindled off markedly: seven divisions in October, two in November, and then, a division a month in spring 1942.[20] The main reason for the decline was that most of the armored units had been used up and were in the process of being reconstituted. But the destruction still continued. By the time Stalin gave his commemorative speech of February, the 28th Armored Division had been destroyed (in January), while the 112th Armored Division was wiped out on February 7.

Taken in isolation, the data on the destruction of the Soviet tank force is not conclusive. Divisions were refurbished, retrained, equipped with new vehicles, and sent back into action.

But the most cursory reflection suggests that this process does not happen overnight, even in the best of armies. In the short term, that is to say, by the conclusion of the first six months of the war, Stalin had lost approximately four fifths of his vaunted tank force: fifty-six divisions had been destroyed out of the theoretical seventy-two that the Red Army possessed.

Shortages were already manifesting themselves in September, when the panicked Meretskov found himself critically short of tanks; as the Red Army hastily reorganized itself in December, the vehicular strength of tank brigades shrank dramatically, reflecting the shortage. In December an armored brigade of forty-six was down to sixteen T-34/76 medium and ten KV-1 heavy tanks. By January the number had decreased to forty-two, and by the time of Stalin's speech the brigades of the armored divisions consisted of only twenty-seven tanks, a recognition of their scarcity.[21] Although part of this shrinkage was based on the inexperience of the commanders and their staffs (smaller units were all they could manage), it also reflected the shortage of armored and soft-skinned vehicles.

Now although the declining loss rate suggests dwindling resources, it could also suggest a better-organized army and more effective one: the Soviets lost fewer armored divisions in the winter months not only because they had fewer to lose, but also because their combat performance had improved.

That this had happened was the theme of Stalin's major public speeches during this period. In the violent battles around Moscow the Red Army had thrown the Germans back and was now moving to the offensive. One would assume, therefore, that German casualties should reflect this claim: better Soviet tactics and a fiercer resistance, the "violent" struggles, should by definition result in heavier German losses, which is why they were defeated in their bid for Moscow.[22]

The casualty reports tell a different story. In August, the Wehrmacht had 39,456 men killed, the highest total recorded for 1941. Already in September, there was a marked decline: 28,499 dead. That trend continued. In October losses came to 23,837, and in November and December there was a marked drop-off: 17,865 men in the former, and 14,949 in the latter. Nor did the figure rise in January.

Although Stalin quickly transformed the stalled German drive on Moscow into a great battle that the Red Army had won, anyone looking over the casualty reports would conclude that the fighting peaked in September and then slowly wound down. Relatively speaking, of course: by the levels of the German campaigns in the west the losses were significant, but the point here is that the casualty figures do not support evidence of any major battle in the last quarter of the year. What they suggest is a relative lull in the fighting while the Germans settled into their positions for the winter and Stalin tried to rebuild his shattered army.

By December 1941 the Germans had 3,906,995 prisoners of war, roughly four fifths of the total prewar size of the Red Army. Even given the Soviet penchant for skipping basic training entirely and giving civilians uniforms and directing them toward the front line, the sheer distances involved in the transport meant this would take time.

The trend line for Russian soldiers taken prisoner by the Germans presents a somewhat different trend from the casualty data. The single greatest total for any reporting period was the final ten days of September: as the Germans mopped up around Kiev they counted 550,961 prisoners. But the month that saw the highest total was October, in which there were 1,037,778 prisoners. In November there was a marked decline: only 291,934, and in December the number had diminished dramatically, down to 75,440.

So the German casualty records, like their records for prisoners taken, suggest that the fighting, rather than intensifying, was winding down. This trend is not contradicted by the other reported data. The number of German soldiers missing in action peaked in July, and then began to diminish: by November it was half of what it had been in the summer and was in any event extremely small, only 34,547 men for the whole of 1941, a total not much higher than the one for the comparable period in 1914, and for a vastly larger army.

Similarly, the figures for wounds cases peaked in September and then began to fall: in the final two months it was less than half of what it had been in August. As common sense suggests, the number of soldiers gone missing, like the number of wounds cases reported and soldiers killed outright, are accurate indicators of the intensity of combat. Taken together, they are determinative. Action reports that use subjective terms such as "heavy losses" or "fierce fighting" may reflect the emotions of the people on the scene, but they have little other value.

So there is no concrete data supporting the contention of intensified resistance, desperate fighting, or great battles fought during November and December 1941. In fact, compared to September or August, there was a notable lull in December. Moreover, in absolute terms, some of the figures are misleading.

So were the figures for Soviet troop strengths. True, the maps at Stalin's headquarters in Moscow showed new Soviet armies deployed. The Germans, aware of that fact through their field intelligence services, counted the numbers with growing anxiety. At least twelve new armies were created in the final months of 1941, nine of them deployed in a cluster to the east of the threatened capital, three more to the east of Leningrad. On paper, the numbers were impressive, or depressing, depending on whether they were being looked at from Moscow or Berlin.

But the reality was somewhat different. Stalin had already come to the sensible conclusion that the massive armies of June 1941 were unmanageable by his field commanders. He was correct. Since he killed most of them off, their replacements were by definition inferior, at least in the short term. So the new armies were substantially smaller, five or six woefully understrength divisions, a sort of Potemkin Village of the military map room.

Unfortunately for the Russians, Stalin's illusion, or his desperation, continued unchecked. The last months of 1941 had been a catastrophe. In 1942 not only would the carnage continue; it would get much worse.

THE HOLLOW VICTORIES OF 1942

> We civilians, as you know, have a very bad way of deciding whether a battle was won or lost. Those who retreat after a battle have lost it is what we say.
>
> Tolstoy, *War and Peace*[1]

In one of those fascinating historical coincidences, the day after Stalin threw all the reserves from his Far Eastern armies into the meat grinder, the Japanese attacked the American naval base at Pearl Harbor. For Stalin, the Japanese attack at Pearl Harbor was welcome news, particularly since it was only one part of a coordinated series of major offensives in the Pacific that would tie up Japan's resources for some time to come. The Japanese and the Russians had engaged in sporadic but bloody battles in the Far East for several years. But given the direction and complexity of the Japanese thrust into the Pacific, there was no possibility that they would be able to take advantage of the greatly weakened Red Army forces in eastern Siberia. Stalin now had the not inconsiderable luxury of a one-front war.[2]

As the analysis of German casualties in December suggests, Stalin's offensive to relieve Moscow was a blow that had essentially expended its energies on thin air, as von Bock's troops were already pulling back. But Zhukov's attacks accelerated their movements, and now a dangerous gap opened up on von Bock's left flank. With his troop concentrations fixed on Moscow, and von Leeb's on the Volkhov bridgehead northeast of Leningrad,

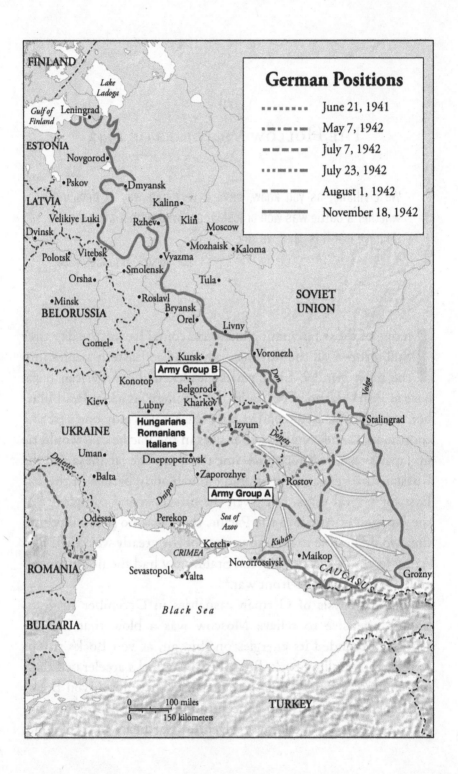

German Positions

········	June 21, 1941
─·─·─	May 7, 1942
─ ─ ─	July 7, 1942
·─··─	July 23, 1942
─ ─	August 1, 1942
━━━	November 18, 1942

FINLAND

Lake Ladoga

Gulf of Finland

Leningrad

ESTONIA

Novgorod

Pskov

Dmyansk

LATVIA

Kalinn

Velikiye Luki

Rzhev

Klin

Moscow

Dvinsk

Polotsk

Vitebsk

Vyazma

Mozhaisk

Kaloma

Orsha

Smolensk

Tula

Minsk

Roslavl

BELORUSSIA

Bryansk

Orel

SOVIET UNION

Gomel

Livny

Kursk

Voronezh

Army Group B

Konotop

Belgorod

Kiev

Lubny

Kharkov

Don

Volga

Stalingrad

Hungarians Romanians Italians

UKRAINE

Izyum

Uman

Donets

Dnepropetrovsk

Balta

Zaporozhye

Rostov

Dnipro

Army Group A

Dniester

Odessa

Perekop

Sea of Azov

Kuban

Kerch

CRIMEA

Maikop

Sevastopol

Yalta

Novorrossiysk

CAUCASUS

Grozny

ROMANIA

BULGARIA

Black Sea

0	100 miles
0	150 kilometers

TURKEY

neither of the overstretched army groups was able to form a continuous front with well-defined boundaries between von Bock's left and von Leeb's right.

In a war fought over such an enormous front, gaps were more or less inevitable, although the causes varied in different gaps. On the Soviet side, Red Army commanders lacked the tactical skills, the training, and perhaps above all, the communications systems, to maintain continuous fronts. To a certain extent the clustering of large formations may have reflected the Red Army's offensive-mindedness of the prewar period, with its emphasis on delivering great smashing blows of the sort that demanded a concentration of forces, the vague and confused memories of Tukhachevsky's concept of deep battle.

But the Red Army's strategy was also dictated by the underdevelopment of Russia, its terrain, and its climate. All three factors affected both the defenders and the invaders. Insofar as there were any amenities of civilization in the Russian countryside, they were confined to the historic fortress towns and trading centers that had been developed over the centuries. There was nothing like the dense network of villages and small towns, all interconnected by minor roads, that was a feature of western Europe. The railroad boom that had characterized czarist Russia in its final decades had if anything intensified the situation.

In the older days of warfare, the speed of tactical deployments was dictated by the number of kilometers a foot soldier could march in a day, almost a constant. Garrisons that got wind of an approaching enemy could reckon on having the time to sally forth and meet him in battle, or in waiting until they were reinforced. But mechanization meant that the rate of enemy movement could be wildly variable: gaps that the enemy found could be exploited in a matter of hours, or, more realistically, days, as opposed to weeks.

In the first months of the war, the Germans had repeatedly driven through the gaps that had thus developed, moving with such speed that the hapless Soviet units found themselves cut off, stranded behind the rapidly moving German front. Early on, back in July, German staff officers had begun to worry about the resulting chaos, debating whether their armies should press on or stop and consolidate their gains. Their better commanders, like Guderian, were by temperament aggressive and inclined to push forward and let someone else clean up behind them.

In the relatively small arena of the west in 1940, and the Balkans in 1941, the Germans had enough forces to achieve both breakthrough and consolidation. In this vastly larger area, in a country that was still largely terra incognita, to achieve both was impossible, certainly in the short term and probably at all.

As Tolstoy shrewdly observed, generals in retrospect tend to fight the battles that they wish had happened, as opposed to the ones that occurred. Luck, accident, and error play a great part in determining the outcome, as much or more than skill. The German decision to press on after October meant it was inevitable that the same gaps would develop on its side as on the Soviet, and that at some point, given Stalin's obsession with attack, those gaps would be discovered.

The vaguely defined boundary between the two northern army groups afforded just such an opportunity, one made all the worse by the boggy terrain to the southeast of Leningrad, which meant that von Leeb's forces essentially had no right flank. In that sense Hitler's idea of striking out from the Volkhov, on the north side of Leningrad, was sensible: the bog barrier was a sort of Pripet Marsh situation in miniature, so the only way to secure a front was to be on one side or the other of the bog. Nor was there any discernible set of anchor points for a position on the northeastern (or Soviet) side.

To make matters worse, as von Bock's final push on Moscow developed, it resembled a left hook, because he was approaching Moscow from the northwestern quadrant, with his main force between the Volga and Moskva Rivers. Not only did that lengthen the period of vulnerability for the withdrawing troops, but as the pressure to the south of Moscow eased accordingly, the Russians were able to move forward. Tactically, this was the worst possible situation in which to have to conduct a defense, and the weather hardly helped. So as the Germans pulled back (given the casualties, one can hardly say they were defeated), their 4th and 9th Armies found themselves being squeezed between the bogs to the north and the Soviet advance to the south.

German officers had always been inclined to conduct highly elastic defensive battles, the idea being that bulges in your lines as the enemy penetrated made him vulnerable to attacks from the flanks, provided two conditions were met. The bulge, or potential breakthrough, had to be on a small enough front that it could be contained, a hole in the dike as opposed to collapse of an entire section. The enemy offensive had to be small enough in scope so that your neighbors could come to your aid. In this case, neither condition was met. The gaps in the German deployment were too great, and von Bock's neighbors were already overstrained, as they were under attack themselves.

In retrospect, Smolensk, with its envelopment and destruction of whole Soviet armies, established the pattern of future German offensive successes, and Rostov defined the pattern of future offensive failures, Tikhvin being a second example of failure. The Germans were able to seize their objective, but they lacked the forces to hold it, and their commanders, unwilling to get their men killed for no good reason, would then pull back, with or without Hitler's permission. The only result was a growing body count.

Zhukov's December Moscow offensive set the pattern on the Soviet side. He saw the opportunity and seized it, but he was unable to exploit it. On the one hand, his commanders lacked both the men and the tanks required. But Russian commanders not only lacked the resources, they lacked the skills. This inexperience was hardly surprising. By December 1941 there were precious few officers left, period, much less with extensive experience.

That was just as true of Georgi Zhukov as his subordinates. At Khalkin Gol, where he had defeated the Imperial Japanese Army on August 15, 1939, he had enjoyed the luxury of fighting a grossly underequipped and technologically deficient enemy that was, to make their situation worse, also vastly outnumbered. His achievement there was hardly the stuff to suggest a Bolshevik Napoleon or Wellington; rather he was the only Soviet general who had ever actually directed a victorious battle. Such experience is not to be discounted. As Stalin had now discovered, neither political reliability nor peacetime achievement was a guarantor of success in wartime.

But the command and coordination of entire army groups (or fronts, as the Soviets called them) was a whole different order of magnitude from directing a few divisions on the battlefield. Although Zhukov was considerably more intelligent than Stalin's phalanx of aging Red Cavalry generals, he suffered from the same deficiency. So the result of the first phase of the midwinter offensive was somewhere between a check and a draw. The threat to Moscow was removed, and the Germans ceded ground, scrambling, or rather stumbling, back to some sort of defensive position hacked out of the frozen earth.

As we have seen, Hitler had, rather sensibly, been willing to halt the offensive drives in October 1941. The impetus for further actions came from his two northern commanders, von Bock and von Leeb. Both men were convinced that the grand prizes of Moscow and Leningrad were within their grasp. As is well known, German troops fought their way into the suburbs of the former, and completely surrounded the latter. By the standards of previous wars, when the capital cities were the chief prizes, the Russians would have been compelled to sue for terms.

Not unreasonably, the generals felt they were on the verge of victory, particularly given the appalling losses the Red Army had suffered in men and equipment. So Zhukov's poorly executed attacks, coupled with Stalin's willingness to sacrifice every last Russian soldier, was a rude shock to the senior German commanders. To their men, it was a devastating psychological blow. It was one thing to be told to stop and regroup, settle in for the winter: by mid-October that would have been a welcome development, given that the Wehrmacht had been in intensive combat for four months (even longer for the units that had been in action in the Balkans in spring 1941).

It was quite another to be on the verge of victory and then, faced with what seemed to be an inexhaustible horde of enemy soldiers willing to sacrifice themselves in droves for a few meters of frozen ground, be subjected to a series of contradictory orders as the traditional German reflex of tactical disengagement came into conflict with Hitler's determination not to cede ground.

Given the terrain, the lack of any sort of supporting infrastructure of towns and roads, the weather, and the amateurishness of the Red Army, Hitler's decision was correct. European Russia was not like France or Italy, where the defenders could fall back a few kilometers to the next village or ridge. He was correct in another way as well. His combat experiences in the First World War, when British soldiers had been massacred over and over again as they tried to penetrate the German lines, convinced him that the attacking Russians would suffer the same fate. Meanwhile, his forces would be replenished and regroup: when the spring came, they would end the war.

There is no doubt that Hitler's analysis was correct. He had been right from the start, and his senior commanders were wrong. However, the command conflicts of the campaign of compromises that developed in fall 1941, and led to the impasse before the gates of Moscow, wreaked psychological havoc with the rank and file of the Wehrmacht. Deprived of victory, facing an enemy whose savagery contravened all the traditional rules of warfare, and above all confronted with an endless and featureless terrain that seemingly alternated between mud and ice, the soldiers oscillated between panic and depression.

From that point on, sometime in December 1941 or early January 1942, a great gulf developed between the subjective impressions of the course of the war as seen by the men in the German military who were fighting it and the somewhat abstract and distant perspective revealed by the body count. Subjectively, those accounts, taken in conjunction with Stalin's boasting of great victories and advances of hundreds of miles, suggest a situation that the losses do not support. Casualties in the first reporting period for January 1942 definitely rose: 7,070 German soldiers were killed, as opposed to the totals of 6,545, 4,358, and 4,026 for the three reporting periods of December 1941. However, although the total was higher, and certainly reflective of the increased fighting in midwinter, the casualties were significantly lower than in any of the periods prior to December: losses in the first three months of the war had been significantly higher.[3] Far from suggesting either intensified Soviet resistance or tactical proficiency, the figures suggest the opposite.

The German successes of spring and summer 1942 would to a great extent restore the Wehrmacht's confidence in its military abilities. As we shall see, right up until the final days of the war, the Germans were inflicting massive blows on the Red Army, so the confidence was justified. But their confident outlook, their belief in an ultimate victory, disappeared in the snow and ice of European Russia, and never returned. It was replaced by a grim realization that all they could do was fight to stay alive, and, failing that, inflict as much damage on the enemy as possible. The deathride was underway.

But the Germans, even in the panic and confusion of midwinter, were too nimble, or their opponents too slow, for Soviet forces to exploit the tactical advantage that Stalin and Zhukov had seen. The Red Army in the twentieth century resembled nothing so much as the behemoth that had lumbered into Moravia to fight Napoleon, the bravery of its officers and men exceeded only by the excruciating slowness with which they performed the most elementary maneuvers.

In that bygone era, when generals felt they were defeated, they quit the battle, one way or another, and there was, as Tolstoy's character remarks in *War and Peace*, a simple way of determining victory. But as the wars that followed made sadly clear, the standards had changed. The results of battles became increasingly ambiguous: armies, their generals, the states they represented tended to fight on regardless.

So although Zhukov may very well have thought that he had won, his opponents hardly thought they had lost. Or, more correctly, in both cases (von Leeb and von Bock) they felt they had suffered a kind of abstract defeat of the sort that led Erich von Manstein to entitle his memoirs *Lost Victories*, a title that itself recalled the account penned by his predecessor on the Eastern Front in the First World War, Max Hoffmann, when he wrote *The War of Lost Opportunities*.

This was a mind-set that automatically led to the search for excuses, and in the Second World War, one was conveniently at hand. As we have seen, all three of the German army group commanders were constantly involved with Hitler, wrangling with him, lobbying him, and complaining bitterly about what they perceived as his amateurish meddling. Although in retrospect their decisions hardly seem to represent better alternatives, Hitler was definitely meddling in what German commanders had traditionally felt was their exclusive preserve.

So was Stalin, the difference being that the price of disagreeing with him, or in some cases even agreeing with him, was hardly trivial. No Russian officer at any level was going to do anything that would result in his being arrested, tortured, and then probably executed, with the knowledge that his family would perish as well. Not surprisingly, then, as the Russians broke through the gaps in von Bock's position, they simply came to a halt, waiting for orders as to what they should do next, and thus lost the brief window of opportunity that existed for them to make even deeper penetrations, to seal off the Germans as their comrades had been sealed off in the preceding months.

Leaving aside for the moment the territory regained in this offensive, it is worth remarking that the pattern of Soviet offensive efforts was firmly set. There would be the inevitable breakthrough, but then everything would grind to a halt while the field commanders waited for instructions. How long would it take to get to Berlin? In this war the answer would be forty months and 25 to thirty million dead Russians.

Stalin announced a great victory, and the Battle of Moscow was enshrined as one of the turning points of the war: Hitler had failed to take Moscow. As we have seen, whatever Hitler's original and somewhat changeable interests in the two cities had been, the main impetus to take both, once the fighting started, always came from his senior generals. Hitler's inclination to shut down offensive operations until spring, whether correct or not, was certainly indicative of his priorities, which were revealed soon enough, once his armies had survived Stalin's midwinter offensives.

But the general position of von Bock's troops was bad, particularly for the two armies that now inadvertently found themselves strung out in a salient sticking out of the new German lines and running about 200 kilometers up past the obscure and insignificant town of Rzhev (whose only claim to fame is that its inhabitants believed that theirs was the northernmost town on the Volga River).

Such salients, or bulges, were by now a typical feature of the Eastern Front, given that neither side had the manpower to maintain a continuous defensive line. Von Bock's troops had advanced as far as they could, and then, meeting Soviet resistance, had halted, without much regard for the precariousness of the bulge. Although the Soviet high command was unable to execute the sort of double envelopment that would have sealed off the salient and created a pocket, its existence could hardly be missed, and so they hurled masses of men and armor against the beleaguered Germans there.

Von Bock understandably wanted to pull back still more, and certainly to get his troops out of the salient. Hitler saw matters differently. He argued, with some justification, that the Red Army's losses in trying to fight the Germans head-on would vastly exceed any gains that might be made. At this point in the war, he had considerably more confidence in his soldiers than he did in their generals.

In the event, he was more or less correct, a fact often obscured by the combination of anger, panic, and bitter recrimination that characterizes all German accounts of the midwinter fighting.

By January, Stalin still had enough troops left to mount offensives against the other two army groups, so it was the turn of von Leeb and Army Group North. The offensive began on January 7, and Soviet forces drove through the separated German units holding positions stretching out to the southeast of Leningrad. North of Novgorod there was a substantial gap, and the Russians crossed the Volkhov River. Further south, on the eastern side of Lake Ilmen, German units suddenly found themselves surrounded. The only thing von Leeb could think of was to have the units to the southeast of the lake withdraw to the river chain that flowed into the southern part of the lake, and on the 12th, he asked for permission to pull back from what he correctly regarded as his overextended and in some cases surrounded positions. Hitler refused, and von Leeb resigned (on the 16th). He was replaced by Georg von Küchler, who had previously been von Leeb's 18th Army commander.

Von Küchler was an experienced infantry commander, aggressive and highly respected. The command he inherited was in desperate straits: the German forces at Kholm and Demyansk, insignificant villages south of Lake Ilmen, were surrounded by early February. There were nearly 100,000 German troops in the pocket, so the Soviet armies of the Northwestern Front seemed poised for the same sort of victory that had characterized the German advances of 1941.

Instead, the Luftwaffe supplied the surrounded troops from the air, and von Küchler cobbled together more fighters, creating combat units out of service and supply troops, as well as air force ground personnel and Baltic volunteers. For about sixty days, the hastily improvised defenses of Army Group North fought the Soviets to a standstill. And then, somewhat astoundingly, given the desperate situation the Germans had found themselves in at the end of January, went over to the offensive.

By the middle of March, nearly twenty Soviet divisions had been wiped out, and the German positions stabilized. The January breakthrough south of Leningrad could have been a real Soviet triumph, one that would have dwarfed Stalingrad, given both the symbolic importance of Leningrad and the number of German troops involved. Instead, it was Tikhvin in reverse: the hapless Soviet soldiers who survived found themselves pretty much back where they had started in January, with only the false consolation that they had achieved a great victory. In reality, the commanders of the two Soviet fronts had had enough: the positions of Army Group North stayed where they were for the next two years.

Army Group North in the first quarter of 1942 thus sets yet another pattern: the battered Germans, desperate to survive, were not only able to absorb the Soviet battering, but, surprisingly, were able to go over to the offensive. The tactical advantage gained ended up being the status quo ante. Since the obvious Soviet objective was to lift the siege of Leningrad (at the very least), the offensive was a failure, its only real achievement to run up the body count. That was considerable: buried beneath the labyrinth of official Soviet accounting, the various operations against Army Group North during this period come to almost 400,000 dead, a total that is roughly equal to the number of Russian soldiers Stalin had brought in from the Far East.

The dimensions of the Soviet failure were either hidden or lost in overall conflagration, as well as by Stalin's determination to make the course of the war hinge on the battle for Moscow, and in the confusion of battle, the Rzhev salient became a kind of code name for fighting to the southeast of Leningrad that continued all the way through the year.

But the battles between the Red Army and Army Group North in the first months of 1942 were an ominous portent for the future. Although Stalin may very well have believed what he said in public, that the Germans were getting weaker and he was getting stronger, January 1942 was his best shot at victory. In reality his armies neither regained enough ground nor killed enough Germans to make an impact on Hitler. On the contrary, von Küchler's success emboldened him considerably. Clearly, the problem was at the top, with his senior generals: find the right man, and the situation would be corrected. Tactically, the success of the Luftwaffe in supplying the Germans inside the pocket centered on Kholm and Demyansk suggested that such encirclements were only temporary reverses. His troops could fight their way out of any predicament, turn the tables on the enemy, and slaughter him in large numbers regardless of how bleak the situation appeared.

It would be a mistake to say that the fighting stopped in March 1942. What happened was that the Germans stabilized their positions and the Red Army, exhausted, was forced to wait until its stocks of men and equipment were replenished. Both sides were planning for major offensive operations once the ground dried out.

Stalin claimed, and possibly may have believed, that his armies had won great victories. The reality on the ground was different. On the map, the territory seized back was impressive, provided one overlooked the fact that with the exception of Tula to the southeast of Moscow, and Rostov at the mouth of the Don, the Germans still held every major city they had captured in the fall. In a war in which armored columns could achieve penetrations of well over 100 kilometers in a day, as the Germans had repeatedly done, the loss or gain of distances that by the standards of earlier wars were staggering was of little significance.

Although Stalin had concentrated on Moscow, the most serious breakthrough in the Soviet midwinter offensives was actually in the south. As we saw earlier, after von Rundstedt had been dismissed at the end of November 1941, he had been replaced with Walter von Reichenau, who evacuated Rostov and organized a successful defense along the Mius River.

On January 12, 1942, von Reichenau, who was something of a fitness fanatic, went out for a run. He returned to his headquarters at Poltava and collapsed. On the 17th, von Reichenau, still unconscious, was flown to Leipzig. The plane carrying him either crashed or made an extremely rough landing; in any event, von Reichenau was dead, and von Bock was hauled out of retirement to replace him.

The replacement came just in the nick of time. Red Army units had found gaps in the German front between Kharkov and Izyum, a city on the Donetz River a little over 100 kilometers to the southeast of Kharkov. The advance penetrated deep into Ukraine, turning the small town into a salient. But the same situation prevailed in the south as in the north, only more so: although the Germans were sorely pressed and ceded ground, they were neither cut off nor beaten. The Soviet offensive essentially ran out of steam, leaving the Germans to patch together a defensive line of sorts, and creating a potentially dangerous bulge to the northwest of Izyum. Neither von Bock nor Timoshenko, commander of the Soviet front, was insensible to the dangers posed by this substantial bulge. On the Soviet side, the salient represented an opportunity to cut right through Ukraine and seal off the bulk of

Army Group South and its Romanian allies. Von Bock saw that the massing of forces inside the salient for a breakthrough gave him a similar opportunity. Both men began gathering resources to exploit it.

At this point, as the ground began to thaw, the two dictators intervened, each making plans that would determine the future course of the war. Before we consider those plans, and their results, we should consider the balance of power between the two sides. Given the intensity and scale of the fighting, not to mention the horrible conditions that prevailed, one is entitled to wonder just what resources were left for both sides to assemble.

Stalin was certainly entitled to put the best possible face on the situation, and as his February 1942 public speech makes clear, he did: he had saved Moscow and Leningrad, thrown the Germans back, regained hundreds of square kilometers of sacred Russian land, the hated Hitlerites had suffered their first real defeats. The tide had turned, and from now on, the Germans would be on the defensive, driven out of the country in short order.

As Stalin saw the situation, perhaps this was true, but the cost was high. Of course there is no evidence that he was concerned about how many dead Russians his insistence on endless and usually futile offensives cost. He either genuinely believed that his manpower was sufficient to withstand his losses, or the nature and extent of his losses were concealed from him. He was however certainly aware that his forces were running out of equipment, but again, it is far from clear to what extent his appreciation of Hitler's situation diverged from the reality, only that it did. Every scrap of information that suggested the Germans were getting weaker was clutched at.

In the Soviet Union there was an additional fillip to this understandable tendency of straw clutching: because Stalin said the Germans were getting weaker, they had to get weaker. Because Stalin said that they had lost over four million men, Soviet reporting had to reflect that. Because Stalin said the Germans were getting weaker and the Red Army was getting stronger, the data had to agree.

Although from then on Soviet estimates duly confirmed that in 1942 the Red Army was twice the size of the Wehrmacht (5.3 million Russian soldiers to 2.7 million Germans), Hitler and his generals knew very well that they had over eight million men in the German military machine, and nearly a million more in the armies of their allies. They were hardly running short of manpower.[4]

So although the Soviet side makes a surprisingly seamless argument; with the data offered (and accepted) supportive of the general idea that the Germans were getting weaker and the Red Army was getting stronger, it suffers from the unfortunate flaw of being absolutely backward. Not only were the Germans not getting weaker, but in terms of firepower, the only measurement that really counts, they were getting stronger in new and potentially disastrous ways.

For example, the German tank situation was improving dramatically. Given the continuous fighting and the distances covered, one would assume that the Wehrmacht was in nearly as bad shape as the Red Army by March 1942. Worse, because Soviet factories would turn out tanks in enormous quantities that Germany could hardly match.

A beguiling notion, but rather far from the truth. There were definitely fewer German tanks on hand. At the end of June 1941 the Germans had 4,824 vehicles, and at the end of January 1942, they were down to 4,254, a loss of nearly 12 percent, although given the prevailing accounts of the situation, even that figure comes as a bit of a surprise.[5]

But during those opening months, the composition of those numbers had changed substantially. The modified Mark 3 tank with a reasonably potent 5 centimeter gun now formed nearly 40 percent of the tank force, and the number of poorly and inadequately armed Mark 2 and Mark 3 tanks had decreased accordingly, while the number of Mark 4 tanks remained almost exactly the same. In other words, the slight decrease in the raw numbers was more than compensated for by the change in the composition of the tank force, in which larger and more powerful vehicles replaced inferior ones.

But even there the numbers are misleading. Although the number of Mark 4 tanks was stable, the new ones coming off the assembly line as replacements were equipped with a much more potent version of the 7.5 centimeter gun, and very much the match in hitting power for the standard Soviet tank. For the first time since the fighting had begun, German tankers would be able to take on the T-34/76 Soviet tank.

Moreover, despite the vehement objections of leading tankers like Guderian, the Germans had begun manufacturing much cheaper and surprisingly effective armored tracked vehicles. A great part both of the weight and complexity of German tanks lay in the revolving turret, whose specifications also limited the size of the main tank gun. As a result of an internal dispute long before the start of the war, the Mark 3 tank turret had been designed to take a much more powerful gun than the puny 3.7 centimeter weapon that equipped all the initial Mark 3 tanks, so upgunning the Mark 3 was a relatively simple task.

The appearance on the battlefield of the Soviet KV and T-34/76 series tanks had been a considerable shock; once again German ground commanders were forced to fall back on the 8.8 centimeter antiaircraft guns that were an integral part of all combat units, despite being crewed by air force personnel. But the famous flak 88 was a wheeled vehicle with a very high profile, so its mobility and vulnerability made it problematic; nor were its Luftwaffe crews enthusiastic about becoming antitank gunners.

The Germans had been experimenting with mounting heavier guns on surplus tank chassis even before the start of the war, and their experiences against the Red Army had accelerated that development. There were three distinct different vehicle types, none of which had any Soviet counterpart until well into the war. To counter the more heavily armed and armored Soviet tanks, the Germans began to produce tank destroyers. Initially based on the chassis of the obsolete Mark 1 and Mark 2 tanks, at first they were little more than gun platforms, their armor useless against larger than small arms fire. But this was only a stopgap measure; subsequent models, although still based on the tank chassis, were well-armored, low-profile vehicles mounting extremely powerful high-velocity guns (mounting the gun in the hull as opposed to the turret meant that a much more powerful weapon could be deployed).

At the same time, seeing the great difficulty with which towed artillery kept up with the armored columns, the Germans began to put more energy into the development of what is nowadays called the self-propelled gun: a medium howitzer mounted on a tank chassis. This category of weapon was supplemented in the direct ground support role by another tracked gun carrier, which really had no exact equivalent in anyone else's army, the assault gun. The Germans mounted the low-velocity 7.5 centimeter gun designed for an infantry support role on a Mark 3 tank chassis.

The aim, as with the design of a whole family of partially tracked personnel and transport vehicles (the equivalent to the American half-track) was the replacement of wheeled and towed field and antitank guns as well as the elimination of truck-borne infantry. Essentially, the only guns that would be towed would be the heavy guns that were never intended to be in the immediate vicinity of the battle.

It would be incorrect to infer that these decisions happened quickly, and that suddenly the Wehrmacht's combat divisions were transformed into masses of assault guns, half-tracks, and the like. German industry, even after the ascent of the highly organized Albert Speer in spring 1942, never managed to produce the new weapons in the vast quantities the military needed. However, the number of tracked gun carriers that had been produced even by January 1942 was significant: 6,370 assault guns, 760 self-propelled guns, and 2,042 tank destroyers.[6] By contrast, even according to its own highly questionable production statistics, the Soviet Union had produced 117 vehicles in all three categories.[7]

So in the Russian campaign, to their already high level of development in the coordination of armor, infantry, and airpower, the Germans brought into the field another element: highly mobile artillery and antitank weaponry that could keep pace with the infantry over rough ground, and offer direct support of their assaults. The assault gun was in fact revolutionizing small unit tactics: for the first time infantry could rely on direct artillery fire delivered against a strongpoint that would otherwise have required either a costly assault or time-consuming and sometimes unavailable artillery or air strikes.

The German forces in Russia were now not only more experienced, but they were better armed than a year earlier. And as had always been the case, regardless of the war or the theater, as the ground dried out, they were first off the mark.

Hitler, who had never been enthusiastic about his generals' fixation with Leningrad and Moscow, had emerged from the wrangling compromises of the fall with the determination to seize control of the war. This time the offensive efforts would be entirely on the southeast. The plan, code-named Blau, envisioned a drive deep into Russia, seizing control of the rest of its agricultural heartland, Black Earth Russia, centered around Voronezh and stretching east to the major cities on the Don (and even the Volga), all the way to the oilfields in and around the Caspian Sea.

To that end, the two northern army groups were stripped of men and the all-important armor, one estimate being that they were almost cut in half. Everything went to Army Group South, and once again the Germans aimed at a vast pincer movement, with the right wing striking out from Rostov into the Caucasus and thence to the Caspian, while the left wing advanced to the Don and then to the Volga, striking deep into the Russian heartland.

The German commanders were familiar with this tactical maneuver, although the scale of it was unlike anything they had ever attempted. The problem was the objective: instead of sealing off armies (or in this case, groups of armies), Hitler aimed to seal off Stalin's economic resources, from the oilfields of the Caspian and the Caucasus to the remaining heartland of Soviet agriculture. As a bonus prize, the movement, if successful, would also deprive the Bolsheviks of their last remaining warm water ports.

These objectives were consistent with Hitler's intentions, but it seems fair to say that his generals never completely grasped their importance, thinking still in terms of the annihilation of armies and the conquest of capital cities. Consequently, the point of the summer offensives of Blau, the great sweep whose left wing finally came to a halt on the banks of the Volga River, at Stalingrad, is misunderstood.

The importance of the objectives merits a brief explanation. But then so does the sequence of events in this enormous theater of operations: before what Hitler intended as the death blow to the Bolsheviks could begin, he acceded to the requests of his local commanders who wanted to deal with the bulges that had resulted from Stalin's midwinter offensives.

There were two of these in particular. The bridgehead the Soviets had established on the western side of the Kerch Strait gave them a foothold on the Crimean Peninsula, where the talented Erich von Manstein, together with a large Romanian force, was laying siege to Sevastopol. In February, Stalin had listed Kerch (the town at the eastern end of the peninsula) as yet another Soviet victory. It now became the site of a massive Soviet defeat. In early May, von Manstein launched a surprise attack on the Soviet bridgehead and wiped it out, destroying the bulk of the two Soviet armies there, and taking over 160,000 prisoners.[8]

To the north, von Bock aimed to take care of the Izyum salient before proceeding to Blau. His attack was set for May 18, but for once the Red Army was first into action, and began its own offensive on the 12th. Initially the Russian penetration boded for success: as had been the case in January around Moscow and Leningrad, the German troop concentrations left all sorts of gaps, and the Soviet columns piled into the Izyum salient, began to break out of it, and penetrate still deeper into Ukraine.

The result, like von Manstein at Kerch, was a sort of Smolensk in reverse, with the Soviet troops advancing recklessly forward, not realizing that they were vulnerable to the same pincer movement on offense as had been the case when their units had been bypassed by the advancing Germans. Von Bock wanted to seal off the developing bulge right away, but Hitler overrode him, and waited. Essentially, the Russians trapped themselves. The German 6th Army attacked their right flank and von Kleist attacked up from the south with the 17th Army and the 1st Armored Group.

As had been the case with Kiev that fall, Stalin hesitated, ignoring the pleas from his staff to call a halt. At midnight on May 18, a nervous Khrushchev called Stalin personally to beg him to call off the offensive. Stalin refused to talk to him, shouting out that "Military orders must be obeyed.... Khrushchev's poking his nose into other people's business.... My military advisers know better."[9]

By May 24, the Germans had once again executed a vast pincer movement, and cut off the advancing Russians. Five days later the entire offensive spearhead had been destroyed. Army Group South counted 240,000 prisoners and over 1,200 tanks destroyed or left on the battlefield.[10] It regrouped, and on June 28 began to execute Blau.

Stalin, far away in Moscow, had miscalculated on two levels. Convinced that the main effort would be directed toward Moscow, he had shifted his resources north.[11] At the same time, he apparently was so convinced of the successes of his midwinter offensives that he believed he could ignore the dangers of having his troops in highly vulnerable salients such as Kerch and Izyum. But as a result, with the loss of 400,000 men as prisoners alone, and nearly 2,000 of his precious tanks, his forces in the south were in no position to stop the onslaught of Blau.[12]

Even after he saw the developing threat, shifting whole armies from Moscow to the southeast was no easy task. It would take time, and that was precisely what the Germans were not giving him.

In his subsequent speeches, he blamed the failure on the Allies; if only they had opened a second front, Blau would either have never gotten off the ground or would have been a colossal failure. The one Soviet accomplishment was that, for the first time in the war, their units retreated instead of destroying themselves in futile counterattacks (or holding in place and being taken prisoner as the Germans swept around them).

But in the meantime, the Germans were moving quickly enough. By July 7, they had reached the Don along most of its length, were at Voronezh, the key city of the Russian (as opposed to Ukrainian) agricultural heartland, and had occupied Rostov once again.

Von Bock, based on his experience with Army Group Center in November, was cautious. He was, like most senior German officers, with the exception of von Manstein, dubious as to the quality of the Romanian, Italian, and Hungarian forces tasked with safeguarding the flanks of the offensive, and although Hitler had told him to bypass Voronezh and keep heading east, he instead decided to take the city.

Unlike von Reichenau, who had finessed Hitler's refusal to let von Rundstedt retreat after Rostov, or von Leeb, who had gritted his teeth and obeyed, von Bock simply ignored Hitler's directive. He was determined to proceed at his own pace.

Hitler had already decided to change the command structure in the south, to break up Army Group South into two groups, both of them in theory operating in parallel with North and Center. Army Group A, under the command of Sigmund Wilhelm List, would execute the southern side of the pincers, and B, under the command of Maximilian Maria Joseph Karl Gabriel Lamoral Reichsfreiherr von Weichs zu Glon, the northern. Given the size of the forces committed, and their radically different objectives, the decision made sense. But Hitler took advantage of the reorganization to eliminate von Bock, who was eased out of command on July 13.

List, a cautious and methodical commander with extensive experience in Asia Minor, had a laundry list of objectives: to secure Rostov and the entire eastern coast of the Black Sea, then the oilfields that stretched from the Caucasus over to the Caspian Sea. All in all, an advance of nearly 1,100 kilometers on a broad front, with Soviet forces on three sides. Moreover, given the transparency of his objectives, List's armored columns would largely be denied the opportunity to bypass Russian units and cut them off, as they were driving straight into a funnel, with the narrowest tip being Baku, the center of the Soviet oil industry.

In partial compensation, List had three outstanding commanders, each of them a master of mobile warfare as well as traditional tactics: von Manstein, commanding the 11th Army; Hermann Hoth, of the 4th Armored Army; and von Kleist, of the 1st Armored Army. List not only knew Asia Minor well, but he was the most experienced and capable of all the senior generals when it came to dealing with Germany's Romanian and Hungarian allies, whose mountain troops, together with their Italian counterparts, would be crucial in the advance. On the other hand, he was new to the Eastern Front (his last command had been in the Balkans), detested Hitler, and was unenthusiastic about his mission, the point of which he failed to grasp.

Nevertheless, his armies set out, with the by now usual success. Von Manstein took the fortress city of Sevastopol on July 2.[13] Three weeks later List broke through the defenses around Rostov, and captured the city, together with 240,000 prisoners. But it was still a long way to Baku, and after the fall of Sevastopol, Hitler pulled the 11th Army out of Group A and sent it north, while Hoth's armor was transferred to Group B. So List was down to two armies, von Kleist's armored force and Richard Ruoff's 17th Army.

By August 10, List's troops were in Krasnodar and Maykop, the center of the oilfields of the western Caucasus, and on August 22, in a moment subsequently made famous (or notorious), German mountain troops raised the swastika flag on the crest of Mount Elbrus, the highest peak in the mountain chain. Heady stuff, and List's troops continued to accumulate real estate: the Taman Peninsula fell into their hands by September 6, along with the Soviet naval base at Novorrossiysk, the only major Black Sea port still in Soviet hands.[14]

Although the Red Army was doing its best to stop them, the real problem for the Germans and their allies was space, not resistance. The distances in the Caucasus were staggering, even measured by the scale of northern Russia. From Rostov at the mouth of the Don to Baku on the Caspian was over 1,100 kilometers, through terrain that made the steppes of Ukraine and the forests of the Baltic look like a city park in Vienna or Munich. Rostov itself was at the end of a very long supply line, almost 2,000 kilometers from Berlin. There was only one main rail line from Rostov south toward Baku. The mountain chain that gave the region its name bisected the region, running all the way from the Black Sea to the Caspian. The mountains were a formidable obstacle, one that had deterred even the energetic railroad engineers of pre-revolutionary times.

Historically the Russians had settled the region the same way that South America had been colonized. They had located along the water and largely ignored the interior, whose inhabitants had fought the invaders for centuries, as indeed they do to this very day. So the czars had little incentive to develop the region. As we have seen, the infrastructure of European Russia, by contrast with western Europe, was woefully underdeveloped. But when the advancing Germans fanned out from Rostov, they found themselves on what was more of a trek, a safari, than an invasion, traversing a formidable countryside. Like the bewildered Macedonians who had followed Alexander the Great in ancient times, well might they have asked what they were doing here at the ends of the earth.

Alexander could provide no easy answer, and Hitler's was both complex and abstract. It was no wonder that his increasingly exasperated generals saw the foray as a wild-goose chase with no concrete goal they could use to mark their success.

But they were wrong. Both the southern and northern extremities of the pincer movement were of vital importance to Stalin. If he lost them, he lost the war. Stalin understood that, although characteristically, he phrased it differently. When Stalin sent Nikolai Baibakov, deputy commissar for oil production, to the Caucasus to supervise the destruction of the oil wells should it be necessary, he told him that Hitler "has declared that without oil, he'll lose the war."[15] But that statement cut both ways: Stalin's tanks needed fuel just as the German ones did.

With the advent of the internal combustion engine, the Caucasus and the Caspian suddenly became important. Petroleum, hitherto a minor natural resource, suddenly became as important to the modern industrial state as coal had been.

Russia on the eve of the Great War and the October Revolution, sustained by a dramatic surge in agricultural development of the same sort that had been the prelude to the Industrial Revolution in Great Britain, was now poised for modernization and industrialization. The abundance of iron ore, petroleum, and precious metals, all of which Stalin had traded off to Hitler in enormous quantities, could provide the Soviet state with the basis for transforming itself into a modern state.

Conversely, whoever had possession of those as yet still poorly exploited natural resources would dominate Europe in a way not seen since the coming of the Roman legions. In the short term, without that precious oil, the lavish bounty of tanks, locomotives, and motor vehicles that Churchill and Roosevelt were bestowing on an ungracious and rapacious Soviet state (over a million tons by May 1942) would be worthless: the Red Army would lack the means to continue the war.[16]

Southeastern Russia had an importance that had been recognized long before the automobile. The country's two mighty rivers, the Don and the Volga, flowed diagonally across the interior, providing a a vital transportation route linking otherwise inaccessible parts of the vast countryside not only with each other, but also with the outside world. The mouth of the Don opened onto the Sea of Azov and thence to the Mediterranean, via the Strait of Kerch and the Black Sea. The mouth of the Volga opened directly onto the Caspian.

Peter the Great had attempted to remedy Russia's lack of free access to the oceans by building Petrograd, a port city that connected to the Baltic via the Gulf of Finland. He had succeeded in building a great city, but there was nothing he could do about the Gulf of Finland: an estuary of the Baltic that was so shallow it mostly froze over during the winter and whose shipping channels had to be constantly maintained.

By contrast, Sevastopol and Rostov were not only deep water ports that were accessible year-round, but both were connected to the interior by the Russian riverine network. The railroad lines built by the czars that connected both cities to the rest of Russia had furthered that connection.

Unfortunately for the Bolsheviks, both cities, together with the entire Black Sea, were now dominated by German and Romanian armies: the landlocked body of water was now in danger of becoming a German lake, and with the fall of Sevastopol in July, indeed was one to all practical intents.

So the Volga connection into the Caspian became even more

significant for the beleaguered Bolsheviks. Once again, geography dictated strategy. Technically, the city of Astrakhan was the dominant center of the Volga as it entered the Caspian. But the czars had developed a town some 380 kilometers upstream to guard their far southeastern border, since Astrakhan was isolated from the rest of Russia, dependent on the river for communications with the interior. Given the landscape on either side of the river as it flowed toward the sea, building the northern town was a wise decision.

The town, Tsaritsyn, offered all sorts of advantages. The area was more heavily settled, the climate more salubrious, and the city only about seventy kilometers from Salatch, on the Don River. A spur from the main rail line connected the two, which facilitated commerce greatly. Consequently, in the Civil War, both the Reds and the Whites had fought for possession of Tsaritsyn. It was the key not only to the region, but given the importance of the two rivers as the only links to year-round warm water ports, key to the security of the Bolshevik state as well.

Stalin had been instrumental in directing the fighting there, and as his grip on Soviet power increased, he had the city renamed after himself. Stalingrad (Khrushchev would rename it Volgograd), thus became even more important. Its location made it a prime spot for industrial development, and Stalin's desire to make it the showcase for the successes of his regime, however it fed his vanity, was quite rational. After the German invasion, the city became even more important. The sprawling tractor factory on the west bank, like the locomotive works and diesel plant at Kharkov, was one of the chief sources of T-34 tanks.

List was doing his best to break through to the Caspian, but as the summer days began to shorten, it became clear that Grozny was still a long way off, much less Baku. At the end of August, Hitler, extremely dissatisfied with the progress of Army Group A, summoned List to his advanced headquarters at Vinnitsia in Ukraine. Alfred Jodl, technically chief of the army staff, but now simply a figurehead, was sent to List's headquarters (in early September).[17] The net result of this back-and-forth: Jodl and Hitler got into a serious altercation, List was sacked on September 9, along with the chief of the general staff, Franz Halder, and Hitler himself assumed command of Army Group A. This curious state of affairs lasted until November 21, when he handed command over to von Kleist.

But for all that, Grozny and Baku remained tantalizingly out of reach. Nor was the failure surprising. The advance of Army Group A was more on the order of a safari than an invasion, defeated not so much by resistance as by logistics.

The most efficient means of conquest would have been to land a force on the southern side of the mountains, where a rail line ran from the coast of the Black Sea directly east toward Baku, and the terrain was less desolate. But there was no German naval presence in the Black Sea, nor, by mid-1942, any way to get one there. Although Hitler had ordered plans drawn up for the invasion of Malta as well as Great Britain, there is apparently no evidence that any similar action was contemplated here, although an amphibious landing would probably have worked: the Red Army south of the mountains was hardly a potent fighting force.

In any event, despite having taken over as commander of the forces of Army Group A, Hitler essentially ignored the army and switched his attentions to Group B, the northern side of the pincer movement that characterized Blau. To say that the situation was confused is an understatement. The Germans now had four separate army groups (called North, Center, A, and B), but von Weichs, in charge of Army Group B, was told to divide his forces so as to execute another envelopment move. In the north, the left wing would go around the beleaguered Soviets fighting on in the ruins of Voronezh, the key city for Black Earth Russia. Meanwhile, the right wing would envelop Stalingrad and thus control the Volga, cutting Stalin off from his last remaining year-round access to the ocean.

Although Stalin had hardly abandoned his obsession with re-lentless suicide offenses, the losses of the summer and early fall had temporarily forced him to pause, as the surviving armies of the southern fronts were hardly in any position to stand and fight. But the lull, if indeed there was one, was caused simply by the slowness of Red Army deployments to meet the new threat posed by von Weichs, whose objectives were apparent to anyone looking at a map.

As Army Group B closed in on the two cities, a new danger arose. Although the concentration of Soviet industry around Sverdlovsk and Chelybansk would still be far outside of the range of the short-range bombers the Luftwaffe possessed, operating from airfields to the west of the Volga, they would rapidly destroy the fragile Soviet transportation infrastructure the country desperately needed. Soviet forces operating to the south of Stalingrad would find themselves cut off from the rest of the country, as the terrain of Astrakhan to the east of the Volga hardly facilitated supplies reaching them via some circuitous Asiatic route.

To make matters worse, Stalingrad was 600 kilometers due north of Grozny, so the advance there would shield the progress of Army Group A. They could advance to the east and southeast without worrying about a vulnerable left flank.

Stalin's own plan remained in place, despite his losses in the south. He planned a major offensive in the same general area to the southeast of Leningrad that had seen so much fighting in the midwinter operations. Presumably a successful thrust would cut off Army Group North entirely and force a further withdrawal of Army Group Center, force Hitler to draw off armor from von Weichs and List, and give the Red Army time to build up its forces on the eastern bank of the Volga.

Stalin had already launched a major offensive around Rzhev (at the end of July), and when that bogged down, as Soviet offenses habitually did, he launched a second and much larger one to the north, on August 19.

Unfortunately for the attacking Soviet forces, Stalin neglected to take into consideration the developing plans on the German side. Hitler, after the successes of the summer in the south, having dispatched von Weichs in his drive to the Volga and the Don, had decided to deal with Leningrad as well, as that city remained one of the chief objectives of his senior generals; all the more so now that Moscow was out of reach. So Hitler directed von Manstein, fresh from the conquest of Sevastopol, and clearly one of the Wehrmacht's outstanding generals, to move to the north and finish off the city.

As a result, while the Red Army troops were engaged with the German 18th Army around Leningrad, they became vulnerable to von Manstein, whose units were moving into position for an attack on that city scheduled for September 14. Offering an exposed flank to any of the senior German armored commanders was to afford them a fatal blow, and von Manstein promptly delivered one. Most of the Soviet 2nd Shock Army (the impressive name given to its newly formed assault units) was destroyed: seven of the sixteen infantry divisions, six of the nine independent infantry brigades, and four out of the five armored brigades.[18]

Blau was definitely over, its main achievement being to run up an enormous number of Soviet casualties. Even by the highly suspect scheme of Soviet accounting, admitted losses in dead and missing came to over 1.2 million men, as opposed to German losses of well under 200,000. The Wehrmacht was by no means running out of steam. On the contrary, the casualties during this period were in most instances lower than they had been in the preceding summer and early fall.

Although in his two anniversary speeches that November, Stalin repeated his initial boast that "over eight million enemy soldiers and officers" had been put out of action, and spoke of the "heroic defenders of Moscow and Tula, of Odessa and Sevastopol, and of Leningrad and Stalingrad," his main objective was to explain the reason for the German successes: "the absence of

a second front in Europe enabled them to carry out their operations without any risk."[19]

The thread of the second front ran through that November
speech, which as a result contains a surprisingly technical analysis of previous campaigns and wars. This analysis was highly
misleading in three senses. As Stalin very well knew, in the First
World War the Germans had beaten the Russians so badly that
Lenin had been forced to agree to a peace under the most humiliating terms, and this despite the fact that imperial Germany and
Austria were fighting in France, Italy, and the Balkans as well as
in Russia. So Stalin's dismissal of that parallel ("the comparison
is inappropriate"), although typical of Marxist-Leninist debate
rhetoric, hardly stands up to any scrutiny.[20]

Nor is there any mention in the speech of the fact that, thanks
to Japan, Stalin was free from worrying about his own second
front in the Far East, and had been able to rely on the Soviet
armies of the Far East to defend Moscow in his midwinter offensives. But the tactic of launching a complaint about a situation that he himself had taken advantage of was by 1942 second
nature to the dictator, who knew the British were every bit as
desperate as he was, and certainly in no position to quibble over
rhetorical fine points.

The only question is the extent to which Stalin knew at this
point that Hitler had drawn down his forces in the east to shore
up the Mediterranean. As early as fall 1941, Hitler had ordered
the transfer of air force units from Army Group North to Sicily. One of von Manstein's numerous complaints about Hitler was
that in early August, prior to sending him to Leningrad with his
11th Army, Hitler had stripped out the 22nd infantry division,
with the aim of converting it back into an airborne unit and sending it to Crete, "where, though one of our best formations, it was
to lie more or less idle for the rest of the war."[21]

By 1942, the Germans had a substantial investment in the
Mediterranean. In his speech, Stalin downplayed that commit-

ment ("four German divisions and eleven Italian"), but this understates the matter to the point of misrepresentation.

On the contrary, by January 1942 the German armored forces in North Africa had been upgraded, now called the 5th Armored Army. Although the quantity of their equipment never matched the massive British force (much less what the Americans deployed that fall), in actual fact there were only six of these powerful units in the Wehrmacht. Keeping one of them in North Africa, along with Erwin Rommel, usually considered one of Hitler's best generals, was definitely a handicap, as was sticking one of von Manstein's best combat divisions in Crete. Moreover, with the exception of the elite mountain troops, Africa also tied up the best of the Italian army as well. Stalin could deny it with impunity, and did, but he was already benefiting from the so-called second fronts.

The speech is thus both an excuse for failure and a plea for help. It was also a tacit admission that the Soviet Union could not win the war against Hitler on its own. At this point, Stalin needed more than hollow victories. For that matter, he needed more than decisive ones.

Unfortunately, the plan that his only remaining senior general of any competence had drawn up, and that the great dictator had himself approved, was hardly going to meet that requirement. In fact, in the final months of 1942, the Red Army was on the verge of experiencing yet another great defeat.

THE PLANETS AND PARADOXES OF 1942–1943

In view of the operational situation at the end of the German
summer offensive [of 1942], the strategic aim of encircling the
German southern wing was so palpably evident that it could not
possibly be overlooked. The idea of breaking through the front of
the allied armies was also a very obvious move. In other words,
not very much genius was required on the Soviet side to draw
an operations plan in the late autumn of 1942.

Erich von Manstein[1]

The point man for the northern side of the great pincer movement directed by von Weichs at Army Group B was Friedrich Paulus, commander of the 6th Army, a force that was
comprised of four allied army groups: two Romanian, one Hungarian, and one Italian. Paulus was charged with driving to the
Volga. Since in order to get to that river he had to cross the Don,
which was to the west of the Volga, in effect his troops would
cut off European Russia from its warm water outlets. With the
war in the Pacific, it would be no exaggeration to say that Stalin would be cut off from the outside world completely. Given its
position as the key city astride the southern leg of the great Russian river, Stalingrad, historic Tsaritsyn, was the key to the operation. If Paulus could reach that city, seize control of it, as well as
the adjacent stretches of the river, and then hold it, Stalin would
slowly strangle to death.

Although von Weichs, as a cavalry officer from the Great War, could justifiably be presumed to be the very man to direct such a bold foray, when one surveys the ranks of the senior German commanders, it would be difficult to find a general less suited to the task of conducting what was basically a cavalry raid on a colossal scale than Paulus.

His military career had been almost entirely as an adjutant or a staff officer, and it was as this last that he had come to the attention of von Reichenau, who, after he had assumed command of the now defunct Army Group South, had persuaded Hitler to let Paulus assume command of the 6th Army.

Career officers like Paulus exist in every army, the key difference here being that by all accounts, within the context of his assigned duties, Paulus was more than competent. Given that he went down in military history as the first and only German general to surrender his forces at the end of a battle, there is no shortage of criticism of the man, and much of it is justified. However, the short of it is that he was, like many staff officers, temperamentally unsuited to be a field commander, and a great deal of the responsibility for the German defeat at Stalingrad is traceable to his waffling.

The problem emerged quickly enough in fall 1942, as Paulus threw away one of the great German advantages in combat, its speed of maneuver. That speed was particularly important on the Eastern Front, given the cumbrous maneuvering of the Red Army, the inexperience of its commanders, and its excessive dependence on orders from Stalin. The trick was to get to the objective before the Russians could organize a defense of it, and that was particularly important when it came to Russian towns and cities. German commanders understandably preferred not to have to fight their way building to building, and Hitler had been incensed at von Bock's surprising decision to do just that at Voronezh.

The problem, both at Voronezh and then at Stalingrad, was that in both cases the cities not only straddled a river, but did so at the most logical crossing point. Bypassing the city and sealing it off was thus not so easy as it might appear at first glance. If the Germans and their allies crossed the river above and below the city, enveloping it from three sides, their bridgeheads across the river would not only be vulnerable to flank attacks, but the city itself would become a staging area for attacks, what a German general in a previous war had called a postern gate, an opening in a fortification that enabled the defenders to sally forth and surprise the besiegers.

There were only two ways to prevent powerful counterattacks from developing. The first was to use your mastery of the air to deliver such crippling blows in your enemy's rear that his attacks either were completely destroyed before they could be launched or broken up so thoroughly that they could easily be beaten off. The other tactic was to move so quickly that by the time the enemy had organized his attack, your bridgeheads had been expanded so dramatically that you had the room to maneuver and parry his blows.

In their earlier campaigns, up to and including summer 1941, the Germans had used both simultaneously. But increasingly, the Luftwaffe was unable to carry out the air-to-ground support that was required. As we have seen, part of this failure was that by summer 1942 its forces were dispersed all over Europe, a tendency that was accelerated by the Allied determination to open a new front, the airspace over Germany. But the main reason, once again, goes back to the failure to get a heavy long-range bomber into service, the Ural bomber project that had languished after Wever's death.

The development of such a plane was now, belatedly, getting attention, as the Germans began to realize its utility. The ability of the heavy bomber to drop enormous amounts of explosives on ground targets, when coupled with its range, meant that it could be used as an extremely effective ground support aircraft, and indeed, in June 1944, the Allies would do precisely that, giving the French rail and road system such a terrific pounding that German units attempting to get to the front were severely hampered and in some cases destroyed.

Although the Germans still had command of the air, and although their tactical ground attack planes strafed the river crossings with impunity, they lacked both the range and the payload to destroy the Red Army's troop concentrations where they were the most vulnerable, at their assembly points far behind the river.

Paulus's troops had reached the outskirts of Stalingrad by September 2. He had moved far too slowly. Not only had he given Stalin and Zhukov time to deploy their armies to face this new threat, but as the hours of daylight began to shorten, as the weather worsened, tactical air support diminished. The air forces of the Second World War were severely hampered by night and fog, and the dependence of the Luftwaffe in Russia on hastily improvised unpaved airstrips with no hangars was hardly helped by the rain and the steadily decreasing temperatures.

Given all these factors, Paulus had lost the battle for the city even before it began. Had any of Tukhachevsky's disciples of deep battle still been around, the Red Army would have been able to snuff out the threat to the key city of the regime in early September: the vast German advances into the interior had created the perfect opportunity for the deep, rapid thrusts that the murdered Soviet marshal had envisioned. By summer 1942, the enormous advances of Army Groups A and B had dramatically increased the dimensions of the front. In May the southern portion of the front had extended down from Belgorod to the German positions on the Mius River, about 600 kilometers.

Since the front extended northwestward some 1,900 kilometers from Belgorod to Leningrad, to say that the armies of the Germans and their three principal allies were overextended is putting it mildly. For that matter, the very use of the word "front" implies a situation that was not the case. The best analogy would be with the American frontier after the Civil War, in which isolated detachments of the American army held forts scattered throughout the vast region, while law and order (such as it was), for the various territories was administered from a handful of towns. Like all analogies, this one breaks down in numerous ways, but it is a useful corrective to the situation implied both by lines drawn on maps and the word itself.

But after the collapse of Timoshenko's thrust in May and the consequent German rush east and south, the situation changed dramatically. As Army Groups A and B surged forward, their advance extended the German penetration of Soviet territory considerably: about 800 kilometers due east of Rostov at the mouth of the Don, and a roughly equal distance to the southeast, into the Caucasus. In fact if a semicircle with a radius of 800 kilometers was drawn, with its center point being the German position at the mouth of the Kalmius River, it would be a surprisingly good approximation of the shape of this portion of the front in late summer 1942.

This enormous new area of conquest was both an opportunity and a liability for each of the two combatants. One more German surge on the scale of its predecessors, and Stalin would no longer be able to feed his armies or supply them with fuel. His only access to his new allies, Britain and the United States, would be through the precarious northern and Far Eastern ports. He was beginning to recognize that while the paired ideas of his unlimited resources and growing strength sounded good in speeches, that was hardly the case on the ground. Already, in June, he was turning savagely on Timoshenko for the losses at Izyum, rather disingenuously forgetting, or ignoring, that he was himself responsible for not pulling the Soviet forces back when he was warned of the impending disaster. Perhaps more ominously, the Red Army was forming its first brigade of female soldiers, a sign that at some level Moscow was beginning to realize it did not in fact have unlimited manpower to waste.[2]

In any event it is difficult to imagine how Stalin could fail to notice the German pattern: regardless of what he was told, or what he had thought, or how he excused it to himself, each of the two successive German summer offensives had chewed off enormous pieces of valuable Soviet territory. Given the extent to which Stalin was familiar with the previous war, it is highly unlikely that he failed to see a rather obvious pattern: your generals kept assuring you that the Germans were on the ropes, running out of resources, only to find themselves trying to explain why the supposedly enfeebled opponent had managed to deliver another crippling blow. But at the same time, if your armies could deliver an equivalent massive blow, you might be able to drive them back, and relieve the growing pressure on the areas you depended on to continue the war.

By September 1942, Hitler's armies were in position to deliver the final blow in the south. But that same position exposed them for the first time to a serious vulnerability. Although the changing nature of the front (to use the least misleading word) in the first year of the war sometimes disguises the fact, the line of demarcation between the two armies can be seen as an irregular line hinged on Leningrad, the far end moving along the Black Sea until it reached the outskirts of Rostov. From time to time there were bulges, or salients, which exposed one side or the other to a situation where its forces were likely to be trapped. But as impressive as those bulges seemed on maps, they were simply too small, in relation to the overall size of the front, for the Red Army thus far to be able to take proper advantage of them.

But now the situation had changed. The German advance had created yet another enormous bulge, a great arc stretching out to the southeast, so as the German advance reached the Volga and Stalingrad, an enormous expanse of flank, almost 500 kilometers, was exposed. By early September, the head of the German thrust was centered on the Volga, all twenty divisions of it, Paulus's 6th Army. Strike behind that armored head and not only would Paulus be cut off, but the entire German bulge would be threatened. The Germans would have only two choices: withdraw or be destroyed. Of course the ensuing battles, assuming they refused to withdraw, would be bloody. But the threat to the oilfields, to the Volga, would be removed.

Stalin could see the opportunities he was being offered, knew timing was critical, and may well have realized the dramatic opening given the Red Army by Paulus's stuttering advance to the Volga. But instead of throwing all his remaining forces into action in the south, Stalin continued on the same course he had employed since June 1941. Instead of concentrating the Red Army's divisions for one great blow, he and his generals replicated the lesson he had absorbed from the Great War: to mount a whole series of coordinated hammer blow offensives all along the front, and thus relieve the pressures on the critical southern sector.

The problem with this strategy was that it would work only if the Germans obliged the Red Army by doing exactly what it wanted them to do: abandon their operations in the south, fail to mount a successful defense, and then fight to the last soldier to defend the threatened areas of the Baltic and Belorussia they had occupied. Thus far the Germans had done nothing to suggest that there was any validity to such assumptions. As we have seen, both of the northern army groups (North and Center) had become the stepchilds of the Eastern Front, forced to cobble together the resources to beat off the Red Army's offensives, and had always managed. The Soviet plan, in other words, was based on wishful thinking, a best-possible-case scenario.

The key assumption was that there was no way the Germans could manage in the north without shifting all their available resources there. Since at this point Army Group Center was as threadbare as North, it would be unable to offer any real help. Moreover, as the Soviet offensive developed, it would be driving through the boundaries between the two German army groups.

Compounding the difficulties of the German commanders was Hitler's determination to respond to perceived threats elsewhere.

In August, the German high command, reacting to the Dieppe raid, went into a panic and shifted Germany's premier super-unit, the Leibstandarte armored SS division, to France. In fact, Berlin intended to ship the army's premier combat force, the Grossdeutschland, there as well, and the overstretched Luftwaffe was diverting valuable resources to the Mediterranean in response to the Allied threats there. Given the German dependence on tactical airpower, the decision was bad news indeed. The omens for Stalin were favorable.

The plan being hatched in Moscow in September 1942 was nothing if not ambitious. It was a grandiose scheme to end the war outright. Stalin approved the idea of two coordinated offensives on September 26, 1942. Zhukov would direct Mars, the northern offensive, and Aleksandr Mikhaylovich Vasilevsky would direct Uranus, an operation designed to cut off the 6th Army at Stalingrad. Once Mars was well underway, there would be a supplementary operation, Jupiter, designed to prevent the forces of Army Group North from coming to aid its beleaguered colleagues in Army Group Center. Assuming all went reasonably well with Vasilevsky and Uranus, there would be a fourth planetary operation, Saturn. Tentatively scheduled for mid-December, this offensive would drive all the way to the Sea of Azov and, it was hoped, complete the destruction of Army Groups A and B.[3]

So the planetary operations, and specifically Uranus, were planned not simply to relieve the pressure on Stalingrad and the Volga. The aim was to begin that operation at the same time as Mars, so that Hitler would be unable to send forces from one part of the front to stave off defeat on the other (the forces in the Caucasus were simply too far away to redeploy to the north). There would be two great hammer blows that would split the front wide open, followed by two more that would complete the annihilation of the German forces in the east and win the war outright.

It was as though the Allies, instead of spreading their successive invasions of Europe over the nineteen-month period from

November 1942 to June 1944, decided to execute them over the space of three months. In this plan, Stalingrad was a small part of a huge offensive albeit a valuable part.

The analogy with an Allied hypothetical is imperfect, but it illuminates the grandiose nature of Stalin's thinking, as well as how far removed from the reality of combat on the Eastern Front he and his generals were. Thus far, the Germans had repeatedly bloodied the Red Army at every turn: each offensive had been successful at wresting key Soviet territory, and the Red Army's own attacks had achieved little more than a mountain of dead Russian soldiers.

Out of denial, because the information that was reaching him was being massaged for positive effect, or simply because the notion conformed to preconceived ideas nurtured in isolation in the decades before the war, Stalin now assumed that these offensives would reverse the fortunes of his dwindling forces. All would happen as foretold: military reality would conform to the plan, just as economic reality had.

If the Soviet official records are to be believed, Zhukov would have an impressive armored force at his disposal, possibly as many as 2,000 tanks, and in fact, the forces earmarked for Mars were somewhat more powerful than the ones given to Vasilevsky for Uranus. The USSR supposedly produced 25,175 tanks in 1942, including 12,553 T-34 and 2,533 KV heavy tanks, but Zhukov and Vasilevsky between them had at the most only 4,000, which illustrates another key weakness in the four planetary operations.[4] The Red Army lacked the material resources to support these ambitious schemes.

Nor did the two Soviet commanders have the experience in directing large battles: Vasilevsky, a senior staff officer whose ascent began after the Terror, was the Soviet counterpart to lackeys like Jodl and Keitel in Berlin. But as Stalin had cut his teeth on the fighting around Tsaritsyn (as Stalingrad was then called) during the Civil War, he presumably did not feel in need of any military expertise. Vasilevsky was precisely what he required: someone to do his bidding.

By contrast, Zhukov had field experience in combat, but whatever talents he possessed, Stalin's micromanagement had precluded him from exercising any independent action. He certainly had the character to try to warn Stalin of the impending disasters of 1941. Given Stalin's tendency to shoot not only the messengers but those who ushered the messenger in, this was character indeed. But it did not necessarily translate into generalship; on the contrary, in the inverted world of the Bolshevik cadres, it suggested obtuseness rather than intelligence.

Uranus was set to begin on November 19–20 as a pincer movement that would surround the 6th Army, together with its Romanian, Hungarian, and Italian allies, cutting all of them off from the German lines. Zhukov was, however, slow off the mark: Mars only began on November 25, 1942.

The resulting battles over the next four months (December 1942–March 1943) were all interrelated, the result of Stalin's four great offensive breakthrough operations, and the desperate German attempts to contain them. As a result, these four months form the most confusing and complicated period of the war on the Eastern Front. So clarity of exposition demands treating the four planetary operations and the German countering moves sequentially, even though almost everything was happening at the same time.

Although Uranus began before Mars, Zhukov's offensive occurred in isolation from events elsewhere and was broken off while the repercussions of Uranus were just being felt. So it makes sense to describe the events there first.

Zhukov's plan was, like Vasilevsky's, to strike on both sides of the salient, as the Germans had been doing to the Red Army since June 1941. The southern edge was the boundary between Army Group Center and Army Group North, so Zhukov aimed initially to drive a wedge between the two German deployments, then pinch them off by envelopment.

As we have seen, von Kluge's forces, designated to receive the heaviest blow, had already been picked clean for Blau. So the fighting was desperate indeed. But Zhukov's plan foundered in the face of the tough German resistance; instead of a grand envelopment, by the first week of December 1942 it had degenerated into two smaller encirclements, one at Velikie Luki and the other at Vyazma, an otherwise strategically insignificant piece of real estate that lay in the Luchassa Valley. The area just to the north and east had been fought over the previous winter in combats for the Rzhev salient. But the names are misleading: in December 1942 the Russians and the Germans were fighting for the same meaningless area as in December 1941. The only rational reason for the combats was that the German troops there, although quickly enveloped, were making the attackers pay a heavy price: instead of withdrawal, a withdrawal that Zhukov obviously hoped would precipitate a collapse of the entire front, the Germans stood and fought, even though they were at first completely cut off, surrounded by the offensive surge.

At one level, Zhukov was correct: a German defeat in the Luchassa Valley would mean that the Red Army would be able to drive a deep wedge into the northern sector, conceivably reverse the course of the war. So Zhukov sent waves of tanks and infantry, often operating in complete isolation from one another, against the German defenders. The finesse of Mars deteriorated into a series of kamikaze attacks.

Despite their supposedly overstretched lines and meager resources, the Germans slaughtered the attacking Russians. By the end of the year, the two German commanders recorded the destruction of somewhere between 1,500 and 2,000 Soviet tanks, and counted 100,000 Russian dead. The Germans estimated total Soviet casualties at close to a quarter of a million men. Given how many Soviet units were ultimately drawn into the fighting, it is impossible to evaluate the extent of the losses precisely, but since Zhukov had 667,000 men and nearly 2,000 tanks for Mars, the notion that the six armies involved were essentially destroyed is probably accurate enough. In the final attempt to destroy the Germans in the Vyazma pocket, for example, the Red Army committed "44,000 men and 500 tanks and during the attacks they lost 42,000 men and 183 tanks destroyed."[5]

So Mars, justifiably seen now in the West as Zhukov's greatest defeat, wound down because he no longer had any forces left to fight with. Moreover, by January 1943, every available Soviet unit was needed for Uranus and the remaining two planetary offensives.

German losses in the fighting to contain Zhukov's offensive were significant. Casualties for all three army groups for the last four months of the year came to 427,622 dead and missing, nearly 80 percent of the casualties on the whole front for the entire year.[6] In November, for the first time, the numbers of the missing in action (as opposed to those killed) began to rise appreciably: in December they actually exceeded the number of those killed, a good indicator of the intensity of the fighting.

But the Germans were still right where they had been at the start of Mars. Their casualties were far less than Soviet casualties no matter how computed, and their units, although depleted, would soon recover. Mars was a major defeat for the Red Army, and a hard-fought victory for the Germans, made all the more remarkable by the disparity in numbers and the lack of reinforcements.

Before continuing on to an account of Uranus and its aftermath, it is worth explaining why it was that Mars failed so completely. The question is not only interesting in itself but helps to explain what happened from January 1943 on. By December 1942, three developments were firmly in place that transformed both the nature of the Wehrmacht and the nature of how the war would be fought. The Rzhev meat grinder, the struggle for the Luchassa Valley, the fighting in the Vyazma pocket, all three events are pretty accurate predictors for the rest of the war.

The numbers of tanks and guns and men cited in accounts of these battles and those that followed are highly misleading. On paper, German divisions were fighting Soviet armies, infantry divisions having to fight off armor. How could the Soviets lose? German intelligence appreciations afterward pinpointed one of the key Soviet weaknesses:

> Indeed the enemy has learned much, but he has again shown himself unable to exploit critical favorable situations. The picture repeats itself when operations, which begin with great intent and local successes, degenerate into senseless, wild hammering at fixed-front positions once they encounter initial heavy losses and unforeseen situations. This incomprehensible phenomenon appears again and again.[7]

Indeed this perceptive analysis applies not simply to the failure of Mars, but to the failures of all subsequent Soviet offensives to achieve their objectives with any sort of minimal loss of life.

That explains the massacres, but it hardly explains why the Germans were not driven from the battlefield. Although several historians have argued that the position was unstable, and the Germans were too weak to hang on in the long run, the actual sequence of events hardly supports these notions.[8]

The first development in the Wehrmacht was the growing deployment of independent Abteilungen based on powerful new weapons that in general were not being parceled out at the divisional level. This tendency had begun in 1941 with the growth of the assault gun units. By fall 1942 it had accelerated, to the extent that the Wehrmacht reached a sort of tipping point: its most potent firepower lay not in its regular divisions, whether armored, motorized, or other, but in a growing forest of independent armored units.

In spring 1942, in addition to the assault gun units, the Wehrmacht began to deploy new Abteilungen based on a formidable new weapon, the Tiger 1 heavy tank. The vehicle was slow and ponderous, characteristics that made it ill suited for the great sweeping armored thrusts of 1939–1941. But with its 8.8 centimeter main gun, it could destroy any Soviet tank with one shot, while its heavy armor meant it was vulnerable only to the most accurately placed shell delivered at close range.

Soviet offensives like Mars, in which the Red Army simply hurled dozens of tanks at the Germans, frequently unsupported by infantry, played to the Tiger's strength. The Tiger tanks were able to stand off at great distance and pick off Soviet tanks before they could get into range. Of the three units formed in 1942, one, the 502nd, went into action with Army Group North in May 1942. Its tanks were heavily engaged in Zhukov's offensive, inflicting losses on Soviet armor out of all proportion to the size of the unit: three of its tank commanders accounted for nearly 400 Soviet tanks.[9]

By and of themselves, these new units, despite their hitting power, were not enough. But in this same time frame, the army was changing in yet another way. A brief examination of the evolution of one of the more important German combat units is illuminating. The premier infantry regiment in the German Army was the Grossdeutschland. It began the war as an infantry regiment, but rapidly expanded. By September 1942 it was no longer a regiment, but appeared in the order of battle as a motorized infantry division, which most people would take to mean that its soldiers were transported by trucks instead of their own feet. But this meant that the division had its own self-propelled artillery. More importantly, it now had its own armored units, consisting of assault guns and tanks.

In the order of battle, the division was an infantry division with some trucks. But its armor made it easily the match for a Soviet mechanized corps, since in 1942 an entire Soviet corps would have only 175 vehicles at its disposal.[10] Moreover, an enumeration of the sheer numbers (so many men, so many guns, so many tanks) disguises the increasing concentration of hitting power in German combat units, and this power in turn was magnified by the integration of infantry, artillery, and armor (and airpower), battlefield components that in the Red Army were still functioning independently. It did little good to deploy great hordes of tanks if they had no close infantry support: they could penetrate but not occupy, and without infantry support they were targets not only for other tanks but for antitank gunners.

By fall 1942, the main weapon of the Mark 3 assault guns of the Grossdeutschland had been upgraded: their new high-velocity 7.5 centimeter guns were effective tank killers, and their Mark 4 tanks had been similarly modified. As the Wehrmacht's best unit, the division was in a privileged position with respect to the quantity and quality of its equipment and personnel.

By comparison with its Soviet adversaries, the Grossdeutschland was a sort of super-unit, with hitting power out of all proportion to its nominal designation. That imbalance only increased as the new heavy armor and potent antitank weaponry began to appear in spring 1943. Not coincidentally, it was precisely this unit that was the keystone of the German defenses that stopped Mars in the Luchassa Valley (the key area in the Vyazma pocket).

For the sorely pressed officers and men of this division, those two names brought bitter memories of the heavy losses and savage fighting. Losses included two regimental commanders, and the quasi-official divisional history concludes its discussion of fall 1942 with the following sentence: "of all Grossdeutschland's battles in the Second World War, Rzhev is the battle upon which the survivors look back with unmatched horror."[11] But that remark, true as it may be, helps to explain why morale remained so high even when, after July 1943, Germany's strategic fortunes were clearly waning. November 1942–January 1943 was really the worst period of the war as far as most German units were concerned.

Our detour for Mars left Paulus on the approaches to Stalingrad. Given its urban sprawl, the size of the Volga, and the relative absence of places to cross upstream, Paulus had no choice but to fight his way into the heart of the city. Fortunately for the Germans, both the city center and most of the industry (including the tank factory) was on the western side of the city.

Vasily Ivanovich Chuikov's 62nd Army had withdrawn into the city in early September, and the Germans began a deliberate and methodical attempt to seize control of it. By September 20 they had taken Mamayev Hill and the main railroad station, cutting the Soviet defenders in half and reaching the Volga.

By September 26, Paulus's troops had seized the main buildings in the city square, and units of the 4th Armored Army, initially attached to Paulus but not technically part of his command, cut Chuikov off from the Soviet 64th Army to the south, and largely cleared the southern part of the city. By the end of November, at the point at which Mars began, the Germans had every major building still standing. Insofar as Stalingrad can be (misleadingly) described as a fight for the physical possession of an actual city, by early December that battle was over.

But already the second phase of the fight had begun. Paulus had the core of the city, but he was unable to secure his flanks, or to cross the river. Of course in terms of the original German idea, it was hardly necessary to cross the river in order to cut Stalin off from his last remaining warm water port. Tactically, however, the failure to cross to the eastern bank meant that Chuikov could keep feeding troops across the river and try to regain the city. Although the Luftwaffe was exacting a terrible toll on the Red Army at the river crossings, it was unable to shut down either the flow of reinforcements into the city or the movements across the river to the north.

So the German positions in southeastern Russia now consisted of two great bulges protruding into Soviet territory: Stalingrad and the Caucasus. Such salients were problematic for both sides, rather like a coiled rattlesnake, ready to lash out and deliver a death blow with lightning speed. Although there is no evidence that Stalin himself had begun to appreciate this aspect of the Wehrmacht, the survivors of the first eighteen months of slaughter were beginning to grasp the implications. The only effective way to kill a rattlesnake, namely, to sever the head from the coiled body, applied as surely in the steppes of Russia as in the wilds of the American Southwest. Although all analogies are imperfect, they can also be illuminating, and in this case, the striking power of the 6th Army, like that of Army Group A in the Caucasus, was concentrated in the tip of the salient, the head. Sever the head and most of the lethal force of each component would rapidly become useless.

By the time Zhukov launched Mars, Vasilevsky's columns had broken through on Paulus's flanks and were driving far past the 6th Army. Given how thinly held the flanks of the 6th Army were, the danger of being trapped inside the city had always existed. But Paulus, instead of holding his relatively small armored force back so it could counter any flanking move by the Red Army, had instead committed it to the reduction of the city. Before he realized his situation, he and his men were trapped in yet another pocket, and would either have to hold on until relieved or fight their way out.

Vasilevsky's initial penetration seemed to indicate success: unlike Mars, which had run into trouble almost from the outset, Uranus was actually going according to plan. The German forces to the south, Army Group A, were on the verge of being cut off completely as the Red Army struck toward their left flank, now completely up in the air. No matter how the ensuing battles developed, the threat to the oilfields and to the mouth of the Volga had been checked, if not eliminated.

Hitler was quicker to react than Paulus, no more blind to the precariousness of his armies than Stalin was. At this moment, the last days of November 1942, the two dictators were briefly not only in accord, but were setting in motion perfectly complementary deployments. As Stalin had Zhukov unleash Mars, Hitler ordered Paulus to stand fast. Just as Stalin's intention was to trap the Germans inside the salients and then drive deep into occupied territory, Hitler's preemptive response was to have his soldiers continue to slaughter their attackers.

Hitler's calculation was that his men could hold out indefinitely. Nor was this assumption without foundation. As we have seen, during the previous winter, there had already been situations in which units in Army Group North had been cut off, surrounded by the Red Army. They had been supplied by air drops, and had given such a good account of themselves that the Soviet troops surrounding them had ultimately been forced to disengage.[12]

The precedent was not entirely convincing, given the distances involved and the size of the 6th Army. But Hitler's confidence had another basis as well. Part of Stalin's calculation had been that by launching two great offensives simultaneously (Uranus and Mars) he would deprive the Wehrmacht of its great tactical advantage, the ability to shift forces rapidly from one part of the front to another, and thus snuff out any offensive threat.

If that calculation proved correct, the Red Army's massive thrusts of November 1942 would destroy the German forces completely, and send the survivors reeling back into their 1940 borders.

Hitler's plan was therefore simple, and forced upon him. The German units that were surrounded would stand and fight. The threat to the overextended forces at the far southern end of the front was the most critical. So Hitler tapped von Manstein, who was back in Leipzig with his family, having buried his son Gero, a lieutenant in the 51st Grenadiers, killed in action in October. Army Group Don was definitely ad hoc. The main force consisted of two detachments, each named after its commander. The first, under the leadership of Hermann Hoth, consisted of the 4th Armored Army and what was left of the 4th Romanian Army. The other detachment, under Karl-Adolf Hollidt, consisted of the 6th, 11th, and 22nd Armored Divisions, the remnants of half a dozen infantry divisions, and what was left of the Italian Expeditionary Force and the Romanian 3rd Army. A fourth armored division was en route, and Berlin had ample reserves in the west, as there was a belated recognition in the German high command that the Dieppe raid was not in fact the prelude to an Allied invasion of France. But all in all, even with the increased striking power of the German units, von Manstein hardly commanded an overwhelming force, given the ten Soviet armies Vasilevsky had hurled into Ukraine.

But just as breaking the siege at Stalingrad was only one of the objectives of the planetary operations, and a minor one at that, von Manstein's two main tasks were to stabilize the German defenses and prevent Army Group A from being cut off in the Caucasus. The relief of Stalingrad was a lesser priority: given the immense difficulties that von Manstein was facing, and the catastrophe that would befall Army Group A should he fail, what happened to Paulus was rather beside the point.

Von Manstein, like the other senior generals actually on the Eastern Front, preferred to see him break out of his encirclement and fight his way back to the German positions.[13] However, von Manstein was of the belief that by the time Paulus asked for permission to break out (on November 22), "the vital hour may have already been missed," a tactful way of saying that Paulus was too slow to react.[14]

Decisive action at the command level was needed. Paulus, regardless of whether he was slavishly following Hitler's orders or making a reasonable tactical decision that coincided with those orders, was incapable of the decisive actions required. In all fairness, his situation was deteriorating rapidly and the army high command, which in von Manstein's view was equally culpable, was hardly helping the situation. Army Group Don was not getting what it needed to reach Paulus, nor, as the days of January 1943 slowly lengthened, was there any real chance of it doing so.[15]

Moreover, Vasilevsky was still attacking vigorously all the way up to Voronezh, so von Manstein's first priority was still to stabilize the German positions, which always seemed to be on the verge of collapse. As he himself admitted, "whether in this situation Don Army Group and Army Group A, which was now withdrawing from the Caucasus, could be saved at all seemed doubtful."[16] So Hitler's insistence that Paulus was tying up Soviet units that otherwise would be used to exploit the breakthroughs was not entirely off base. The larger part of seven Soviet armies was still involved in trying to reduce the German forces trapped inside the Stalingrad pocket.

By mid-January, with the last of the three main airfields lost that the Luftwaffe had relied on to keep Paulus supplied, von Manstein wrote the situation off. In his view the only solution was capitulation. But it must be said that Hitler's appreciation of the situation was essentially accurate: given what was already known about the fate of German prisoners of war, capitulation was hardly much of an option: the officers and men of the 6th Army could either die quickly in fighting or die slowly in captivity.

But in late January, Paulus, who after his initial and tardy request to withdraw had behaved as though he'd fight to the bitter end, suddenly reversed course. On February 3, he surrendered. The timing was curious. At that point von Manstein was only sixty kilometers from the city, close enough to make it possible for the 4th Armored Army to disengage and rejoin the German forces.

As Paulus was surrendering, the Red Army mounted a shriveled version of Saturn, one last blow aimed at the increasingly exposed left flank of Army Group A. The key position in the south was Rostov, at the mouth of the Don. It had become both a bridgehead and logistical center for the German and Romanian units to the east.

But von Manstein, who had managed to stabilize the critical middle section of the front (the right flank of what was left of Army Group B and the left flank of the adjacent Army Group A), now smashed into the nine Soviet armies that were threatening Rostov. Although elements of the Red Army were within twenty kilometers of Rostov, Army Group Don stopped the Russian offensive dead in its tracks.

Saturn was the last gasp effort of the operations with which Stalin had planned to end the war and destroy the German army outright. One reason it failed was that the Soviet high command now lacked the reserves to exploit any breakthrough, or to throw into action to reverse the course of a battle. This problem had been inherent in the disposition of the forces in November, when Stalin had authorized Zhukov's ambitious plan. Since Mars and Uranus were launched at the same time, the units engaged in one operation could not be withdrawn and sent to the other, either to stave off defeat or reinforce success. And with the holding back of what was left of the Soviet reserves to launch Saturn, Stalin had committed every available soldier and every working gun and vehicle to the scheme. Although not by nature impulsive, and not inclined, as Hitler was, to taking wild risks, Stalin had banked on the success of the four grand offensives. He was now having to face an extremely unpleasant reality: failure.

The problem extended past the depleted units and destroyed vehicles. The Red Army had never paid much attention to logistics, and until Uranus, it had never advanced far enough to outrun its supplies. The bitter experiences of the first eighteen months of the war had apparently made the senior Soviet commanders aware of what the martyred Tukhachevsky had been articulating when he spoke of deep battle. The successive German thrusts of summer and fall 1941, and summer 1942, were good examples of the concept, and the Soviets were responding in kind.

But they had failed to understand that if the men and vehicles conducting those deep armored thrusts were not lavishly supported by an ever-extending system of supply, reinforcement, and maintenance, the whole advance would eventually peter out. And at that point, unless the enemy had abandoned the battlefield and was running away, the advancing units would become extremely vulnerable to any determined counterattack.

Nor was this simply theory. Vasilevsky's units had surged past Stalingrad, had taken Kharkov and Belgorod, key cities to the northwest. But now they were dangerously overextended. The units that should have advanced to relieve and reinforce them had all but ceased to exist, committed to the capture of Rostov.

Von Manstein, who quickly saw the Soviet vulnerability, now delivered the third blow. The first had stabilized the front. The second had stopped the advance on Rostov. The third was the most ambitious: von Manstein hurled the battered but resilient Army Group Don toward the two cities, surprising the exhausted Russians, who were now in the same situation that the defending Germans had been at the start of Mars, fending off a vigorous attack on their own. By mid-March both Kharkov and Belgorod had fallen to the Germans and there was very little left of the massive spearhead that Vasilevsky had deployed to envelop Paulus at Stalingrad and then advance to Kharkov. Soviet official records admit the loss of over 1,000 tanks and 100,000 dead.

Both dictators now had to face some rather grim prospects. Hitler was not any closer to grasping the heart and lungs of the Soviet Union in March 1943 than he had been six months earlier. Stalin's aims had been equally dashed: given the enormous distances of the front, the extent of the German penetrations into

Soviet territory, surprisingly little had changed. The Russians still had Stalingrad and the Germans still had Rostov.

Whatever illusions the two men had nurtured thus far, they were not blind to the disturbing results of those four bloody months. Their responses were complementary. Hitler admitted to von Manstein that the defeat at Stalingrad was his responsibility, as indeed in one sense it was: not only had he let von Reichenau talk him into giving Paulus command of the 6th Army, but in fall 1942, as we have seen, he had reduced the striking power of his armies in the east by shifting key units to the west in response to potential threats there.

In so doing he had crippled the Wehrmacht in three different but vital areas: the SS super-unit he had sent to France (the Leibstandarte) was easily the equal of the Grossdeutschland. Its presence on the Eastern Front would have vastly increased the hitting power of the combat units there. Given how close von Manstein got to Stalingrad, even with the cobbled-together forces available, the notion that if he had additional units he would have broken through is hardly speculative.

Much of the success of those units was based on the careful integration of tanks with infantry and tactical aircraft. Hitler had subtracted both of those components as well. The successes of Army Group Don in those four critical months (December 1942–March 1943) are truly astonishing. As we shall see, Hitler implicitly recognized that success, as his next move would be an expansion of one of von Manstein's ideas.

Stalin, like Hitler, was sobered by the bloodbath. He at last recognized the cost of his obsession with mounting constant offensives. After the fall of Kharkov, the Red Army was essentially bankrupt. It lacked the men and the equipment to mount another offensive. Thanks to the increasing shipments of Allied aid, the bankruptcy was only temporary; and although the statistics are wildly inflated, there is no doubt that Soviet factories were turning out more armaments in 1943 than in 1942. But for the moment, the only sensible strategy was to go over to a completely defensive posture. Stalin temporarily recognized reality and acceded to Zhukov's pleadings.

The inner workings of Stalin's mind remained, as always, veiled and obscured. But it is instructive that Zhukov, the architect of the planned offensives, not only kept his head on his shoulders, but his advice was now, at least in the short run, taken seriously. That suggests that Stalin, in his own circuitous way, was beginning to shoulder some of the responsibility for the failures of the Red Army. So while Hitler planned his next move, Stalin did a masterful rewrite of recent events.

During Stalinist times, there was a wry Soviet quip to the effect that the future was fixed and known, it was only the past that was constantly changing; the same insight that Orwell deployed in 1984, albeit the Bolsheviks were far less successful in practice than Orwell's Ministry of Truth.[17] Stalin now proceeded to create a fictional masterpiece in which the chaos and confusion of those four months became a neatly ordered and highly persuasive narrative.

The failures of Mars, and indeed the whole planetary scheme, to end the war, disappeared into the memory hole, with the tacit acceptance of the Red Army's senior commanders: Zhukov certainly wasn't eager to acknowledge how badly he had been beaten. Stalin's disappearing act was greatly aided by the Germans, although not for the same reason. Von Kluge and von Küchler, the commanders of Center and North respectively, failed to realize the damage that their stubborn defense had done to the Red Army, mainly because they were conscious of their own losses. For the Germans, Mars was another in a series of bloody conflicts in the same general theater of operations. It failed so utterly in its aim of destroying their armies that they never realized its intentions.

So the whole notion of the four great offensives disappeared.

When finally their existence was uncovered fifty years later, Stalin's replacement legend was so firmly embedded in everyone's ideas of the war that the disasters of Mars, like the aims of Uranus, became minor footnotes: historical annotations to a novel.

In the story Stalin wrote, everything that happened from September 1942 through February 1943 was about Stalingrad. The German attempts to take the city, and the subsequent surrender of the hapless Paulus, became the center around which all other events revolved. The legend was all the more convincing because this time Stalin had a concrete and undeniable event to which he could point: Paulus had surrendered, the 6th Army had been defeated.

Moreover, the story fit neatly enough into the existing narrative, which emphasized Hitler's failures to take Moscow and Leningrad. That legend in turn fit nicely into the whole classical notion of campaigns and battles directed against major cities. It was the sort of story that anyone who had read about the Fall of Troy could understand, a practical illustration of Stalin's genius at taking the complex ideas of Marx and Lenin, often, or even generally, expressed incoherently, and reducing them to simple sentences that anyone could understand.

He was an excellent storyteller in a unique position both to weave a compelling tale of Soviet triumph and to ensure that no one would contradict him. The bewildering and complex sequence of events between December 1942 and March 1943 only made the task all the easier.

Paulus's surrender in February was clearly a German defeat, particularly when plucked out of the context of Stalin's ambitions, the debacle of Mars, and von Manstein's astonishing offensives.

The magnitude of the defeat is surprisingly difficult to measure. In terms of casualties, January 1943 was the worst month of the war: the Wehrmacht lost 164,596 men dead and missing, only 37,000 of these being killed in action, a figure consistent with von Manstein's estimate of 90,000 6th Army prisoners, as well as some of the later official Soviet figures. The losses in tanks were heavy as well: 2,115 vehicles, but these losses were for the entire theater, not simply those incurred at Stalingrad.

The Romanian 3rd and 4th Armies, the Hungarian 2nd Army, and the Italian 8th Army, holding the flanks of the German positions at Stalingrad, all suffered heavily. Although from the cursory references in most accounts one would assume that these soldiers simply ran away, or offered only feeble resistance, the few available accounts of their combats contradict that notion. Many of the casualties they suffered were in the attacks and counterattacks spearheaded by Hollidt, where they proved themselves surprisingly tough fighters: two senior Romanian officers were awarded the *Ritterkreuz* as a result, and the Wehrmacht did not award those medals lightly, even to its own officers.

The Romanians suffered 158,854 casualties in the three months of fighting (November 1942 through January 1943).[18] Although it is sometimes said that the Hungarian 2nd Army was virtually wiped out in the Stalingrad fighting, actual losses came to 35,000 dead and missing, of which about 25,000 were prisoners (by contrast only 3,000 Romanian soldiers were captured at Stalingrad).[19]

In the midwinter fighting, three German armored divisions were wiped out, but only one (the 22nd) ceased to exist; the 24th, whose survivors surrendered at Stalingrad, was re-formed by the end of the year.[20] Against those very real losses must be balanced the equally real additions: in 1942 the Wehrmacht created no fewer than four new armored divisions, in addition to the three it had formed in 1941, new units that were in addition to the deployment of three Tiger I units in 1942. Moreover, in the first months of 1943, five more new Tiger I units and two new assault gun units were created and deployed.

Despite the losses sustained in the midwinter fighting, by April 1943, the armored divisions had more of the workhorse

Mark 4 tanks in service than they had in September. Then too, the majority of the tanks lost in January and February 1943 were Mark 3 vehicles. The net effect was that through combat losses the Germans were replacing the vehicles they had found to be outmatched and obsolete with newer and more powerful designs. Even so, their industry was producing more vehicles than they were losing. Hitler's armored divisions possessed more of these tanks than they had possessed a year earlier.[21] Hitler's war machine was hardly shrinking.

On the Soviet side, an exact accounting of the butcher's bill is probably impossible. The semiofficial American army account of the war noted in 1968 that "the Soviet Union has not made public its own losses," and the official figures eventually released have little credibility: 485,777 killed and wounded from November 19, 1942, to February 2, 1943.[22]

A better indicator of the actual scale of loss is to be found in the official figures for armored losses. Those numbers are surprisingly high: 2,915 vehicles for the same operation as above, a figure substantially higher than what is admitted either for the September–November defense of Moscow or the June–July 1942 fighting around Voronezh. But in both the earlier cases the human losses were considerably higher than the vehicular: 513,338 in the former and 370,522 in the latter. That observation leads to the deduction that a good estimate for total number of soldiers killed during Uranus is probably in the neighborhood of the admitted total for all casualties, slightly under half a million men.[23]

This brief accounting suggests that, placed in the proper context, Uranus was a bloody draw. The shape of the front remained pretty much the same and in March 1943 neither dictator was any closer to his goal than he had been in the previous year. At best, considered in isolation, Stalingrad was a Pyrrhic victory.

Of course if one assumes that Stalin's resources in men and munitions were immense and Hitler's were dwindling, then it is easy to come to the brutal conclusion that the very idea of such a victory had no meaning in this war. However, as we have seen, Stalin's resources were not only finite, but they were dwindling. By December 1942 the Red Army was ordered to

> reexamine all command personnel whose state of health has previously marked them as unfit for line [combat] duty. Use command personnel who are identified as fit for line duty by the reexamination to fill vacant positions in army operating units, in accordance with their training.[24]

Such orders, when viewed in the context of reports of self-mutilation, desertion, drunkenness, and summary executions, suggest an army in serious difficulties.

The official figures for the expansion of the Soviet military during this period, at first blush quite impressive, a 67 percent increase between 1941 and 1943, indirectly allow us to grasp the dimensions of Stalin's problem.[25] By 1943, Stalin had 11,858,000 men and women under arms, certainly a major increase over the 1941 figure of 7,100,000. In 1942 the same reporting system shows a strength of 11,340,000. So the increase between 1942 and 1943 was only 5 percent. On the other side, matters were quite different: in 1941 the Germans alone had a strength of 7,309,000; in 1942 this total had risen to 8,410,000, and in 1943 it had risen yet again, to 9,480,000.

In other words, Hitler's forces were increasing at a more rapid rate than Stalin's. The ominous reality for the Soviet dictator, then, is that even using his own data, as the war progressed his margin of superiority was shrinking. In 1942 he had 135 Russians in uniform for every 100 Germans. In 1943 he only had 125 Russians for every 100 Germans.

As we have seen, at the start of the war, Stalin ordered a massive relocation of Soviet industry deep into the heartland, where it would be well out of the range of the Luftwaffe's short-range bomber fleet. Statistics attesting to the amazing accomplishments of these newly relocated industries promptly appeared, but, as we noted earlier, the discrepancy between the number of tanks available for Zhukov and Vasilevsky and the official Soviet tank production data suggests that these figures are mostly fictional.

When it came to even more basic military matériel, the situation in 1941, at the start of the war, was appalling. In his famous 1956 speech Khrushchev would reveal that

> At the outbreak of the war we did not even have sufficient numbers of rifles to arm the mobilized manpower. I recall that in those days I telephoned from Kiev to comrade Malenkov and told him, "People have volunteered for the new Army [units] and are demanding weapons. You must send us arms." Malenkov answered me, "We cannot send you arms. We are sending all our rifles to Leningrad and you have to arm yourselves." Such was the armament situation.[26]

Although there is a tendency to assume that Khrushchev was exaggerating to make his point, the evidence suggests the contrary. Here is the account from a soldier who enlisted as a reserve and then became part of the Soviet 11th Guards Division:

> We were being armed and fitted out on the road. Trucks would drive up, the column would stop, and packs would be thrown down from the vehicles so we could be issued with their contents straight away. Initially, we had been a motley and colorful crew, armed with Polish rifles, then some old German models, though there was no ammo for them.[27]

That same shortage persisted well into 1943, when a German sniper from the 3rd Gebirgsjäger noted that

> The Russian units were created very quickly. . . . They were put into uniform jackets with civilian clothes beneath them, and received just two days' training in the use of small arms. Their equipment and training was so rushed that not all of them even had weapons. Calculating the losses expected during the attack, only the first waves were given guns. The soldiers coming behind them had to set out unarmed and pick up the weapons of the fallen.[28]

By extending the ranks of the army to include all males between the ages of fourteen and sixty, by calling back into combat duties the disabled, and by increasingly relying on women, the Soviets were able to preserve Stalin's fiction of an inexhaustible pool of cannon fodder. But the situation was not only grim, it was getting steadily grimmer.

Reading between the lines of Stalin's 1943 May Day speech it is possible to discern a recognition of that reality. Although Stalin defiantly proclaimed that "No amount of clamor can do away with the fact that the camp of the fascists is really going through a grave crisis," the tone of the speech is revealing, the window dressing for the command decision to stand completely on the defensive that Zhukov had persuaded him to make in March.[29]

What is notable in this speech is the absence of any of the hard figures that had characterized his earlier discourses. The address ends with a series of blunt orders, which, despite their verbosity, may be summarized easily enough: soldiers and their commanders need to "perfect" their skills, the army needs to "consolidate and develop the successes of the winter battles," and the "guerrillas" need to intensify their efforts. These sound like the words of a man aware of his own grave crisis.

By contrast, the Germans, although profoundly shaken by the carnage, were not only realistic, but grimly confident. Von Manstein summed up the situation succinctly:

> The armies of the enemy's Southwest Front had received such a beating that they were temporarily incapable of further offensive action. . . . The Russians had still not succeeded in winning their decisive victory over the German southern wing, the destruction of which could probably have never been made good by our side. By the end of the winter campaign the initiative was back in German hands.[30]

The situation by the time of Stalin's May Day speech was thus a curious paradox. In failure the Germans were becoming more powerful; in victory, the Soviets were becoming less so. If Stalin was aware of the situation, so was Hitler. Hitler felt he now had the means to deliver the final blow, and he was determined to do so.

Summer 1943: The Turning Point

The result of the whole combat consists in the sum total of the results of all partial combats; but these results of separate combats are settled by different considerations.

Von Clausewitz, *On War*[1]

The best measure of the exhaustion of the Red Army can be seen in the sharp dip in the German losses in the spring and early summer of 1943: the total number of soldiers killed for April, May, and June was the lowest of the war, so low that the sum of all three months together was only slightly more than during the three winter months of 1941–1942. From the point of view of the senior German generals, the sensible thing to do was to consolidate their defensive positions. That would involve mounting a series of small local offensives to straighten out their lines, what German officers thought of as a strategic defensive, with an eye toward wearing down the Red Army still further and forcing a stalemate.

Von Manstein had his eye on the one obvious spot, a large bulge located roughly at equal distances from Orel and Belgorod, which, as he records in his memoirs, was just "begging to be sliced off." During the German counterattacks of February and March 1943, the Germans had seized all the lost territory from Belgorod to Kharkov, and then along the Dnieper River all the way down to the Kalmius River and Taganrog. But to the north of Belgorod the front curved back to the west, and then to the northwest, forming a line from Serny up to Sems, and then turning back to the northeast, eventually looping around Orel before resuming its northwesterly course.

The result was a salient roughly 200 kilometers wide that projected some 150 kilometers into the newly stabilized German lines, an area that corresponded roughly to the czarist province named after the only town of any importance in the area, Kursk. The Germans had occupied the city in November 1941 and then lost it during the chaotic days of March 1943. Now mostly in ruins, it was almost at the base of the projecting salient. Although another historic Russian town, and an important railroad junction since 1868, it had no particular strategic significance. The main rail line that ran through the city lay along a north–south axis. Given the physical shape of the front, and the condition of the railways themselves, the line was of no use to either side by this point in the war. Nor was there any serious industry there: the area was almost entirely agricultural, the chief crop being sugar beets and the mills needed to refine them.

But the absence of urban centers and the developed agriculture created an ideal terrain for mechanized warfare. Given the inadequacies of the Soviet logistical system, the Red Army preferred to locate both its troops and its matériel as close to the front as possible. So the bulge was both a sack in which a sizable Soviet force was trapped and a launching platform for yet another Soviet offensive.

But the Germans felt that Stalin was not going to make any further offensive moves until the Allies had begun their invasion of Europe. As we saw at the end of the last chapter, their conclusion was correct. Stalin was all for loosing another wave of attacks, but he lacked the resources to do so, had no choice but to stand on the defensive and wait for the Allies to replenish what he had squandered with his relentless offensive operations.

By February 1943 he had already received approximately $376 million worth of tanks and motor vehicles, and the flow of matériel was increasing rapidly: deliveries in the first four months of 1942 had averaged 149,500 tons a month, but for the same period in 1943 the average had increased dramatically, to 270,350 tons, and that was only the data for shipments from Canada and the United States.[2] As the Allied shipments began to arrive in such great quantities, Stalin realized that if he waited a few more months, the United States and Great Britain would have given him a whole new air force to replace the one he had lost, and a whole new motor pool to give his army the mobility it had never possessed: 2,411 tanks, 120,330 motor vehicles, 1,901 bombers, and 1,555 fighter planes arrived by July 31.[3] So there was a window of opportunity for the Germans, and it coincided, fortuitously, with the good weather of the Ukrainian summer.

Meanwhile in May 1943 the German and Italian armies in Tunisia finally surrendered to the Allies, clearing the way for further Allied offensives. It is a long way from Tunisia to Kursk, but by May 1943 Hitler's concerns about the Mediterranean increasingly had an impact on operations in Russia. During the war Stalin was desperate for a second front; afterward his propagandists bombarded the world with the claim that the Allied delay in opening one had forced the Russians to bear the brunt of the resistance against Hitler, which in turn enabled them to claim that the Red Army had defeated the Hitlerites, indeed would have done so on its own.

Although this claim was dutifully accepted and even endorsed by Western historians, it seems more an example of circular reasoning than of fact-based analysis.[4] But as we have seen, the reality of multiple fronts was very much in Stalin's favor from fall 1941 on. Hitler and the German high command were constantly reacting to Allied threats, whether imagined (the Dieppe raid as a possible prelude to an invasion) or real (the escalation of the war in North Africa).

After the Allied invasion of North Africa in November 1942, the threat to Hitler was very real, and he responded accordingly.

In January 1943 the Wehrmacht recorded 125,596 men missing in action, which is consistent with the generally accepted figure of 90,000 prisoners of war taken when Stalingrad capitulated. In May 1943, the same documents record 74,500 men missing, the German soldiers trapped in Tunisia and forced to surrender there. That loss was a much worse disaster than what had taken place in the east because of the loss of a sizable number of Germany's latest tanks and the remnants of Italy's mechanized and armored divisions as well as its airborne troops.

As Hitler reacted to these threats in the west, the army group commanders in the east were deprived of key elements at critical moments in the war, such as the loss of the Leibstandarte SS division to France in autumn 1942. Moving an armored division across the length of Europe was hardly a trivial exercise, and the increasing Allied bombing raids hardly helped. Once the Leibstandarte was in France, it would literally take months to get it back to the Eastern Front: like the American cavalry in movie Westerns, the SS did arrive, just in the nick of time, and thus was able to spearhead von Manstein's spring offensive. But its impact would have been far greater had it been deployed as part of Army Group Don in early December 1942.

Air force units could be transferred much easier than armor, and Hitler took advantage of that fact: from fall 1941 on, the Luftwaffe units in the east were culled out and sent elsewhere, generally to the Mediterranean, which Hitler was apparently determined to hold on to, judging from the steady flow of planes, tanks, and men into a conflict that it seems unlikely he could have won.

Soviet aircraft losses were, even by the official counting, astronomical. But as the war continued, the Germans began to lose the absolute control over the airspace that was essential to the success of their ground operations, partly because of an increasing level of competence on the part of Soviet pilots, but also because German pilots and ground crews were being sent to the Mediterranean to keep the supply lines open to German and Italian armies in North Africa.

It is impossible to assign a relative weight to these two factors, although after the war Stalin was told that the overwhelming majority of Soviet aircraft lost during the war was lost owing to mechanical defects of some sort, and it appears that as late as mid-1943 Soviet pilots were going into combat with less than five hours of flight time.

One advantage of Stalin's account of the war was that it was simple to grasp: the very words "second front" conjured up an image of an enormous ground campaign evocative of the Western Front in the First World War. It was a compelling image, much easier to sink one's teeth into than the complex world of threat response and preemption, or of a war based on the seizure of resources rather than cities.

Both during the war and afterward, there was a heated debate about whether the Allies should have concentrated their efforts on the Mediterranean. Even before the operation was approved, the Americans were increasingly of the opinion that operations there would not have an effect on the outcome of the war commensurate with the cost. That the British were by and large simply repeating a strategy from the First World War, and one that had not been much of a success, certainly makes the notion of an invasion of Europe via Italy, as Churchill urgently desired, rather dubious. It would be difficult to find a concentrated geographic area of Europe where the vast Allied superiority in mechanization and logistics would be less useful, and hardly anyone judges the Allied campaigns in Sicily and Italy as anything other than a slog.

However that may be, Hitler reacted nervously to those threats. From Stalin's point of view, Hitler's nervousness, already a handicap, would prove invaluable as the German advanced their own plans, which were the mirror image of Zhukov's, although the similarity was superficial.

The German high command and the army group commanders favored strategic defense, which von Manstein explicates clearly in his memoirs (for those familiar with tennis). The decision was whether to wait for a Russian offensive and then

> hit them hard "on the backhand" at the first good oppor-
> tunity, or whether we should attack as early as possible
> ourselves and, still within the framework of a strategic
> offensive, strike a limited blow "on the forehand." The
> Army Group preferred the former solution as one of-
> fering better prospects operationally. . . . The plan did
> not meet with Hitler's approval. . . . Consequently
> our minds now turned to the idea of a "forehand
> stroke."[5]

The two views are not so much opposed as existing on different levels of grand strategy. From the level of the theater itself, the initial proposal—to respond forcefully—was sound, almost inarguable, as was Zhukov's plea to stay on the defensive and let the Germans exhaust themselves in an attack. At a higher level, however, when the other theaters were considered, Hitler was right: better to get in the first blow before the Mediterranean collapsed.

That was not the end of the disagreements however. From von Manstein's point of view,

> The whole idea had been to attack before the enemy
> had replenished his forces and got over his reverses
> of the winter. At the same time it was certain that the
> longer we took to launch the operation, the greater
> must be the threat to those of Southern Army Group's
> armies in the Donetz-Mius salient which had to hand
> over all their available forces and, most of all, to the
> Orel bulge as the jumping-off base of Central Army
> Group's Ninth Army.[6]

Although the logic seems impeccable, there is a flaw. If the salient was such an obvious candidate for a German attack, the only way it could be imagined that the Soviet high command had not noticed this as well was to postulate a level of unimaginable ineptitude.

Although Stalin had a tendency to misread Hitler's intentions and insist that far too many of his troops be in the wrong place, the basic Red Army problem thus far had been as much tactical as strategic. Even when the Red Army units were in the correct position, they were unable to maintain it in the face of German envelopment tactics, or to counterattack quickly enough to force the Germans back. Even when it massed a force of men and armor, it was unable to coordinate the two components for a successful attack. Its commanders were not able to respond quickly enough to the "backhand" strokes that had characterized German defensive doctrine since 1914. By mid-1942 the Red Army had some excellent weapons available in quantity, but the men who operated them were badly trained and badly led, while their opponents were not only increasingly better equipped but more experienced.

Anyone looking at the map could see that the salient was an obvious candidate for a German offensive, and as the war entered the end of its second year, the local remedy for the deficiencies of the Red Army was equally obvious: a static defense in depth. So simply by positing basic competence on the other side, the most reasonable assumption to make would be that the Red Army would dig in at precisely the hinge points of the salient, since that was where an attack, if successful, could do the most damage. In other words, there was no possibility of surprise, nor any room for maneuver: any offensive would have to strike at the two points where the salient rejoined the main Soviet lines.

A successful attack at both points would not only pinch off the salient and trap the defenders inside, but the German forces would then be in a position to drive deep into Soviet territory and turn the bulge inside out: instead of pointing into German space, it would now point into Soviet space, and based on their combat experiences, the German commanders were confident that once they broke through, their superior mobility would enable them both to strike deep and expand the salient, forcing a complete rupture of the Soviet position.

To succeed, the Germans would have to be committed to joint offensives (the two sides of the pincers directed at the base of the salient). All that was necessary to mount a successful defense was to slow down the attack long enough for the forces held behind the salient to strike back at the weak spots that developed in the attacking forces.

Of course given the speed with which the Germans executed operations, for the Red Army responding forcefully was a bit like the helpful hint that the best way to disable a rattlesnake was to grab him behind his head after he had struck. However, there was one feature of the bulge that favored the Russians. The actual juncture points of the salient (the two areas where it turned back into the lines) were, by the standards of the Eastern Front, minuscule. The northern hinge was hardly twenty-five kilometers across, and on the southern side any attack would have to develop to the northwest of Belgorod, where it would be constricted to slightly under a forty-kilometer front.

There was no way that even the blundering Soviet armies could miss the uncoiling German armored columns, simply because there was no way the Germans could get around them. If the Germans went in one direction, back toward their own lines, they would achieve nothing. If they went in the other direction, they would not only risk being cut off and surrounded, but the whole point of the envelopment would be lost.

So the geographical and chronological context of the planned German offensive differentiates it dramatically from the previous ones. Absent the element of tactical surprise, deprived of any room to maneuver around the defenders, the only way the forehand blow would succeed was if it emulated the great offensives of the earlier war, when the aim had been to deliver an opening blow on a small front so powerful that it destroyed the defensive positions, hopefully annihilating the defenders and thus allowing a massive penetration of their lines, what the French termed a *coup de bélier*. So Citadel, as the German offensive was called, despite the reliance on airpower and internal combustion engines, was a return to the tactics of the earlier war. In consequence, both sides were trying to build up their forces for the inevitable battle. The Soviets were digging in, the Germans arming up.

Von Manstein, writing in retrospect, argued that this delay was the fatal flaw. Hitler's directive outlining the operation was dated April 15, 1943, and specified the earliest possible start date as May 3. As the German offensive did not begin until two months later, and as Hitler in the order emphasized the importance of surprise as "to when the attack will begin," accounts of the resulting battle have echoed and amplified von Manstein.[7]

But as the timeline for Hitler's earlier offensives suggests, delays were largely irrelevant to their success: Hitler had directed that the offensive in the west start as early as October 1939. It was then repeatedly delayed, but no one argues that the delay occasioned a failure. Quite the contrary; nor was surprise some crucial element of the success of that offensive. In May 1940 the Dutch knew precisely when they were to be attacked. What surprised the Allies was the speed of execution rather than the timing of the attack.

Thus far in the war, neither time nor resources had been of much help to the Red Army. As we have seen, every German offensive effort thrust deep, exploiting both the inevitable gaps in the lines and the Red Army's slow response time and surprising lack of mobility. There was no evidence that the situation was suddenly going to change. What had changed was the drastic shrinkage of the zone of operations on both sides of the salient, which transformed the battle, and thus demanded that the Germans deliver a blow so powerful that it could not be successfully resisted.

So how effectively Zhukov was able to build up his forces is somewhat of a red herring in this debate. The real question was the extent to which Hitler could build up his forces to make the offensive blow so massive that it would rupture the front. Given the developments on the German side, holding back made sense. The Red Army was undoubtedly getting better at the basics of combat and combat support, and its rate of improvement was probably dramatic, but the Germans were getting better as well.

For the first fifteen to eighteen months of the war, the Germans had not only been grossly outnumbered, but most of their basic tools, tanks, antitank weapons, and field artillery, were, for a variety of reasons, either inferior to the weaponry of their opponents or equivalent. Their numerous battlefield successes could hardly be attributed to any technological advantage save one: in June 1940 the Wehrmacht deployed over 600,000 motor vehicles. By contrast, even by the official reckoning, there were only 800,000 trucks in the entire Soviet Union.[8]

But in the fall of 1942, with the deployment of limited numbers of the new Tiger 1 tanks and the upgrading of tank and antitank weaponry, that situation began to change in tangible ways of great importance to success on the battlefield. As we have seen, the impact of the one Tiger 1 unit on the battlefields of northern Russia in fall 1942 was significant, as was the intervention of the expanded and upgraded super-unit, the Grossdeutschland.

By spring 1943, both the quantity and the variety of powerful new weapons had dramatically increased. By May, monthly production of the Tiger 1 had increased sixfold over December 1942, and production of a new and powerful main battle tank, called the Panther, had begun in earnest. With its sloped armor, high-velocity 7.5 centimeter gun, and mobility far in excess of the Tiger, the Germans felt they had finally built the decisive main battle tank. So in addition to the additional Tiger 1 units formed up in spring 1943, the Panthers would be distributed to key armored divisions, supplementing the upgraded Mark 4 tanks, which until that point had been the army's main battle tank.[9]

At the same time, a greatly expanded family of assault guns and tank destroyers was going into service. Unlike Germany's tanks, assault guns were being mass-produced. In 1942, for example, 994 Mark 4 tanks were produced versus 3,041 assault guns.[10]

The true tank destroyer (Jagdpanzer) was still being developed, and only began to appear in spring 1943, but a number of highly successful stopgap designs had been built in 1942, and in reasonable quantities: over 2,300 vehicles mounting either a high-velocity 7.5 centimeter German gun or an equally powerful captured Soviet weapon were in service.[11] Although often ignored in enumerations of tank strength, and bitterly resented by leading German tankers such as Guderian, these vehicles gave the infantry an overwhelming advantage on the battlefield, both in protecting them against enemy armor and in demolishing fixed strongpoints that otherwise would have held up the infantry.[12]

Although the best of the tank destroyers, the Czech-built Hetzer, had not yet gone into service, Ferdinand Porsche had developed his own unique variant, mounting an 8.8 centimeter gun that was even more powerful than the one on the Tiger. Called the Ferdinand or the Elephant, these large and formidable vehicles, like the Tiger tanks, were deployed as independent Abteilungen.[13]

As we have seen, the formation of independent units with potent new weapons was paralleled by the systematic upgrading and expansion of the premier combat divisions, whose firepower was of a whole different order than that of an ordinary German armored division, which in turn was roughly the equivalent of a Soviet armored corps. In the bitter fighting of Mars in 1942, the overstrength Grossdeutschland Division was instrumental in blunting the massive Soviet offensive. By early 1943, the four premier SS divisions had, despite their technical designation as motorized infantry divisions, all been given armored components that made them even more potent than the Grossdeutschland. It was this massive force that von Manstein was able to throw into his Kharkov-Belgorod offensive in early spring 1943. Those cities were captured by units of the SS Armored Corps, which consisted of those four divisions. The uniformity of equipment and size of units in the German army was never as consistent as people imagined and was rapidly becoming meaningless.

The two armies were evolving in different directions. A Red Army mechanized and armored corps had a tank strength that was hardly equal to anyone else's armored division, while for the Germans the situation was reversed. The hitting power of these super-units was wildly disproportional to their nominal identification as divisions, and was becoming only more so, since they received the latest tanks first.

The new vehicles were only just beginning to appear in quantity in 1943, but Hitler's appreciation of their importance was not that wide of the mark. As we shall see, in combat they proved themselves deadly out of all proportion to their numbers. So by the start of Citadel, Hitler had an armored force whose hitting power was unlike anything the Germans had fielded in earlier offensives.

In other words, Hitler was trading off Soviet replenishment time for German and counting himself the winner. The notion is debatable, but then command decisions generally are. The point is not that he was right and his critics were wrong, but that his decision was a reasonable one. Since the idea of a German attack into the salient in early summer could hardly be assumed to be a surprise, the other alternative was to attack in such strength that surprise didn't matter, as the Germans had done in their May 1940 offensive in the west.

Given the basics of the operation, Citadel was going to be two distinct battles separated by nearly 200 kilometers, and those battles were going to be divided into two distinct phases: the initial German "forehand" blow, and the Soviet return.

Although they knew the German attack was coming, Zhukov and Stalin once again misread the situation in a way that had the potential to be disastrous. They had guessed that the main German effort, or the more successful one, would be from the north, and so had positioned the bulk of their mobile reserves ready to strike there, strung out in an arc centered on Tula: the 11th and 14th Armies, the 3rd and 25th Armored, and the 2nd Mechanized Corps. Another bloc of reserves was stationed directly behind the salient itself: the 5th, 27th, and 53rd Armies, with the 4th and 10th Armored and the 1st Mechanized Corps. Finally, in the south there was a much smaller grouping, opposite Belgorod and Kharkov. But these units, the 47th Army and the 5th Armored, were over seventy-five kilometers from the front, and widely scattered.[14]

The Soviet disposition of forces was not only heavily skewed to the northern side, but left a remarkably wide gap opposite the southern hinge, and this was precisely where the most powerful German armored force was positioned to strike. Von Manstein had all five of the German super-units there; the plan was to mount a great northeasterly blow that would drive deep into the interior.

The Soviet disposition of forces favored him. By contrast, Walter Model, commanding the 9th Army, which would be attacking the northern hinge of the salient, would find himself in an increasingly awkward position: the deeper he penetrated the Soviet position, the more vulnerable his men would be to flanking attacks from the massive armored reserves Stalin and Zhukov had positioned on the northern side of the bulge.

Model, one of the few German generals who was a perfervid National Socialist, a true believer, was also an energetic, ruthless, and extremely competent armored commander, the anti-Paulus. In any ranking of German field commanders he would be very close to the top, as he had the perfect combination of opportunism and prudence: he knew precisely when bold moves were called for and when caution was advised.[15]

Given the constricted space and the obviousness of the bulge, the twin offensives Model and von Manstein launched were going to be different from anything thus far seen on the Eastern Front, and to a certain extent in the war overall, General Bernard Montgomery's defensive victory at El Alamein (October 23–November 5, 1942) excepted. In the earlier battles, breakthroughs had been measured in substantial distances. Repeatedly in 1941 and 1942 the advancing Germans had achieved penetrations of over sixty kilometers in one day, and in the midwinter offensives of 1942–1943, both sides had established deep thrusts of the same sort. But those thrusts had a simple cause: the area of the front was simply too vast to be manned in sufficient strength everywhere to hold off an attack in force. Perhaps the Red Army, unlike the Wehrmacht, had the manpower to hold a continuous front, but Stalin's insistence on massive attacks at any cost precluded that.

That being the case, the standards for judging the progress of the offensive are different from those of the earlier offensives. Despite its subsequent reputation as the greatest tank battle ever seen, in reality the first phase of both offensives, which began on July 5, 1943, resembled the offensives the Germans had conducted on the Western Front in the First World War.

In the north, the armored units of Model's 9th Army got off to a bad start. The area of the front under attack was less than twenty kilometers wide, so there was no way a thrust by such an enormous mechanized force (no fewer than five armored divisions) could achieve much in the way of surprise. Nor did they: for the first time in the war, the Germans had to advance through an artillery barrage. There was another problem as well, one the Allies would discover in France in 1944: the emphasis on armor and mechanization created a shortage of infantry, but in both instances (Kursk in 1943, Normandy in 1944) that was precisely what was demanded by the nature of operations.[16]

Nonetheless, within forty-eight hours, Model's attack had smashed through the Soviet defenses, achieved a penetration of almost twenty kilometers in some places, an average of about fifteen. Stalin's instructions had given May 10 as the deadline for completion of a traditional layered defense with successive positions, one behind the other. It was now July 5, so the Russians had had adequate time to prepare the positions. Given that, together with the small area of the front involved, and the fact that the basic defensive deployments in such instances were well understood by all concerned, the German progress was substantial. Model was deep enough to have ruptured the Soviet defenses.

Almost every chronicler follows the general Soviet narrative: Model's attack stalled out in the face of determined resistance and heavy losses of men and armor, so Kursk was a Soviet victory in which the Soviet operational plans at last entered the realm of modern warfare, and battlefield performance met Moscow's expectations.[17]

So it is worth deviating briefly from the normal chronology of battles to note that the loss figures for both sides hardly bear out this narrative. The official Soviet record of the battle admits total casualties of 177,547, while the German records show losses in the same categories coming to 49,822.[18] Losing soldiers at the rate of 3:1 when holding prepared defensive positions in expectation of a known attack hardly constitutes battlefield success.

Model's attack paused not because it was thwarted or stalled, but for a reason familiar to any commander from the earlier war: having penetrated the main defensive positions, he now had to pause in order to make the next leap forward. He was also aware of the precariousness of his situation: the more deeply he penetrated the defensive positions on the northern hinge, the more vulnerable he would be to a counterattack. Of his intentions there is no doubt. Model aimed for a second surge on July 12. But that assault never took place.

The official Soviet account that has continued to define the Kursk narrative rests on an interesting sleight of hand. Citadel was divided into two separate operations, so the figure of 177,837 dead, wounded, and missing tells only part of the story. The reason is obvious enough: when the other operation is added, Red Army losses in dead and missing alone come to 182,859, and total losses to 607,737.[19] So the 3:1 exchange ratio understates the case considerably, even granting the reliability of the Soviet figures, an extremely dubious assumption.

By minimizing the heavy Soviet losses, and (as we shall see below) by wildly exaggerating the German ones, Stalin controlled the narrative of the battle, recasting it the same way that he had created a battle of Moscow and a great triumph at Stalingrad. In two particular senses his story of the Battle of Kursk was an even taller tale than the earlier ones. Hitler had certainly aimed to seize Stalingrad, and the German high command had definitely wanted to take Moscow; but nobody on the German side had the slightest interest in taking Kursk: the town was already in ruins and had no military significance. Nor was Citadel some epic tank battle. On the contrary, the constricted spaces involved left the armor on both sides with little room to maneuver: rather the tanks and assault guns were utilized either for infantry support or to fight off Soviet tank attacks, these last occurring sporadically and involving small numbers of vehicles on both sides.

Zhukov and Stalin, their eyes fixed on Orel, had always planned to mount a massive offensive as a riposte to the expected German thrusts. As Model, ever wary, paused before his second surge, they began that assault, known as Kutuzov. Their attack began before the beginning of Model's second surge: the artillery preparations started during the night of the 11th, and the attack itself began on the same day (July 12) that Model's second-wave attack set out.

Given the sinuous nature of the front, if Zhukov seized Orel, he would be behind Model, whose attacking forces would then be in grave danger of being cut off from the rest of the front. So Model shifted his priorities, disengaged from the offensive, and turned north to cover his flanks and rear. Unfortunately for historians, Model did not live to see the end of the war (he shot himself on April 21, 1945, rather than fall into Soviet hands), and thus left no account of his intentions. Based on his earlier campaigns against the Red Army, he apparently intended to beat off Kutuzov and then resume Citadel.

He had good reason to assume that he could do this, because the main blow had already fallen on the southern hinge, where von Manstein had all the German super-units and the bulk of the heavy armor. Despite the obvious conclusion that follows from the German disposition of forces, to a remarkable extent the Soviet obsession with the northern sector influenced subsequent accounts of the fighting, some commentators going so far as to imply that Kursk was Model's battle to lose, seeing the pause as a sign that he indeed lost it.[20]

But the German pincers had two sides to it. As Model was moving south, von Manstein was moving north by northeast, and at the same time, which is why Kursk is two simultaneous engagements. Evaluating one without the other is misleading.

Von Manstein's Army Group South had the most powerful armored formations, the five super-units of the Waffen-SS and Grossdeutschland. Together they constituted the bulk of the new German armored force. It is therefore not surprising that von Manstein was making much better headway on the south hinge than Model was on the north. Moreover, the Soviet reserves in the south were too far back to be able to intervene effectively. By the time they were able to mount a counterattack, von Manstein had already smashed through the Soviet defensive positions and was on the verge of breaking into the open.

His new heavy armored units were simply slaughtering the Soviet tankers. The tanks of the Leibstandarte SS destroyed 487, and the armored units of the Grossdeutschland destroyed 263 Russian tanks; in the first two days of the battle the Tiger I tanks of the 505th Heavy Armored Unit destroyed 111.[21] By July 13, von Manstein's intelligence officers reckoned they had 24,000 prisoners and had destroyed 1,800 tanks.

Although Model lacked the new tanks that von Manstein deployed, he was not entirely without new weapons. He had the newly formed 563rd Heavy Antitank Unit, which went into action with the 9th Army for the first time. Composed of Ferdinand Porsche's cumbrous but deadly tank destroyers based on the Tiger tank chassis, the unit destroyed 320 Soviet tanks, and this despite the numerous mechanical difficulties that beset the new vehicles. As one of their commanders subsequently reported:

> One gun under Lieutenant Teriete destroyed 22 tanks in one engagement. The total number of tanks destroyed is high and the Ferdinand contributed substantially to the defense, just as with the penetration. One gun commander destroyed seven of the nine American-built tanks that approached him. The main gun is very good. It destroys every tank with one or two rounds, even the KV2 and the sloped American ones.[22]

This report calls attention to another often ignored fact: by July 1943 the Soviet armored situation was so critical that they were using American tanks, and as this report suggests, the Germans found their design to be noteworthy, despite subsequent Soviet claims as to their inferiority.[23]

What in effect was emerging as the shape of the battle by July 13 was the worst possible development for the Red Army. One of the elegant things about the pincer envelopment the Germans favored was that if one jaw succeeded, it would divert pressure from the other. As the Soviets surged forward toward Orel, they became increasingly vulnerable to a sweep from the south. In other words, Model's force became a sort of hinge, or pivot, for von Manstein's advance. If Model could hold off the Soviet offensive, the attacking Russians would find themselves deployed too far to the north of the bulge to be able to move to stop von Manstein's breakthrough.

Given that Model was bearing the brunt of the attack, this was going to be no mean feat. But at that point, the Luftwaffe, which thus far had been unable to maintain air supremacy over the battlefield, launched a major air-to-ground offensive in support of the hard-pressed Germans. This was an all-out effort that dwarfed the massive tactical air strikes of May 1940, as in the intervening years the air force had been steadily developing its ground attack capabilities.

The original ground attack aircraft, the dive-bomber, or Stuka, had an extremely sturdy airframe to enable it to withstand the force exerted when it pulled up out of its dive. The dive directly into the target below was responsible for the accuracy of the delivery (as opposed to the haphazard nature of level flight bomb release). However, the standard dive-bomber, the Junkers 87, designed in 1936 and first tested in 1937, was thus rather slow, and vulnerable to enemy fighters. It was effective only when the Luftwaffe controlled the airspace over the battlefield, and German designers were never able to come up with a successful replacement for this aging warhorse.

What they did manage to do, however, was to transform it from a dive-bomber into a tank killer. By 1943 the Ju 87G, armed with an extremely high-velocity 3.7 centimeter gun, was in action, as its chief enthusiast, Hans-Ulrich Rudel, had proved that armed with this weapon he could destroy a T-34 tank with one shot. It is a measure of how successful this new development was that over the course of the war Rudel was credited with destroying 519 Soviet tanks, incidentally flying more combat missions than any other pilot in the world.[24]

However, to return to the key moment at Kursk, as Zhukov launched his attack in the north, von Manstein was punching completely through the southern defensive positions on the other side of the salient. The breakthrough was the one aspect of the battle in which the new technology of mechanization transformed the exploitation phase: when von Manstein broke through the layered Soviet defenses in the south, there would be nothing much to stop him. Consequently, Zhukov would have to pull back or risk being surrounded himself. In that sense, Citadel was yet another nasty surprise: despite careful preparation and their allegedly superior intelligence regarding the Germans, the Soviet high command had misread the capabilities of the German forces on the southern flank.

So by July 11, Zhukov was in the unenviable position of having committed the bulk of his forces to destroy Model, only to discover that von Manstein was smashing through the southern flank of the bulge, posed to move on Voronezh and thus cut off not only the Soviet defenders in the salient itself, but the bulk of the armor committed in the north.

Although in most accounts of the fighting the Germans are seen as too weakened, too exhausted, for this maneuver to be a possibility, the combat records of the key units involved do not support this claim. As late as July 17, for example, the Grossdeutschland still had 107 tanks in action, of which forty-four were the new and potent (although breakdown-prone) Panthers.[25] Although the losses had been heavy enough for some units to be temporarily merged, the Germans were very fast at repairing their vehicles, and that, taken with the fact that the majority of the Tiger tanks were still running, suggests that the armored force necessary for the exploitation phase was largely intact.

At this key moment in the fight, von Manstein received unpleasant news. He was summoned to Hitler's headquarters, arriving on July 13. Here is von Manstein's account of the meeting:

He [Hitler] opened the conference by announcing that the Western Allies had landed in Sicily that day and that the situation there had taken an extremely serious turn. The Italians were not even attempting to fight and the island was likely to be lost. Since the next step might well be a landing in the Balkans or lower Italy, it was necessary to form new armies in Italy and the western Balkans. These forces must be found from the Eastern Front, so "Citadel" would have to be discontinued. . . . The commander of Central Army Group, Field-Marshal von Kluge, reported the Ninth Army was making no further headway and that he was having to deprive it of all its mobile forces to check the enemy's incursions into the Orel salient. There could be no question of continuing with "Citadel" or of resuming operations at a later date. Speaking for my own Army Group, I pointed out that the battle was now at its culminating point, and that to break it off at this moment would be tantamount to throwing a victory away.[26]

Implicit in von Manstein's reckoning was the idea that if what he called the "mobile reserves" of the Red Army were destroyed completely, the pressure on Orel and the 9th Army would obviously be relieved. The only Soviet forces left would have to disengage or be cut off by the German advance from the south.

It is hard to resist the inference that this conference was rigged. Von Kluge, who had never been enthusiastic about the operation, was already in a funk, overwhelmed and depressed. Autocratic and distant from the scene, he had already ordered Model to break off his offensive.[27] Model's absence from the conference is important. In January 1942 he had gotten into a nasty argument with Hitler about what the 9th Army needed in order to beat off the Soviet attacks around Rzhev, in which he essentially dared Hitler to make him do something he didn't want to do, and Hitler had backed down.[28]

It is impossible to believe that Model would not have sided with von Manstein. In fact, that was probably why he had not been invited. As was almost always the case, Hitler's summons meant he had made a decision that he was now decreeing. It was certainly possible to argue with him, as Model had successfully done before. All Model had to do was fight off the Soviet offensive until the breakthrough to the south relieved the pressure around Orel. Having battled the Red Army to a draw in the winter of 1942–1943 at Rzhev, under far worse conditions, he would most likely have succeeded.

The evidence suggests that von Manstein's appreciation of the situation was correct. The heavy armored units were still intact, and they had shredded the Soviet tank force. The Soviets subsequently admitted the loss of 4,253 tanks, 4,821 artillery pieces, and 1,563 aircraft during Kursk, the worst losses since the start of the war for any one operation.

As von Manstein's account makes clear, Hitler was not particularly upset by the loss of Sicily per se. He was looking ahead to the next Allied moves, and pessimistic about the Italians. It was now mid-July (1943). It would take months for one of the armored divisions to disengage and be shipped to Italy, the same situation that had prevailed after the Leibstandarte had been shipped to France and then moved back to the Eastern Front. A decision made after the Allies declared themselves by mounting another invasion would be far too late. Moreover, in Hitler's view, the Allies might well try to land in the Balkans and seize the Romanian oilfields. In consequence, he had multiple threats to consider, the support of his armchair generals in Berlin, and cover from Günther von Kluge. So he ordered Citadel broken off and the massive concentration of armor dispersed to meet threats real and imagined.

It is often said that journalists write the first draft of history.

Stalin went that aphorism one better: he was not only the chief actor, but he wrote the script. Kursk may well be the first battle in history where one side declared itself the winner from the start of the engagement.

How this myth developed is an interesting insight into how Stalin operated. From the start of the German offensive, Moscow mounted a surprisingly successful and surprisingly specific internal propaganda campaign. At the end of the first day's fighting, it was claimed that the Germans had only managed to "penetrate slightly into our defense lines," and that the Red Army had "crippled or destroyed 586 enemy tanks."[29] On July 6 the loss of 433 tanks was claimed; the next day, 530; by the 8th, the Red Army had gone over to the offensive and the Germans had lost 304 tanks, and on July 24 the "final liquidation of the German summer offensive" was announced: the Wehrmacht had 70,000 killed, and had lost 2,900 tanks.

These figures duly made their way into the historical record: the title of one widely read account of the battle is *The Tigers Are Burning*, in line with the Soviet claim that 700 of them were destroyed during the fighting.[30] Unfortunately for the argument, this claim founders in the face of an inconvenient detail. In July 1943 there were only 262 Tiger I tanks in existence, and fewer than 150 were deployed in Citadel.

In fact, Hitler's hopes for the success of his new weapons were hardly dashed. The Tigers, although used only in small numbers in fall 1942, had already proven themselves formidable weapons. On July 5, 1943, the 505th Heavy Armored Abteilung, numbering about three dozen Tiger tanks, destroyed forty-two T-34s; over the course of the fighting, nearly the whole month of July, the losses of all the heavy tank units involved came to around twenty vehicles.[31]

Although for decades all analyses of the battle were based on the assumption that the German armor was fatally crippled, given the German records, and even the official Soviet figures, it is more probable that it was the other way around. Curiously enough, despite the usual claims, the disposition of forces revealed by the map in the Soviet official history suggests that von Manstein's armored columns had nothing much standing between them and Voronezh; Khrushchev, generally the most realistic of the senior Soviet leaders, was convinced that was the case.[32]

Kursk was not a German victory. On the other hand, the claim that it was a defeat seems wide of the mark. The fact that Stalin crafted his story of a victorious defensive battle right from the start tends to raise suspicions as to how the outcome would be presented on the Soviet side. Although the Soviet defense was tenacious on the northern wing, that a battle consisting of a sequence of large-scale engagements fought over an area this size could be decided in a few days is highly unlikely. It is doubtful that Allied landings at Anzio and in Normandy could withstand this kind of scrutiny: in both cases weeks passed and the invasion forces were still stuck inside a narrow bridgehead.

Although no one knows precisely what was in Hitler's mind when he called off the offensive, there is no evidence to suggest that he was not telling von Manstein and von Kluge what he actually thought, just as he told Guderian what he thought in August 1941 when he observed that his generals knew nothing of economics and thus failed utterly to understand his objectives in the war against Stalin. The only way he could keep the Allies from overrunning Italy and the Balkans was to transfer troops there. Those troops would have to come from the eastern armies, and did.

So although the misleadingly named Battle of Kursk was in no sense a German battlefield defeat, Hitler's decision to protect his southern flanks against Allied threats played neatly enough into Stalin's tale. Citadel was the last of the three great German summer offensives in the east; the commanders there now lacked the resources to conduct the sort of powerful thrusts of the previous campaigns. They were reduced, in other words, to precisely the situation von Manstein had articulated, defensive jabs and parries that would forestall any serious Soviet penetration.

So it was easy enough for Stalin to stand the affair on its head, claim a great victory in a battle given a name that was irrelevant to the fighting. He was the supreme dictator, could rewrite history as he went along. What he couldn't do was pretend his armies were in Germany when they were still east of the Dnieper. Berlin was a long way off. It would take the Red Army almost two more years of desperate combat and millions of dead Russian soldiers to get there.

DEADLOCK: THE GREAT RETREAT

"It's not treachery or rascality or stupidity: it is just as at Ulm . . . it is . . ."—he seemed to be trying to find the right expression. "C'est . . . c'est du Mack. *Nous sommes Mackés*," he concluded.[1]

Prince Bilíbin

When Hitler got wind of the great Allied invasion force that was sailing toward Algeria (Operation Torch, November 8, 1942), he theorized about their objectives to his courtiers.

"The enemy will land in central Italy tonight. There he would meet with no resistance at all. There are no German troops there, and the Italians will run away. . . ." It would never have occurred to him not to associate such a landing operation with a coup. To put the troops on land in safe positions from which they could methodically spread out, to take no unnecessary risks, that was a strategy alien to him.[2]

As the telling phrase "it would never have occurred to him" makes clear, Albert Speer, the witness to this monologue, obviously intended it as an example of a fundamental weakness in Hitler's strategic thinking. Fair enough, and there has never been any

Soviet Offensives, 1943–1944

———— July 4, 1943	·······—··· August 19, 1944
·—·—·—· December 1, 1943	········· December 31, 1944
– – – – April 30, 1944	

shortage of adjectives when it came to describing the scope of Hitler's alleged aims.

As we have seen, Hitler boasted that no one would ever know what he was thinking. But it is possible to divine how he thought about strategy by analyzing key statements. One of the more interesting deductions to be made from Hitler's exposition on the Allied invasion of North Africa is the extent to which he paid the British and the Americans the compliment of attributing to them the mirror image of his own strategic vision. A "methodical" plan that takes "no unnecessary risks" can be characterized as predictable and unimaginative. It is also a recipe for needlessly prolonging the suffering of a war.

From the very first Hitler had demanded bold strokes that bypassed the normal notions of strategy as the professionals of his military conceived them, aerial assaults against the Netherlands and Belgium in May 1940, the thrust into the Balkans in April 1941, the airborne invasion of Crete in May of the same year, as well as the expansion of the original objectives of Barbarossa. Complications set in because the objectives Hitler set out were alien to the thinking of most professional officers. Hitler not only demanded imaginative solutions to problems, but frequently the problems he wanted solved were outside the comprehension of his subordinates.

As Tolstoy's use of the hapless Austrian General Mack illustrates perfectly, cleverness can become its own trap. So it was in July 1943, when Hitler announced he was stopping Citadel, not because he was particularly concerned about the loss of Sicily, but because he had leapt to the conclusion that the Allies would launch precisely the sort of bold stroke he had expected a year earlier, invading Italy or the Balkans.

Von Manstein saw that as confirmation of his essential correctness in arguing that the offensive should have been mounted in May: he reckoned that by mid-July the Red Army already would have been beaten in the field. Whether von Manstein was right is an interesting question with no easy answer, but Hitler grasped the crux of the matter. It would take several months to get the heavy armored units into Italy and the Balkans, even without their equipment. If there were to be German units in position to resist an Allied invasion, they would have to begin redeployment immediately, and the Germans would have to hope that the Allies waited a few months before mounting their third major offensive.

By attributing to the Allies the same bold moves that he himself favored, Hitler did more than pay them a compliment. He did himself in, and in that peculiarly military way that Tolstoy described, a sort of strategic version of outsmarting yourself. His concerns about an Allied offensive in the western Balkans and Italy led him to deploy German units to both areas.

Unfortunately for the commanders of the eastern army groups, Hitler moved more than men. As the war in Russia had evolved, the Wehrmacht recapitulated the decentralization and fragmentation that had characterized its organization in the previous war. While the elite units in the Wehrmacht and Waffen-SS deployed the formidable Tiger tanks in 1942, the bulk of those vehicles were organized into Schwere Panzer Abteilungen, heavy armored units, as was also the case with the powerful tank destroyers based on the Tiger tank. Like the super-divisions, the Abteilungen had an impact on the battlefield that greatly exceeded their size. The first of the Tiger 1 units, in service with Army Group North after May 1942, destroyed 1,400 Soviet tanks during its career. Together with the armor of the Grossdeutschland, it was responsible for much of the success the Wehrmacht had in stopping Mars in 1942, and in von Manstein's operations in the first half of 1943.[3]

As previously mentioned, one of the reasons Mars was such a brutal affair for the Wehrmacht was that Hitler, concerned about another bold stroke after the disastrous Dieppe raid, had ordered the Waffen-SS Leibstandarte to France. Given the hitting power of the super-units and the heavy armored Abteilungen, transferring even one of them to another theater had a dramatic impact. When Hitler ordered the formation of the 424th for action in Tunisia in fall 1942 and moved the Leibstandarte to France, he cut the heavy armor available to the three Eastern Front commanders by a third.

Now, faced with a much more real prospect in the Mediterranean theater, he did the same thing, sending one of his precious heavy tank units (the 508th) to Italy and essentially disbanded the Waffen-SS armored corps that had been the heart of von Manstein's spring offensive at Kharkov with the aim of shipping it south as well.

The effect was to cripple the eastern army groups. The problem was not just armor. German industry was not able to equip the German army with the armored, tracked, and wheeled vehicles it needed to be a truly mechanized force. However, it was capable of producing enough of these vehicles to equip its elite units, whose combination of firepower and mobility had enabled them to check the ponderous and slow-moving Soviet offensives.

The army high command's concept of a strategic defensive in the east, its ability to deliver what von Manstein had termed "backhand strokes," depended heavily on being able to move these core units to threatened sectors. So when Hitler began stripping them away, he not only ended any chance for offensive operations, he crippled the army's defensive capabilities as well. Without the powerful armored units, army group commanders lacked the mobile armored reserves that could snuff out Soviet units that broke through.

This need was becoming all the more pressing since Hitler had already been picking away at the Luftwaffe, deploying its units to the south long before he began to worry about an actual invasion. As a result, the Germans no longer had the absolute mastery of the air that they had enjoyed in the two years of the war, which had enabled them to annihilate Soviet units that otherwise would have broken through and moved to exploit their success.

Unlike his French counterpart in May 1940, who was convinced that he had no air force whatsoever, the perception of the German foot soldier in the east was that the mere appearance of German planes overhead would send the Soviet aircraft scuttling off. However, by mid-1943 their appearance could no longer be relied on. The Luftwaffe was more overstretched than the army. Its transport capabilities had never recovered from the losses during 1940–41; nor was it able to replace its aging fleet of cargo planes with designs that were adequate for the tasks at hand.

Although following Stalingrad, Zhukov and the other senior Soviet commanders had managed to dissuade Stalin from his kamikaze assaults, the lull was only temporary. Stalin fully intended for the defensive phase of Kursk to be exploited in exactly the way that Zhukov had proposed in the planetary operations. The victorious outcome would be followed up by two massive offensive operations, Kutuzov on the northern flank, and Rumiantsev on the southern.

Zhukov's attacks on Model's 9th Army were driving the Germans back. But the Germans had a defensive position, somewhat misleadingly called the Hagen line, along the west bank of the Dnieper River. So von Kluge, under heavy pressure from Zhukov, withdrew to that line, which he reached in good order by mid-August.

Now Hitler's transfers began to bite in earnest. The Soviet left hook after Citadel, Rumiantsev, aimed to smash all the way through to the Black Sea. That operation began on July 17, forcing von Manstein to give ground. Without the Waffen-SS armored corps, there was little he could do other than emulate von Kluge, retreating step by step, and exacting a high price in the process.

By August, von Kluge was determined to retreat rather than let his forces be drawn into costly defensive battles. His wariness was given new impetus: Berlin shifted his five most powerful divisions to von Manstein, so that he could block the expected Soviet offensive in the south and withdraw the Romanian and German armies that would once again have been trapped had the Soviet drive succeeded. Von Kluge now demonstrated the passive-aggressive cleverness that had earned him the malicious although probably justified sobriquet of "Der kluge Hans," clever Hans. He warned Berlin that without those units he would be unable to stand off the Soviet attack, and then used that excuse as the justification for a series of retreats. By September 17, the Red Army had advanced to Bryansk. Smolensk was abandoned a week later, so Center was now holding a defensive line, known as Panther, in Belorussia, roughly along the northern reaches of the Dnieper River.

Stalin's determination to remain perpetually on the offensive had not slackened. A new offensive began on October 3. However, von Kluge, who now apparently felt that events had justified his inclination to retreat the last three months, dug in. Although there were some minor successes, this last Soviet offensive of the fall slowly petered out as the peculiar combination of mud and ice that characterizes October in Belorussia set in.

The weather did in von Kluge as well. On October 28, his driver lost control of his vehicle, and in the resulting accident the commander of Center was badly injured. He was replaced by Ernst Busch, and did not return to the Eastern Front. When he was recalled to active duty in late June 1944, it was to assume command in the west.[4]

Meanwhile, von Manstein, now in command of what was once again known as Army Group South, managed to stabilize the shaky German position in Ukraine, although given the force he had available, and the length of the front, his only real option was to prepare for further withdrawals in the face of the next Soviet attack.

However, Ukraine, even in October, was a much better place for maneuvering than Belorussia. By the end of that month, the Soviets had broken through the misleadingly termed defensive line on the west bank of the Dnieper in an offensive centered around Dnepropetrovsk, which they seized, advancing over 100 kilometers on a broad front, but creating another dangerous bulge.

A further advance, or an offensive launched out of the salient, would cut off the anchor point of the Army Group South's position in Ukraine, the line they had been holding along the Mius River as it flowed into the Black Sea. So von Manstein launched a limited counterattack in mid-October that annihilated the Soviet 5th Guards Army, driving them back and destroying some 350 armored vehicles and taking 5,000 prisoners.[5]

Stalin demanded more offensives, and the Russians obediently organized themselves for their third midwinter offensive. As with the previous ones, operations would begin in December, when the ground was frozen. Not by coincidence, the fighting tapered off while Stalin was in Tehran in November, meeting with Roosevelt and Churchill.

By late summer 1943 the Soviet script of a steady stream of offensive operations, each one pushing the Germans back further, was highly developed, precisely defined by Stalin in his November speech celebrating the twenty-sixth anniversary of the October Revolution. The extent to which its opening paragraphs defined all subsequent accounts of the war is notable:

> Shortly after the October days of last year [1942] our troop[s] passed over to the offensive and struck a fresh powerful blow at the Germans, first at Stalingrad, in the Caucasus, in the area in the middle reaches of the Don, and then, at the beginning of 1943, at Velikie Luki, at Leningrad, and in the area of Rzhev and Vyazma. Since then the Red Army has never let the initiative out of its hands. Its blows throughout the summer of this year became increasingly strong, its military mastery grew with every month. Since then our troops

have won big victories and the Germans have suffered one defeat after the other.[6]

The rhetoric, amply supported by the official Soviet claims of a series of successful offensives, each one inflicting crippling blows on their enemy, is to a great extent given credence by the highly subjective accounts of the Germans themselves, who increasingly began to see the Eastern Front as one Thermopylae after another.

To read what is by far the best autobiographical novel of the Eastern Front, Guy Sajer's *The Forgotten Soldier*, is to be immersed in month after month of endless suffering and calamity, in which ragged and grossly underequipped bands of Germans heroically battled the Soviet masses in a tragic struggle whose brutality and suffering dwarfs that of such classics as Erich Maria Remarque's pacifist fiction *All Quiet on the Western Front*. This meme, albeit on a considerably less emotional and compelling level, is duly repeated by military historians.

The record of Wehrmacht losses tells a different story. Expressed as a percentage of the armored force (thus accounting for its growing size), losses in 1943 came to 13 percent, including Stalingrad and Tunisia. To put that figure in perspective: in the offensives of 1939–1940 armored losses had been almost 10 percent, and in 1941, 8 percent. In 1942 losses had come to 5 percent; and in 1944 losses were still only 10 percent. Personnel losses, which track the losses of armor, do not support the apocalypse of the final period of the war. On the contrary, the average death toll was slightly higher during the opening months of Barbarossa (1941) than it was during 1944.

Given the dramatic increase in equipment losses from 1942 to 1943, it is easy to see why German soldiers and their officers felt their losses were heavy: by comparison they had more than doubled, and from July 1943 on, the Germans were conducting nothing but fighting retreats. Moreover, everyone concerned was writing in hindsight, knowing that the war had been lost and

Germany defeated. No matter how honest the chronicler is, that retrospective vision always contaminates the story. In the case of the Eastern Front, that contamination was greatly exacerbated by the strenuously vetted paeans of triumph that emerged from Soviet sources from July 1943 to the present day.

Moreover, the relatively scanty photographic evidence we have conforms to the model suggested by the numbers. Candid photographs from 1944 are scarce, but in general they support the image that dominates the photographs from 1943. German officers and men, far from looking beleaguered and overwhelmed, are smiling cheerfully into the camera, often posing on their tanks, which in many cases appear to be brand-new examples of the latest models. The few images of larger groups reveal heavily armed soldiers and armored columns vastly more potent than comparable images from May–June 1940.[7]

Although this contrast between objective evidence and subjective impressions appears to be a contradiction, it reflects the difficulties of evaluating combat, difficulties that became increasingly evident in modern warfare. The clipped but eloquent words of one exasperated American officer to his commanders in an earlier war sum up the problem perfectly: "'losses are heavy' may mean anything. Percentages or numbers are desired."[8]

From the point of view of the average soldier and his commanders in the field, this confusion is understandable. The retrospective accounts of the surviving German generals are a different matter. They were of course unlike their Soviet counterparts, and free to say what they wished, and they would have been less than human if they had not indulged themselves, taking no responsibility for failure and patting themselves on the back for successes, whether real or imagined.

Thus one thread runs through every account: Hitler was to blame. At some level, given his wickedness, everyone wants to believe that is true, and at some level it is. But as we have seen, many of the claims made by the surviving generals are extremely disingenuous, and many of Hitler's military decisions were quite sound. One distinguished historian puts the matter fairly:

> Anyone reading the memoirs of the German generals and field marshals might conclude not only that Stalin was able to arrange for it to snow and become freezing cold only on the German side of the front, while the Red Army enjoyed balmy weather, but also that any successes attained by Germany were due to the brilliance of the generals and all the defeats the result of Hitler's unwillingness to listen to their invariably wise advice.[9]

The other obvious justification is the perfect complement to Stalin's boasting: we lost because we were outnumbered, our brilliant successes were achieved in the face of overwhelming odds.

Thus every account details in often tedious fashion the extent to which German divisions, or ad hoc battle groups, had to fight off whole Soviet armies, thus reinforcing Stalin's claim of his vast resources. And now that the Great Retreat had begun in earnest, this notion became set in stone.

Stalin was perfectly entitled to claim the credit, but the great shift he spoke of was partially a function of his willingness to slaughter his soldiers for what in the First World War had been cynically and accurately referred to by the French as engagements for the sake of the communiqué. The main reason for the retreat was Hitler, who had shifted his priorities from the east to the south and to France. Although subjectively, the end result for the German armies in the east was a great weakening of strength, this weakening was mostly (not entirely) a function of the extent to which Hitler was steadily stripping away their resources.

In point of fact, as remarked early in this chapter, the average strength of the German armored force, a key indicator of the armaments industry's progress, was steadily increasing. In May

1943, with the African losses, Germany had only 3,195 tanks (in both quantitative and qualitative terms that number exceeded the deployment of May 1940). But by October, despite the allegedly crippling blows inflicted by the victorious Red Army, the number had risen to 4,460; six months later it was nearly 6,000.

The army was definitely sustaining losses, but the average monthly losses in 1943 were lower than in the first months of the war, and hardly different from the averages for the previous year. The Wehrmacht had yet to see its annual death toll in the east exceed half a million, while on the Soviet side the number of soldiers killed in action in 1943 was higher than in 1942: nearly 7.5 million men as opposed to seven million. Of course the official Soviet data makes a different claim, but even if the official figure for 1943 is accepted, it comes to almost 2.5 million men killed or missing.

The Soviet official records reveal a steady stream of offensive operations, thus fulfilling Stalin's constant mantra of relentless attack. The names chosen for the July offensives, recalling as they did images of the wars of the Napoleonic era, were clearly intended as a reminder of those bygone days of triumphant glory.

On paper, both in the official documents locked away in Moscow and in the stream of literature that followed, the result was a steady Soviet surge that ended with the victorious Red Army raising the flag in the ruins of Berlin. The Germans, exhausted by their successive defeats, were sent reeling back in a series of great hammer blows.

Officially, there were no fewer than fourteen separate offensives in the last half of 1943. On paper the amount of territory recaptured was impressive, and Stalin boasted about it in his anniversary speech of 1943. After Stalin's death and eclipse, Soviet historians deconstructed his claims, making the argument that the offensives had been sequential, and thus revealed some degree of strategic acumen: at each point the Red Army brought an overwhelming superiority of force to bear, which thus explained its triumphs.

However, this narrative was simply another aspect of the Soviet pseudo-reality that prevailed even after Stalin's demise. In actual fact Stalin reverted to his initial concept, ordering up continuous attacks at every point on the front, and thus guaranteeing that the Red Army would never be able to bring to bear the manpower and the armor to deliver a truly crushing blow. Although the Soviet dictator may well have believed that the planetary operations of the winter and the Kutuzov and Rumiantsev exploitations after Kursk had been triumphs, they were successful only because the German commanders preferred a fighting withdrawal, were willing to trade off territory for the integrity of the beleaguered combat units insofar as was possible.[10]

If the planning and execution of the Soviet offensives was pedestrian, the casualties were not. They were, as usual, heavy. As a result, Stalin's new offensive operations were on a much smaller scale. Six of the operations involved less than half a million men, and only four involved more than a million. The average numbers committed to the four large-scale operations (Smolensk, Donbass, Chernigov-Poltava, and Lower Dnieper) were substantially lower than the large-scale operations of the past.

In line with the official story that the Red Army was getting better and the Germans were getting weaker, Soviet casualties appeared to be declining. As we have seen, Soviet casualty figures, like Soviet claims about German losses, have little relation to reality. But even accepting the official accounting for the dead and the missing as being barely half a million men in the last months of 1943, the Germans were still winning the exchange rate handily.

Subjectively, of course, the situation after July 1943 was a dramatic, perhaps even traumatic, change for the Wehrmacht, which up until Stalingrad had seen itself as moving inexorably from one victory to the next. The ability to check the Russians at every turn, regardless of the number of men and tanks they threw into battle, only reinforced that perception. In his Secret Speech, Khrushchev spoke of this problem:

> Before the war, our press and all our political-educational work was characterized by its bragging tone: When an enemy violates the holy Soviet soil, then for every blow of the enemy we will answer with three, and we will battle the enemy on his soil and we will win without much harm to ourselves. But these positive statements were not based in all areas on concrete facts, which would actually guarantee the immunity of our borders.[11]

As everyone listening to the speech knew, the reality was horribly, tragically different. For the first years of the war, it was the Germans who could rightfully brag about their prowess (as well as the intriguing ratio of 3:1 Khrushchev mentions).

But in the space of the first six months of 1943, the German army underwent a severe trauma. As the hard data shows, the trauma was not so much physical as psychological: the surrender of the 6th Army at Stalingrad and the army in Tunisia. Moreover, regardless of whether his reasons were right or wrong, regardless of the situation on the ground in July 1943, when Hitler halted the Citadel offensive he left his soldiers deeply frustrated, and stripping them of their armored reserves hardly helped.

Subjectively, then, all the accounts of the war began to focus on the inexhaustible Soviet manpower pool, and how beleaguered and outnumbered the Germans were. Conversely, those first six months of 1943 enabled Stalin to resume his bragging, and he did so.

So from mid-1943 on, the war in the east assumes a certain schizophrenic character. Objectively speaking, the Germans were exacting a heavy toll on the attacking Russians. By its own accounting, the Red Army lost over 5,000 tanks in the second half of 1943, over twice as many as the Germans lost. Certainly, the psychological importance of regaining lost territory is not to be discounted. But Stalin was frittering away his resources with these constant offensives, just as he had done earlier in the war. The only difference was that now his troops were actually advancing and able to hold on to their gains.

As a result, it is assumed that after Kursk, the Red Army had entered the modern era, had learned how to conduct offensive operations. The deliberate pace was seen, approvingly, as a sign of the army's increasing expertise, and when the losses were noted, they were largely dismissed because, after all, the Germans were losing heavily as well, and unlike Stalin, could not afford the losses.

It would be difficult to find a finer example of innumeracy. This appreciation of the situation defied demography. Stalin could not afford to sustain losses of more than 2:1 without eventually running out of cannon fodder.[12]

As we noted earlier, the Red Army had started forming female units as early as December 1942, and the following months saw the deployment of nearly a million women in the Red Army. Since the American and British armies used women in auxiliary roles, it is easy to assume that the Soviets did the same. That assumption would be false: Soviet women served as snipers, fighter and bomber pilots, machine gunners, and tank drivers. Although the specific figures are unknown, there is no dispute about the use of women in combat in the Red Army.[13] As the months went by, the ranks of the combat forces were sustained by adding old men, teenagers, and men who would have been judged medically unfit in any other military. Again, although this combing out of the civilian population occurred in all the other armies in both world wars, to assume that there was an equivalent process going on in the Reich would be an error.[14]

Stalin was not innumerate. As we shall see later, he took care to ensure that the numbers supported his claims, arresting those who failed to come up with the proper data. But Hitler apparently understood the basics himself, and thus his insistence that the Germans expend their energies in killing lots of Russians.[15] Eventually Stalin's reserves would be exhausted. That was particularly the case if he kept frittering them away as he was doing.

The problem, which even Stalin was beginning to understand, was that once the retreat began, the Germans were willing to cede enemy territory to gain the upper hand. The mobility of armies had increased dramatically since 1914, but the distances were formidable obstacles in and of themselves, particularly for the primitive logistical system of the Red Army. From Kiev to the frontier of the Reich was over 800 kilometers, from Smolensk to Warsaw twice that. Moreover, as the Germans retreated, not only did their interior lines of communication grow shorter, but the front they had to hold decreased, so they would no longer be spread so thin.

Other than the negative impact of continuous retreat on morale, the chief disadvantage to this strategy was that the natural obstacles of the terrain did not give the defense the advantages that it automatically had in Sicily, Italy, the Balkans, and Normandy. There were no mountains north of the Tatras and the Carpathians, and the rivers were undependable—at some times of the year impassable, at other times, when they froze over, almost irrelevant. Nor did any part of the area have the dense network of towns and villages that afforded natural strongpoints. In 1941, Stalin had ordered everything the Red Army left behind to be destroyed, which hardly improved the situation militarily for either side.

Consequently if there was a breakthrough, the defenders could easily find themselves trapped, just as the Soviet troops had experienced from the very first of the war, and the Germans as well. One of the reasons von Manstein was able to destroy the encircling Soviet forces west of Dnepropetrovsk in October 1943 was that by now such operations were almost routine: both sides aimed at envelopment and encirclement. Tactically the war had thus deteriorated into a series of repetitions on both sides.

One of the unit histories of the Grossdeutschland provides us with an illuminating description of the German tactics during this penultimate phase of the war:

> Defensively, the Germans adopted the World War I tactic of holding the front lines with small numbers of troops who then withdrew unnoticed to the main line of resistance. When the Soviets had spent their fire on abandoned trenches and their troops and tanks were out in the open, artillery would open up on them from carefully worked out fields of fire, isolating them from their support and cutting off their withdrawal.[16]

Of course the situation rarely worked out quite so perfectly, but up until the end of the war, Soviet tanks and infantry were so poorly coordinated, their operations so rarely synchronized, that their advances were nothing more than a series of lurches with noticeable pauses. The erratic nature of their offensives thus allowed for further German retreats.

Consequently, German personnel losses began to decline from their July 1943 high: December losses were only a little over 30,000 (dead), and had stabilized. Although the Germans were steadily losing territory, they were hardly being routed.

By this point, two years into the war with Stalin, both Hitler and his generals, regardless of their differences about strategy and tactics, understood their adversary very well. Stalin would keep attacking until he had no more soldiers left, and whatever their initial successes, his commanders would never be able to exploit them. His resources were being augmented daily by the vast flow of British and American aid coming into the USSR. In the first half of 1943, Stalin had received 1,775,000 tons of aid; in the second half of the year he received 3,274,000 tons, a considerable increase.[17] Given that aid, and his willingness to see his citizenry slaughtered, the struggle would be bitter.

But by standing on the defensive in the east, the Germans were reverting to a strategy that had served them very well in the previous war, trading off enemy territory that was of relatively little value, a tactic that enabled them to control the tempo of the enemy advance, seizing opportune moments and inflicting crippling losses in return. Despite tanks and airplanes, the Red Army of 1943 was the same slow-moving and cumbrous entity that the British and French armies of the previous war had been. Now that Hitler had lost the chance to seize the Don basin and Stalin's oil supplies, he was content to fight to a draw.

So although historians are more or less correct in the idea that in the first half of the war Stalin was able to check Hitler, keep him from attaining his key objectives in the south, by the same token, logically speaking, it has to be said that in the second half of the war Hitler was just as successful in holding off Stalin. It was only in the final two or three months of the war that the front imploded, as the Allies pressed forward from the west across the Rhine.

Or, to put it another way, in less than twelve months, Hitler had seized almost all of what historically was European Russia and Ukraine. In June 1943, a year later, Stalin had recovered hardly any of it. His achievement had been to keep Hitler from chewing off still more. Given that the last turn of the screw would have ended the war, this was no mean feat, but there is a reason we differentiate victories and defeats from draws. The situation in mid-July 1943 was a draw. Hitler was checked but Stalin had not been able to achieve any more than that.

Unfortunately for Moscow, the midwinter offensives of 1943–1944 were in every way a repeat of the last six months of the prior year. By the end of December 1943, the Red Army had advanced from its line outside Orel all the way past Kiev, slightly over 400 kilometers. Kiev was recaptured at the end of December. South of the ancient Ukrainian city, however, the German defense hugged the Dnieper intermittently down to the Mius defensive line and thence to Taganrog.

The recapture of Smolensk had relieved Stalin's concerns about the safety of Moscow, so he now authorized a major strike into Ukraine. The Russians threw most of their armored force in this offensive, which dragged on until the end of April 1944. By that month the Germans had been expelled from Ukraine, had lost Odessa and the Crimea, and had retreated back to the old Soviet frontier of August 1939. But the Red Army lost about two thirds of its tank force and half of the soldiers it had committed to the operation.[18] Such losses were repeated all throughout the winter and spring of 1944: in a five-day period in late winter, the tanks belonging to the German 503rd Heavy Tank Unit and the 11th Armored Regiment destroyed 267 Soviet tanks, at the cost of seven of their vehicles.[19]

At the same time, Stalin mounted an attack on Army Group North. Von Küchler had been systematically denuded of resources in order to support von Kluge's October battles, and at the same time his best combat division, the 1st Prussian, was sent to support von Manstein. So the only military solution to this problem that von Küchler could see was to do what his colleagues in the south had done, withdraw. Unfortunately, the 18th Army commander, Georg Lindemann, disagreed, and Hitler, sensing there was genuine difference of opinion, insisted that North hold fast. Given that a third of von Küchler's strength consisted of air force ground personnel, not line infantry, and that he essentially had no reserves, this was an impossible task.

The upshot of the fighting was that von Küchler's chief of staff ordered a withdrawal in his absence; Hitler belatedly approved it, but von Küchler was sacked, and replaced by Model, who then did exactly what his predecessor had been arguing for and retreated to what was rather optimistically called the Panther defensive line, a position that ran from the Baltic and Lake Peipus down through Vitebsk.

The siege of Leningrad was finally over, and by Soviet standards a rather economical victory, as hardly more than a third of the soldiers dedicated to the operation had been put out of action and only enough tanks lost to equip two mechanized corps.

Although the Germans could have maintained their defensive position along the Mius and Kalmius Rivers indefinitely in the face of frontal attacks, in the face of Soviet advances to the north, they abandoned the position, withdrawing to the west. This withdrawal left their units in an extremely vulnerable situation, strung out along southern Ukraine. By the time the Soviet offensive began, after Christmas, the Germans had managed to retreat far enough to the west and south so that the Soviet offensive was more on the order of an advance than an attack.

There was one exception. The German 8th Army was still occupying a salient stretching roughly from Cherkassy to Korsun. Zhukov saw the opportunity for another Stalingrad operation, albeit on a smaller scale, and the forces of the 1st and 2nd Ukrainian Fronts mounted attacks on both sides of the salient. By January 28, 1944, the resulting Soviet drives had the Germans surrounded.

Von Manstein was just as conscious of the potential as Zhukov. In a series of ferocious attacks, he relieved the pressure on the encircled German troops, most of whom were then able to escape back toward the German lines. By February 16, the battle was over. The Cherkassy pocket was hailed as another great Soviet victory. Moscow claimed to have killed 55,000 Germans, captured 15,000 more, and destroyed over 500 German tanks.[20] Like most Soviet claims, this one was highly implausible: the figures for losses in both areas exceeded total German losses for the entire Eastern Front as well as Italy for the period in question.

Official Soviet losses came to 80,188, but no armor, yet another illustration of how such data should be regarded.

Although the Red Army units moved to encircle the Germans much more expeditiously than at Stalingrad, von Manstein's armor moved much faster as well, suggesting that if he had had the forces at his disposal the year earlier that he had now, Stalingrad might have turned out differently. Not that it mattered: Stalin demanded victories and he was being given them. The real significance of Cherkassy was that it represented one of the very last times the Germans were able to assemble their mobile reserves in order to mount a major counterattack.

Von Manstein was essentially at the end of his tether with Hitler. So was von Kleist, commander of Army Group A. The two men had cooperated in the evacuation of the Kuban Peninsula in the fall, thus ensuring that the German forces in the south would be able to fight on; their encirclement and annihilation would have been far worse than Stalingrad and Tunisia combined.[21] All through 1943, von Manstein had sparred with the dictator, and although he never admitted it, it appears that Hitler's Citadel decision was a turning point for von Manstein as well. After his desperate relief efforts at Cherkassy he went to Hitler, who was now at the Obersalzberg, and argued with him about his insistence that no ground be given. Hitler was adamant.

By the time von Manstein returned to the front, yet another major German force, the 1st Armored Army, had been cut off. So von Manstein went back to Hitler and said that he would resign if Hitler did not authorize a breakout. Hitler gave in, and Hans Hube, the 1st Army commander, fought his way back to the shrinking German lines, eventually reaching their relative safety on April 6.

The situation was roughly the same for von Kleist, although he assumed the responsibility and gave the orders that saved the 6th and 8th Armies from encirclement, ordering them to withdraw from their precarious positions on the Bug River. Hitler, faced with yet another fait accompli, authorized the withdrawal on March 27.

On March 30, Hitler summoned von Manstein and von Kleist to his mountain retreat, gave them medals, congratulated them, and relieved them both of their commands. The interchange was curious as well as surprisingly cordial. Von Kleist told Hitler that his recommendation was that he come to terms with Stalin. Hitler's answer is revealing: there was no need to do so, because the Red Army was rapidly being used up.[22]

Von Manstein was replaced by Walter Model, and Army Group South became Army Group North Ukraine. Ferdinand Schörner, a tough tactician and National Socialist known for his ruthlessness, replaced von Kleist at what was now named Army Group South Ukraine.

Despite his toughness, Schörner was as much a professional officer as any of the others. In February he had personally led the 40th Armored Corps (which, together with other units had been hastily redesignated Kampfgruppe Schörner) across their exposed positions on the eastern bank of the Dnieper at Nikopol. Given the situation, this was no mean accomplishment. It demonstrated that Schörner was a realist about the situation: he would willingly surrender territory to save his men so they could fight another day.

However, in April he was forced to accede to Hitler's determination to fight for the Crimea, where the Red Army attacked on April 8. Two days later the Germans and Romanians were falling back on Sevastopol, so Schörner pulled a von Manstein: accompanied by the commander of the 17th Army, Erwin Jänecke, he went to the Obersalzberg to lobby for a general withdrawal. The result was the same: Hitler held back, Schörner tried to buck up the defenders, Jänecke was sacked, and by May 8, Hitler finally gave in, allowed a withdrawal, but demanded that the successive 17th Army commanders be court-martialed. Presumably if Hitler had listened to his army group commander, the entire force would have been saved, although the most recent accounts, by Romanian scholars, suggest that the whole matter is considerably more complicated than was initially made out. No one really knows whether Hitler's decision was totally wrong or partly right.[23]

As a result, despite their supposed victories, by May 1944, the Red Army was by no means poised on the threshold of victory: that would depend on the success of the next major offensive.

Not that Stalin waited. On the contrary, he was shrewdly aware of the importance of claiming triumph after triumph. He had begun celebrating his apocryphal victories while the Battle of Kursk was still going on, orchestrating the news releases so they revealed a great German defeat, and then crowning his achievement with a formal public celebration.

> Stalin jovially asked Antonov and Shemenko: "Do you read military history?" . . . Stalin . . . went on: "In ancient times, when troops won victories, all the bells would be rung in honor of the comrades and their troops. It wouldn't be a bad idea for us to signify victories more impressively." . . . Stalin . . . punctiliously worked out the salutes to be given for each victory.[24]

Shortly thereafter, on August 5, 1943, with the recapture of Orel and Belgorod, Stalin had an artillery salvo fired in a sign of victory. As most churches had been closed down, their bells long since converted to scrap, this was the best thing available.

There was one war Stalin could easily win, and that was the war for world opinion. From August 1943 on, he never failed to seize the opportunity to announce yet another victorious offensive, yet another crushing German defeat.

Stalin was certainly entitled to take the credit in public for checking Hitler's advance, and the Russian people were entitled to learn news from the front that was both true and concrete, after two years of obfuscation and fantasy. However, events after the end of Citadel were not nearly as encouraging as the artillery salvo might suggest.

When Hitler told von Kluge and von Manstein he was stopping the offensive and moving troops to the Balkans and Italy, the field marshals set about organizing a series of withdrawals, forcing the Russians to battle their way through Ukraine and toward the old frontiers.

The strangely erratic and halting nature of these post-Kursk Soviet offensives tends to be obscured by the undeniable fact that the Germans were being rolled back, nor were the Germans able to hang on to the best defensive position in Ukraine, the west bank of the Dnieper. However, the reason for that abandonment had little to do with any Soviet initiative; rather it was because von Kluge had to send five divisions to von Manstein so he could extricate the German forces in southern Ukraine. Consequently von Kluge lacked the troops to defend his position. But the Soviet advance masked the lost opportunity. Von Kluge failed to hold the Dnieper, but, further south, von Manstein still managed to retreat safely.

The failure to execute the potential of what the original plan for Saturn had envisioned was a serious failure. Giving the Germans the time to organize (or regroup) was a mistake, often with fatal consequences for many of their opponents. In that sense, Uranus had been either a shrewd master stroke or a lucky shot in the dark: it cut off the 6th Army and deprived them of any room to maneuver, or to extricate themselves.

But Uranus was essentially a unique operation. Afterward, Zhukov returned to the by now predictable technique of massing forces for a great hammer blow that always succeeded in a breakthrough, but was never able to move on to any sort of true exploitation. He could envelop the Germans, but as Nikopol and Cherkassy showed, envelopment was not in and of itself enough.

Paulus had been willing to quit, but his fellow commanders were made of a different mettle. Von Manstein had estimated that during his abortive Citadel offensive, his troops had won the exchange ratio to the tune of 4:1; even using the rather dubious Soviet official data, that exchange ratio held throughout the rest of 1943. The Germans were just as successful at killing their enemy in retreat as in attack.

The Soviets seemed to be learning little about combat tactics. Meanwhile, despite the Germans' growing feeling of panic as they were forced into retreat after retreat, actual losses after Citadel peaked in August 1943 and then began to decline, reaching a low in December. The losses in deaths for 1943 were the same as for 1942, to the point of being statistically insignificant.

One reason for the sudden slowing of the pace of losses was probably the lack of basic resources for the Red Army. As noted earlier, the forces available in fall 1942 for Zhukov's grand offensive operations suggest that the Soviet tank force, despite the astounding production figures, was only some fraction of what was allegedly leaving the factories. Most of that had been lost by May 1943, as we have seen in the preceding chapter, despite the hordes of tanks emerging from Soviet factories in 1943. At Kharkov in March and at Kursk in July, the Germans were noticing more and more American vehicles, which suggests that once again the Red Army was short of tanks.

There had never been any serious attention paid to the movement of infantry, artillery, and supplies by truck in the Red Army. In the constant retreats of the first two years that lack had been masked by the simple fact that as they retreated, the Soviets were more and more able to depend on interior lines of supply, notably railroads. One basic reason for the slow tempo of Soviet offensives was the need to build up matériel in support, and the lack of trucks to move supplies from railheads to the troops poised for the attack.

Once the tanks broke through, there was no easy way for the

infantry to follow them, and both components found themselves on their own, without the steady stream of supplies and heavy artillery they needed to consolidate their advance. Consequently, the exploitation phase of any breakthrough was limited to the speed with which the average soldier could advance on his own two feet.

The vast flow of Allied equipment was beginning to have an impact. But the fact that Studebaker and Willys became words with which every Russian of that generation was familiar is a telling reminder of the fact that the Red Army was essentially dependent on imported trucks. Given the voracious appetite of modern armies for mechanized transport, imports could not meet Russian needs.

Then there is the curious fact that Stalin apparently began to lose interest in the immediate direction of the war, increasingly satisfied by his generals bringing him news of triumphs and successes. The one technique he had impressed on them since July 1941 was to attack. So as long as they continued to do that, they could hardly be faulted, and since the Germans were slowly withdrawing, it was easy to proclaim the success of each offensive.

However, by the start of 1944, Stalin was either gradually realizing that these small efforts were not going to succeed, was impressed by the gains of the Ukrainian offensive, or, most likely, was beginning to give ground to Zhukov. The Soviet marshal may not have been a military genius (very few men who were survived around Stalin), but then it took no great genius to realize what was required, and that these incessant waves of small-scale offensives were hardly going to win the war.

The Red Army lacked the command expertise, the logistics, and the training that would enable the exploitation of whatever openings those attacks created. The spring encirclements suggested that there had definitely been some improvement, because Soviet forces had managed coordinated envelopments. But they were repeatedly unable to close the circle and annihilate the Germans inside the pocket.[25]

What was needed was an offensive on the grand scale of the planetary operations that had resulted in Stalingrad: one final blow that would crack the German front completely and end the war. The offensive in Ukraine had been the test case. What was required was an even greater effort. Left unsaid was the disquieting observation that it would have to succeed, given the losses thus far. Three years of war, and except for the airwaves that faithfully transmitted Stalin's boasts, the Germans were still fighting on, inflicting staggering losses on their enemy.

Death of the Phoenix:
The Last Eleven Months of the War

The great superiority of the German Army comes from its organization and instruction.

Marshal Marie Emile Fayolle, April 13, 1918[1]

B y April 1944, Stalin was confident of an eventual victory in the east. Now that he was assured that the Allies would mount an invasion of northern France in summer 1944, he knew a fourth front would be opened up against Hitler (Italy and the airspace over Germany being the second and third). There was no possibility that Hitler could mount another offensive in the east, and indeed he was already weakening his beleaguered army groups there, preparing for anticipated invasions not only of France but of the Balkans.[2]

At his meeting with the two Allied leaders in Tehran in November 1943, Stalin had taken the measure of their relationship. He had already sized up Churchill, but the Americans were a different matter. Now he began to realize the extent to which he could take advantage of the American naïveté typified by Franklin Roosevelt. But he also grasped the essential slipperiness of the American political leader: he failed to gain a commitment from Roosevelt regarding Poland, which the ailing president told him would have to be put off until after the November 1944 presidential elections.[3]

So Stalin's strategic reasoning was transparent (although apparently not to Roosevelt). Ukraine and Bessarabia had been a part of the USSR before the start of the war. In the case of the Romanian province, only by the merest of technicalities, but Stalin felt assured of retaining it intact, assuming he could pry it away from the Germans. The situation was the same in the Baltic. Stalin, who had tested Roosevelt's grasp of world affairs by engaging him in a discussion about the British in India, found him sorely wanting, and was confident that these obscure parts of the periphery of the old czarist empire were his for the taking, and would hardly be challenged.

Poland was a different matter. Its national existence had triggered the war, the revelations about his pact with Hitler had cost him dearly in world opinion, and from September 1939 on he had been fixated on the destruction of that country. So his mind was set. He would take advantage of the forthcoming Allied invasion of France to seize Poland, and present Roosevelt with a fait accompli.

But at the same time, there was the temptation of Romania and the Balkans. By the start of 1944, Tito and his Yugoslavian communist forces had finally established their ascendancy over their (mostly) Croatian enemies. During the Great Terror of 1937–1938, Stalin had eliminated not only the vast majority of the old Bolsheviks in the Soviet Union, but their counterparts in other countries, carefully preserving only the most benign and slavish. The survivors were, as Stalin taunted them after the war, "kittens."[4]

But the Yugoslavian leaders had, through a combination of circumstance and prudence, managed to survive the persecutions of their government during the 1930s, Stalin's deathly embrace, the vicious fighting of the civil war after 1941, and Hitler's own highly effective terror campaign. Stalin now had to face an unwelcome development: a victory led by men who were out of his control. To most outsiders, the fact that they were all communists papered over the problem. The notion that world communism was a monolith controlled completely by Moscow was as mistaken as the official line that the parties in the various countries were independent and quasi-spontaneous manifestations of the universal desire for socialist justice.[5]

On the other hand, Stalin hardly wanted Tito to be defeated outright, and by spring 1944, this was a distinct possibility. As discussed previously, Hitler's concerns about an Allied invasion of the Balkans in July 1943 had led him to divert German combat units there. Not by coincidence, their arrival resulted in yet another series of major offensives that came surprisingly close to destroying the Yugoslavian partisans completely.

What Stalin wanted was a communist Balkans, albeit one safely under his thumb in exactly the same way he planned for Poland, the only difference being that he had murdered almost every Pole who could try to assert that nation's independence, including (especially) Polish communists. The best way to accomplish what he wanted was to overrun the Balkans with the Red Army. As a happy by-product, that would deliver the rest of Ukraine into his hands and create enough of a panic in Bucharest that the Romanians would probably change sides. When that happened, Hitler would be deprived of the greater part of his oil supplies. His military machine would literally run out of gas.

The problem Stalin now faced was essentially the same problem that his adversary had faced: there were two grand prizes to be had, but they were at opposite ends of a very long front, and increasingly at the ends of very precarious supply lines. Moreover, despite the rhetoric about limitless resources, when it came to troops on the ground, the same situation prevailed as with the ratio between the enormous number of armored vehicles Soviet factories allegedly produced and the numbers of tanks available for any one operation.

As a result, by early spring 1944, the Germans were still in possession not only of most of Poland, but of a goodly portion of Belorussia, as well as the Baltic and points further south. While

Stalin was feting the Allies in Iran, his armies had continued their war of attrition, and although they were pushing the Germans back, there had as yet been no serious breakthrough.

Undeterred but somewhat more realistic, Stalin decided to capitalize on the convergence of the Allied landings in Normandy, scheduled for June 1944, and the differing climatic conditions at the two ends of the front. By spring 1944, the German and Romanian troops in the south had finally been forced out of Ukraine and were now occupying a defensive position along the 1939 Romanian frontier with the Soviet Union. So Stalin ordered an offensive for early April that he hoped would smash through the German and Romanian positions in eastern Romania, overrun the oilfields in the southwestern part of that country, and move directly into Yugoslavia and even Greece. That offensive would be followed by one in the north, to take place in June; he lacked the resources to mount two such major operations simultaneously.

German combat units were now scattered all over Europe, as Hitler had continued to thin out the forces on the eastern front so as to fight on elsewhere. By the projected date for Stalin's first attack, the Germans were spread very thinly indeed. So Stalin unleashed his April offensive against Romania. Unfortunately for the Red Army, although the German units in the south were, in terms of manpower, mere shadows of their former selves, the surviving core constituted the worst possible case for any adversary: experienced and heavily armed combat veterans. By the time the offensive was called off, the armies of the Ukrainian fronts had been severely mauled, and none of the key objectives had been accomplished: Yugoslavia was still a long way away.

But then so was Bucharest. The Soviets had failed even to take Iassy, and in early June the German forces in the Balkans just missed capturing Tito himself (he was wounded but escaped). Moreover, the sequential nature of the two offensives meant that Hitler could now shift forces; if need be he could abandon Romania and defend the eastern border of the Reich, hoping to fight to a bloody draw, and that is precisely what he did when the Soviet offensive in the north developed in June.

The Soviet response to the failure of the Romanian offensive was exactly the same as the response to the failures of earlier offensives. The whole operation was consigned to the memory hole, so that even the most basic data remains deliberately obscured: the best current estimate is that in roughly six weeks of fighting the armies of the Ukrainian fronts had a casualty rate of slightly under 20 percent, roughly 150,000 men, as opposed to German and Romanian losses of about a third of that.[6] Given the convoluted way in which the basic Soviet data was hidden, and the general ratio between the official figures researchers finally teased out and the more objective estimates (for say, Rzhev), it is difficult to conclude that the ratio was that low.

That the Red Army after this many years of combat was still suffering lopsided casualties suggests that little had been learned. Internally, Soviet commanders admitted this. The report of the 2nd Ukrainian Front is surprisingly candid in this regard:

> The enemy began extensively employing separate groups of tanks and self-propelled guns, which often operated very carefully from ambush . . . opening fire on our combat formations from a distance of two kilometers or greater. In these instances our forces were inadequately prepared . . . in some cases, our infantry and tanks simply halted their attacks. . . . After discovering that the enemy's tanks (self-propelled artillery) were outside of their direct fire, our accompanying artillery became silent and, since they were incapable of towing the guns forward . . . our tanks . . . conducted the fight . . . alone. . . . Our infantrymen and artillerymen, who are poorly trained in target identification . . . conducted their fire in disorganized fashion and frequently without any observation.[7]

The most logical conclusion, given Soviet obfuscation and denial about losses, is that casualties in the failed Romanian offensive were consistent with those sustained in other offensives. On the other hand, the observation that attacks simply "halted" in the face of superior enemy fire might provide an alternative explanation, that increasingly Red Army local commanders were reluctant to get everyone killed.

So the war ground on, and the Romanian failure, like the earlier ones, was expunged from the record, as Stalin turned his attentions to the north. By most ways of reckoning, Bagration, the name for that offensive (tagged after another famous Russian general of the Napoleonic Wars) would be the largest single operation of the war for the Red Army, but then the prize was enormous: an entire country.

It was also true that the Belorussian front was the most problematic part of the new German defensive position. Thanks to the advances in the spring, it now vaguely resembled the Kursk bulge in reverse, or at any rate it could be attacked from three sides. An offensive that broke through the front there would cut off the remnants of Army Group North, forcing the Germans to fall back on Germany proper. Thanks to the wedge that had been driven through the Germans to the south, so that the front was now from the southwest of Odessa up past Tarnopol (also in Soviet hands), Hitler was now deprived of his best resource, the ability to shift German units from one part of the front to the other to seal off any developing breakthrough. Both the northern German army groups would have to fight off the Red Army on their own.

As the Germans had retreated after July 1943, the strengths of the original three army groups relative to one another had remained pretty much the same. Even though its armor had been drastically pared down, the scattered components of what had initially been Army Group South remained the strongest of the three. Given Hitler's concerns about his oil supplies, that suited him perfectly. If the Red Army reached southern Romania, the German war machine would grind to a halt, not instantly, but in a few months at most. The Allies were going to have to battle their way across France and up Italy (where they were having an exceedingly difficult time of it). The idea that Hitler could fight them all to a draw was not at all unreasonable, provided he could keep the Allies from establishing themselves in France.

To prevent that, Hitler had deployed seven of his armored divisions to France, including the bulk of the super-units, the armored divisions of the Waffen-SS. The only remaining unit in the east of equal size was the Grossdeutschland, with Army Group South. The issue now plaguing the Germans, as more and more of their new and powerful armored vehicles came into service, was almost the obverse of what it had been at the start of the war. In 1941 their armor had been sorely lacking, but they had been vastly superior to the Red Army in mechanization and effective tactical airpower, as well as in training, leadership, and logistics.

As we have seen, as the war went on, the effective firepower of the army, as seen by the transformation of its armored component, increased dramatically. However, the effective combat mobility of its infantry failed to keep pace. Only the infantry of the elite units was transported by vehicles capable of keeping up with tanks and assault guns, and to a surprising extent, the Wehrmacht was still dependent on horses for transport. Given the speed and power of the Germans, there is a natural tendency to assume their forces were highly mechanized. However, that was not the case, nor had it ever been.

Conversely, the Red Army had entered the war completely lacking in the means to transport its infantry over rough terrain, which, given the abysmal nature of Russian roads, was the entire country. Nor, despite its sporadic doctrinal emphasis on offensive thrusts, had any provision been made to equip it with the level of mechanization necessary to keep the mobile armored columns supplied with fuel, ammunition, and spare parts.

This logistical failure is one of the main reasons that even when its commanders were able to envelop the German defenders, thus demonstrating their competence in modern warfare, they were rarely able to finish them off, or to exploit their breakthrough. They would quickly outrun their primitive logistical support. Nor were local commanders allowed to take the initiatives that were essential in exploitations.

But in one key respect the situation was improving. The three quarters of a million trucks and jeeps flowing to the Red Army from the United States and Great Britain gave the Soviets a transport capability they had never had before. During the spring retreats of 1944, the Germans began to discover that, for the first time, the Red Army, thanks to the largesse of its allies, was able to advance more quickly than the Germans were able to retreat, and as the ground dried out, as the German forces in Romania and Ukraine braced for their stand astride the original frontiers of the USSR, they were grimly aware that the situation was only going to get worse for them. The roads of Hungary, Romania, and Galicia were as far above those of Ukraine and Belorussia as they were below the roads of Germany and Belgium.

The German armies of the east still had plenty of firepower. The lion's share of it was contributed by the independent Abteilungen of Tiger tanks deployed there, six in all, as one, the 510th, had only been created in June 1944. In clashes of armor, they were difficult to best. The three initial units that entered combat in midwinter 1942–1943 accounted for 4,000 Soviet tanks, and their presence on the battlefield is one of the main reasons that the only Soviet successes came when they were able to bring an overwhelming superiority of force into play.

These units, and the new generation of assault guns and tank destroyers, could all easily stand off and destroy any tank they encountered, as Soviet tank losses for 1943 make clear. But the Germans lacked the supporting infantry, and thus were not able to seize the inevitable lull that followed any Soviet penetration.

As the ground mobility went, so also went the Luftwaffe, already overstretched to the maximum, since it was responsible for defending German airspace against the increasingly heavy Allied bombing raids.

Although the German air defense system was exacting a high price on the British and American bombers, the diversion of resources was costly. The Luftwaffe had from the first been designed as a tactical air force, with its main emphasis on the support of army operations in the field. Essentially it was now forced to become an air defense air force, switching missions in mid-war. Given the far-flung nature of its operations, its commanders were doing a remarkable job, but something had to give, the something in this case being the Eastern Front.

The German prospects, in other words, were grim. The only good news in all this was that in the winter of 1943–1944, despite the bombing campaigns, the production of armaments finally began to accelerate. In fact, by April 1944, the German tank inventory was actually larger than it had ever been, and more powerful: over 40 percent of its armor now consisted of the new Panther and Tiger tanks, and most of the remaining armor consisted of the modified Mark 4 tanks. The new low-profile tank destroyer based on the Czech 38(t) chassis, called Hetzer, was beginning to appear in numbers as well. Given the killing power of the new armor, it would take more than an overwhelming superiority to best the Germans.

The problem was that the flow of powerful new weapons of all types was mostly going everywhere but to Army Group Center, which had never recovered from the deployment of its mobile units for Citadel. On paper it was the largest of the army groups, at almost 800,000 men. But in terms of firepower, it was the weakest. Its thirty-eight divisions were almost entirely footbound infantry units formed by the reorganizations of the winter, and it had less than 10 percent of the German army's armor.

To make matters still worse, Center had no air support. By one estimate the 6th Air Fleet, tasked to support the army group, had fewer than fifty fighter planes.[8] Although the Germans had always been adept at manning defensive lines with inferior troops, their success had been predicated on being able to back them up with first-line combat units that could throttle any offensive successes. On the Eastern Front those units had to have a high degree of mobility, i.e., mechanization as well as armor. By May 1944 Army Group Center had none whatsoever.

This last factor was important. No one gives high marks to the command abilities of Ernst Busch, who had taken over from von Kluge after his automobile accident in October 1943. But as we have seen, he had reorganized his command successfully, and his army commanders had fought off a series of Russian attacks through the winter and early spring. Busch had taken an army group with a high percentage of support units and managed to patch them together into a competent defensive formation.

But his basic problem was insurmountable. Once their defensive positions were broken through, his units lacked the mobility to regroup and strike back, and Busch lacked the reserves to reinforce them. Nor were there any prospects of this situation changing by way of reinforcements arriving from elsewhere.

Hitler's insistence that the embattled German units stand their ground is almost always seen as a knee-jerk response that went against the grain of an officer corps trained to withdraw and regroup rather than be overwhelmed. But now there was very little else for the defenders to do but hang on and fight to the bitter end.

The situation was exacerbated by the obviousness of Germany's situation. It hardly took much military training to reckon that the Wehrmacht had to brace itself for four, or even five or six, major offensive surges as summer 1944 arrived, each one aimed at a different part of Hitler's slowly shrinking empire. The eventual Allied breakout from the Anzio beachhead meant that the Allies would try to drive up the Italian peninsula, while the Italian real estate they acquired would enable them to launch even more air raids. Given the naval resources they had tied up in the Mediterranean, they would probably mount an invasion either of southern France or the Balkans as well. By fall 1944, the most the German commanders could hope for was to make the Allies pay an extremely high price for the territory gained, as they had been able to do in Italy.

All these future difficulties would add to the two major problems looming: there would be both an Allied invasion of France and a major Soviet thrust in the east. From Hitler's perspective, then, the problem was how to defend against all of these threats, and the difficulty of doing that with too few resources was compounded by the fact that it was not easy to reckon the precise impact area of the two major threats. In theory, the Allies could invade France almost anywhere along the northern coast, and since the Germans were not sure just where that would be, they had to divert more resources to the defense than would have been the case had they known the location.

The same applied in the east: thus far, the Soviets had tended to mount massive simultaneous attacks everywhere, one reason why their successes were so marginal. If they continued the pattern of the fall and spring, the result would probably be yet another stalemate. On the other hand, if they decided to throw all their resources into one massive offensive, where would they strike?

Hitler was convinced that Stalin's next offensive would be directed toward the oil reserves. His assumption was not unreasonable but it was wrong. At the same time, the German dictator was increasingly focused on the coming struggle in the west. So although the German command, both in Berlin and at Center, could see the Soviet plans for Bagration unfolding, there was really little it could do about it other than wait for the offensive to begin.

Little but not nothing. Although the German high command

no longer had the mobile reserves its generals had traditionally held back as reinforcements, the enormous length of the front in Russia meant that it was still possible to move units laterally from one area to another. Although such moves were risky, by this point the Germans were confident that their opponents were simply too slow to move and would be unable to take advantage of the opportunity offered by such shifts from one area of the front to another. So in early May, Berlin proposed a preemptive strike in the direction of Tarnopol, correctly estimating that this was the place to blunt any planned Soviet offensive. Busch's 56th Armored Corps started receiving reinforcements so it could mount such an operation. Busch's right flank (opposite Tarnopol) in theory connected with the left flank of Model's Army Group Ukraine. So in late May, Hitler, convinced that the main blow would fall on the two southern army groups, transferred the 56th Corps to Model, who accordingly was now responsible for part of Busch's right flank. But Model now acquired all of the new armor Berlin had sent, together with about a third of Busch's artillery.[9]

Compounding the problem for Busch was Hitler's decision that the key center part of his front, an arc formed by the cities of Vitebsk, Orsha, Mogilev, and Bobruysk, was to be defended to the bitter end. There was to be no withdrawal from them in the face of a Soviet attack. That decree also put an end to the sensible proposal made by the 9th Army's acting commander, Hans Jordan, to shorten the defensive line by a withdrawal to the next logical defensive positions, along the Dnieper and the Berezina Rivers, thus ensuring that any Soviet offensive blow would essentially expend itself into the void, as well as compressing the front by over 200 kilometers.

In late May, Busch went to Hitler and personally made the proposal. But Hitler's view was that by staying where they were and fighting on, the Germans tied down more Russians than if they retreated. The logic is interesting: despite being overextended everywhere in the east, the Germans were stretching the Red Army as well, and given the casualty exchange rate, they were still winning the war of attrition.

Hitler's orders created the conditions for a genuine catastrophe if things started to go wrong. And as we have seen, all the conditions for such a scenario were in place: Center lacked the armor and airpower to beat back a Soviet offensive even partially, and its orders to stand fast at all costs more or less guaranteed its destruction should it fail to hold. Nor did the condition of its greatly weakened and poorly equipped infantry units suggest that they would hold.

Stalin had decided that Bagration would begin on June 22, the anniversary of the German attack on the Soviet Union. But although he was, as usual, conscious of the symbolism, the timing gave him a very practical advantage. By that date, the Allies would either have established themselves in France or they would have failed. From Stalin's reckoning, the best outcome was a bloody stalemate there that would occupy both sides and allow him to move forward. However, given the June date, he was for the first time in a situation where he could not lose regardless. If Overlord, the Allied invasion of France, died on the beaches in a week or so, it would still take Hitler months to get his divisions back to the Eastern Front. If Overlord broke out of the beachhead, he would be compelled to throw more and more resources into France, just as would be the case if there was a stalemate. In any case, Stalin was doing with Bagration what he had done in September 1939 with Poland, hanging back and waiting to see what would happen before he made his move.

By June 22, it was becoming clear that a stalemate was developing in northern France. The Germans had been unable to throw the Allies out; Normandy was clearly not going to be Gallipoli. But neither had the Allies broken out. Normandy was looking more and more like Anzio: the Allies had landed there on January

22, 1944, and it had taken them about four months to break out of the beachhead. For the Soviets, this was the best possible situation, provided they could exploit it.

Military operations rarely develop as anyone planned, but all the conditions were in place for Bagration to be the exception. It was envisioned as a massive pincer operation that would trap the entire German army group, and that was precisely how it played out.

By June 24, Vitebsk was surrounded. Hitler finally gave Busch permission to withdraw his troops, but it was too late. By June 27, the breakout failed. Two days later the Russians fought their way into Bobruysk. Busch's center was collapsing as well, and Kurt von Tippelskirch, commanding the forces there, took matters into his own hands and ordered a retreat to the Dnieper. Busch, overwhelmed at every level and on both sides, was sacked on June 28 and replaced with Model.

Bagration was a true victory, and in most respects the first one the Red Army had enjoyed. By mid-August the Belorussian and Polish fronts had collapsed, and the Soviets were approaching the borders of the historic German province of East Prussia in the north and were into Ruthenia, the far eastern tip of what had once been Czechoslovakia. Army Group Center was shattered into small fragments, and to claim that it was completely destroyed (the subtitle of the most authoritative study of the Soviet operation) is not at all hyperbole.[10] Given how far the Red Army penetrated after the late June battles, the exploitation phase was, again for the first time, well done.

The collapse of the Belorussian front was the worst German defeat of the war, and the only one not immediately balanced by a Soviet defeat, as had been the case in February–March 1943. As August 1944 was the month in which the Allies broke out of the Normandy beachhead and the Germans abandoned France as fast as they could manage it, it was increasingly clear that Hitler was going to lose the war. The only question at this point was how much longer it would go on. So Stalin's decision to smash through and grab Poland had paid off. All he had to do now was seize Hungary and Romania to complete his conquests and safeguard the USSR from future German attacks. His armies were now the closest to Berlin, and thus poised to take the lion's share of the credit for the defeat of Germany.

But the Soviet victory poses a bit of a puzzle. The Wehrmacht was scattered all over Europe, and engaged in a bitter struggle in every theater. The losses sustained during Bagration were therefore not going to be made up in any meaningful way. That being the case, it is curious that despite this calamity, the war continued for nearly ten months. In early September the Allies were confident the war would be over by Christmas, and although Stalin was much more cautious, he may have entertained the same fantasy.[11]

Part of the answer to the puzzle of why the war kept on going is that, despite all of the claims made about its strength and its newfound experience, the Red Army lacked enough of either to seize the fruits of victory. In Bagration, the Soviets admitted losing 2,957 tanks, while in the offensive launched in July to take Romania they admitted that they lost another 1,269, probably the bulk of the armor available in summer 1944.

Soviet losses for the operation are perfectly tailored: the 770,888 casualties come in as less than the strength of Busch's forces when the fighting started, and since the words "destruction" and "annihilation" are invariably used to describe what happened to his army group, one assumes, logically enough, that the Soviets for once came out on top with respect to losses.

In July and August, the Wehrmacht had 123,000 soldiers killed, and nearly 720,000 missing, the bulk of those taken prisoner. But those losses were for all fronts. The best calculation for Center is that it had somewhere over 25,000 men killed in combat, and well over a quarter of a million men missing, most of those presumably taken prisoner.

That being the case, the debris of the mauled units still formed a sizable force, which explains why the Red Army had to spend the next nine months fighting its way into Germany. Moreover, despite its equipment losses, the German army began September with the same size tank force it had in May, at which point it was both the largest and most powerful armored force the Wehrmacht had ever put into the field.

At bottom Stalin's problem in the east was the same one the Allies faced in the west. By the end of August the Germans in most of France had been routed, retreating as fast as they could. Not only did the Allies believe the war would soon be over, but they aimed to mount an ambitious airborne and armored assault up through the Netherlands in order to get across the Rhine and into Germany. But Montgomery's Market-Garden, as the plan was called, was not a success.

One of the things that Hitler's adversaries missed was the ability of the Wehrmacht to reconstitute itself after the chaos of defeat or even strategic withdrawal. By the time the Allies were able to launch their airborne invasion into the Netherlands in September 1944, the Germans retreating from France, who a month earlier had been a panic-stricken mob, were once again operating in well-organized combat units and holding good defensive positions. They fought back with all their customary dispatch and effectiveness. Phoenix-like, the army kept rising out of its own ashes.

In fairness to the Red Army and its commanders, they were facing the same problem in the east, only more so, since the army groups to the south were still intact. And as the German offensive of December 1944 in Belgium demonstrated, almost until the bitter end, the Germans were capable of inflicting serious punishment.

The Red Army now discovered this problem in earnest as it geared up for the second great offensive of 1944, one that would take it through Romania and Hungary, link up with Tito in the Balkans, and penetrate Vienna, the traditional gateway that separated the developed west from the less advanced east. The third wave would engulf East Prussia, and then Stalin aimed to seize Berlin.

The difficulty was that the only way the Red Army could deliver massive blows like Bagration was by shifting resources from one section of the front to the other, the same technique the Germans had used. That meant, inevitably, that there was a lull as one surge tapered off and the next one was organized. Bagration began on June 22, a smaller offensive that penetrated into Galicia began on July 13, followed by another surge into Romania and Hungary that began on August 20.

The orderly progression of these offensives in the official Soviet record is impressive, but it disguises the fact that the delays gave the Germans time to reorganize.

Hitler took advantage of the temporary lull in the northern and southern army groups to sack Georg Lindemann, the Army Group North commander, who, quite sensibly, seeing that the disintegration of his neighbor to his right had him out on a considerable limb, wanted to withdraw further south. He was replaced by Johannes Friessner, whom Hitler thought had plenty of fight in him, but that general, once he surveyed the situation, decided Lindemann had been right.

When von Manstein, toward the end of his tenure, had proposed to Hitler that there be one overall commander for the east, Hitler's response was interesting.

> "Even I cannot get the field marshals to obey me!" he cried. "Do you imagine, for example, that they would obey you more readily? If it comes to that, I can dismiss them. No one else would have the authority to do that."[12]

Guderian, whom Hitler had brought back from unemployment (along with von Rundstedt and von Kluge), now suggested to Hitler that the easiest way to solve the problem was to shift Schörner to North, replacing him with Friessner. Not that it made much difference. On August 20, the Red Army launched its Balkan offensive, which eventually pushed the German, Hungarian, and Romanian armies all the way back into the Reich. By the end of August, the Romanian army had dissolved, as the government rather fruitlessly tried to save itself by switching sides, thus fatally handicapping whatever chances the Germans had to hang on to the country.

To make matters worse, Hitler had already pulled out the two armored divisions that constituted Friessner's reserves, sending them to the rescue of Schörner. The still powerful and effective units of the Grossdeutschland, which had battered the initial Soviet attempts to penetrate Romania in June and July, had already been shifted to East Prussia to save the situation there.[13]

By late October, Budapest was under siege, the Baltic was lost, and Hitler pinned his entire hopes for survival on one last series of major offensives in the west. With the loss of Romania, his armies were now short of fuel, and when his western offensives failed in the bitter winter of 1944–1945, the war was over, although the fighting continued, as the Germans battled on in the east to the bitter end.

Although official Soviet combat losses obediently tapered off in the final months of the war, the losses in armor tell a much different story: 1,766 tanks destroyed in the fighting for Budapest in fall–winter 1944–1945; 1,267 lost in the battles to cross the Oder River that took place at the same time; 3,525 destroyed in the attacks into East Prussia; 1,027 in the fighting in Pomerania; and another 1,997 in the final struggles for Berlin, the last three operations extending well into 1945.

Until the end the German units exacted a heavy price. In the March 1945 defense of the Lauban area, the 6th Volksgrenadiers, hardly an elite unit, as the name suggests, destroyed 100 Soviet tanks, while the remnants of the 8th and 17th Armored Divisions between them destroyed another 250 vehicles.[14]

By April 1945, the armies in the east were essentially down to the forces holding out around Berlin, the 9th Army, whose troops, desperate to avoid the fate of being Soviet prisoners of war, attempted the final breakout to the west as Berlin fell. Few of them made it. By this point in the war, there were no German records being kept. The Soviets claimed to have killed 60,000 Germans and taken another 120,000 prisoner, thus completing the absolute destruction of the 9th Army, as well as of the Wehrmacht itself. Most probably, the destruction of the 9th Army was the last large-scale combat of the European war.

It is instructive however to note that the two Soviet armies operating against the Germans at Halbe, the area where the last remaining German force in the east was destroyed, record 293,315 Soviet casualties during that operation.[15] Nor is this surprising. Although the period of the heaviest losses for the Red Army was 1941, when casualties came to the staggering total of 38,031 a day, and losses in 1945 came to only 28,792, using the same data, it appears that this last figure was actually higher than the period 1942 through 1944.[16] Whatever had been gained in the way of tactical skills, Stalin had squandered in the lives of his soldiers. He truly was, as General Volkogonov sadly remarked, entirely ignorant of the first principle of the military art. Thanks to the Allies, he had destroyed Hitler, but as we shall see, in the process he had also destroyed the system his ruthlessness had created.

THE WAR OF EXTERMINATION:
ALLIES, PARTISANS, CRIMINALS

"I have never believed it for a moment," answered Bärlach. Watching unconcernedly as Gastmann lit his pipe, he went on: "I couldn't convict you of a crime you committed; so now I shall convict you of one which you have not committed."

Friedrich Dürrenmatt, *The Judge and His Executioner*[1]

No part of the war between Stalin and Hitler is as complex, as misunderstood, and as morally repellent as the war against the populations of central Europe and European Russia. Outside the Soviet bloc, this aspect of the war was submerged in the unfolding horrors of the Holocaust. Rightly so: over 70 percent of Europe's Jewish population lived inside the zone occupied by the German armies; by the end of the war, of those 6.5 million people, 4.5 million were dead.[2] Three quarters of the Holocaust murders took place in the territories over which the Wehrmacht and the Red Army fought.

Paradoxically, inside the Soviet bloc, Hitler's war against European Jewry was given scant attention, subsumed and minimized in the legend that Stalin was creating of a systematic war of extermination against the Soviet people. In his November 6, 1942, speech, "On the 24th Anniversary of the October Revolution," Stalin set the tone:

The German fascist invaders are plundering our country, destroying the cities and villages built by the labor
of the workers, peasants, and intelligentsia. The Hitler
hordes are killing and violating the peaceful inhabitants
of our country without sparing women, children or the
aged.[3]

In this same speech, Stalin spoke of a "war of extermination,"
a phrase that after the end of the war began to resonate with a
world slowly beginning to understand the dimensions of the
Holocaust.

The relatively late date of Stalin's 1942 speech allowed him to
make the claim that the sufferings of the inhabitants led them to
resist the Germans, and created a climate that naturally led to in-
surgencies and armed struggle. Inside the Soviet zone after 1945,
the notion of that resistance was systematically cultivated. Examples of the depredations of the invading Germans, their cruelty
and barbarism, were endlessly repeated. So too was the bravery,
the sacrifice, and the accomplishments of the partisans, who epitomized the resistance of the Soviet people. Decades after the end
of the war, long after Stalin's death, the unity of the invaded peoples in the face of the Hitlerites was still being celebrated. Most
likely, this aspect of Stalin's mythmaking will prove the most
durable.[4]

In the West, these accounts were largely taken either at face
value or at a slight discount, with the general emphasis, when
there was any serious mention of these topics at all, being on how
Hitler and his minions had squandered whatever goodwill the
Germans might have enjoyed by their campaign of terror and bla-
tant racialism. As is the case with many assumptions about this
war, this one is both true and false. The advancing Germans were
in possession of lands where they had historically been seen as
occupiers and invaders. Nor is there any doubt that the aim was
to instill fear from the very first.

The Wehrmacht envisioned the maintenance of a strict and ruthless order in the zone. A May 1941 directive from the high command makes this explicit:

> The application of martial law aims in the first place at instilling discipline.... This is possible only if the troops take ruthless action themselves against any threats from the enemy population.... Guerrillas will be relentlessly liquidated by the troops, whilst fighting or escaping.[5]

To say that the May directive envisions draconian measures would be to understate the case considerably. Nor is there any doubt that from September 1, 1939, regular army units had systematically violated the norms that had customarily been observed by European armies.[6] Not the Red Army, of course; as we have seen, from the very first neither its commanders nor its soldiery had paid much attention to such niceties, and Lenin had exhorted them in terms bolder than any of Hitler's orders.

The Wehrmacht order is interesting however in that it assumes counterinsurgency warfare as a matter of course. The Germans had a good reason for this assumption. Hidden beneath Stalin's rhetoric about a civilian population polarized by German savagery was a systematic Bolshevik plan for insurgency.

The Red Army had had a center of instruction for irregular warfare since 1933, and in early 1941 there had been an intensification of those efforts. By June 29 of that year the Central Committee of the Communist Party had called for the formation of "Partisan Units and Diversionary groups" to wage a "pitiless war ... to the last drop of blood."[7] Already, in August 1941, the security services were parachuting agents behind the advance of Army Group Center in Belorussia. Stalin's aim was for them to help organize Red Army forces trapped behind the German lines as well as raise destruction battalions and guerilla units from the local population. In this they were to be aided by the local Communist Party functionaries. There were numerous examples of partisan units created from bypassed Red Army soldiers.[8]

The advancing Germans were encountering partisans early on. Reports sent out by the SS Cavalry Unit in Belorussia are explicit: "42 Partisans were shot and 16 taken prisoner" (September 23, 1941), "11 Russian soldiers and 13 Partisans taken prisoner" (September 27), "74 prisoners, 5 Partisans shot" (September 29).[9]

The chronology is suggestive: even if it were granted that a spontaneous response to German atrocities occurred in the occupied territories, in late September 1941, the Germans had not yet overrun Belorussia and Ukraine.

So while there is no doubt about the wickedness of the German military and civil apparatus, the chief object of Hitler's war of extermination in the east was the Jewish population. That campaign allowed Stalin to claim a similar program directed at the Soviet people by the Hitlerites. Thus Hitler folded the Holocaust into a larger war of extermination fueled by racial hatred: Hitler aimed not only to eliminate the Jews, but also the Poles, together with other Slavic peoples as well.

There is no doubting Hitler's ultimate aim with regard to the Slavs of central Europe. To observe that Stalin had been engaged in his own war of extermination against them, as evinced by the Holodomor and the Great Terror, in no way lessens Hitler's infamy. But neither does the racial nature of Hitler's savagery differentiate it from Stalin's murderous acts. The people who endured the Bolshevik regime, whether after 1917 (Ukraine, Belorussia) or 1940 (the Baltic states and Bessarabia), were quite conscious of being victims of Bolshevik terror.

Given the actions of the leadership of the Third Reich, and the peculiarly repellent nature of its racial ideology, Stalin's claims were logical and persuasive, but in reality the destruction of which Stalin spoke was the result of neither collateral damage nor German ruthlessness: it was almost entirely caused by Stalin himself. As one expert analyst has observed, most of the civilian deaths inside the zone of occupation were caused by Stalin, not Hitler.[10]

From the very first, he directed that when the Red Army retreated, it would destroy everything it left behind. On November 17, 1941, one of Stalin's many decrees specified that

> All settlements in the rear of the German troops, [together with those settlements] 20–60 kilometers deep behind the front line and 20–30 kilometers to the right and left of the roads, must be destroyed and burned to ashes. . . . In case of necessity of withdrawal of our detachment in a particular locality, all Soviet population must be taken away too, and all settlements without an exception must be destroyed lest the enemy should use them.[11]

So as the Red Army withdrew, it systematically destroyed every physical object it could lay its hands on. Not simply bridges, railroad junctions, and storehouses containing essential supplies the advancing Germans could use, but major buildings, monuments, and even (especially) farm equipment.

But much of the damage was not the result of combat or unavoidable collateral damage. Most of it occurred early on and had nothing to do with the actual fighting. A good idea of the extent of the destruction that resulted from Stalin's directives can be gathered by examining the difficulties of the remaining civilians in the German zone in the immediate aftermath of the 1941 offensives. By early October 1941 the Germans were aware of a major problem they faced:

> It has been our experience that the Russians remove or destroy systematically all of the food supplies before retreating. The urban population of the conquered cities thus will either have to be fed by the Wehrmacht or it will have to starve.[12]

Although the authors of this report were willing to permit starvation, the Germans apparently ended up importing food into the zones they occupied.

From a purely military view, the death of millions of civilians, Belorussian families starved and frozen while their Jewish counterparts were beaten to death, has little to do with the course of the war, unless one subscribes to the view that it was a diversion of Hitler's increasingly scarce resources.[13] Stalin, however, planned to do considerably more. His intention was to involve the civilian population of the German-occupied zones in a separate war directed against the German military. His actions deliberately ensured that their suffering would be maximized. Not content with destroying their towns and their food, from the very first he demanded their active participation in the war, in effect forcing the civilian population to fight and thus amplifying their suffering.

"Demanded" is not an exaggeration. In his May 1943 address he issued the following directive:

> I order . . . that men and women guerillas strike powerful blows at the enemy's rear establishments, communications, military stores, headquarters and factories; that they destroy the enemy's telegraph and telephone lines; that they draw the wide strata of the Soviet population in the areas captured by the enemy into the active struggle of liberation, and thus save Soviet citizens from extermination by the Hitlerite beasts; that they take merciless revenge on the German invaders.[14]

By this time, even if he was not aware of it earlier, Stalin could hardly have failed to notice one of the nastier aspects of German policy. There were savage reprisals for any signs of resistance in the local population: the taking of hostages to ensure their good behavior, the destruction of houses and even villages, and the summary execution of anyone suspected of any act of resistance, or simply as acts of intimidation.

After the assassination of Reinhard Heydrich on May 27, 1942, the Germans retaliated by murdering all the adult males in the Czech village of Lidice outright; the women and children were sent to the camps, where they perished as well. This highly publicized reprisal, a war crime in every sense of the word, was, like the taking of hostages to ensure that the locals remained studiously neutral (another war crime), no less effective for its wickedness.

Stalin was familiar with this technique. Lidice was neither the first example of brutal reprisal nor was it an isolated one. From September 1939 on, the Wehrmacht shot enemy soldiers who had surrendered, took hostages to ensure the good behavior of the locals, massacred civilians and destroyed their homes in reprisals, and maintained public order by summary executions. These atrocities began before Barbarossa. They were by no means restricted to the SS, and they seem to have been widespread.

By December 1941, when the plan to assassinate Heydrich was conceived in London, the extent to which reprisals and other atrocities were an integral part of the Third Reich's means of waging war was hardly a secret. The only aspect of it that was arguably veiled in secrecy was the systematic mass murder of European Jewry. It is impossible not to conclude that in planning the assassination of a relatively minor Hitlerite, the British simply did not care what the consequences were: they had decided that killing Heydrich would send a message to the leadership and proceeded accordingly. Insofar as they reckoned on any adverse consequences for the Czechs, they figured that demonstrations of Hitlerite brutality would only inflame the population, radicalize them, make them more resistant.

Once the war began, Stalin did the same thing, only on a much grander scale. There was a logical reason for his desire. There is a general incomprehension in the West about the histories of the people inside the zone. Each case is different, and in an enormous geographical area inhabited by a hundred million people (almost 150 million, if we include Moldova, Bessarabia, Yugoslavia, and Czechoslovakia), inevitably any generalization is a drastic simplification.

If the numbers are large, the histories are complex, and for most Westerners completely obscured. Few of us, regardless of education, know much about the aspirations of the Belorussians to have their own country, much less that they briefly achieved independence in 1918, only to be swallowed up in the savage fighting that swept across the region. The extent and savagery of the fighting in Poland, Hungary, and the Baltic, or for that matter, that there was a brutal war there at all, is a missing chapter in the history of modern Europe.[15]

Their individual histories may be bewildering, but there is a common thread. Whether they were Czechs, Slovaks, Slovenes, Ukrainians, or Estonians, they wanted their own nation. The success of the Czechs, the Poles, and the citizens of the three Baltic states after the end of the First World War in achieving that independence further obscured the desires of the remainder, scattered across the Balkans and central Europe. The success of the October Revolution compounded the frustrations of most of them.

Although he was publicly committed to the idea of autonomous socialist republics, Lenin's intentions with regard to the newly emerged independent Lithuania make clear what in his view that meant: "We must ensure that we *first* sovietize Lithuania and *then* give it back to the Lithuanians," he noted in July 1920.[16] The process of sovietization was a bloodbath, as the Bolsheviks repressed the populations using every means at their disposal.

Stalin did not believe in the concept of nation in the first place. When he was in Moscow after the end of the war, Milovan Djilas, one of the few intellectuals to engage Stalin in genuine discourse, asked him to elucidate the difference between nation and people, a matter of deep importance to the communist leadership of what would shortly become Yugoslavia. Here is Stalin's reply:

> Nation, you already know what it is: the product of capitalism with given characteristics. And people, these are the workingmen of a given nation, that is, working-men of the same language, culture, customs.[17]

So in Stalin's view the whole concept of the independence of a nation was a product of capitalism, and therefore should be rooted out.

In Belorussia and Ukraine, the rooting out had been going on for decades. But in 1939–1940, when Stalin deftly managed to re-acquire all the territory lost in 1917–1920, he expanded his terror accordingly. When the Red Army overran Poland in September 1939, the Soviet security services began eliminating those groups, or classes, that Lenin had identified as inherently opposed to his ideas. Landowners, army officers, the clergy, the wealthy, intellectuals who had not previously embraced socialism, all were systematically repressed. Stalin aimed to eliminate these classes because he believed them to constitute the core of resistance to Marxism-Leninism, and he rejected the notion their patriots had advanced that they were entitled to exist as a state, whether they thought of themselves as Poles, Lithuanians, or Ukrainians.

Inside the USSR, the terror kept people in line; in the zone it gave them a reason to join the other side. The Katyn Woods Massacre noted earlier was simply the tip of the Gulag iceberg. In the weeks before the invasion, and after it began, Stalin's security services embarked on an orgy of terror. On the night of June 13, 1941, a week before the German offensive began, Soviet security services personnel descended on the three Baltic states, arresting 20,000 Lithuanians, 10,000 Estonians, and 15,000 Latvians, 3,315 of whom were children.[18] At the same time, the main unit of what had been the Latvian army, transformed into a Soviet unit after the occupation, was surrounded, its members either shot outright or shipped off along with the others, to disappear into the Gulag.

As the Germans advanced, seemingly unstoppable, Soviet security services personnel abandoned their headquarters in the major cities, but before they ran off, they slaughtered their prisoners. In some cases there were survivors, and for the first time Soviet citizens were able to grasp the true nature of Stalin's rule over them. Graves were exhumed as family members searched for relatives among the corpses.[19]

Not surprisingly, when the Wehrmacht swept into the Soviet Union in June 1941, the natives had decidedly mixed reactions. The Bolshevik terror, whether recent or of long standing, had polarized the population, as had been the case when the Red Army had moved into Poland in September 1939. At that time, the Jewish inhabitants of eastern Poland had been pleased, Bolshevik sympathizers and party members overjoyed; but for the Ukrainians and Belorussians who formed a large element of the population of the new Soviet zone, one oppressor had been replaced by another, and many of the natives felt that the German one would be an improvement: "Consequently, in most areas from the Baltic north to the Ukrainian south . . . the Germans . . . were generally well received by the local population," is how one prominent historian of the Holocaust puts it.[20]

The idea that the invasion was a catalyst for the Soviet people, igniting their traditional patriotism, which was then intensified by Hitler's savage treatment of them, is, like the notion of Hitlerite brutalism in the zone, largely a Stalinist myth. The brutality was there, but it was, with two important exceptions, Stalinist.

The evidence suggests a population, whether Russian or otherwise, whose response was about as far from supportive as it is possible to get from people living under a rule of terror.

For example, there is no evidence that either the Red Army or the population of the USSR responded with enthusiasm to Stalin's exhortations. By early 1942, his security services had detained 638,112 soldiers, detainment being a euphemism for imprisonment without the formality of any charge; out of that number 82,865 were arrested. Over the course of those first months, nearly a year, 994,000 soldiers were condemned, i.e., sent to penal battalions or camps, and 157,593 were executed outright.[21] These figures, when added to the roughly four million soldiers who had surrendered by the end of 1941, suggest an army with very little motivation to support the cause.

The lack of enthusiasm for the cause was equally marked among the civilian population. In 1940, when the labor laws were tightened, 2,081,438 workers were convicted of absenteeism and leaving the job without permission, and 322,000 of those were given prison sentences.[22] In 1941, the number of convictions fell to 1,769,082, but the number of prison sentences doubled; moreover, after the war began there was a new decree in addition to the earlier ones, and that resulted in additional convictions. Consequently in 1942, the first full year of the war, the number of convictions for shirking, 1,692,859, was the same as the prewar rate.

However, let us not become too sympathetic to the Slavic peoples of central Europe. There was a dark side to the German liberation, one that helps explain the veil of silence and obfuscation that characterizes this part of the war, and goes a long way toward explaining why Stalin's mythmaking went unchallenged.

Since the bulk of the killings aimed at European Jewry was carried out in the camps, and particularly in the Operation Reinhard camps in the east, it is sometimes assumed that initially the members of the local Jewish community were rounded up and removed from their homes, a process that enabled the Germans to preserve the fiction of relocation and resettlement. Although this process certainly took place, in the occupied territories it was supplemented and even supplanted by other procedures, and those began very early in the war.

Given the imperfect records maintained in Ukraine, Belorussia, and Poland, the death tolls are largely estimates (which is not to say they are not reliable); but in the three Baltic states we have more precise figures: 415,153 Jews were murdered in 1941 alone.[23] Essentially the entire Jewish population was gone by the end of 1941. Taken together with the murders and deportations carried out by the Bolsheviks before the invasion, the population of the Baltic was literally decimated in a few short months.

The same situation was true in Belorussia, where the almost entirely urbanized Jewish population, at least three quarters of a million people, was eliminated. The massacre at Babi Yar, in Kiev (Ukraine), in which about 35,000 local Jews were murdered, is thus unique only in the sheer number of people murdered in a short period of time. As the date of those killings (September 29, 1941) suggests, the extermination campaign was operating early.

There were survivors (the main reason Babi Yar is as well known as it is), but in general these operations were efficient: the number of Jews murdered in the Baltic states during 1941 (415,153) is the same number as the figures reported for the years 1941–1944; the four death camps in the east began operation only in 1942, and the roughly 4.5 million people murdered there had been almost entirely massacred by the end of that year.[24]

Although in popular mythology Hitler's Europe was dominated by sinister black-clad Germans with jackboots and automatic weapons, the reality was quite different. "In 1941 the full-time staff of the Gestapo . . . including Austria and what is today the Czech Republic, was fewer than 15,000."[25] One reason for the reticence of the surviving Estonians, Latvians, Belorussians, and Ukrainians (simply to name the most numerous groups) is that they greeted these killings with a certain amount of enthusiasm. Nor were they simply enthusiastic onlookers: they were active participants.

There was a certain logic to this criminality. On the one hand, the Bolsheviks had eliminated that part of the population that by education and social class exercised any sort of leadership in their respective societies. As that aspect of the terror extended to the clergy, institutional Christianity was stamped out. Stalin effectively deprived the population of any sort of alternative moral leadership or guidance, just as he deprived them of the classes of people around which any sort of independence movement could coalesce. This was the application with a vengeance of his definition of "people, these are the workingmen of a given nation." In his scheme, that would be all that was left, and they would perforce turn to the party for guidance on every issue.

In the east, institutional violence against the Jews had been either tolerated or encouraged by the czars, one reason that Jewish men and women were attracted to the Bolsheviks and were represented in the various communist parties out of proportion to their numbers in the general population. As dedicated party members, they thus participated in the Stalinist repressions; in the mind of the mob, they thus became guilty by association. The extent of Jewish participation in the Bolshevik terror, particularly in Poland after September 1939 and the Baltic after June 1940, is, like the surprising numbers of Jewish officers in the German military (and SS), a deeply disturbing and controversial topic.

In his speeches Hitler routinely linked the two categories, and we find that linkage repeated ad infinitum in SS reports: on August 23, 1941, a report from the 10th SS Regiment notes that "65 Jewish Bolsheviks were shot."[26] Just as Stalin used the murder of the Jews in the east as a fiction to enable his claim of a general war against the Soviet people, Hitler used the association of Jews with the communists as an equivalent pretext. Where both men were in complete agreement was in the necessity of ridding their respective states of their Jewish citizens.

But Hitler's campaign was tightly focused, and had the tacit approval of the population as well as their involvement. The truth, sad and repellent as it is, is that very few people among those 150 million who lived in the central European and Balkan countries affected by the war had any real concern for the murder of the Jews. When the Romanian army took Odessa, there was a massacre of the Jewish townspeople whose scale equaled and possibly even exceeded the murders in Kiev.[27]

The intense hatred and animosities that Hitler exploited were hardly confined to the Jews. What Stalin fictionalized as a starkly contrasted black and white of Hitlerite brutality and murder directed against the abstraction of the Soviet people was in reality a complex mosaic of motivations and fears, sometimes converging or complementary, sometimes bitterly opposed. Although Stalin was successful in convincing the world that there was such a thing as the Soviet people, and, judging by their accounts, historians more than most, in fact there was no such animal, and certainly not in the western provinces.

As a result, the German advance was the catalyst for a sort of civil war, because, in addition to the understandable desire for autonomy and independence, and the lamentable attitudes toward the Jews, there was the fear and dislike each group felt for its neighbors. Largely hidden from view to the outsider, at first ignored entirely and then submerged in the Stalinist-Leninist denial of the whole notion of nationality, those feelings were nonetheless quite powerful. When the great Austrian novelist Joseph Roth wrote *The Radetzky March*, he captured both the complexity of those hatreds and their depth in a few brilliant sentences. Witnessing the general rejoicing in his provincial garrison town at the news of the assassination of Franz Ferdinand,

> [Captain] Jelacich, a Slovene, became furious. He hated the Hungarians as much as he despised the Serbians. He loved his country. He was a patriot. But he stood

there, patriotism extended from helpless hands, like
a flag that you must plant somewhere but can't find a
ridge on which to plant it. . . . He went over to the table
and slapped it with his hand: "Gentlemen, we request
that you continue this conversation in German."[28]

The depth and intensity of those feelings were not realized in the
West until the savage fighting that broke out when Yugoslavia
collapsed in 1991. Unfortunately, the animosities that fighting revealed were not some unique aspect of the Balkans.

Moreover, outside of Yugoslavia, the net result of the war was
a vast redistribution of the ethnic mosaic that had characterized
central Europe for centuries. By contrast with 1920, the Poland
of 1950 was inhabited almost entirely by Poles, for instance. The
ethnic Germans, a surprisingly large group scattered throughout
the region as the result of earlier centuries of emigration, were almost entirely back inside their historic lands, and the Jews, hatred
of whom was the other common thread that runs through the
histories of the region, were now almost all dead.

Although the scale of violence was by contrast minimal,
Czechoslovakia provides us with an excellent example of the complex and largely ignored realities of central Europe. Of the 13.5
million inhabitants of the new country in 1921, over three million
were ethnic Germans, two million were Slovaks, and there were
in addition about 1.5 million Hungarians, Poles, and Ukrainians.
The Czechs constituted only half of the population. Officially
committed to the idea of a Swiss-style federalism, the Czech majority managed to alienate all the major ethnic groups. Although
after the Munich agreement of 1938 the perception was that the
country had been abandoned by Great Britain and France, the sequence of events, like the underlying reality of simmering ethnic
tension and repression, reveals a much different story.

When the Wehrmacht advanced into western Bohemia, the
ethnic Germans celebrated, and the Slovaks seized the opportu-

nity to declare their independence. Like the Hungarians, the Slovaks were forced to turn to Hitler for guarantees: whatever their dislike of the Germans, they feared their Slavic neighbors more.

Behind the fiction of repression and resistance, there was a splintered reality of indifference and alliance. Slovakia, formally allied with Hitler, contributed two combat divisions to the war in the east. As we shall see, the three million ethnic Germans, like their cousins in Alsace (where ethnic Germans constituted roughly three quarters of the population), contributed soldiers by the tens of thousands. The number of ethnic Germans scattered outside of the Reich was hardly trivial, and may have numbered as many as ten million people.[29]

Postwar, the communist government of Czechoslovakia assiduously fostered the notion of Czech resistance to the Hitlerites, going to absurd lengths to reshape national history to conform to the Stalinist legend, while at the same time papering over their own ethnic cleansing. The government was even more reticent about discussing what happened to the three million ethnic Germans who had been driven across the borders into Bavaria, losing their possessions, and in a surprisingly high number of cases their lives. Like the notion that the Slovaks wanted out, the seamier side of national history was simply expunged. Except for a few cranks, the unity of Czechoslovakia was accepted as sober fact in the West. When in 1990 the Slovaks announced their intention to split off, form their own country, there was considerable shock in the West.

But the Slovak desire had a long history; like the creation of Belarus, Ukraine, and Moldova, the re-creation of Estonia, Lithuania, and Latvia, it finally made public the long hidden desires of these people to have their own state, a desire that gave the lie both to Stalin's intellectual conceit and the success of his repressions.

The largely ignored or even unrealized aspects of the history of the Czechoslovak state make clear the depths of confusion and misunderstanding that existed in the West. That such fundamental misunderstandings could exist about a country whose capital was an easy drive from Munich or Dresden, was literally in the heartland of western Europe, is troubling.

But Czechoslovakia serves as an example of more than Western ignorance about the Slavs and their neighbors. Hitler was not well disposed to the Czech people. One of his more pertinent observations was that

> Every Czech is a born nationalist who subjugates his interests to all other obligations. One must not let oneself be deceived, the more he bends, the more dangerous he becomes. . . . Of all the Slavs, the Czech is the most dangerous one, because he is diligent.[30]

Yet the despised Czechs who lived in the protectorate after 1939 suffered hardly any persecutions at all, the reprisal for Heydrich's assassination excepted. The armaments industries of Bohemia became an important component of Hitler's war machinery. Their productivity in armored vehicles outstripped the factories in Germany proper.

The Czech example suggests that National Socialist policies were rather more flexible than one might imagine, and indeed this was the case in a number of ways.[31] Hitler may very well have planned to eliminate the Czechs eventually, just as he planned to purge the world of the Jews. Nor did he much care about the fate of the other Slavs. But the actual occupation of Czechia (as it was then called) was surprisingly benign.

In the Stalinist mythos, not only were the natives roused to revolt by Hitlerite savagery, but they were extremely successful, and had the support of the vast majority of the oppressed peoples. The numbers hardly bear this out. In Belorussia, by most estimates there were well under 10,000 partisans in early 1942, out of a population of 5.5 million. Even at the end of the war, the number of people who were alleged to be in the partisans was, as we shall see, substantially less than the number of locals actively involved in the German military or police.

In his November 1941 speech, Stalin explicitly spoke of the German rear

> being undermined by our partisans, who are utterly disorganizing the supplies of the German army. . . . That is why our army has turned out to be stronger than the Germans expected, and the German army weaker than could have been supposed.[32]

As was invariably the case Stalin's public exhortation was simply the public indication of decisions already made: it indicated not a plan, or a determination, but a directive to intensify. By 1942 the Central Staff of Partisan Warfare had been established in Moscow. Technically subject to the Soviet high command, it was actually run by a trusted Belorussian political leader, Panteleimon Kondratevich Ponomarenko, and was controlled by party members rather than army officers.[33]

Since Stalin had decreed there would be guerrilla warfare, there was. And since he had decreed its success, it would be highly successful. If the official Soviet history is to be believed, there were vast areas in the German zone under partisan control, and the disruption of rail traffic significantly hindered the German war effort, particularly in the crucial summer of 1943.

Over the course of the war, the official history claims that the partisans eliminated the entire Axis force in the east, inflicting over 1.5 million casualties on the "fascists," and destroying 6,543 tanks, approximately half of the losses sustained during the entire war.[34] The use of the term "fascists," as opposed to "Hitlerites," is, perhaps unintentionally, revealing. In Bolshevik ideology, anyone actively opposed to Marxism-Leninism was a fascist, a definition that therefore included those millions of Ukrainians, Belorussians, Poles, and Lithuanians who simply wished for national independence, and therefore resented the Stalinist state, whether they took up arms against it or not.

Such figures are clearly fantasies of the most transparent sort, like the numbers of slaughtered Germans that Stalin announced at regular intervals. But the purpose was to create the impression that serious damage was done, even making allowances for gross exaggeration. Making the same sort of correction that brings other official figures in line with reality produces some horrifyingly low figures, a few hundred tanks, a few tens of thousands of casualties. Although Stalin's claims represent an extremely clever rhetorical ploy, in analytical terms they mean that the precise extent of the damage is unknowable.

There is some German testimony regarding the difficulties caused by partisan activities in Belorussia during July and August of 1943, when there was a concerted campaign to disrupt railroad traffic. The extent to which this campaign was actually disruptive is uncertain, but given the location of the fighting in summer 1943, which was at the other end of the front entirely, its impact on the war was in any case of little significance.

In terms of logistics, the main German difficulty was a function of the grossly underdeveloped rail and road system of the Soviet Union and the great distances munitions and supplies had to be transported. In the zone, the partisan activities were a nuisance, not a threat; Yugoslavia was the only place where the contrary was the case.

From December 1942 until the end of April 1945, Hitler required a stenographic record to be kept of his military conferences, and these verbatim transcripts reveal a concern with minutiae. At one point in the July 25, 1943, briefing, Hitler is calculating how many rounds of 8.8. centimeter ammunition were fired against Allied bombers attacking the area between Kiel and Flensburg:

Führer: How many 8.8. barrels are there?

[Major Eckhard] Christian: In total, there are 54 heavy batteries here.

Führer: Are these sextuple barrels or normal barrels? Generally it's been sextuple barrels so far. So let's say 40 8.8s. That's 240 barrels. So 100 rounds per barrel, which is very little in an hour and a half. Very little has been shot.[35]

Conspicuously absent from this extensive record of Hitler's growing micromanagement of the war is any mention of insurgents, guerrillas, or partisan activities, nor does the matter get much attention in the accounts of the surviving generals.[36]

Until the end of the war the Wehrmacht was able to shift reserves around with surprising ease: as we have seen, after fighting the Soviet offensive in northeastern Romania in June 1944, the Grossdeutschland was transferred all the way to the other end of the shrinking front, and fought its last battles in East Prussia. The Tiger tanks of the 503rd Heavy Armored Abteilung fought at Kursk in July, then were shipped to the west, and then, after the German collapse in France, were deployed in western Hungary. Of course the lightly armed partisans were hardly able to take on first-line German combat units, even in transit, but as the equipment of these units, and the supplies they needed to function in combat, had to be transported entirely by rail, the effectiveness of partisan attacks on the rail lines in the east seems minimal.

There were areas behind the lines that the partisans controlled for long periods of time, probably the most significant being a large section in Belorussia, from the south of Polotsk down to the north of Lepel. It was subsequently claimed that this "Partisan Zone" comprised nearly a quarter of a million kilometers, but as the two towns, neither one of which fell into the hands of the

Bolsheviks until Bagration, are less than thirty kilometers apart, this claim seems exaggerated.[37] In any event, a German offensive in April 1944 wiped out most of the partisans and reclaimed (temporarily) the area.

Taken all together, it seems highly unlikely that the partisan movement contributed much to the Soviet war effort on the Eastern Front. The locals, who already lived in fear of Stalin's security services, now simply had more to fear. Matthew Cooper's conclusion to his pioneering study of the movement is worth quoting:

> It would be pleasant, for the writing of this book, to conclude by proving that the German occupation policy in the East, far from pacifying the population, brought upon the practitioners the full fury of guerilla warfare, warfare that severely dislocated their supply lines and led to severe strategic consequences for the course of the war. This however would be only partially true.[38]

It hardly seems true at all.

What little reliable evidence we have suggests that in the main, guerrillas were mostly concerned with two basic tasks. The first was simply staying alive. This was no easy feat, as the records of the German units involved in maintaining order make clear. On December 3, 1941, for instance, the records of the SS Cavalry unit record a firefight with partisans. The Germans had three men killed, counted seventy-three dead partisans, and took another ninety-three prisoners; five days later, another futile attack resulted in one dead German and seventy-three partisans killed.[39]

Simply obtaining food became a high priority. Nikolai Ivanovich Obryn'ba, a Muscovite Red Army man in Belorussia, records one such operation, in which the men he was with relieved the local villagers of their cattle. "Sergei spelled it out for the old man: 'We're Partisans and we've come to take the cattle from the Germans.'"[40] That the cattle belonged to the villagers, who were thus being condemned to starvation, seems not to have entered anyone's mind.

The other activity of partisans speaks to the civil war aspect of the whole struggle: the execution of those who in some way collaborated with the Germans. The rather ingenuous account of Obryn'ba in this regard speaks volumes:

> The first thing we had to do was to call at a village near Antunovo, to execute a woman who, according to her fellow villagers, was seeing a Polizei in Lepel. . . . By visiting her Polizei sweetheart in Lepel, the woman was spreading alarm among those in the village with Partisan connections. People were in fear for their lives. And so, seen in this way, our brutal orders became understandable: to protect those fighting the invaders.[41]

Leaving aside the questionable logic employed, it is difficult to see what this planned execution might have accomplished in terms of the war effort, other than the obvious result of stirring up existing hatreds still more.

There were, as noted earlier, perhaps as many as ten million ethnic Germans living outside Germany and Austria, the result of emigrations during the Middle Ages into the present-day nations of Estonia, Poland, Hungary, Romania, Serbia, Moldova, and Ukraine.

The men from those areas were incorporated into the military in four different ways. It appears that most ethnic Germans who were residents of Hungary, Slovakia, and Romania served in those armies, as the three states were allied with Hitler. Judging from the situation in Alsace-Lorraine, where the draftable males mostly served in the regular army, a similar situation existed in the other areas immediately adjacent to Germany proper.

One peculiarity of the Hitler regime allows for a certain insight. For most of the war, Heinrich Himmler, head of the SS, was greatly restricted in his recruiting of the citizens of the Reich. He therefore had to turn to neutral and occupied countries to expand its ranks. In its expansion, the SS distinguished three racial categories: Germans, Germanics, and non-Germanics.

In this as in every other way, the Third Reich was a complex and confusing state. Although most ethnic Germans who went into the SS were amalgamated into the initial four "German" divisions, the 7th SS division, Prinz Eugen, was composed almost entirely of ethnic Germans from Yugoslavia.

Technically, the term "Germanic" was intended to denote not only the ethnic Germans scattered throughout central Europe, but volunteers from western European countries like Denmark and the Netherlands. That particular subset, like the non-Germanic category, is somewhat easier to trace. The numbers are surprising. Taken all together, the Waffen-SS, the military arm of the SS, raised almost 250,000 combat troops in the non-Germanic category, about three and a half times as many as Himmler contrived to raise from western Europe.[42]

The total of 316,000-odd troops thus derived in both categories for the Waffen-SS is strictly for combat troops. Clearly the number of combat troops thus raised is not trivial. Nor does this figure include police and support units, or members of the killing squads formed to murder the Jewish population as the army advanced. It also excludes reasonably large numbers of soldiers in other categories, such as the Russian defectors and converted prisoners of war that the captured Soviet general Andrei Andreevich Vlasov attempted to organize.[43]

The best estimate is that in addition to the quarter of a million combat troops raised just from the zone of German occupation, roughly another three quarters of a million men served in police detachments, as prison camp guards, and support troops. Of this nearly one million men, about a quarter of a million were Ukrainians, 110,000 were from the Caucasus, another 110,000 from the southeast, as well as some 70,000 Cossacks.[44]

The numbers are difficult to quantify, for a number of reasons, not least being the savage reprisals exacted by the Bolsheviks as they recovered the territories and completed their subjugation of the locals: three years after the end of the war there were two million people in the prison camps inside the USSR; two years later the number had increased by nearly half a million.[45] Stalin thus ensured that there would be very few survivors to fashion an alternative to the legend he created.

When mentioned at all, the contributions of those central Europeans who threw their lot in with the invading Germans, like those of the Hungarian, Italian, Slovakian, and Romanian armies in the east, are dismissed; they are said to have been engaged only in support or police duties, and in any case, it is alleged, their numbers were dwarfed by the Red colossus. Given the situation after 1945 in all of the countries affected, no one was going to be able to challenge Stalin's account, and attempts to correct the record after 1990 have been severely handicapped by the nearly half a century of Soviet control over the records.[46]

However, in those cases where evidence survived, it runs completely counter to the Stalinist myth. In Latvia, a very small country with a population well under two million souls, units formed from the survivors of the former Latvian army were deployed as early as October 1941 in support of Army Group North, operating south of Lake Ilmen.[47] By fall 1943, an entire Latvian brigade was in action on the German side in the Baltic.

In combat the Latvians revealed themselves to be first-class soldiers, an observation that allows us to appreciate Stalin's genius. By creating the illusion of an army of inexhaustible resources and an apparently limitless number of divisions, he not only filled desk-bound mediocrities in Berlin like Franz Halder with dismay, but he diminished the very real contributions of Hitler's allies: what was a brigade or a few divisions when confronted with the hundreds of divisions of the Soviet giant?

In terms of training, firepower, equipment, and the ability to kill their opponents, few of the units allied with Hitler were comparable to the Wehrmacht. On the other hand, the same could be said about the British and French troops who had opposed the Germans in 1940–1942, and the Americans in 1943. Although such matters are difficult to quantify, using the figures derived by several respected analysts, it would seem that one brigade of reasonably competent soldiers (a conservative judgment of the Latvians) would have roughly the combat effectiveness of two Soviet divisions.[48]

The notion that these units were ineffective, good only for support duties, is analogous to the idea that Hitler committed his entire army to Barbarossa and was running out of men after the first few months of the war (he had about six million people in the German military machine at the end of 1940, and nearly eight million by the end of 1941).[49] Not only was it not true, it was in fact exactly the opposite of the reality. No comprehensive history of these allied units exists, but the few accounts we do have of individual units reveal distinguished combat records, an effectiveness out of proportion to their numbers.[50]

Regardless of whether Stalin intended to provoke a German response or assumed that Hitler was the same as he was in this regard, the result was a bloodbath. And since right up until the end of the war the number of Russians taken prisoner exceeded the number of captured Germans five or six times over, Stalin lost that exchange just as he was losing the one on the battlefield.

That civilians were caught in this carnage, the victims of all sorts of criminal acts, is indisputable. However, leaving aside the Holocaust, Stalin himself was responsible for the vast majority of the deaths inside the zone. It is scarcely conceivable that he was unaware of the consequences of his "orders," and the catastrophic effects they would have on the peoples of the occupied territories. Regardless of the military effect guerrilla activities had on the German ability to wage war, the costs would inevitably be enormous.

They were. Alexei Tolstoy, whose careful calculations of the Soviet war dead in the late 1970s have proven to be accurate (if anything the errors are on the side of caution), concludes that for every two civilians killed by the Germans during the war, at least five were killed indirectly or directly by Stalin's deliberate policies.[51] And of course this calculus does not explicitly address the core issue: no one has any idea how many of the civilians who died were murdered as an indirect result of Stalin's determination to open a front behind the German lines.

That determination was not subject to compromise. Stalin's clever rubric, that Hitler was waging a war of extermination, papers over the dubious morality and ruthless cynicism of his own actions quite effectively, as it implied that neither he nor the Soviet people had any choice in the matter. But this notion is not really true either. The Germans were much more open to negotiations on these matters than is usually understood.

Milovan Djilas, one of the leaders of the Yugoslavian resistance during the war, makes a telling observation about the subject of reciprocity. The Yugoslavian leadership entered into negotiations with the Germans in order to get them "to recognize the rights of the Partisans as combatants so that the killing of each other's wounded and prisoners might be halted."[52] They did not inform Stalin of this, as they knew he would never approve. So the deaths of a few million from the former czarist provinces, where the locals had already established a profound resistance to his power, was not simply to be accepted, it was to be desired.

The notion of a war of extermination is apt, provided we realize that it was as much Stalin's war as Hitler's. In this connection the judgment of Djilas about the Bolshevik leader sums up the situation nicely:

> Every crime was possible to Stalin, for there was not one he had not considered. Whatever standards we use to take his measure, in any event, let us hope for all time

to come, to him will fall the glory of being the greatest criminal in history.[53]

That this judgment was penned by a dedicated communist who had fought the Germans for four years in a war noted for its savagery is more telling than mere numbers.

Conclusions:
False Victories, Mistaken Beliefs

Perhaps there is a reasonable excuse for believing the Stalinist
story. The real story, the truth, was entirely unbelievable.

Martin Amis[1]

D rawing conclusions from wars is a risky business. The war
on the Eastern Front represents an even trickier proposition, because the reality of it is so difficult to discover. One
of Stalin's shrewder insights was that the best way to control any
debate where you couldn't actually kill your opponent was to attack him at every level on every issue, producing a sort of rhetorical quagmire. Not content with the recognition that the Soviets
had finally prevailed in this grim struggle, Stalin and his disciples
wanted the world to believe that the Red Army alone was responsible for Hitler's defeat, that the story of the war after summer
1941 was forty months in which the Germans had been bested at
every turn. Hitler's treacherous and unprovoked aggression was
proof not only of his wickedness but of his foolishness in thinking he could defeat the Soviet Union.

Although after Stalin's death his role as warlord was considerably diminished, his successors nurtured all the other legends of
the Great Patriotic War carefully, sticking to the same basic outline. As we have seen, the result was that even relatively simple
and straightforward matters such as the number of Soviet war
dead and the existence of the August 1939 pact between Hitler

and Stalin were hotly contested.[2] After Stalin's death the leadership still exercised tight control over everything that was published, and continued an extremely aggressive defense of its views. Nor did that denial of basic realities stop with the collapse of the Soviet Union.[3]

Their aggressiveness was made considerably more effective by their control over the basic facts. As we saw in the introductory chapter, it was not until the mid-1960s that there was any quasi-official admission, even in private, as to the scale of Soviet losses, and nearly forty years passed before any serious analysis of those losses emerged.

A discussion of the Soviet war dead data began this book, but the basic figures bear repeating. In the sense that we know almost exactly how many American servicemen were killed in the Second World War, precise figures for losses on the Eastern Front will never be known. But we have a series of estimates from a variety of different sources, most of them working independently of one another: the figure of 27 million Soviet war dead must therefore be taken as the minimum figure for military deaths, as opposed to the German figure of 2,416,784 killed and missing, this latter category including all prisoners of war, some of whom eventually returned alive from the Gulag. While there are obvious complications caused by the lack of reliable information as to the exact death toll for the Romanian, Hungarian, Italian, and other units fighting on the Eastern Front, the conclusion that the exchange ratio was wildly lopsided in favor of the Germans and their allies is inescapable, and undercuts the notion of a great Soviet victory.

Although time has considerably dimmed the notion that Stalin was a military genius, the notion that he was, at least by contrast with Hitler, a strategic thinker of some weight has a surprising persistence.[4] Khrushchev's scornful remarks in his Secret Speech are closer to the mark. But during Stalin's lifetime no one was about to suggest any sort of deficiency, as the following interchange between the Montenegrin intellectual and partisan leader

Milovan Djilas and Marshal Ivan Stepanovich Konev illustrates. The marshal was blunt in answering Djilas's question as to why all the senior Soviet commanders in 1941 had been replaced:

> Voroshilov . . . was incapable of understanding modern warfare. . . . Budyonny never knew much and he never studied anything. He showed himself to be completely incompetent and allowed awful mistakes to be made. Shaposhnikov was and remains a technical staff officer.
> And Stalin? I asked.
> Taking care not to show surprise at the question, Konev replied, after a little thought: "Stalin is universally gifted. He was brilliantly able to see the war as a whole, and this makes possible his successful direction." He said nothing more, nothing that might sound like a stereotyped glorification of Stalin. He passed over in silence the purely military side of Stalin's direction.[5]

Taken collectively, this seems to be a fair assessment of the military capabilities of the commanders of an army that staggered to victory on mountains of its own dead.

Given the unfamiliarity of modern audiences with the First World War, comparisons would be more bewildering than illuminating; however, it should be pointed out that Stalin's approach to fighting the Germans both echoes the approach of the Allied generals of the First World War and was a conscious emulation of those ideas: the way to beat the Germans was to attack them incessantly, rationalize your own heavy losses by claiming that the other side was suffering much worse, that its morale was crumbling, that one more big push would break through and end the war.

Stalin was vastly more successful at this tactic of spinning and fictionalizing than his British and French predecessors. The use of terror ensured there were no leaks, no dissenting views, and hardly any contrary thoughts. Moreover, as Marshal Konev's smoothly diplomatic assessment of Stalin's ability to see the war as a whole suggests, Stalin did grasp one essential truth: that in order for him to win, the war would have to be fought on other fronts, and after Stalingrad the timing of his offensives was carefully synchronized with the series of massive Allied invasions.

But as Helmuth von Moltke the Elder once remarked, "The theory of strategy scarcely goes beyond the first principles of common sense."[6] Hitler and Stalin both grasped one of the more basic ideas that dominated Allied military thinking in 1914–1918, that the way to win a modern war was to kill as many enemy soldiers as possible, a war of attrition. Stalin explicitly invoked this concept in his public addresses, and it was why Hitler was so reluctant to let his generals conduct local withdrawals: by remaining in place they could inflict more losses on their opponents.

If in recent years the tendency has been to see the senior Soviet commanders as being less talented, there has been a countering movement in which it is argued that at the lower levels the Red Army had steadily improved, and, taking advantage of its greater resources, was able to match the Germans on the ground and beat them in battle. However, as we have noted, the losses in the final months of 1945 were actually heavier than in 1941. There are of course alternative explanations for that, but the basic fact that this is so makes any sort of conclusion highly dubious other than the one already mentioned: there was improvement, but the gap was never really closed, because the Germans were getting better as well.

There are also disturbing features of the Red Army during those last months of the war that undercut the notion of a disciplined and well-trained combat force. As it advanced into the Reich, Russian soldiers engaged in loot and pillage on a scale that was unprecedented in the modern age. Although for obvious reasons there are no figures on the extent of the looting, the information we have on one aspect of that behavior, rape, is quite revealing. Although widespread raping was well known in Germany and central Europe, it hovered beneath the radar of military historians for decades. As one of them recently admitted, he was

> "shaken to the core" to discover that Russian and Polish women and girls liberated from concentration camps were also violated. "That completely undermined the notion that soldiers were using rape as a form of revenge. . . . By the time the Russians reached Berlin, soldiers were regarding women almost as carnal booty."[7]

The incidence of rape was not confined to isolated situations; rather it was, as the above remarks suggest, on the order of an epidemic. It is worth noting in this regard that in 1914, there were precisely two cases of rape recorded in the czar's forces in East Prussia.[8]

But it is difficult to argue that an army of rapists and robbers is an army with the level of discipline required to function effectively on the modern battlefield. The universal regulation of soldierly behavior rests not on a concern for morality, but on a concern for order and discipline. Practically speaking, the loss of basic control evinced by this epidemic also helps explain why the casualty exchange ratio remained so lopsided up to the end of the war.

There is also the disparity in weaponry; like the shocking indiscipline of the Red Army, it is rarely noted. Although later Soviet tank designs, notably the JS-2 heavy tank, were impressive-looking weapons, in combat they apparently had severe defects; nor, regardless of how well designed, were they any match for the Tiger tanks developed some years earlier. On January 14, 1945, Tiger tanks from the 507th Abteilung destroyed twenty-two JS-2 tanks at almost point-blank range without suffering a single loss.[9]

The notion that Stalin won the war does not, however, rest on evaluations of tactics or strategy, or purely military considerations, but on three fundamental points that go far beyond those concerns.

He beat Hitler because he seized Berlin and a sizable piece of Germany as well, it is argued. He did most of the fighting, the proof being that millions of Russians died trying to stop Hitler's mad scheme for world conquest. He deserves the lion's share of the credit because Allied aid did not begin to arrive in any quantity until 1943, at a point when Stalin had already defeated the German invasion.

Although the general idea, like all legends, to a certain extent defies logic or analysis, and will continue to do so, none of the reasons generally alleged in support of Stalin's claim has much merit. The final Soviet surge occurred because the victorious and powerful Allied armies in the west were not allowed to press forward and overrun the rest of the Reich. Given how the Wehrmacht was still piling up the bodies of Russian soldiers until the very end of the war, the notion that the Red Army would have gotten to Berlin first had there been an actual race seems doubtful. This decision was part and parcel of the same general approach initiated by Churchill and Roosevelt after June 1941, the idea apparently being that Stalin was a reasonable fellow who could be satisfied, or perhaps civilized, by being welcomed into the comity of the great powers. Churchill, even though he despised Stalin and justifiably feared his ambitions, was still willing to sit down at the table and negotiate with him. Churchill's preeminent historian puts it this way:

> He [Churchill] had the impression, he said, that Stalin and the Soviet leaders "wish to live in honorable friendship and equality with the western democracies. I also feel that their word is their bond."[10]

Chamberlain and the French had felt the same way about Hitler at Munich, an appeasement conducted with far more justification.

Stalin repaid the Anglo-American largesse by egging on Kim Il-sung, the dictator of North Korea, who went to Moscow expressly to ask Stalin's permission to invade South Korea. "Stalin encouraged him, but shrewdly passed the buck to Mao. . . . He thus protected his dominant role but passed the responsibility."[11] Kim would never have dreamt of doing anything on his own, and Mao, although itching to establish his hegemony over East Asia, lacked the means to wage such a fight on his own. Stalin was clever in hiding his control behind the scenes, but his willingness to start the Korean War is a fact of some inconvenience for the notion of his peaceful intentions.

That the Bolsheviks bore the brunt of Hitler's aggression is a deeply flawed idea once we understand that Stalin was planning to attack him. But leaving that equally inconvenient fact aside, the notion stands the actual situation on its head. From December 1941 on, Stalin derived an enormous benefit from America's entrance into the war. Initially, as we have seen, this benefit consisted of the half a million soldiers he was able to transfer from the Far East once he was assured that the Japanese army was committed to Southeast Asia.

The aggressive, risky, and surprisingly successful American responses in 1942 to Japan ensured that country's attentions would be fixed elsewhere for the rest of the war. The extent to which this freed Moscow from a serious dilemma is difficult to overemphasize. So there was a second front in the global sense long before there was one in the narrow sense that it was interpreted, and that Stalin demanded. But even there, the notion that Stalin had to fight on alone until June 1944 hardly withstands examination. As we have seen, Hitler steadily drained off resources from the east to meet threats in France, the Balkans, Italy, and the Mediterranean. It makes no difference whether those threats were real or imaginary. The result was the same, to weaken the combat capabilities of the Wehrmacht in the east.

The controversy surrounding Allied aid to the USSR provides a perfect illustration both of the ferocity and tenacity with which the Stalinist position has been maintained, and the reason why it has been so successful. From early on Bolshevik writers made concerted attacks on the whole notion that Allied aid was significant. These arguments, like all communist propaganda, make for incredibly tedious reading, and can be easily summarized.[12] The argument goes that the amount of aid, although of some value in 1942, was of diminishing importance as the war progressed, owing to the enormous increases in Soviet production of what was needed to win the war. The problem is that military historians seem unaware of the problematic nature of Soviet statistics. One of the warrants on which this study has been based is that accounts of the war must be seen in the broader context of the history of the Soviet Union, in which one of the few flourishing industries was the production of numbers.

The extent to which these numbers are distorted and unreliable is difficult to convey, mainly because each case is somewhat different. But as the following examples demonstrate, the situation was pervasive, and began with Stalin himself. On November 6, 1941, Stalin made a public address on the occasion of the twenty-fourth anniversary of the revolution, in which he gave the following figures:

> In four months of the war we lost 350,000 killed, 378,000 missing, and have 1,078,000 wounded men. In the same period the enemy lost over 4,500,000 killed, wounded, and prisoners. There can be no doubt that as a result of four months of the war, Germany, whose manpower reserves are already becoming exhausted, has undoubtedly been considerably more weakened by the war than the Soviet Union, whose reserves are only now unfolding to their full extent.[13]

By the time of Stalin's speech, German casualty reports came to 144,575 dead and 29,010 missing; the Germans counted 3,539,391 prisoners of war; the estimate of Soviet casualties for 1941 is currently 4,308,094 dead.[14]

Nor were such wildly exaggerated claims simply put forth as propaganda. When Stalin declared something to be true, it was officially true. As is the case with many direct statements about the Soviet Union, this one sounds like a wild generalization. But consider the following example, which is of fundamental importance to any understanding of the Stalinist world.

In January 1934 Stalin made a speech to the 17th Party Congress in which, along with many other things, he said that one of the great achievements of socialism was the rapid increase in the birth rate, owing to improvements in the life of the workers. In Stalin's speeches, whether to the world at large or to the party leadership, he was never content with vague, general statements, but gave precise figures. The results of the next census, he said, would show that the population had grown from 160.5 million at the end of 1930 to 168 million by the end of 1933. The logical conclusion was that by the time the next census was completed, the population would be higher still.[15] However, when the actual census was completed, in 1937, the data showed quite the contrary: instead of the 170 million odd that Stalin had forecast, the actual figure was 162 million.

Stalin's reaction was instructive. The data was released to the Politburo in January. In March everyone in a position of authority in the census office was arrested, and in September the census was declared invalid, the work of "wreckers" aiming to destroy the realities of socialist achievements. Not surprisingly, the next census, held in 1939, showed a population of . . . 170 million. Just to make sure that there were no more factual embarrassments, there was no subsequent census during Stalin's lifetime. The next Soviet census was taken in 1959.

Today no one really knows what the actual numbers were for the prewar population, nor is there any agreement as to how the data should be weighted to compensate. So although no one actually believes the official figure to be accurate, it is used as a baseline in calculating wartime losses, simply because it is the only figure we have.[16]

The 1937 census is one of the few instances in which we have concrete proof of how Stalin manipulated the basic data. Clearly it is not a trivial example. Nor is it an isolated one. The numbers used internally to make decisions were just as suspect as those proclaimed to the outside world. Again, the following example is instructive. In October 1952, Georgi Malenkov had reported to the 19th Party Congress that the Soviet grain harvest had been 130 million tons, which, he claimed, meant that the agricultural problems of the country had been conquered.

But in 1958, Khrushchev revealed that the actual grain harvest had been only 92 million tons, or almost 40 percent less than claimed. Far from representing the triumph of socialist agriculture, the amount "did not satisfy the current requirements of the government, let alone permit the creation of necessary reserves" in Khrushchev's words.[17]

Although in noncritical areas at the lower levels, Soviet reporting may have been as accurate as in France or Canada, when it came to critical areas relating to agriculture, the economy, and industrial production, the figures bore only some vague relationship to the actual situation. In fact, in one of the more important economic analyses of post-Soviet Russia, the authors devote an entire chapter to the issue of distortion in the government's statistics. Their arguments are extremely technical, but the conclusions are clear enough:

> Since the end of the 1920s official statistics have systematically overstated data on growth rates of the physical volume of production.... The scale of statistical

> distortions has been so significant that sometimes the ordinal numbers were changed for particular periods, i.e., 30 percent instead of 3 percent. The greatest distortions overstating real growth occurred in the 1930s. Real industrial growth was distorted most; data on the dynamics of agricultural production were distorted least.[18]

Since in one of the most documented examples grain production was overstated by 40 percent, the argument in the last sentence seems something of an understatement.

When we look at the broader context of Soviet data then, it is clear that the numbers were manipulated in order to conform to what Stalin believed should be happening, regardless of what the actual situation was. The consequences of giving Stalin information he didn't want to hear could be fatal. The census staff was, one supposes, lucky simply to be arrested and imprisoned: the chief of the air force staff was arrested, tortured, and then shot, after he told Stalin something he didn't want to hear, that the reason there were so many crashes was that Soviet aircraft were riddled with defects. Given that environment, that all Soviet data was not systematically altered to meet Stalin's expectations is unlikely.

Stalin had determined that the USSR won the war, and that it did so largely on its own. By definition British and American aid was trivial, and the data dutifully showed that to be the case. After Stalin's death the pattern continued, as the position he had defined resonated with resurgent nationalism.[19]

Debates on the importance of Allied aid to Stalin have essentially been comparing the numbers of actual working armored vehicles that the British and Americans loaded onto ships and transported to the USSR with the theoretical numbers of armored vehicles that the tank factories claimed they had produced in order to satisfy Stalin's demands. Even on that comparison, however, the shipments were substantial: 12,575 British and American tanks were sent to the Red Army, enough to equip 273 tank brigades based on the theoretical Soviet organizational charts of December 1941, an armored force substantially larger than the one Stalin had lost in the first six months of the war.[20] So the notion that this massive injection of armor was insignificant does not bear scrutiny.

In their argument that Allied aid was trivial, Soviet writers were careful not to rest their argument entirely on statistics. As is the case with any clever rhetorician, they advanced other claims as well, independent of numbers. Not only was the number of tanks sent insignificant in the context of massive Soviet production but the turning point victories had been reached before the aid began to arrive in quantity.

As we have seen, on inspection these victories largely evaporate. Moreover, the German evidence establishes pretty clearly that the Red Army was deploying American tanks in July 1943 in sufficient quantity for the Germans to notice. That observation casts a good deal of light on the often quoted assertion that not only was the aid slow in coming, but the equipment was inferior to what the Soviets were producing themselves. These claims are almost entirely without merit. American medium tanks, although inferior in theoretical design, were substantially more reliable than their Soviet counterparts, and the lighter American tanks were at least as good or better than their Soviet counterparts. And, of course, one reason the Red Army needed so many tanks was that it had failed to develop the specialized tank recovery vehicles that other armies (the Germans and Americans in particular) employed. All of those came from the Allies.

Finally, Soviet writers, who have been allowed to frame this debate for the last half century, engaged in another sleight of hand: while denigrating the quantity and quality of the tanks they were sent, they passed over in silence the substantially larger numbers of wheeled and tracked vehicles shipped to them. There was a good reason for this. The Allied shipment of tracked artillery (self-propelled guns) was roughly the same as the Soviet production of the Red Army's standard 76.2 millimeter self-propelled gun during the key period of the war.

For various reasons, Soviet factories were unable to produce heavy trucks in any number, and those that were built were based on ancient models, grossly inferior in every way to the 363,080 trucks sent to the Red Army.[21] To frame the proper comparison, the German firm of Opel, the primary supplier of trucks to the Wehrmacht, only produced 82,356 trucks during the entire war.

The Soviet Union never managed to find the resources to build tracked personnel carriers that would enable the infantry in a tank brigade to keep up with the tanks. That was one reason for the heavy Soviet losses of armor, as well as for the ubiquitous pictures of Soviet infantry clustered on tanks. The 7,179 personnel carriers the Allies sent over had no Soviet counterpart. But of course the Germans had one.

To put these other figures in perspective: a Soviet tank brigade, for example, was supposed to have not only forty-six tanks, but 156 trucks for its infantry component (no tracked vehicles existed to transport them). Insofar as the Red Army had any meaningful wheeled transport capacity, it came from the approximately half a million vehicles the Allies supplied.

The idea that Stalin could have prevailed in his war against Hitler without the massive quantities of Allied aid, while probably the perfect example of how his apologists framed the terms of any substantive debate to the Soviet advantage, is without merit. On the contrary, his victory was built as much on mountains of Allied matériel as on the mountains of Russian corpses.

This last was the real key to the Soviet victory, the one factor that Stalin could control. From the very first everyone had subscribed to the notion that the manpower of the Red Army was essentially inexhaustible, and several generations of Germans, including the veterans who had survived, wrote about their experiences in ways that reinforced the notion that Stalin had infinite human resources.

It is impossible to do any calculation, using any realistic set of numbers, in which the German army was not killing off Russian soldiers at a rate that greatly exceeded what the manpower at the disposal of the two dictators could withstand. As mentioned at the start of this book, the only real question is an abstract one, the determination of what the precise ratio was, not the fact of the imbalance itself.

So from the traditional perspective of professional soldiers, Stalin was, as the Soviet general Dmitri Volkogonov observed, entirely ignorant of the basic principle of the military art: to secure objectives with the least losses. The same could be said of Hitler, and was, by military professionals trained to see victory in terms of the seizure of national capitals. But on a higher level, a level beyond the comprehension of those same critics, both leaders understood grand strategy perfectly. Hitler knew that the way to win was to deprive Stalin of the means to wage war. He came close to doing so, and one reason he failed, one of the more significant, was that he failed to reckon on the enormous amount of Allied aid that Stalin would get. The Soviet ruler could replace everything he lost in the disasters of the first months and still keep fighting.

Stalin understood something of equal importance: he could win if he sacrificed enough Russians, if he kept on demanding attack after attack. Finally he would prevail. The actual numbers of Russians killed was irrelevant to him. In that regard Churchill's conversation with him is revealing, and worth quoting in full:

> "Tell me," I asked, "have the stresses of the war been as bad to you personally as carrying through the policy of the Collective farms?"
> The Subject immediately aroused the Marshal.

"Oh no," he said. "The Collective Farm policy was a terrible struggle."

". . . because you were dealing with . . . millions. . . ."

"Ten millions," he said, holding up his hands.[22]

So Stalin had some idea of the cost, and a rather precise idea, given what we now know about the number of deaths caused by the "struggle."

So he concluded that the key to victory was to press on regardless of the cost, that the Germans couldn't kill the entire Red Army, and that, failing to do so, they would eventually lose. Despite Stalin's excellently articulated and convincing tale of how the Soviet Union won the war, the evidence suggests that this war was Hitler's to lose, that he came very close to winning it, that Stalin was the victor only because he was willing to sacrifice approximately 27 million Russians, and, at that, largely by default. That those of his field commanders who contrived to live through the first years of the war learned the rudiments of mechanized warfare is certainly true: there was a learning curve, albeit an extremely bloody one.

In the main, Hitler lost his war against Stalin because of decisions that he himself made, not because he was overwhelmed and defeated on the field of battle by a superior enemy. On close examination, many of Hitler's decisions that have been criticized as mistakes were on the contrary shrewd strategic moves. Although the general Stalinist outline of the war has the Germans staggering from defeat to defeat, the evidence suggests that by summer 1943 they were on the verge of a genuine breakthrough of the sort that their predecessors and opponents had dreamed of throughout the First World War.

Seen in that light, Citadel was a victory unachieved, and although as we have seen, the Germans had more difficulties on the battlefield there than they had encountered before (no thanks to Stalin), the offensive did not fail. It was broken off, not because of the judgment of the field commanders, who on the contrary believed they were on the verge of a real victory, but on Hitler's direct orders.

So until July 1943 the prospect of victory was tantalizingly close. At that point, the massive Allied invasion of France was a year into the future, and American troops had yet to set foot on any part of the mainland. Their performance in North Africa in spring 1943 could be dismissed, and, despite the decision to emphasize the war in Europe, the Pacific theater was where most of the fighting was going on. Indeed, for Hitler, it was the Pacific theater that seemed the one into which all of America's massive resources were being directed, as the conquest of the strategic islands held by the Japanese was now in full swing after the bitter fight for Guadalcanal (which ended only in February 1943). It was reasonable for Hitler to assume that the Allies could hardly mount simultaneous efforts everywhere at once, and that he had plenty of time left in which to bring the Soviet Union down completely.

In the aftermath of Citadel, the Soviet Union claimed that the Red Army had defeated the German offensive soundly. Since they controlled all the accounts of the battle, they were able to paint a convincing picture of that failure and their success. It was not a lack of resources that brought the offensives to an end; it was what Hitler did with those resources as a result of his July decision. But Hitler's decision of July 1943 to break off Citadel was a mistake, one of the very few that he made, and perhaps the one with the most damaging consequences.

At the grand strategic level, both Hitler and the Allies understood the importance of airpower as one of the keys to victory, which in turn meant that one of the objectives of both sides in both theaters was control of territory from which bomber attacks could be launched.

Leaving aside the numerous flaws in this reasoning made by both sides when applied to specific cases, Hitler's decision to move into the Balkans in spring 1941 was as justified as the British move into Greece that triggered the attack. In this peculiar game, the larger islands of the Mediterranean—Crete, Sardinia, Sicily—became important. For the Allies, they were simply large aircraft carriers on which their strategic bombers could be based for attacks on the economic heartland of Hitler's empire, or, as was the case with Sicily, used as the guard post for an invasion of the Italian mainland.

With the collapse of Italy in 1943, Hitler realized that the Germans would have to block the Allied acquisition of the Mediterranean islands, and moved to that end. The loss of Tunisia in May 1943 was an additional stimulus, as it meant that the Germans had now lost control of North Africa, and would have to mount a more concerted defensive effort on the northern side of the Mediterranean. As the summer days went by, that need became more and more urgent in Hitler's mind, and was clearly one reason why he broke off Citadel and began shifting troops into the southern and western borders.

Hitler kept pouring precious military resources into the Mediterranean, to the point that he doomed the last great German offensive effort in Russia by his insistence that resources be shuttled there, first in the futile efforts in Tunisia, and then, in July, with his misdirected efforts to hold Sicily, Italy, and the Balkans.

Defeats, like catastrophes, have many causes, and Hitler's decision in July 1943 was certainly not the only reason the Germans lost in the east. Allied aid and Stalin's willingness to fight to the last Russian prolonged the struggle. After summer 1943 other factors tipped the balance, the two most significant being the two most obvious. The successive Allied invasions (Sicily, Italy, and Normandy) stretched the Wehrmacht to the point that it was impossible to mount more than holding actions on any front. Although the impact of the strategic bombing campaign is, despite the claims of its apostles, quite problematic, it certainly had some effect on Germany's ability to prolong the war, as did the overall failure of Germany's technical experts to produce weaponry in the quantity that would give the army and air force the technical superiority it desperately needed on the battlefield. But an outright German victory in July 1943 would have rendered these other matters moot. The point is not that German victory was a certainty. In warfare very little is certain. But the possibility was real, the promise of success tantalizingly close.

After 1945 the Red Army, as a result of its victory over the Wehrmacht, a victory enormously magnified by incessant propagandizing, was transmogrified into an unstoppable military machine. Its numerous deficiencies were ignored, the striking defeats of its lavishly trained and equipped surrogate armies brushed aside, and when incontrovertible evidence of the deficiencies surfaced, as it occasionally did, the rationalizations were so ingenious as to form a whole subgenre of intelligence literature.

After all, Stalin had won. Germany was divided, its capital split in two, the barricades around the Brandenburg Gate, like the moonscape where Speer's chancellery had once stood, perpetual symbols of that victory. But nowadays Stalin's great victory is perhaps not so clear cut.

EPILOGUE:
THE GREAT PATRIOTIC WAR AND THE COLLAPSE

The war solved no problems. Its effects, both immediate and indirect, were either negative or disastrous. Morally subversive, economically destructive, socially degrading, confused in its causes, devious in its course, futile in its result, it is the outstanding example in European history of meaningless conflict.

C. V. Wedgwood, *The Thirty Years War*[1]

Almost every phrase in Wedgwood's brilliant conclusion to her seminal study of that horrible conflict could be applied to the war between Hitler and Stalin. Although the passage of time and Stalinist secrecy make comparisons difficult, the devastation in the Soviet empire the Germans occupied during the Second World War was in many ways much worse than what was experienced in the German lands during the Thirty Years War. In fact, the debates and controversies surrounding the effects of that war provide a salutary framework for any attempt to get past the intuitive feeling that the effects were "either negative or disastrous," to use her memorable phrase.

Three centuries later, historians of the Thirty Years War are still uncertain as to the exact dimensions of the extent of that devastation. Their uncertainty is a sobering reminder of the difficulties of moving past vague general statements that in themselves often become exaggerations.[2] In one sense, however, the task of modern scholarship on such distant subjects is easier: three centuries gives us a perspective that is only just becoming possible sixty-five years after the end of the Second World War and barely two decades after the collapse of the Soviet Union. Consider, for example, the case of the British Empire. As the First World War still raged, General John Pershing recorded the following brief interchange with Georges Clemenceau, the French prime minister:

> Clemenceau observed Great Britain was finished as a world power. Not merely because of the "immense drain of the fighting," but because "the experience of her Colonial troops in the war will make their people more independent and she will lose her control over them."[3]

True enough, but the loss of the largest and most prosperous parts of her colonies occurred only after the end of the next war: for India (and subsequently Pakistan) in 1947, for southern Africa even later.

Had foreigners been allowed to travel inside the Soviet state, the physical evidence might have led them to the conclusion that the empire was slowly collapsing. But in the decade following the end of the war, as in the decade preceding it, there was simply no independent travel permitted, and very little guided and controlled travel. So it is hardly surprising that either the dimensions of the depredations or the implications of Stalin's scorched-earth policy for the future were noticed.[4] There was no objective assessment of the actual damage suffered during the war. No one knows whether the usual Soviet figures citing the destruction of 1,700 towns, 70,000 villages, and housing for 25 million people are accurate.[5]

At the same time, the Bolsheviks never ceased to flood the world with evidence showing the incredible achievements of socialism. The result was a series of blithe assumptions about the durability and slowly improving standard of living that went on right up until the collapse of the Soviet Union. Consequently, that the Soviet Union would simply implode was unthinkable. The consensus, shared by friends and foes alike, was that the system was as close to a fixed point in the political and social universe as could be found.

Twenty years later, considerations of the exact causes for the Soviet collapse, still largely unrealized and not really understood, have to a great extent eclipsed any serious investigations into the long-term effects of the war on the defunct state. The scholarly rigor that would allow definitive answers to the question may well be impossible. Certainly the war was not the sole cause of the collapse, but a brief consideration of the chief candidates illuminates its importance, certainly as the primary indirect cause.

Probably the most significant direct cause of the collapse is the one that generally gets short shrift from analysts. The economic assumptions that governed the state's decisions proved unworkable. Another festering sore was the problem of the ethnic minorities who wanted true independence. From its origins in Marx on through Lenin and beyond, the Bolsheviks had been curiously blind to the power of local, regional, and tribal allegiances. "The official view, circa 1985, was that nationality issues formed a comparatively minor and easily manageable problem," is how one observer worded it.[6]

Then of course there was the grim fact that Stalin had maintained order by a rule of terror. In the six years preceding the war, roughly twenty million people had been arrested, and of those, a good one million were murdered, the blow falling disproportionately on those with skills: "During Stalin's time party officials were even more in fear of the security people than ordinary citizens were."[7]

There was Stalin himself. The more that we learn about his life, the more difficult it is to avoid the conclusion that he was, as the composer Dmitri Shostakovich claimed, an extremely jealous man whose jealousy took the form of murdering the hapless objects of his insecurities. In *The Possessed*, written nearly a century before, Fyodor Dostoevsky had described what would come to pass and prophesied the inevitable result:

> Every member of society spies on the others, and it is his duty to inform against them. . . . All are slaves and equal in their slavery. . . . The level of education, science, and talent is lowered. . . . In the herd there is bound to be equality.[8]

All on his own, Stalin created a climate that fostered men whose abilities were extremely modest. The Tukhachevskys were all either dead or so fearful that they hardly dared to breathe in his direction.

Moreover, the insulated life of privilege that was increasingly enjoyed by the nomenklatura, particularly at the higher levels, produced a leadership that was both naive about the world and out of touch with the pressures that were slowly creating the great implosion to come.[9] Stalin had often baited his subordinates about their innocence, and he had a point, although of course to a great extent he was responsible for that himself.

The exact weight to assign to each of these causes is unknowable. However, one interesting observation follows: the Great Patriotic War was the major cataclysm closest to the ultimate collapse. In a system that was clearly moribund and stagnant, with chronic shortages of practically everything, carefully vetted and worded memoirs, histories, and studies of the war were one of the few flourishing enterprises.[10] The victory of the Red Army over Hitler was both the vindication of the system and its one clear and unambiguous triumph, the depredations of the Hitlerites the excuse for every shortcoming: "The history of the war thus emerged as a bizarre cocktail of facts, falsifications, and, above all, omissions," is how one recent Soviet historian put it.[11]

In ascending order of importance, the war had four catastrophic effects on the Soviet Union: the enormous physical damage to the infrastructure, the diversion of scarce resources caused by Stalin's desperate efforts to move Soviet industry out of German reach, the negative impact of his systematic forced relocations of entire populations, and the demographic holocaust that resulted from the deaths of tens of millions of Russians, primarily and almost exclusively those from western, or European, Russia. Although it is possible that the state might have survived one of these, taken together, they reinforced the downward spiral that was in turn exacerbated both by the applications of Marxist doctrine and the Leninist-Stalinist depredations of the decades before the war.

As we saw earlier, Stalin decreed widespread destruction in the occupied zones, and as the German retreat began in 1943 very little was left intact. Valuable (and in the case of the USSR, extremely scarce) farmland was contaminated by chemical residue (from explosives) and lubricants, the soil compacted by the pressure exerted on it by military vehicles, the isolated farmsteads and small villages destroyed. The net effect is actually worse than aerial bombardment.

A comprehensive and systematic analysis of the resulting damage is at this point impossible, but the isolated evidence seems persuasive. For example, there was the startling collapse of the electrical grid. Although the Soviet data is, as we have seen, highly questionable, in 1940 the official figure for the total electricity output of what would become the occupied zone was slightly over 2.5 million kilowatts.[12] When the Germans looked into the generating situation they discovered that there were only 300,000 kilowatts available. Although it is impossible to verify the Soviet figures, the data suggests widespread destruction no matter how the official figure is adjusted.

The German-occupied zone produced one fourth of the total electricity generated in the USSR, which gives a rough idea of its importance to the country as a whole: the wealthiest, most populous, and most developed part of the country had been lost, including the areas that produced, by one reasonable estimate, about two thirds of Soviet coal, iron, steel, and aluminum.[13] The depth and breadth of the destruction of human and physical resources in what had been the wealthiest and most developed portion of the Soviet Union is appalling. So the proposition that in itself the damage was a burden that eventually proved too much to bear is a reasonable conjecture. It is probably overlooked by analysts because most people are unaware of just how much of the Soviet Union the Germans rolled over in 1941–1942. True, the German advance was eventually stopped before Moscow and Leningrad, but only after the Germans had occupied what was essentially an entire country—and indeed, after the collapse of the Soviet Union, no fewer than six separate countries came into being that lay inside the former German zone.

The access allowed foreigners was less rigorously controlled in those countries, so it was possible to measure the extent of the recovery from the war, albeit in a highly subjective way. But even superficial inspections revealed an infrastructure that was still scarred from the war. What one saw looking across the Wall into East Berlin from the West was not entirely misleading: surprisingly large parts of the city of Dresden still consisted of ruins or overgrown lots half a century later. Even driving down the streets of prosperous towns it was easy to see buildings still in ruins, walls pockmarked with shell splinters.[14]

The state of affairs inside the Soviet Union was much worse. Indeed, the varying rates of recovery of the countries behind the Iron Curtain was one of the chief irritants for the Russian nomenklatura.[15] As the years rolled by they had increasing difficulty in understanding why the quality of life in East Germany and Czechoslovakia, and even in Hungary and Poland, was so much better than in Russia itself.

There were many causes for the lag in the reconstruction of the USSR, but one of them was the result of the decisions Stalin made at the start of the war, to relocate industries and forcibly remove entire populations. Those decisions had long-term effects both on the infrastructure of the country and on its demographics, all of them negative or disastrous. Combined, they went a long way toward ensuring that the country would never fully recover from the heavy blow occasioned by the war.

With proper development of the transportation infrastructure, those inefficiencies could have been remediated to a great extent, and in the years before the war, the Bolsheviks had duly touted such projects, just as they had talked at great lengths about the need for the mechanization of agriculture and the electrification of the countryside. The extent to which anything of value had actually been accomplished is unknowable, but anecdotally, the evidence suggests that serious development and modernization were pretty much still where they had been in 1914, aside from a few grandiose projects whose value was both highly questionable and of extremely limited impact.[16]

But behind the banners and slogans of modernization, surprisingly little had been accomplished. The various Soviet schemes of the 1920s and 1930s emphasized the importance of railroads, and this emphasis was duly invoked to explain the appalling condition of the road system as well as its startling inadequacies: until 2004 there was no all-weather road equivalent to the Trans-Siberian rail line built by czarist engineers, and there is still no all-weather road linking the important Siberian city of Irkutsk with the rest of the country.[17]

As we have seen, the lack of a road system worthy of the name, a constant problem for the invading Germans, had hardly helped the Red Army as it stumbled westward, and was one reason for its frequent halts, pauses that enabled the embattled Germans to regroup, and thus raised the Soviet death toll considerably. Given that foreigners were not allowed to drive on it (and very few Russians were allowed to drive outside the USSR), the appalling state of the road system was unnoticed. When the journalist Serge Schmemann visited his family's ancestral village in the 1980s, he found that "the road to Koltsovo was paved only after my first visit in 1990; before that, there were days when the nearest town, Ferzikovo, 8 miles away, could be reached only by tractor."[18] And this was in an area less than 150 kilometers southeast of Moscow.

Although the emphasis on rail lines was used to explain the lack of all-weather roads, the rail lines too were problematic. By 1939, for example, the amount of railroad track had increased by only about 35,000 kilometers since 1917, and much of the existing 100,000 kilometers was for various reasons unusable. Given the enormous expanse of Russia, this was markedly insufficient: before the start of the First World War, France had 60,000 kilometers of track and the United States, whose area was more directly comparable, had nearly 400,000.[19]

So the base from which the USSR had to start rebuilding the most developed and the most devastated parts of the country was already extremely low, which meant that enormous resources were required. Stalin's relocations drained off those resources and put enormous strains on a system that was already woefully inadequate, badly maintained, and poorly thought out.[20]

So Stalin's decision to relocate such a major part of the Soviet industrial base, although justified at the time, was a great step backward in the long term. The industries thus relocated could not simply be moved back to the west once the war was over, and the evidence, scanty as it is, suggests that neither Stalin nor his heirs ever thought about doing that. So the development of the eastern interior of Russia, begun out of wartime necessity, continued apace, resulting in monstrous inefficiencies of human and physical resources. By contrast, in Poland and East Germany, the two countries most devastated by the war, not only was the physical infrastructure more highly developed to begin with, but the new and smaller borders dictated that whatever resources there were could be utilized more efficiently.

Stalin's other great decision involved the forcible relocation of millions of Soviet citizens. These massive population shifts have been documented only recently, so neither the magnitude nor the implications have been realized. Magnitude: the number of Soviet citizens forcibly shifted from their home territories to the interior eventually amounted to around three million souls, the culmination of a drastic resettling of the Soviet state that by Stalin's death had resulted in the physical removal of about six million people.[21]

The number of human beings involved is actually significantly higher, because while entire ethnic groups were being exiled from their traditional areas, other, presumably more politically reliable or ethnically acceptable, people were being dragooned into the vacated space.

Although in all probability Stalin would happily have let those 3 million people starve to death, and that may well have been his intention, his heirs were less inhumane. As we have seen, Khrushchev actually worried about feeding the population sufficiently, and starting in the 1960s the government bombarded its citizens with statistics purporting to show how their standard of living was increasing, as in some measure it was.

The disastrous agricultural situation was not helped by the false ideas about agronomy championed by Lysenko in the 1930s. That fundamental wrong turn, discussed in the opening chapter of this study, insisted that a crop that could flourish in only one area could be transplanted into any other area. Not only was that not true, but the areas in question were parts of the country where there was a basic reason why settlements had traditionally been sparse: neither Siberia nor Kazakhstan (the two major destinations) was particularly hospitable. At best they could support limited numbers of people, and those relatively sparse numbers had adapted their lifestyles accordingly. Not even a rich agricultural area could easily take the shock of such wholesale migrations, much less one that was already marginal.

The idea of the development of the hinterlands of central and eastern Russia, and the concomitant decentralization of industry, was, like the obsession with industrialization per se as the magic wand that would improve the standards of living, part of a process that had begun before the war.[22] But the massive relocation of people and resources during the war accelerated the process considerably, straining an economy that was already staggering under the burden of fixing the damage in the wealthiest and most populous section of the country.

Finally, there was the human cost. One of the warrants for this account of the war, as noted at the beginning of this book, was the startling and dramatic imbalance between the number of dead Russians and dead Germans, the inference being that accounts of great Soviet victories and a triumphant Red Army were the stuff of legend. The question here, however, turns to a different point, the extent to which it can be argued that those 27 million dead Russians, taken in concert with the enormous destruction wreaked on the countryside's infrastructure, became a significant factor in the collapse of the Soviet state.

Such an argument is complex and technical by definition. It is not made any easier by the realization noted in the preceding chapter that the census data after 1937 was falsified, and that there was no census at all until 1959. As we noted at the start of this chapter, historians trying to measure the impact of the Thirty Years War have more data, and more reliable data, to work with. Although Stalin's successors no longer executed those who brought them bad news, the habit of making the data fit the plans announced by the state continued. Consequently, it was not until the 1980 census data reached the West that enough of a trend line was established to see the dramatic negative impact of what Stalin had called the Great Patriotic War on the Soviet population.

The losses during the war were now clearly visible, because in the 1980 census there was

a severe deficit of males aged 55 and over. . . . The effect of World War II is also reflected in the deficit of births in 1940 to 1945, reflected in the "pinching" of the pyramid in the 35–39 age group of both men and women ... The effects of World War II can be seen in the data from the 1959 and 1970 census on the percentages of males by age group.... These differences appear in all the Slavic and Baltic republics, but not in the Transcaucasian and Central Asian republics. This probably reflects the much heavier World War II military losses suffered in the northern areas.[23]

The extraordinarily high rate of loss in the males resulted in a noticeable drop in the birth rates, and this drop was most marked in those areas of the country most affected by the war.

There were three practical consequences of this deficit on postwar Soviet society. First, as noted above, one of the unintended consequences of Stalin's forced relocations was to strain the Soviet economy severely. Those moves, when taken with the severe deficit in the population of European Russia, dramatically increased the percentage of the population at the eastern and southern peripheries of the state. Their increasing share of the population led them to demand more resources, which in turn meant a further diversion of increasingly scarce assets into the edges of the country and away from its traditional center of western, or European, Russia (including Belorussia and Ukraine).

Second, Stalin's wartime deportations had the understandable result of reducing entire populations to the sort of abject dependency that would require generations to overcome even in a state with lavish resources to devote to their improvement.[24]

But the state lacked those resources, particularly in terms of manpower. That deficit affected successive cohorts of the able-bodied males who formed the core of the Soviet Union's workforce, as well as its military manpower pool. That shortage in turn lowered industrial and agricultural productivity: there was simply not enough skilled labor available to produce what any modern society required, the third practical consequence of the war.

As early (or late) as the 1970s, a French analyst had noticed the disastrous consequences of the Soviet economic system, which he compared with the reality of a science fiction novel. The inherent unworkability of the system was now exacerbated by the manpower shortage. Again, agriculture provides us with a succinct example of how the two negative tendencies, one in population, the other in the basic structuring of the state, combined.

The early Soviet leadership was aware of the inefficiencies of Soviet agriculture, which, as noted earlier, employed twice as many people as Germany or the United States, but whose productivity was only about four fifths as great. One of the solutions fashioned was to mechanize agriculture. Not only was it intended to replace human labor with machines, but the idea was to build very large machines, thus reducing the labor costs still more.

Superficially this solution mimicked what was going on in the West. By and of itself it might have eventually been made to work, but in consequence, agricultural productivity became more and more dependent on machine operators for tractors, harvesters, and transport vehicles, and the mechanics to keep them running. But it was precisely that category of the Soviet workforce that had been hit hardest by the war, and in the areas that were most suited to the growing of basic crops.[25]

The result was a slowly developing death spiral, the dimensions of which went unnoticed until the very end of the regime's life. The French analyst who, in 1976, predicted that the system would collapse by the end of the 1980s, was regarded with derision, but events proved him right.[26]

Catastrophes have complex causes, and it would be simplistic to see the death toll during the war as the only factor; however, as its effects were experienced over successive generations, it was probably determinative. It went unnoticed because of the nature of the phenomenon, which was only identified by demographers four decades later. It is significant in this connection that the trends only became clearly visible in the 1980 census, right on the threshold of the collapse.

Then too there are the intangibles, difficult to measure in any way, but no less profound for all that. Shostakovich expressed it perfectly when he explained the paradox:

> And then the war came and the sorrow became a common one. We could talk about it, we could cry openly, cry for our lost ones. People stopped fearing tears. Eventually they got used to it. There was time to get used to it, four whole years. And that is why it was so hard after the war, when suddenly it all stopped. . . . I wasn't the only one who had an opportunity to express himself because of the war. . . . That wasn't the situation everywhere, and in other countries war probably interferes with the arts. But in Russia, for tragic reasons, there was a flowering.[27]

Although the war brought terrible suffering to untold millions, it was also, paradoxically, a time when Stalin was forced to loosen his stranglehold on the citizenry, if for no other reason than he needed both hands to throttle the Red Army and its leaders. In terms of how people felt, of their freedom to breathe, the war was actually a brief interlude.

Of course at the end of it, Stalin began all over again, planning a new round of terror, carefully fashioning his own holocaust, and terrorizing the few artists and intellectuals who were still alive.[28] The end of the war was the end of any hope that the situation would improve. With each year that went by, the USSR moved inexorably backward to 1937. It was during those years that Nikolay Bulganin remarked to Khrushchev (as they were en route between Moscow and Stalin's country estate), that when you visited Stalin you never knew whether you'd come back.

So there's a grim irony in the manner of the great tyrant's death: lying there after a crippling stroke, unable to summon help, the servants too terrified to do the obvious, the critical hours in which prompt treatment might have prolonged his life going by, that same terror being replicated all the way up through the leadership. The great criminal was finally undone in part by the consequences of his own criminality.

But not before his obsessions had permanently disfigured Russian life. The days of the camps had hardly ended with the end of the war:

> On 1 January 1948 there were 2,199,535 prisoners in camps and colonies. . . . on 1 January 1950 there were 2,550,275 prisoners. . . . These figures . . . do not include the prison population.[29]

When, after Stalin's death, the releases began, the result was to create a country in which a significant minority of adults had been in prison, often with actual criminals. Given the turnover in the Gulag, and the extensive population losses of the war, losses that affected traditional Slavic Russia the most heavily, it is probably the case that as many as one quarter of the male population in those areas consisted of former convicts. Whatever their guilt or innocence, they had been immeasurably coarsened by the ghastly living conditions and cruel treatment.

The result was to define lawlessness down. As Vladimir Bukovsky records, with a certain grim humor, "Khrushchev wasn't very far from the truth when he said in one of his speeches: 'If people stopped stealing for even a single day, communism could have been built long ago.'"[30]

By sending millions of Russians to certain death on the battlefield, by condemning countless others to incredible suffering by his insistence on the "destruction" of whole categories of human and material resources, Stalin ensured the eventual collapse of the

Soviet state. Whether Lenin's legacy deserved to be called "great" is arguable. But whatever chances the Soviet state had to achieve its dreams of prosperity and equality for its citizens, a realized utopia based on socialist principles, those visions perished along with tens of millions of Russians in the Great Patriotic War.

NOTES

CHAPTER I: INTRODUCTION: PSEUDO-REALITY AND THE SOVIET UNION

1. My translation. In the standard English translation from the nineteenth century the passage appears as "In appearances everything happens as it does everywhere else. There is no difference except in the very foundation of things." *Letters from Russia* (New York: New York Review of Books Classics, 2002), 126. A little later on he says much the same thing: "En Russie, les noms sont les mêmes qu'ailleurs, mais les choses sont tout autres" (Book 1, 3rd Letter, 204).

2. See the repeated linkage in Hitler's speeches on Bolshevism in Adolf Hitler, *The Speeches of Adolf Hitler*, edited by Norman H. Baynes (London: Oxford University Press, 1942), 1:674, 676, 682, 686, 695, 700, 710, 713, and the editorial note on 1.721. Nor was this linkage fantasy. As Hitler's listeners knew, Ernst Toller, initial leader of the Munich soviet, was Jewish. So was Eugen Leviné, who succeeded him. Béla Kun, who ran the Hungarian Soviet Republic, was Jewish, and so were most of his immediate subordinates. See as well the shrewd insights by one of Hitler's first and best biographers, whose work was written before the world knew of the Holocaust: Konrad Heiden, *The Führer*, translated by Ralph Mannheim (New York: Carroll & Graf, 1999 [1944]), 21–22, 455–59.

3. The phrase is taken from Mark Harrison, "The Soviet Union: The Defeated Victor," in *The Economics of World War II: Six Great Powers in International Comparison*, edited by Mark Harrison (Cambridge: Cambridge University Press, 1998), 269.

4. *The Rise of the Roman Empire*, translated by Ian Scott-Kilvert (London: Penguin, 1979), Book 12, Paragraph 15 (page 45).

5. Walter Laqueur, *The Dream That Failed: Reflections on the Soviet Union* (New York: Oxford University Press, 1994), 99–100.

6. From Foreword to the 2004 edition of Dmitri Shostakovich, *Testimony: The Memoirs of Dmitri Shostakovich*, as related to and edited by Solomon Volkov, translated by Antonina W. Bouis (New York: HarperCollins, 2004 [1979]), xlii.

7. Custine, *Letters*, 8.

8. Malcolm Muggeridge, *Chronicles of Wasted Time I: The Green Stick* (New York: Morrow, 1973), 244. Muggeridge was one of the disillusioned: he went to the USSR as a true believer, looked around, and realized what a horrific enterprise it was. See the extensive discussion in François Furet, *The Passing of an Illusion: The Idea of Communism in the Twentieth Century*, translated by Deborah Furet (Chicago: University of Chicago Press, 1999), 62–92.

9. There is an informative and horrifying account of such matters in James E. Oberg, *Soviet Disasters* (New York: Random House, 1988). His account of the way the Soviets manipulated the air safety data (125–28) is recommended to anyone who believes that Soviet archival data is an accurate depiction of the reality it purports to represent. See the example recounted by the dissenter Vladimir Bukovsky in *To Build a Castle: My Life as a Dissenter*, translated by Michael Scammell (New York: Viking, 1978), 272. In *From the Yaroslavsky Station*, 3rd edition (New York: Universe, 1989), Elizabeth Pond has other examples of how the news was manipulated through denial (69).

10. David Remnick, *Lenin's Tomb* (New York: Random House, 1993), 25.

11. From Winston Churchill's address to the British Conservative Party Conference, Brighton, October 4, 1947.

12. Joseph Stalin, *The Great Patriotic War of the Soviet Union* (New York: International Publishers, 1945). These addresses and reports are in chronological order; Stalin's legends began in July 1941, right at the start of the war. Although after his death accounts of the war eliminated his presence almost completely, the narrative stayed the same, as revealed by the six-volume official history: Institute für Marxismus-Leninismus beim Zentralkommitte der Kommunistischen Partei der Sowjetunion, *Geschichte*

des Grossen Vaterländischen Krieges der Sowjetunion (Berlin: Deutsche Militärlervlag, 1962), whose general outline is carried over in the classic two-volume account of John Erickson, *The Road to Stalingrad* (London: Cassell, 1975) and *The Road to Berlin: Continuing the History of Stalin's War with Germany* (Boulder, Colorado: Westview, 1983). After the collapse, researchers who had access to Soviet archives were able to refine and often contradict many of the details of the existing account, the most notable being David Glantz, beginning with *When Titans Clashed* (Lawrence: University Press of Kansas, 1993) and *Zhukov's Greatest Defeat* (Lawrence: University Press of Kansas, 1993). Glantz was the first scholarly analyst to evince any serious skepticism about Soviet factual claims, and the first to call attention to the extent to which every setback was covered up, noting that "as much as 40 percent" of the war consisted of "forgotten battles" that Soviet historians had rather conveniently forgotten because the "failure seemed to tarnish the luster of the Red Army's newfound and lofty fighting reputation as well as the reputations of the senior commanders who planned and conducted the offensive[s]." David Glantz, *Red Storm over the Balkans: The Failed Soviet Invasion of Romania, Spring 1944* (Lawrence: University Press of Kansas, 2007), xiii.

13. Furet, *Passing of an Illusion*, 350, and elsewhere. Furet was making explicit what everyone had conceded to be true: the military achievement of the Red Army was the real basis of Soviet prestige and power.

14. Jean Dutourd, *The Taxis of the Marne*, translated by Harold King (New York: Simon & Schuster, 1957), 195.

15. David Lloyd George, *War Memoirs* (London: Odhams, 1938), 2:1313.

16. "Special Report to the Twentieth Congress of the Communist Party of the Soviet Union," February 24–25, 1956. Widely available: quotations taken from the version at www.uwm.edu/Course/448-343/index12.html.

17. Robert Musil, *The Man Without Qualities*, translated by Sophie Wilkins and Burton Pike (New York: Knopf, 1995), 1:390. "Pseudo-Reality Prevails" is their translation of the title of one of Musil's chapters (83). "World history undoubtedly comes into being like all the other stories. Authors can never really

think of anything new, and they all copy from each other. That is why all politicians study history instead of biology or whatever. So much for authors" (390).

18. The orange-growing incident is detailed in Hungarian film director Peter Bacso's blackly humorous account of Stalinist times, *The Witness* (1968). The film was shelved for fifteen years. When I interviewed Bacso in Budapest in July 1988, he was adamant that "the parts that you think are the most unbelievable are the ones that really happened," and he referred, somewhat vaguely, to equivalent projects elsewhere.

19. There is an extensive technical discussion of Lysenko's many meddlings in Zhores Medvedev, *The Rise and Fall of T. D. Lysenko* (New York: Norton, 1969), Chapter 8, "Lysenko's Agrobiology," 151–94. As Medvedev records, Lysenko proposed "the summer planting of sugar beets in Central Asia . . . on tens of thousands of hectares at once. These absurd plantings in parched soil . . . the shoots perished despite Lysenko's assertions" (165–66). Such notions explain the origins of Khrushchev's bizarre proposal to grow Jerusalem artichokes, as well as watermelons, in parts of Russia where climatic conditions made their cultivation impossible outside of greenhouses. The same principle as trying to grow oranges in Hungary, but not nearly as illuminating an example. As Roy Medvedev remarks, "it was a good thing that such experiments were tried only on small plots." *Khrushchev*, translated by Brian Pearce (New York: Doubleday, 1983), 53. See also William Taubman, *Khrushchev: The Man and His Era* (New York: Norton, 2003), 227. And for a more detailed analysis of Lysenko and Lysenkoism, see David Joravsky, *The Lysenko Affair* (Cambridge: Harvard University Press, 1970).

20. "There is a persistent myth, sometimes repeated even in Western literature, that collectivization was inevitable, that it made the country strong, and, therefore, that it was at least partially successful." Data from Zhores A. Medvedev, *Soviet Agriculture* (New York: Norton, 1987), 237; quote from 95.

21. Dmitri Volkogonov, *Autopsy for an Empire*, translated and edited by Harold Shukman (New York: Free Press, 1998), 104. See also Robert Conquest, *Harvest of Sorrow: Soviet Collectivization and the Terror-Famine* (New York: Oxford University Press, 1986), esp. 299–319, where Conquest estimates the death

toll and the extent to which what the Ukrainians call the Holodomor was systematically ignored in the West. In "Ukrainian Genocide," Tony Halpin, writing in the London *Times*, estimates that 25 percent of the population died from starvation (June 23, 2008), and provides a succinct sketch of this rather bizarre debate. Compare this horrifying reality with this blandly dismissive reference: "Collectivization was an ideological choice and had to be forced through against stubborn resistance from peasants. . . . Despite the opposition and the poor performance, by 1940 well over 90 percent of all peasants were collectivized." From the chapter on agriculture in Roy Mellor, *The Soviet Union and Its Geographical Problems* (Atlantic Highlands, New Jersey: Humanities Press, 1982), 90.

22. For the full story of the *New York Times* correspondent's Stalinist slant, see S. J. Taylor, *Stalin's Apologist: Walter Duranty, the New York Times's Man in Moscow* (New York: Oxford University Press, 1990), esp. Chapter 12, "The Famine Is Mostly Bunk" (210–23). Martin Sieff, UPI senior news analyst, has called Duranty's claim "arguably the most infamous piece of reporting or analysis ever to appear in that great paper." See his "Commentary: Gareth Jones, Hero of Ukraine," United Press International, Washington, D.C., June 12, 2003, available online at www.upi.com/view.cfm?StoryID=20030611-012334-4255r.

23. Alain Peyrefitte, *The Trouble with France*, translated by William R. Byron (New York: New York University Press, 1986), 33–34.

24. Pauli's remark has its philosophical antecedent in Bertrand Russell, who observed that "some propositions even lack the capacity to be false," to use Jean-François Revel's succinct distillation: *The Totalitarian Temptation*, translated by David Hapgood (New York: Penguin, 1977), 17.

25. See the extensive treatment in Allen Paul, *Katyn: The Untold Story of Stalin's Massacre* (New York: Charles Scribner's Sons, 1991), which provides information that was not yet available when Alexandra Kwiatowska-Viatteau wrote *Katyn, l'armée polonaise assassinée* (Paris: Complexe, 1982).

26. Office of the United States Chief of Counsel for Prosecution of Axis Criminality, *Nazi Conspiracy and Aggression: Opinion and Judgement* (Washington, D.C.: U.S. Government Printing Of-

fice, 1947), 59. There is an excellent brief summary of this aspect of the Nuremberg trials in Furet (*Passing of an Illusion*, 540, note 15).

27. See the examples of regular German soldiers shooting prisoners of war belonging to signatories of the Geneva Convention in John Mosier, *Cross of Iron* (New York: Holt, 2006), 228–42.

28. The judgment is from Paul (*Katyn*, xii). For the Shostakovich quote, see *Testimony*, 3.

29. Both quotes and data from Pavel Polian, *Against Their Will: The History and Geography of Forced Migrations in the USSR* (New York: Central European University Press, 2004), 118–19. The Stalin quote was directed against the ethnic Germans, not the Poles. "All ethnic Germans residing in the Volga German SSR and in the Saratoc and Stalingrad Oblasts are subject to resettlement," is how the decree read (quote and decree in Polian, 127–28). The total number of Germans thus "resettled" was about 438,000, mostly to Kazakhstan and Siberia.

30. John Earl Haynes and Harvey Klehr, *In Denial: Historians, Communism, and Espionage* (San Francisco: Encounter, 2003), 20. Compare with the Soviet official history's description of Stalin's invasion of Poland: "the advance of the Red Army to protect the lives and property of the peoples of western Ukraine and western Belorussia," *Vaterländischen Krieges*, 1.381 (the essay elaborating on this fabrication is on 291–96).

31. Haynes and Klehr, *In Denial*, 20. In the 1970s and 1980s, "some Western Sovietologists claimed that the importance of the purges and forced labor had been grossly overstated, both quantitatively and qualitatively," is the comment by Laqueur (*Dream That Failed*, 134). Compare the detailed and objective account of the responses to the 1979 Sverdlovsk public health crisis in Oberg (*Soviet Disasters*, 3–22) to the authoritative explanation of the causes of that crisis by Matthew Meselson et al., "The Sverdlovsk Anthrax Outbreak of 1970," *Science* (Summer 1994), 1202–1208. Although the deductions made by defectors and others about this disaster were inaccurate in many respects, the thrust of their claim, that the outbreak was caused by an accident in a facility engaged in bacteriological warfare development, has since been confirmed. The point is not to highlight the apologia offered up by sympathetic or unwitting foreigners, but to

call attention to how persuasive their highly fact-based accounts always were. The ingenuous air of objectivity that cloaks many of the more ideologically charged statements makes them quite deceptive: "The Second World War had a drastic effect: estimates of 14–20 million war deaths have been made." Indeed. Quote from Mellor, *Soviet Union and Its Geographical Problems*, 48.

32. The details of this incident are to be found in Simon Sebag Montefiore, *Stalin: The Court of the Red Tsar* (New York: Random House, 2005), 344–46. See also his remarks about how industrial accidents were treated as acts of sabotage (211, 215).

33. Quote from Montefiore (*Stalin*, 345). As we now know, Stalin had his own holocaust in the planning stages, but fortunately died before he was able to act on it. See the account in Jonathan Brent, *Stalin's Last Crime* (New York: HarperCollins, 2003).

34. Kolakowski, as quoted by Volkogonov (*Autopsy for an Empire*, 393). There's a prototypical example of the proverb, which is explicitly quoted, by Shostakovich on the first page of *Testimony* (6).

35. See, e.g., the remarks in Allan R. Millett, *Their War for Korea* (Washington, D.C.: Brassey's, 2002): "Russian claims for destruction of U.N. air forces clash with Chinese claims—and the North Korean claims are pure fantasy" (143). This evaluation is if anything understated. Millett's figures (143): the Russians and the Chinese alone claimed to have downed 2,000 Allied aircraft in aerial combat, while the actual data for losses is about 200, a tenfold exaggeration. But the same Soviet apparatus was reporting losses in the Second World War, so what are the grounds for believing the earlier data was any more reliable?

36. Unfortunately, this judgment holds as true for the most recent studies as for those done in the years before the collapse of the USSR. See, e.g., Chris Bellamy, *Absolute War* (New York: Knopf, 2007); Anthony Beevor, *Stalingrad: The Fateful Siege* (New York: Viking, 1998); Richard Evans, *The Third Reich at War* (New York: Penguin, 2009). All three authors, who are British, seem predisposed to accept with almost no reservation any evidence that is put before them—provided it has a Soviet source. Historiographically, the Eastern Front is thus a unique event, as it would be difficult to find any other conflict in which the claims of one side are accepted so uncritically.

37. Dmitri Volkogonov, *Stalin: Triumph and Tragedy*, translated and edited by Harold Shukman (New York: Grove Weidenfeld, 1988), 475.

38. The idea that the Germans were not good at keeping records is counterintuitive. Historians typically assume that German records at every level were meticulously kept: "Seventeenth-century Germans were scrupulous record keepers, and the Thirty Years' War did little to change their habits of meticulous documentation," is how the standard English language account of that conflict puts it. Quote from Geoffrey Parker, editor, *The Thirty Years' War*, 2nd edition (London: Routledge, 1997), 187. In the twentieth century, the accuracy of German casualty reports was accepted by Winston Churchill, André Maginot, the French government, and the statisticians at the British War Office. See the discussion of how British historians attempted to twist the data to their advantage in John Mosier, *The Myth of the Great War* (New York: HarperCollins, 2001), 10–11. See as well the remarks on cross-checking the loss reports of German combat units with their American and British equivalents in Christopher W. Wilbeck and Otto Carius, *Sledgehammers: Strengths and Flaws of Tiger Tank Battalions in World War II* (Bedford, Penn.: The Aberjona Press, 2004), 8. As these figures are extremely inconvenient for analysts intent on recording Soviet triumphs, they are usually ignored; when given at all, they are dismissively characterized as "estimates." See, for example, the June 7, 2008, article in the *Times* (London): available at www.timesonline.co.uk/tol/news/world/europe/article4083467.ece. The characterization is highly disingenuous.

39. This figure, used by the Militärgeschichtliche Forschungsamt, is a good example of a genuine estimate. Under the circumstances (the length of time before many German prisoners were returned, the dissolution of Germany itself) no exact accounting is possible.

40. "In 1947 pro-Soviet writers in the West were accepting a figure of seven million Soviet war dead": Alexei Tolstoy, *Stalin's Secret War* (New York: Holt, Rinehart & Winston, 1981), 280. See also the note (434) where Tolstoy cites both George C. Herring, Jr., *Aid to Russia* (New York: Columbia University Press, 1973), 297, and Isaac Deutscher, *Stalin: A Political Biography* (London: Oxford University Press, 1949), 550.

41. The official data is reprinted in Glantz, *When Titans Clashed*, 292. "Even the soundest works have been vetted ideologically, and the authors have been forced to write their accounts with the narrowest of focuses": David Glantz, "The Failures of Historiography: Forgotten Battles of the German-Soviet War (1941–1945)," (Fort Leavenworth, Kansas, Foreign Military Studies Office, 1997), 1, available at http://rhino.shef.ac.uk:3001/mr-home/rzhev/rzhev2.html.

42. Speech on Red Square, November 7, 1941, reprinted in Stalin, *Great Patriotic War*, 36.

43. See the summary of populations in Mark Harrison, *The Economics of World War II: Six Great Powers in International Comparison* (Cambridge: Cambridge University Press, 1998), Table 1.1, page 3. In *Soviet Agriculture*, Medvedev also uses the figure of 170 million for the USSR (Table 5.11). The 170:86 ratio actually misstates the imbalance considerably, since it eliminates those of Hitler's allies whose armies were entirely committed to the Eastern Front. If the populations of those states are added, the ratio is 170:121. In other words, if Stalin lost more than two Russian soldiers for every German, he would run out of cannon fodder before Hitler did. But even the most favorable (to the Soviets) exchange ratio was almost 5:1.

44. The American study quoted specifies 263,000 Germans and 195,576 Allied soldiers, but given the various uncertainties and parameters (none of which is addressed directly), I have rounded off simply to avoid false precision. The text from which the numbers derive is Charles B. MacDonald, *World War Two* (Washington, D.C.: Army Historical Series, n.d.), 498.

45. Suslov calculation cited in Tolstoy (*Stalin's Secret War*, 280). Newer data taken from Keith E. Bonn, Editor, *Slaughterhouse: The Handbook of the Eastern Front* (Bedford, Penn.: Aberjona, 2004), 11. Totals cited in the following paragraph are taken from this source.

46. The word is used by Glantz (*When Titans Clashed*, 288). Even if one accepts that the carefully massaged data is accurate (a highly dubious proposition), the most that could be claimed is that the Red Army was approaching some sort of rough parity.

47. Aleksandr I. Solzhenitsyn, *The First Circle*, translated by Thomas Whitney (New York: Harper & Row, 1968), 579–80.

CHAPTER II: UNDERSTANDING THE EVIL EMPIRES: TWO CASE HISTORIES

1. As recorded by James Boswell, *Life of Johnson*, edited by R. W. Chapman (Oxford: Oxford University Press, 1970), 628.
2. Lieutenant General Andreas Nielsen, *The German Air Force General Staff* (New York: Arno, 1959; originally published in 1952 as USAF Historical Study 173), 28–30. The quote is on 126.
3. To the extent that in *The Road to Stalingrad* (London: Cassell, 1975) John Erickson brings the point up (6–7). For the most extreme judgment, see, among many other examples, the opening remarks in Victor Alexandrov, *The Tukhachevsky Affair* (Englewood Cliffs, New Jersey: Prentice Hall, 1964), 1. Claims of Tukhachevsky's significance may be sweeping generalizations, but they can also be seen as intuitive responses generated by the deliberately distorted and partially destroyed records relating to the marshal's life and achievements. The brief summary by Richard Simpkin, *Deep Battle: The Brainchild of Marshal Tukhachevskii* (London: Brassey's Defence Group, 1987), 11, sums up his importance nicely.
4. "Theory and Air Doctrine in the Wever Era" is the title of the fourth chapter of James Corum, *The Luftwaffe: Creating the Operational Air War, 1918–1940* (Lawrence: University Press of Kansas, 2000), 126.
5. See the discussion in Corum, who speaks of the "Anglo/American prejudice in favor of strategic bombing" (*Luftwaffe*, 289–90). Appeals by ground commanders to unleash the full force of the heavy Allied bombers against tactical targets were fought all the way up the chain of command.
6. Quotation taken from Martin S. Alexander, "Fighting to the Last Frenchman," in Joel Blatt, editor, *The French Defeat of 1940: Reassessments* (Oxford: Berghan, 1998), 300.
7. Quoted in Corum, *Luftwaffe*, 137.
8. See the extensive account of the May fighting in Dominique Lormier, *Comme des Lions, Mai–Juin 1940* (Paris: Calmann-Levy, 2005), which corrects the errors and misinterpretations of earlier English language histories.
9. Owen Thetford, speaking of the massacre of the Fairey Battles,

in *Aircraft of the Royal Air Force Since 1918* (New York: Funk & Wagnalls, 1968), 233.

10. See, among many others, "Modern Gas Warfare," *Manchester Guardian*. According to this article, it would take only forty tons of gas to destroy much of London, and "London cannot be defended against such attacks. . . . The modern method of aerial attack is deadly in the extreme. . . . Within two or three days, few if any of London's millions would be left alive" (January 3, 1933:13). Or, as the then prime minister (Stanley Baldwin) put it to Parliament: "The bomber will always get through . . . the only defense is in offense, which means that you have to kill more women and children more quickly than the enemy if you want to save yourselves." As reported, without comment, by Denis Richards in the first volume of the official RAF history, *The Fight at Odds* (London: Her Majesty's Stationery Office, 1953), 2–3.

11. Startling, but absolutely true. See the analysis by Robin Higham in his magisterial work *Air Power: A Concise History* (New York: St. Martin's, 1972): "The British, the Italian in theory, the American, and possibly the Japanese Army forces favored 'strategic bombing' but had not the wherewithal to carry it out; when their bluffs were called they were not in a position to do more than engage in a war of attrition on the 1918 scale. The real successes of 1939–42 were won by tactical air forces in cooperation with surface forces. And that includes the Battle of Britain" (13).

12. The chief arguments as to why no bomber was developed were made by Albert Kesselring in 1954 and duly entered the historical record. His arguments are specious: see the analysis in John Mosier, *Cross of Iron* (New York: Holt, 2006), 79–80. The Kesselring statement is reprinted in Cajus Bekker, *The Luftwaffe Wartime Diaries*, translated and edited by Frank Ziegler (New York: Doubleday, 1968), Appendix 11 (374–75). Bekker's own summation of the air war in Russia is to the point: "For attacking targets in Russia the Luftwaffe felt the absence of a heavy, four-engined bomber even more acutely than it did during the Battle of Britain. . . . Russian loss of material was easily replaced," since the Germans were unable to bomb the factories and transport routes (300).

13. For the estimate of German tanks, see the authoritative summary by F. M. von Senger und Etterlin, *German Tanks of World*

War II, translated by J. Lucas, edited by Peter Chamberlain and Chris Ellis (New York: Galahad, 1967), 21–26. For the inadequacy of German antitank guns, see the archival evidence quoted by Dominique Lormier, *Comme des Lions, Mai–Juin 1940* (Paris: Calmann-Levy, 2005), 27–28.

14. Quote taken from an interview in August 1941 with Heinz Guderian, *Panzer Leader*, translated by Constantine Fitzgibbon (New York: Da Capo, 1996), 200. Guderian is a good example of Hitler's complaint, and his memoirs are disingenuous in the extreme. See Gerhard Weinberg's general comment about how the "most mendacious of military memoirs have become widely known, are frequently cited, and have in some instances been translated into English" in the Introduction to *Hitler and His Generals: Military Conferences, 1942–1945*, translated by Helmut Heiber (New York: Enigma, 2003), iv.

15. Quoted in Corum, *Luftwaffe*, 137–38.

16. Quoted in Corum, *Luftwaffe*, 143–44.

17. A fact often disguised by the way bomber specifications were reported to the public. Multi-engined planes with nothing but fuel as their payload had impressive intercontinental ranges, provided they flew at slow speeds and low altitudes. Flying at a speed and altitude that would enable the bomber to survive even the most rudimentary air defense system greatly increased fuel consumption, as did a payload of bombs. The main reason heavy bomber design took years and years of effort was owing to the difficulty of meeting all four parameters: speed, range, altitude, and payload. The effective combat radius of even the later models of the B-17 bomber carrying four to five tons of bombs was only about 1,300 kilometers. This range was achieved relatively late in the war (1943).

18. Both James Corum and Samuel Mitcham give almost the same description of Wever's end: Corum, *Luftwaffe*, 179; Samuel Mitcham, *Hitler's Commanders* (New York: Cooper Square Press, 2000), 175. Neither cites a source, and neither explains why the crash was so deadly, i.e., the magnesium alloy construction of the plane.

19. There is a readable although meandering account of Tukhachevsky's life by Thomas Butson, perhaps somewhat confusingly titled: *The Tsar's Lieutenant: The Soviet Marshal* (New York: Praeger, 1984). In the late 1980s attempts were made to

rehabilitate his reputation as a military thinker, notably by Simpkin, *Deep Battle*, which contains an informative and succinct biography (3–16). Most English language works on the marshal derive either from Lev Nikulin, *Tukhachevsky* (Moscow: VIMO, 1964) or Roman Goul, *Toukhatchevsky, marechal rouge,* translated [from the Russian] by Jacques Civel (Paris: Libraries et Techniques, 1935).

20. A remarkably sturdy set of enduring legends, despite the convincing and authoritative account of Norman Stone: "The real difficulty was not that the armies were not 'ready': it was that they were ready as . . . [the generals] understood it, that is, gloriously unprepared for what was to come." *The Eastern Front, 1914–1917* (New York: Charles Scribner's Sons, 1975), 48. In the Preface to the 1998 edition (New York: Penguin, 1998), Stone makes a succinct comment on why the legends were so enduring: "Whatever you said about the Tsarist Russian Army might get you in trouble" (7). This Preface is one of the few essays to confront the extent to which the sympathies and prejudices of historians have shaped accounts of twentieth-century Russia.

21. Not to be confused with Lev Borisovich Kamenev, another old Bolshevik, who was murdered in October 1936 as the Great Terror got underway. Sergei Sergeyevich apparently died of natural causes, one of the few old Bolsheviks Stalin didn't have murdered.

22. Inside the Soviet bloc after 1945, the fact that the state manufactured heroes was widely known: it is the subject of the Polish filmmaker Andrzej Wajda's *Man of Marble* (1977). Knowing how heroic figures were manufactured for propaganda purposes, one becomes suspicious of tales of great achievements during the war, such as the exploits of female aviators, snipers, and machine gunners celebrated in Henry Sakaida, *Heroines of the Soviet Union, 1941–1945* (Oxford: Osprey, 2003), and even in the more scholarly account to be found in Reina Pennington, *Wings, Women, and War: Soviet Airwomen in World War Two Combat* (Lawrence: University Press of Kansas, 2001). Or, to name a more commercial example, the Soviet sniper whose exploits are chronicled in Jean-Jacques Annaud's film *Enemy at the Gates* (2001).

23. When Richard Pipes wrote his meticulously researched *Russia Under the Bolshevik Regime* (New York: Knopf, 1993), the only

reliable source he was able to find for White casualties was the Soviet demographer Boris Urlanis (Pipes, 138, note 360–61), who gives a figure for White losses of 127,000. The official figure for the Red Army is slightly over 700,000.

24. As quoted by François Furet, *The Passing of an Illusion: The Idea of Communism in the Twentieth Century*, translated by Deborah Furet (Chicago: University of Chicago Press, 1999), 27. One of the many legends of Bolshevism is the denial of the violent efforts to export communism to the rest of Europe in the months following the October Revolution. The evidence (revealed most recently from Lenin himself) establishes conclusively that this was the case.

25. "Lenin grotesquely overrated the revolutionary ardor of British workers . . . and conceived in his imagination phantom armies of hundreds of thousands of German Communists marching to join the Red Army," is how Richard Pipes summarizes some of the secret documents now made public from the Soviet archives in *The Unknown Lenin: From the Secret Archive* (New Haven: Yale University Press, 1996), 7.

26. While no specialist in the field would contest the notion, to a surprising extent the fact that the terror began with Lenin is still not realized, even by history buffs. In addition to Pipes (*Russia Under the Bolshevik Regime*, 397–401), see the authoritative analysis by Anne Applebaum, *Gulag* (New York: Doubleday, 2003), 3–40. See as well Stéphane Courtois et al., *The Black Book of Communism* (Cambridge: Harvard University Press, 1998): "A preliminary global accounting of the crimes committed by Communist regimes shows the following: the execution of tens of thousands of hostages and prisoners without trial, and the murder of hundreds of thousands of rebellious workers and peasants from 1918 to 1922 [that is, while Lenin was still alive]" (9). There is a more detailed analysis on pages 71–81. The most detailed and comprehensive account of the Bolshevik struggles in the Baltic and Poland is to be found in Dominique Venner, *Baltikum* (Paris: Robert Laffont, 1975), 113–54; subsequently revised and titled *Histoire d'un facisme allemand* (Paris: Pygmalion, 1996), 106–44.

27. As Davies remarks, "In official Soviet histories, as in works by E. H. Carr and A. J. P. Taylor, the 'outbreak' of the Polish-Soviet

War occurs in April 1920.... The error cannot be passed over lightly." Norman Davies, *White Eagle, Red Star: the Polish-Soviet War, 1919–20* (New York: St. Martin's, 1972). Based on the recent documents uncovered, we now know that Lenin was preparing to invade Galicia in spring 1920; the Poles simply beat him to it. See the relevant document in Pipes (*Unknown Lenin*, 77–78). The false notion that Poland was the aggressor in the war with the Soviet Union is a useful touchstone for judging the extent to which a historian is toeing the party line, and hence simply echoing what Davies rather tactfully calls the "official Soviet histories." The use of certain phrases is also an indicator; Butson speaks of a "period of Polish opportunism, an imperialistic drive ... adventurism," characterizations typical of Bolshevik rhetoric (*Tsar's Lieutenant*, 80). See, among the numerous examples, the remarkable account of the Polish War in Earl F. Ziemke, *The Red Army 1918–1941: From Vanguard of World Revolution to U.S. Ally* (London: Frank Cass, 2004), 118–28. Not all of the "official" histories were written in Moscow.

28. The problem of the enormous imbalance between the mass of the army and the troops it was able to put into the field was first noticed in 1938 by Erich Wollenberg, *The Red Army: A Study of the Growth of Soviet Imperialism*, translated by Claude Sykes (London: Secker & Warburg, 1940), 44–45. John Erickson has a more detailed perspective, noting that although in 1920 the Red Army numbered five million men, on the two fronts of the Polish War it could only muster 581,000 in all: "at the decisive point, only 50,000 men could be mustered, and that with difficulty." A point that should always be borne in mind when confronted with Soviet figures. John Erickson, *The Soviet High Command: A Military-Political History, 1918–1941* (New York: St. Martin's, 1962), 101.

29. The French did send military advisers and some very limited matériel. More important to Bolshevik and anti-Polish mythmaking, they also sent General Maxime Weygand, who arrived in Poland with the rather grandiose notion that he would be in charge. As Davies observes, "The legend of Weygand's victory is an excellent instance of the principle that what really happens in history is less important than what people believe to have happened" (*White Eagle*, 222). In this case the legend became firmly

entrenched; even independent and supposedly skeptical historians pay homage to it. See, for example, Michael Gardner, *A History of the Soviet Army* (New York: Praeger, 1966): "In a desperate effort, guided efficiently by the French general, Weygand, and exploiting a series of strategic and tactical errors ... the Polish army inflicted ... a decisive defeat at the gates of Warsaw" (45). By contrast, here is what the general said himself, at a point in his life when, as the man who managed to lose France to the Germans in 1940, he needed every victory he could reasonably claim: "the victory was Polish, the plan Polish, the army Polish." See Maxime Weygand, *Memoires* (Paris: Laffont, 1957), 2.166.

30. See the analysis in Pipes, who inclines to the notion expressed in the text: "Lenin's telegram ... helps to explain why Stalin did not move the southern army towards Warsaw to join the siege, inaction that Trotsky later attributed to insubordination and blamed for the Red Army's defeat" (*Unknown Lenin*, 7).

31. The disclosure of casualties is another touchstone, with Bolshevik apologists and sympathizers generally glossing over them or failing to mention them entirely. The 150,000 estimate comes from Brian Moynihan, *Claws of the Bear: The History of the Red Army from the Revolution to the Present* (Boston: Houghton Mifflin, 1989), 44. Davies estimates that Tukhachevsky had lost two thirds of his command (*White Eagle*, 207).

32. As quoted by Martin Amis, *Koba the Dread: Laughter and the Twenty Million* (New York: Hyperion, 2002), 28. Not an isolated example: there's a similar exhortation by Lenin, aimed at a different ethnic group, quoted in more detail in Courtois (*Black Book of Communism*, 72). See as well the brief summary (with pointers to the documents themselves) in Pipes (*Unknown Lenin*, 10).

33. Tukhachevsky's biographers are strangely reticent about his role in suppressing what Simpkin (*Deep Battle*, 8) calls a "counter-revolutionary rising at Kronstadt." Butson gives a reasonable account of the actual events (*Tsar's Lieutenant*, 111–32), but glosses over both causes and the effects, arguing that a frontal assault was the only option. In *Juggernaut: A History of the Soviet Armed Forces* (New York, Macmillan, 1967), Malcolm Mackintosh describes it as "the most severe and bitter fighting of the whole civil war" (48). Battering disorganized sailors into sub-

mission by hurling mass infantry assaults across the open ice is hardly military genius.

34. Again, Tukhachevsky's biographers make short shrift of his role in repressing what Simpkin calls "problems" at Tambov (*Deep Battle*, 8). Butson omits entirely any discussion of the tactics used, and doesn't mention the use of chemical weapons (*Tsar's Lieutenant* 136–40), a perfect example of Bolshevik techniques. The incriminating documents are summarized and quoted in Courtois (*Black Book of Communism*, 116–18) and Pipes (*Russia Under the Bolshevik Regime*, 386–88).

35. Precise figures are difficult to come by. According to Courtois, at least 50,000 people were put into special camps, most of whom died (*Black Book of Communism*, 118). On the basis of admitted Red Army losses, Pipes estimates total peasant casualties at a quarter of a million (*Russia Under the Bolshevik Regime*, 171).

36. The authoritative analysis of the agricultural data, the key to understanding the regime's failure, is Zhores A. Medvedev, *Soviet Agriculture* (New York: Norton, 1987), esp. 119, 237. Pipes has a succinct summary of other relevant statistics in *Russia Under the Bolshevik Regime*, 170–71 and 138.

37. See the pithy summary in Major Charles Picar, *Tactical Deep Battle: The Missing Link* (Fort Leavenworth, Kansas: School of Advanced Military Studies, 1992), 4–7.

38. Triandafilov's contribution, while not suppressed, is presented in such a way that its importance is minimized. See Simpkin (*Deep Battle*, 32). The term "deep battle" is the English translation of a Russian phrase *gluboky boi*.

39. Promotions in the French army before 1914 were rigged to preclude officers whose political sympathies were not judged sufficiently socialist. "Alas, republicanism did not always coincide with competence," is how Arthur Conte sums it up in *Joffre* (Paris: Oliver Orban, 1991), 277. See also Raymond Recouly, *Joffre* (New York: Appleton, 1931), 235.

40. In 1927, Shaposhnikov had written a treatise, *The Brains of the Army*. As Butson characterizes the treatise, Shaposhnikov advocated "a general staff, fully subordinated to the policies of the regime, that devoted itself entirely to a very rigorous planning. . . . [and] the closest possible alliance between the military and the political organs, implicitly admitting the superiority of the latter" (*Tsar's Lieutenant*, 172).

41. *Sentinel of Peace* (New York: International Publishers, 1936), 14.

42. Account in Dmitri Shostakovich, *Testimony: The Memoirs of Dmitri Shostakovich*, as related to and edited by Solomon Volkov, translated by Antonina W. Bouis (New York: HarperCollins, 2004 [1979]), 96.

43. "When Tukhachevsky was rehabilitated twenty years later [1957] it was revealed that several pages of the deposition were stained with blood." Courtois, *Black Book of Communism*, 198. See also the remarks by Robert Conquest, *The Great Terror*, (New York: Oxford University Press, 1970), 206. In his 1994 film *Burnt by the Sun*, Nikita Mikhalkov gives us a thinly disguised portrait of Tukhachevsky's last days, his arrest, and the beating.

44. These gruesome details, ignored by Tukhachevsky's biographers, are in Conquest (*Great Terror*, 204–5).

CHAPTER III: THE DICTATORS' GAMBLE

1. Delivered to the closed session of the Party Congress, February 24–25, 1956. There is an annotated version of this document available at www.uwm.edu/Course/448-343/index12.html.

2. Malcolm Muggeridge, *Chronicles of Wasted Time I: The Green Stick* (New York: Morrow, 1973), 209.

3. Mikhail Bulgakov, *The Master and Margarita*, translated by Michael Glenny (London: Harper & Row, 1967), "The Haunted Apartment," 77. Bulgakov began writing this novel in 1928, and probably finished it well before the Great Terror (he died of a rare inherited kidney disease in 1940). That an elderly English woman (Webb was born in 1858) and a Russian novelist could both notice that people "disappeared" early on is a depressing insight into the situation in the Soviet Union and to how it was generally perceived in the West. Recently released records show that in 1921, 200,000 people had been arrested; 162,726 in 1929; 331,544 in 1930; 479,065 in 1931; 505,256 in 1933—1,791,394 people even before the start of the Terror. Figures from Jonathan Brent, *Inside Stalin's Archives* (New York: Atlas, 2008), 162.

4. As quoted by Muggeridge (*Green Stick*, 261).

5. In *The Great Terror* (New York: Oxford University Press, 1970), Robert Conquest proposed the following figures, indicating that

each one should be prefixed by "about": seven million arrested, one million executed, two million dying in the camps; another one million in prison, and eight million in the camps at the end of 1938. In the revised edition of his work (New York: Oxford University Press, 1990), he discusses these figures, explaining why they still stand (484–87).

6. These figures are taken from Alan Bullock, *Hitler and Stalin: Parallel Lives* (New York: Knopf, 1992), 494. Inevitably there are discrepancies in the grim head count. For example, Steve Zaloga and James Grandsen cite the loss of "60 of 67 corps commanders, 136 of 199 divisional commanders, 221 of 397 brigade commanders" in *Soviet Tanks and Combat Vehicles of World War Two* (London: Arms & Armour, 1984), 106.

7. The *Times* correspondent was Walter Duranty, the saying is reported by Muggeridge (*Green Stick*, 253). In *Stalin: Triumph and Tragedy*, translated and edited by Harold Shukman (New York: Grove Weidenfeld, 1988), Dmitri Volkogonov concluded between 8.5 and nine million (166), and cites the Churchill conversation (167).

8. Khrushchev remarks from Secret Speech; for a typical example of the treatment accorded the effects of the purge on the army, see John Erickson, who begins his classic study *The Road to Stalingrad* (London: Cassell, 1975) in media res, with the aftermath of the Finnish War; he devotes two pages to discussing what he euphemistically terms the "military purge," limiting himself to a brief discussion of the ineptitude of Voroshilov and Kulik (14–16), and giving only one hint that the Terror extended below the upper echelon: the case of General Rokossovskii, who was briefly imprisoned and then rehabilitated (19).

9. In the Secret Speech delivered to the closed session of the Party Congress, February 24–25, 1956, Khrushchev said: "During these years [1937–1938] repressions were instituted against certain parts of our military cadres beginning literally at the company- and battalion-commander levels and extending to higher military centers. During this time, the cadre of leaders who had gained military experience in Spain and in the Far East was almost completely liquidated." The 30th Rifle Division example taken from Conquest, *Great Terror*, 208. In the final years of the USSR, there were attempts by some Western analysts to argue that the original estimates of losses in the officer corps fig-

ured by Conquest and Erickson were exaggerated. See the dissection of these arguments in Walter Laqueur, *The Dream That Failed: Reflections on the Soviet Union* (New York: Oxford University Press, 1994): "Like saying that a corpse was in reasonably good shape, but the head had been severed from the body" (140; attempts to minimize the terror: 136–42).

10. In his March 1939 address to the Party Congress, Lazar Kagonovich noted that "in 1937 and 1938 the leading personnel in all heavy industry was entirely replaced." As quoted in Stéphane Courtois et al., *The Black Book of Communism: Crimes, Terror, Repression* (Cambridge: Harvard University Press, 1999), 194. For a brief summary of the more notable casualties, see Zaloga and Grandsen, *Soviet Tanks and Combat Vehicles*, 107. In *Stalin's Folly: The Tragic First Ten Days of WWII on the Eastern Front* (Boston: Houghton Mifflin, 2005), Constantine Pleshakov gives a brief list of additional casualties in the aerospace industry. In addition to Tupolev, the following men went to the camps: Petlyakov, Myassisichlev, Kleimenov, Korolev, and Langemak, who was actually shot (page 32). With the exception of Tupolev, the armaments industry casualties hardly appear in any account of the period, and their names are mostly unknown even to specialists.

11. Not that the lists of those to be executed stopped at the end of 1939: Stalin was still signing off on them in 1940. But his ruse worked to a surprising extent. Thus "The writer Ilya Ehrenburg met Pasternak in the street: 'He waved his arms around as he stood between the snowdrifts: "If only someone would tell Stalin about it." The theatrical director Meyerhold told Ehrenburg, 'They conceal it from Stalin.'" Examples taken from Simon Sebag Montefiore, *Stalin: The Court of the Red Tsar* (New York: Random House, 2005), 230; for executions running into 1940, page 322. See the disingenuous summary in Montefiore: "There has been a debate between those such as Robert Conquest who insisted that Stalin himself initiated and ran the Terror, and the so-called Revisionists who argued that the Terror was created by pressure from ambitious young bureaucrats. . . . The archives have proved Conquest right, although . . . the two views are complementary" (229). No: Stalin not only directed the Terror, he took care to create or continue the climate of wickedness begun by Lenin, a mind-set that encouraged atrocities at every level.

12. Stalin demanded numerous executions as the debacle of the Finnish War unfolded. Montefiore records that the "whole command" of the 44th Division was shot in December 1940, and that according to the report Mekhlis submitted to Stalin, "the exposure of traitors and cowards continued" (*Stalin*, 329). For the case of Rychakov and Vannikov, see 343–46. Although these cases clearly have a direct bearing both on the military preparedness of the Red Army and how Stalin exercised command and control over it, they are not mentioned in Erickson, *Road to Stalingrad*.

13. Voroshilov had "spoken out" against their formation, in the delicate phrase of Erickson (*Road to Stalingrad*, 15).

14. There's a brief account of this debate in Montefiore (*Stalin*, 343–44), who appends a note to it at the bottom of the page: "This was not the only such madness." In *Soviet Heavy Tanks* (London: Osprey, 1984), 13, Steve Zaloga and James Grandsen give a somewhat different account of this matter, correctly identifying the gun as the 76.2 millimeter weapon (in Montefiore the gun is described incorrectly as 75 millimeter; there was no such gun in the Soviet arsenal).

15. Their comments reprinted in John Milsom, *Russian Tanks, 1900–1970* (Harrisburg, Pennsylvania: Stackpole, 1971), 44–46. The Soviets were masters at staging carefully choreographed events that dazzled Western observers, whether show trials or military exercises.

16. This article in the Soviet *Tank Journal* went on to conclude that the real value of infantry lay in maintaining a "tactical defense" during battle. As quoted at length by Milsom (*Russian Tanks*, 47). Post-1945, Soviet tank experts postulated that this emphasis on cooperation was valid, as was, perhaps confusingly, the idea of the breakthrough. See the analysis in Milsom (*Russian Tanks*, 47).

17. Data and quote from Steven Zaloga and Peter Sarson, *T-34/76 Medium Tank, 1941–1945* (London: Osprey, 1994), 7.

18. The ammunition situation, of critical importance but almost invariably ignored, is discussed in Zaloga and Grandsen (*Soviet Heavy Tanks*, 9, 13).

19. The peak year for tank production in the USSR was 1936, when nearly 5,000 tanks were supposedly produced. Then production dropped sharply: 1,559 in 1937, 2,271 in 1938, 3,110 in 1939, and only 2,666 in 1940. It was only in the first half of 1941 that pro-

duction increased sharply, if the figures are to be believed: 2,413 vehicles were produced. Data taken from Zaloga and Grandsen (*Soviet Tanks*, 108).

20. As the raw numbers make clear (28,000 divided by 61), the number of tanks produced was so great that the Red Army should have had no difficulty in equipping its armored divisions at the required level, even allowing for the deduction of the 1,600 odd tanks lost during the Finnish War and the replacement of older vehicles by the new T-34 and KV-1 tanks. It might be objected that the figures from the early 1930s should be deducted, as these vehicles had worn out, but tanks were expected to have the same working life as locomotives and other pieces of heavy equipment, and in the French and German armies they did.

21. Examples of the 3rd and 6th Corps taken from David Glantz, *When Titans Clashed* (Lawrence: University Press of Kansas, 1993); 19th Corps from Zaloga and Sarson (*T-34/76 Medium Tank*, 11).

22. The various tanks of the BT series formed the bulk of the Soviet tank force because production of the famous T-34 tank did not even begin until 1940 (as was the case with the Soviet heavy tank, the KV-1), and very few vehicles were built until 1941. One reason was the impact of the Terror at the Kharkov plant (often referred to by an acronym of its full Russian name: Kharkovsky parovozostroitelny zavod or KhPZ). Firsov, head of the team that had designed the BT series tanks, was arrested and shot, along with many of his colleagues (no one knows how many). He was succeeded by Mikhail Koshkin, who was in charge of the T-34 design (the name was Koshkin's idea as well). Unfortunately, Koshkin, worn out by his struggles to get the T-34 in production, died in September 1940, and was succeeded by Aleksandr Morozov, which is why the KhPZ design bureau is frequently called the Morozov Bureau. The notion of using agricultural vehicles to tow guns was totally wrong: not only did such vehicles not have the correct performance characteristics (notably speed), but they had no provision for carrying the ammunition and gun crew needed.

23. See the remarks in Zaloga and Sarson (*T-34/76 Medium Tank*, 11).

24. J. F. C. Fuller, *Tanks in the Great War* (London: John Murray, 1920), 309–13.

25. Estimate from Zaloga and Grandsen (*Soviet Heavy Tanks,* 9).
26. In *The Soviet High Command: A Military-Political History, 1918–1941* (New York: St. Martin's, 1962), John Erickson noted the imbalance between the supposed size of the army and the size of the force available for the invasion: the "581,000 [men on the two fronts] represent[ed] only 10 percent of the total Soviet military strength" (101).
27. Quote from David Glantz, citing Soviet sources, *When Titans Clashed* (Lawrence: University Press of Kansas, 1993), 35, (note 16 for his source). Testimony such as this is convincing, because Glantz consistently offers the most favorable interpretation of the situation allowable (favorable to the Soviets, that is). See, for instance, his citation of Zaloga's tank data (329, note 15).
28. Custine, *Letters from Russia* (New York: New York Review of Books Classics, 2002), 177.
29. At first the Red Army relied on standard (that is, civilian) tracked vehicles. Eventually they started using surplus tanks; the only purpose-built recovery vehicles ever used by the Red Army were American M31 armored recovery vehicles. The use of purpose-built vehicles was essential. Not only did they have the weight and power necessary to the task, but they were fitted with the winches and booms needed for lifting heavy parts. See the analysis of this Soviet deficiency in Zaloga and Grandsen (*Soviet Tanks,* 197). As Andrew Cockburn notes in *The Threat: Inside the Soviet Military Machine* (New York: Random House, 1983), "No amount of intelligence assessments, classified or otherwise, can duplicate the insight that comes from talking to the Sashas, Igors, Genadys, and Vladimirs about the lives they lived in bases and garrisons" (27).
30. German tank production figures taken from the tables in Thomas L. Jentz, *Panzertruppen: The Complete Guide to the Creation and Combat Employment of Germany's Tank Force* (Atglen, Pennsylvania: Schiffer, 1996). For the estimates of the value of the Mark 1 and Mark 2 tanks, see the even more authoritative remarks by F. M. von Senger und Etterlin, *German Tanks of World War II,* translated by J. Lucas, edited by Peter Chamberlain and Chris Ellis (New York: Galahad, 1967), 22–23.
31. Of the 2,667 medium tanks in inventory, 845 (32 percent) were 35t and 38t vehicles. About 2,400 French tanks were pressed into German service after the armistice in June 1940. See the figures

in Werner Regenburg and Horst Scheibert, *Captured French Tanks Under the German Flag* (Atglen, Pennsylvania: Schiffer, 1997), Introduction. The French army was lavishly equipped with small tracked vehicles used to tow light weapons. This was a class of vehicle the Germans had never bothered to develop, despite their utility, so roughly 3,000 of these Renault Chenillete d'infanterie UE tracked carriers were put into service as well.

32. *Epitoma rei militaris* (*De re militari*), Book 3, Paragraph 1. My rather crude translation.

33. Once in 1934 and yet again in 1937: both contacts were revealed by Walter Krivitsky, a high-ranking Soviet agent, in *In Stalin's Secret Service* (New York: Harper, 1939), 106. Little attention has been paid to this revelation, probably because Krivitsky defected in 1937, largely in order to keep from being purged (he died in 1941 under mysterious circumstances that suggest he was assassinated). Revelations by Soviet defectors were always dismissed by specialists and then discounted by Anglo-American historians. "Revisionist historiography has often simply encouraged a continued belief in mythic thinking," is how Harvey Klehr, John Earl Haynes, and Fridrikh Igorevich Firsov put it in *The Secret World of American Communism* (New Haven: Yale University Press, 1995), 327. There is no objective reason to doubt Krivitsky's assertions. As Klehr says, "The Soviets made repeated efforts to reestablish closer contacts with Germany, which, according to some observers, became more energetic after Hitler tightened his grip on power." See the analysis of the growing economic ties in Edward E. Ericson, *Feeding the German Eagle: Soviet Economic Aid to Nazi Germany, 1933–1941* (Westport, Connecticut: Praeger, 1999), esp. 16–18 (quote on 17).

34. For Stalin's complex relations with the Chinese at this time, see Jung Chang and Jon Halliday, *Mao: The Unknown Story* (New York: Random House, 2005), esp. 175–78.

35. The single best account of how the Bolsheviks behaved inside the Spanish Republic is to be found in George Orwell's firsthand *Homage to Catalonia* (London: Secker & Warburg, 1938). It's worth noting that Orwell's account was turned down by numerous publishers, impressive testimony as to why thoughtful people remained ignorant of the dark side of the Bolshevik movement. For the definitive scholarly account of the war, see

Hugh Thomas, *The Spanish Civil War*, 3rd edition (New York: Harper & Row, 1986).

36. As Thomas points out (*Spanish Civil War*, 805, citing an article in *Le Monde* of February 19, 1969), on December 25, 1937, Litvinov summoned a French correspondent in Moscow and told him that "the Kremlin had 'established contacts' to initiate a German-Russian *rapprochement*.... No one took the message seriously." As indeed many historians still do not. See note 33 above.

37. See the Associated Press article by Lynn Berry, "Soviet-Nazi Pact Revisited 70 Years Later," originally published on August 23, 2009, complete with highly defensive interviews of Russian officials and descendants of some of those involved, e.g., Molotov's grandson. Available at http://washingtontimes .com/news/2009/aug/23/soviet-nazi-pact-revisited-70-years -later.

38. See the extensive analysis of Stalin's letter in François Furet, *The Passing of an Illusion: The Idea of Communism in the Twentieth Century*, translated by Deborah Furet (Chicago: University of Chicago Press, 1999), 315–22. English historians have largely ignored the letter and the subsequent meeting. But Furet's point is this: "From September 1939 to June 1941, Stalin was Hitler's principal ally; from June 1941 to May 1945, his most determined enemy. It is the second period, authenticated by victory, that has been retained in the selective memory of nations; the first period, however, must also have its historical due if we are to avoid solely a winner's version of the past" (315).

39. As recorded by Furet, who, alone among historians of the era, emphasizes its importance (*Passing of an Illusion*, 321–22).

40. See the extensive summaries of these discussions in John Earl Haynes and Harvey Klehr, *In Denial: Historians, Communism, and Espionage* (San Francisco: Encounter, 2003), 193–226.

41. So the comment by David Glantz that "in anticipation of a Soviet attack the Finnish government had gradually mobilized its forces to the equivalent of 14 divisions" is thus highly misleading, although his basic account of the Soviet disasters that resulted is not (*When Titans Clashed*, 19–23). The best account of the Russo-Finnish War is William R. Trotter's excellent and detailed *A Frozen Hell* (Chapel Hill, North Carolina: Algon-

quin, 1991); information on the bombing raid comes from 48.
See also Tomas Ries, *Cold Will: The Defence of Finland* (London: Brassey's, 1988), 91. There is excellent and hitherto undisclosed information in the appendices to Eloise Engle and Lauri Paananen, *The Winter War* (New York: Charles Scribner's Sons, 1973).

42. The figure is from Zaloga and Grandsen (*Soviet Tanks*, 121). No other overall accounting has been made, but in *Frozen Hell*, Trotter enumerates five specific engagements and gives tank losses for each: 412 tanks captured or destroyed (pp. 121, 137, 140, 169, 221). Using the same ratios as prevailed in Poland in September (for every vehicle totally lost, two others were disabled on the battlefield but repairable), a reasonable total of over 1,200 tank kills can be computed.

43. Notice the qualifying "almost as." This passage is taken from *Khrushchev Remembers*, translated by Strobe Talbott (Boston: Little, Brown, 1970), 155. Trotter, who also cites the Khrushchev figure in the course of summarizing Finnish estimates (*Frozen Hell*, 263), discounts it, but we have no way of knowing how many invisible casualties there were that were not the direct result of battlefield deaths. Given the conditions of the war, we can assume a high proportion of Soviet wounded later died; additionally, it is highly suspicious that no figures have been estimated for the missing. Since 25,000 Finns were killed during the war, the casualty exchange ratio comes to slightly over 10:1 to the disadvantage of the Red Army. Note as well the roughly 5:1 ratio between the official and the actual figures, which suggests that a similar multiplier should probably be used for other Soviet casualty claims.

44. Verbatim quote as recorded by Montefiore (*Stalin*, 415). Stalin's comments such as this must be weighed carefully in evaluating subsequent characterizations of Khrushchev. Given the bogus nature of Soviet statistics, Stalin's condescension has a certain grim humor to it.

45. Air casualty information from Trotter, *Frozen Hell*, 188–91.

46. Data and details of the various pacts can be found in Ericson, *Feeding the German Eagle*.

47. The Hitler quote is taken from Gerald Fleming, *Hitler and the Final Solution* (Berkeley: University of California Press, 1982), 8. As John Lukacs points out, Halder personally confirmed that

Hitler had said those words to Fleming, and Lukacs cites other examples of this statement in *The Hitler of History* (New York: Random House, 1998), 130. See also the additional summary of remarks to that effect on page 47.

48. See, for example, the part of *Hitler 1936–1945: Nemesis* (New York: Norton, 2000), where Ian Kershaw narrates the unfolding of Hitler's plans for the Russian invasion (333–35). The facts are stated well enough, but words such as "obsession" (repeated several times in the course of three pages), "crusade," "imperious," and "crass" are simply highly literate iterations of mental instability appropriate for a distinguished scholar. Less sophisticated writers are even more revealing: thus the remark about "collective lunacy" in Hubert P. van Tuyll, *Feeding the Bear* (Greenwich, Conn.: Greenwood, 1989), 14.

49. A summary of the key interrogations and the deductions of the interrogators, taken from the Wehrmacht records, is contained in Joachim Hoffman, *Stalin's War of Extermination, 1941–1945: Planning, Realization, Documentation*, translated by William Diest (Capshaw, Alabama: Theses and Dissertation Press, 2005), 80–88. See as well Wolfgang Strauss, *Unternehmen Barbarossa und der russische Historikerstreit: mit Dokumenten, Karten und Abbildungen* (München: Herbig, 1998) and Walter Post, *Unternehmen Barbarossa: Deutsche Und Sowjetische Angriffspläne 1940/41* (Hamburg: E. S. Mittler, 1996). In 1990, Victor Rezhun, a defector who had been an officer in Soviet military intelligence, writing under the pseudonym Suvarov, published *Icebreaker: Who Started the Second World War*, translated by Thomas Beattie (London: Hamish Hamilton, 1990). He summarized Stalin's plans and offered as proof the dispositions of the Red Army in forward positions (those dispositions are corroborated by the Wehrmacht interrogations also summarized by Hoffman, *Stalin's War of Extermination*, 65–70). After the collapse of the USSR the intentions enumerated in Hoffmann and Suvarov were confirmed, most notably by Pleshakov (*Stalin's Folly*), but by other Russian scholars as well (see the extensive citation in *Stalin's Folly*, 285). Given the historic pattern of Bolshevik aggression against its neighbors, a pattern that Stalin continued both before and after the war, this revelation should hardly have been much of a surprise. See, for example, the way the issue of Stalin's aims and behavior on the eve of the war is handled in Richard Evans,

The Third Reich at War (New York: Penguin, 2009), 165–66. This sort of evasion ensures the core of Stalinist mythos will be around for a long time.

50. See the data and discussion in Zhores A. Medvedev, *Soviet Agriculture* (New York: Norton, 1987), 95–199, Tables 5.1 and 6). For an analysis of the inflated figures, see the Epilogue to this book.

51. Glantz, for example, speaks of "the Soviet fear of provoking or being provoked," as though it is a national trait, like drinking vodka (*When Titans Clashed*, 42), a classic case of circular reasoning. For the elaborate Polish provocation that Hitler staged, see Leonard Mosley, *On Borrowed Time* (New York: Random House, 1969), 10–27.

CHAPTER IV: INTO THE MAELSTROM: THE FIRST SEVENTEEN DAYS

1. Bernard Law Montgomery, *The Memoirs of Field-Marshal the Viscount Montgomery of Alamein, K.G.* (New York: World, 1958), 75.
2. As quoted by Ronald Lewin, *Hitler's Mistakes* (London: Secker & Warburg, 1984), 118. In 1940, as chief of staff of the German 18th Army Group, Marcks had altered the initial plans so as to prevent Paris from being bombarded in the event the Germans had to seize the city by force.
3. See the map in Steve Zaloga and James Grandsen, *Soviet Tanks and Combat Vehicles of World War Two* (London: Arms and Armour Press, 1984), 226.
4. See the summaries of the initial plans for the Soviet invasion in Samuel Mitcham, *Hitler's Field Marshals* (New York: Cooper Square Press, 1990), 66–68 (for Marcks), 226 (for Paulus).
5. In order to prevent confusion, in this book German army groups are identified by basic English names (North, South, Center), while other, smaller concentrations are identified by plain English names as well, e.g., 2nd Armored Group. German terms are used only where the English translation, whether conventional or not, would lead to confusion, e.g., Abteilungen, which although it means "units" had a special stipulated meaning in the Wehrmacht (explained in due course in the text). The details of the disposition are to be found in Walter Post, *Unternehmen Bar-*

barossa: *Deutsche Und Sowjetische Angriffspläne 1940/41* (Hamburg: E. S. Mittler, 1996), esp. the maps on 423–32. See also the excellent detailed account in Samuel Mitcham, *Hitler's Commanders* (New York: Cooper Square Press, 2000), 33–45 and Mitcham, *Hitler's Field Marshals*, 92–95.

6. General von Thoma as quoted by Basil Henry Liddell Hart, *The German Generals Talk* (New York: Morrow, 1953), 165. Von Thoma concludes by saying that the purpose of organization is to allow one "to maintain one's momentum."

7. An exact count of what units were originally intended for what operation is difficult, owing to the Yugoslavian operation, so I've added them all together: seven armored, three motorized, three mountain, and thirteen infantry divisions were committed for Greece and Yugoslavia. This does not count two units nominally identified as regiments, but which in reality were at divisional strength (the Hermann Göring armored regiment and the Grossdeutschland, the premier army unit, by now motorized) and the airborne division deployed by the air force. Since two of the motorized units were Waffen-SS, it is clear that a substantial proportion of Germany's best (or anyway best-equipped) troops were to be involved.

8. See the data reproduced in Richard Overy, *The Battle of Britain: The Myth and the Reality* (New York: Norton, 2000), 162. The data is for single-engine fighters only, but as we're talking about bombing missions here, the data for bomber crews can hardly be any better. See also Overy's analysis of combat experience on page 125. Curiously, he then concludes that "the Battle of Britain did not seriously weaken Germany and her allies" (113) although the actual evidence cited suggests the contrary.

9. While some senior German officers were familiar with the area from their service in the First World War, others, like Guderian, were familiar with the Baltic as a result of their participation in the fighting there that took place in 1919–1921. For a corroborating Russian assessment of the problematic defensive terrain, see Constantine Pleshakov, *Stalin's Folly: The Tragic First Ten Days of WWII on the Eastern Front* (Boston: Houghton Mifflin, 2005), 60–65.

10. See the grimly ironic summary in Simon Sebag Montefiore, *Stalin: The Court of the Red Tsar* (New York: Random House, 2005): "in 1934 alone there were 62,000 accidents on the rail-

ways! How could this happen in a perfect country?" (211). Entire sections of key lines were hardly able to operate, as all the personnel had been arrested for wrecking.

11. I. T. Starinov, *Miny zhdat svdego chasa* (Moscow: Voenizdat, 1964), 175. Also quoted by Victor Suvarov, *Icebreaker: Who Started the Second World War*, translated by Thomas Beattie (London: Hamish Hamilton, 1990), 73–74. These accounts were easily obtainable inside the USSR, which strengthens the case being made, and explains why Suvarov's critics never talk about his actual argument, but adopt the position exemplified by the Russian aphorism: " 'It can't be because it couldn't ever be,' as the major once said on seeing a giraffe." Quoted with relish by Dmitri Shostakovich in *Testimony: The Memoirs of Dmitri Shostakovich*, as related to and edited by Solomon Volkov, translated by Antonina W. Bouis (New York: Harper & Row, 1979), 246.

12. In *Icebreaker*, Suvarov has the relevant quotations from the interrogations of Colonel-General Alfred Jodl and Field Marshal Wilhelm Keitel, who maintained that "the entire war in the East, to a known degree, may be termed a preventive war. . . . We decided . . . to forestall an attack by Soviet Russia and to destroy its armed forces with a surprise attack" (325).

13. After the attack, these districts were called "fronts." The Odessa District became the Southern Front, Kiev the Southwestern, and the Baltic became the Northwestern Front; only the Western District stayed the same. As the German invasion progressed, there were regroupings and renamings; for the sake of readability, the fronts will be referred to as districts for the first six months of the war.

14. Of the 967 T-34 tanks in service in June 1941, 313 had gone to the 4th Mechanized Corps of the Kiev District, which had 100 of the relatively new KV heavy tanks as well. The 8th Mechanized Corps had 100, and the 15th Corps had seventy-one. Only the 6th Mechanized Corps of the Western District, with 238 of these new vehicles, came close to being as well equipped. Data taken from the invaluable monograph by Steven Zaloga and Peter Sarson, *T-34/76 Medium Tank, 1941–1945* (London: Osprey, 1994), 11–14.

15. An understatement: when in 1937 Yegorov, chief of staff, had proposed one be established, his practical recommendation was then used against him when he was arrested, and he was accused

of defeatism by Timoshenko. See the brief discussion in Pleshakov (*Stalin's Folly*, 83).

16. Once the bombs started falling, Timoshenko called again. When
Pavlov's deputy asked for permission to open fire (!), he repeated
the same mantra, that Stalin "thinks these may be provocations
on the part of some German generals." These examples could be
multiplied indefinitely. The conversation is recorded both by Pleshakov (*Stalin's Folly*, 100, 107) and Montefiore (*Stalin*, 363–66).

17. Quote from Montefiore (*Stalin*, 367), who seems unaware
of Anglo-French efforts (in the last days of August and first
week of September 1939) to negotiate with Hitler over a Polish territorial adjustment, much as they had done with him over
Czechoslovakia. True, these efforts were feeble, and brushed off,
but the precedent had been set.

18. Interrogation record taken from Cajus Bekker, *The Luftwaffe
Wartime Diaries*, translated and edited by Frank Ziegler (New
York: Doubleday, 1968), 219. Interestingly, there is no mention
of the Soviet officer in the extensive indices and citations in John
Erickson's *The Road to Stalingrad* (London: Cassell, 1975).

19. Wever's insistence on a comprehensive ground-to-air defense
system meant both that German combat units had Luftwaffe
air defense troops attached to them and that their airfields were
well guarded. By contrast, the Allies entered the war with the belief that level flight bombers were accurate delivery systems that
were impervious to antiaircraft defenses. They soon learned: on
May 14, 1940, when they tried to destroy the Meuse bridges and
stop the German advance they lost nearly 50 percent of their
bomber force and failed to hit a single bridge. See L. F. Ellis, *War
in France and Flanders* (London: Her Majesty's Stationery Office,
1953), 55–56. By the 18th, the "bombers of the advanced striking force were virtually out of action. . . . Ten squadrons were
therefore now reduced to six" (72); on the 19th, reconnaissance
revealed a large force moving on Arras, but no bombers were left
to attack it (73).

20. As recounted by Luftwaffe captain Herbert Pabst in Bekker
(*Luftwaffe Wartime Diaries*, 221). The punctuation in the English
translation fails to make clear that the entire passage is a transcript of his remarks. The totals in the sentences that follow are
found on page 221. Soviet aircraft deficiencies: Stalin's son Vasily
told him that during the war only 20 percent of the losses were

owing to combat, and as inspector general of the air force he was
in a position to know.

21. As recorded by Pleshakov (*Stalin's Folly*, 126–27). One of the
many suicides during those first days. Given Stalin's reaction to
failure in July (and later) probably preferable, but hardly condu-
cive to the business of fighting a war. German claims as to the
number of planes destroyed seem to be substantially lower than
retrospective Soviet-sourced accounts.

22. Pleshakov (*Stalin's Folly*, 129) records this directive, without
doing justice to its fantasy-like qualities. The units of the Kiev
District who received this order were already desperately trying
to stave off the German breakthrough around Przemysl in Galicia. Lublin was over 150 kilometers away. Stalin might as well
have directed them to take Berlin or Dresden.

23. Jean-Norton Cru, *Témoins* (Paris: les Etincelles, 1929), 20; my
translation.

24. In that total all the new T-34 tanks of the 6th Mechanized
Corps, arguably the most powerful armored unit in the Red
Army, were destroyed in two days outside Minsk. German
data as recorded by Mitcham (*Hitler's Commanders*, 40); Soviet tank losses by Zaloga and Sarson (*T-34/76 Medium Tank*,
14). The German figure quoted is less than the one cited by
Glantz, even making allowances for difference in the reporting period. Glantz lists presumably official Soviet figures of
4,799 tanks and 1,777 aircraft, *When Titans Clashed* (Lawrence:
University Press of Kansas, 1993), 293.

25. Although much is made of their justified panic, the truth is that
they had made the same discovery in May 1940 trying to destroy the heavily armored French tanks; the Wehrmacht's standard antitank gun, which was also used in the Mark 3 tank, was
a pathetic 3.7 centimeter weapon that should never have been
put into service. After the fall of France the ammunition was
upgraded to give the gun better penetration, but it was still totally inadequate. Postwar, the German consensus was that the
Red Army by and large had better weapons than the Germans
did. For an analysis of the 3.7 centimeter gun problem, see John
Mosier, *Cross of Iron* (New York: Holt, 2006), 97–99. For the
German estimates, see B. H. Liddell Hart, *The German Generals
Talk* (New York: Morrow, 1948), 221–22.

26. Example, data, and quote taken from Zaloga and Sarson (*T-34/76 Medium Tank*, 15–16).
27. Information from Pleshakov (*Stalin's Folly*, 187).
28. The exact dates are in most instances not known. Soviet sources have traditionally been reluctant to divulge such information, even when it was known; given the collapse of the local governments and the chaos of the retreat, in many instances no one knew. Richenau supposedly did not fall until July 17, but it appears the town had been abandoned a week earlier.
29. As quoted by Pleshakov (*Stalin's Folly*, 206).
30. This calculation was made by dividing the currently accepted figures for Soviet dead (4.3 million) and missing (2.9 million) for 1941 by the number of days of combat. The first seventeen days would thus have seen losses of 381,000 dead and 265,000 missing, about 24 percent of the total manpower in theater (for the numbers, see Keith E. Bonn [Editor], *Slaughterhouse: The Handbook of the Eastern Front* [Bedford, Penn.: The Aberjona Press, 2004], 10). It is a conservative estimate, but there are no monthly figures available. In *Stalin*, Montefiore says that losses for the first "three weeks" of the war came to two million men (378), a highly improbable figure, given the strength of the entire front and the death toll for the entire year. But running up the figures for the early loss is, in an oblique way, a reinforcement of the basic Stalinist legend of the war: the catastrophe was caused by the surprise attack. No, the catastrophe was years in the making.
31. The figures are Montefiore's (*Stalin*, 378), apparently derived from the same documentary sources as those used by Glantz, although the two are not compatible (see note 24). By the end of the three offensives in the three main areas, which the Soviets concluded came to an end in September, official losses came to 11,703 tanks and 3,985 aircraft, figures that are broadly speaking in agreement with the generally lower German totals (Glantz, *When Titans Clashed*, 293).

CHAPTER V: DEEP BATTLE:
FROM THE BREAKTHROUGH TO THE FALL OF KIEV

1. General Doumenc, on receiving news that the Germans were crossing the Meuse River in May 1940, as related by Andre Beaufré, *The Fall of France*, translated by Desmond Flower (New York: Knopf, 1968), 181–82.

2. Just because that was not what happened, it does not therefore follow that the wildly optimistic prediction was the sign of mental derangement: in September 1944 the Allied high command was convinced the war would be over by Christmas. See the extensive analysis of this interesting belief in Ronald Andidora's aptly titled *Home by Christmas: The Illusion of Victory in 1944* (Westport, Connecticut: Greenwood, 2002). Quote is from Gud, 175.

3. There is a certain grim irony in the fact that although Kirponos, who was still a division commander in March 1940, and had neither the training nor the background to exercise effective military command of what amounted to an entire country (Ukraine), was transformed into one of the heroes of the Great Patriotic War due to his death in combat during the defense of Kiev. That he was brave is unquestionable, that he was particularly competent, much less certain. See the brief summary of his efforts in John Erickson, *The Road to Stalingrad* (London: Cassell, 1975), 168–69. Note: Mikhail Petrovich is the Kirponos referred to in some texts as "M. I. Kirponos," e.g., in Simon Sebag Montefiore, *Stalin: The Court of the Red Tsar* (New York: Random House, 2005), 380; but see index entry.

4. Stalin thus ignored one of the basic lessons that should have been drawn from the Finnish debacle: the extent to which even crude and improvised bunkers and blockhouses were effective defensive measures. When the Allies invaded Sicily, Italy, and France, they found this out to their cost, as the Germans made extensive use of every natural and man-made obstacle. They also took care to blow up whatever bridge had survived the Allied bombers. Curiously, the same Russian alumni of the officer training regime who pointed out the deficiency of the Blitzkrieg seemed completely unaware of the extent to which the Red Army had historically not done this. The relatively prolonged

and bloody siege of the Brest citadel was always mentioned, but not the fact that it was conspicuous by its uniqueness.

5. In most of the eyewitness recollections Stalin used an obscenity. See, among the various summaries, Dmitri Volkogonov, *Stalin: Triumph and Tragedy*, translated and edited by Harold Shukman (New York: Grove Weidenfeld, 1988), 410.

6. David Remnick, *Lenin's Tomb* (New York: Random House, 1993), 25. Or, as Saul Bellow put it: "A great deal of intelligence can be invested in ignorance when the need for illusion is deep." *To Jerusalem and Back* (New York: Crown, 1977), 162. François Furet also uses this quote to the same end in *The Passing of an Illusion: The Idea of Communism in the Twentieth Century*, translated by Deborah Furet (Chicago: University of Chicago Press, 1999), 117.

7. The exact sequence is related by Montefiore (*Stalin*, 374–76), together with the various profane alternatives to "We've lost it forever." His account agrees with that of Pleshakov (*Stalin's Folly*, 245–56), and is as close to the truth as we're likely to get.

8. *Penséres, traits, et bon mots*, as listed in *Dictionnaire des citations françaises* (Paris: Larousse, 1987), 502. My translation.

9. For the details, see Erickson, *Road to Stalingrad*, 173, who also records Voroshilov's enthusiastic response to this insane decision: "Now we'll put that mistake right." By "mistake" he meant the formation of the armored and mechanized units whose German equivalents were rampaging toward Moscow.

10. A Russian scholar recalled the fortunate circumstances that enabled her father, an officer in the Red Army during the Finnish War, to escape prison or death. His colleagues, she averred, were not so lucky. We still don't know just how widespread the reprisals were, but the anecdotal evidence suggests they were hardly a few isolated incidents, as Montefiore, perhaps unintentionally, suggests with the example he cites (*Stalin*, 327). Compare with Erickson's rather bland comments of "upheavals" and the need "for a new disciplinary code," in his discussions of the aftermath of the Finnish War (*Road to Stalingrad*, 16–21).

11. As quoted by Montefiore (*Stalin*, 179). Compare with Erickson's "officers and men coming out of German encirclement should be rigorously investigated by the NKVD" (*Road to Stalingrad*, 176). Here and elsewhere Erickson's bland summaries, perhaps un-

consciously, hardly reveal the depth and breadth of Stalin's new reign of terror.

12. The full appreciation is in Erickson (*Road to Stalingrad*, 178). It is oddly prescient, insofar as the threat analysis goes, too much so: it has the odor of retrospection about it, as it seems based on German advances that at the end of July had not yet occurred, i.e., the true shape of the salient was still masked, and the German offensive there happened only in early September. Montefiore cites the same exchange between Stalin and Zhukov but omits the report (*Stalin*, 379).

13. Heinz Guderian, *Panzer Leader*, translated by Constantine Fitzgibbon (New York: Da Capo, 1996), 200.

14. Samuel Mitcham, *Hitler's Commanders* (New York: Cooper Square Press, 2000), 41, echoing Ronald Lewin, *Hitler's Mistakes* (London: Secker & Warburg, 1984), who is replicating the point of view of Walter Warlimont, whom he quotes favorably: "Hitler was about to send the German army into the Soviet Union, on a four-year wil-o'-the-wisp chase after seaports, cities, oil, corn, nickel, manganese, and iron ore" (119). Compare with this quote from a senior British general who was present at the meetings during which the British and French decided to invade Norway: "We are quite cynical about everything except stopping the iron ore." *The Ironside Diaries*, edited by Roderick Macleod and Dennis Kelly (New York: David McKay, 1963), 215. William R. Trotter uses this same quote in *A Frozen Hell* (Chapel Hill, North Carolina: Algonquin, 1991), 239.

15. See the enumeration and discussion in Matthew Cooper, *The German Army* (New York: Stein & Day, 1978), 281–82. As Cooper points out, these units, except for the two in Africa, could be replaced either by new units being formed and trained, or by third-line units not judged capable of combat. About thirty of the divisions, all infantry, had been excluded from Barbarossa as second-line units; however, as the German surge continued, they became steadily more useful. The notion that the Germans had thrown everything into battle on June 22, and were thus steadily depleting their forces, is no more tenable than the analogous claim that their forces were exhausted and their tanks on the verge of breakdown; that it is routinely repeated hardly makes it true. See, for example, the unsubstantiated claims made by Rich-

ard Evans, *The Third Reich at War* (New York: Penguin, 2009), 187–88.

16. For Spanish assistance in the war, see Gerald Kleinfeld, *Hitler's Spanish Legion* (Carbondale: Southern Illinois University Press, 1979). The contribution of the Italian army to Hitler's war effort is nearly as undervalued as its fighting qualities. See, for instance, Emilio Faldella, *L'Italia nella seconda guerra mondiale; revisione di giudizi* (Bologna: Capelli, 1959) and Giovanni Messe, *La guerra al fronte russo: il Corpo di spedizione italiano in Russia* (Milano: Mursia, 2005). The enormous contribution of the Romanian and Hungarian armies to the war is similarly dismissed, even though, as we shall see, it was the Romanians who laid siege to the important Soviet naval base of Odessa, and took it on October 16, 1941.

17. These units were in addition to those that had been already committed for the June attack. See the units histories in Franz Kurowski, *Sturmgeschütze vor!* = *Assault Guns to the Front!* (Winnipeg: J. J. Fedorowicz, 1999), 31, 40, 67, 77, 87, 89.

18. Data taken from Hartmut Schustereit, *Vabanque: Hitlers Angriff auf die Sowjetunion 1941 als Versuch, durch den Sieg im Osten den Westen zu bezwingen* (Selent: Pour le Merite, 2002), 147. The German army had traditionally used a ten-day period for its casualty reports.

19. If the official figures are to be believed, 1,121 tanks were produced in the third quarter, only 765 in the fourth. But the raw figures are misleading. Most of the production was, understandably, from the Stalingrad factory, so the vehicles had to be shipped, distributed, and the crews trained, since very few tankers, even those who had survived, were familiar with the new vehicle. All of this took time, even in a highly efficient system. Tank production data from Zaloga and Sarson (*T-34/76 Medium Tank*, 17–18). It is worth pointing out that the fact that the Stalingrad factory was producing so many tanks is yet another instance of the extent to which Hitler's critics simply failed to understand the Soviet reality.

20. Claims such as Montefiore's that "although Hitler had won astounding victories . . . none of Barbarossa's objectives . . . had fallen" are thus highly misleading (*Stalin*, 378). The French had not asked for an armistice until late June 1940; Polish resistance

had gone on into early October 1939; in both cases the fighting went on for roughly six weeks. That either Hitler or his generals believed they would be in Moscow by early August is highly unlikely, given the distances the Germans had to go. Such claims are of a piece with the idea that Stalin had so many men at his disposal that casualties were irrelevant, which in turn plays into the subtext of the basic Stalinist legend of the war, as does the notion that Hitler was an incompetent amateur.

21. The incident is described in detail in Montefiore (*Stalin,* 380). Given how many people had already been executed for less, Timoshenko's remark was no exaggeration.

22. At the time, the Germans claimed to have taken 655,000 prisoners. Subsequent Russian claims were that "only" 520,000 had been captured, and that 150,000 had managed to break out, but this retrospective sleight-of-hand (the Germans counted everyone, the Soviets resorted to a legalistic definition of the personnel actually part of the front) could hardly disguise the dimensions of the disaster (figures taken from Erickson, *Road to Stalingrad,* 210).

23. Tank loss data computed from the extensive tables in Thomas L. Jentz, *Panzertruppen: The Complete Guide to the Creation and Combat Employment of Germany's Tank Force* (Atglen, Pennsylvania: Schiffer, 1996), 2 volumes.

24. Data for prisoners of war taken from Hartmut Schustereit, *Vabanque: Hitlers Angriff auf die Sowjetunion 1941 als Versuch, durch den Sieg im Osten den Westen zu bezwingen* (Selent: Pour le Merite, 2002), 149. Although pointed out in the introductory chapter, it bears repeating that the German data makes it impossible to give much credence to the supposedly official Soviet figures cited by Glantz (*When Titans Clashed,* 292), since he cites total Soviet losses for "Killed or Missing" in the "3rd Quarter" of 1941 as 2,067,801. But by the end of September, the Germans counted 2,501,614 Soviet prisoners of war.

25. See, for example, von Manstein's telling assessment of the Soviet dispositions before June 22, which he evaluated as though the Red Army operated like the German army, and could hold itself in readiness to mount an aggressive defense or an actual offensive. Even after the war was over, it apparently had never occurred to him that for the first two years or so, the Red Army lacked both the sort of defensive doctrines he took for granted

and the capability of carrying them out. See Erich von Manstein, *Lost Victories*, translated by Anthony G. Powell (Chicago: Henry Regnery, 1958), 52.

CHAPTER VI: THE CAMPAIGN OF COMPROMISES: OCTOBER–DECEMBER 1941

1. Aleksandr Solzhenitsyn, "Incident at Kretchetovka Station," in *We Never Make Mistakes*, translated by Paul Blackstock (New York: Norton, 1971), 18.
2. Samuel Mitcham, *Hitler's Field Marshals* (New York: Cooper Square Press, 1990), 141.
3. Given the secrecy that surrounded, and still surrounds, Soviet defense industries, an exact calculation of the importance of Leningrad is difficult if not impossible. In czarist times the city, as the capital, was the natural center of armaments production, and its significance was well known. In addition to the heavy tank factories, much of Soviet finished steel came from the factory complex on the western outskirts of the city. The estimate given in the text derives from the maps in Institute für Marxismus-Leninismus beim Zentralkomitte der Kommunistischen Partei der Sowjetunion, *Geschichte des Grossen Vaterländischen Krieges der Sowjetunion*, 6 Bänden (Berlin: Deutsche Militärverlag, 1962), volume 1.
4. "I have nothing against calling the Seventh [Symphony] the Leningrad symphony, but it's not about Leningrad under siege, it's about the Leningrad that Stalin destroyed and Hitler merely finished off." Shostakovich (a Leningrader himself), in Dmitri Shostakovich, *Testimony: The Memoirs of Dmitri Shostakovich*, as related to and edited by Solomon Volkov, translated by Antonina W. Bouis (New York: HarperCollins, 2004 [1979]), 156. A failure to understand Stalin's feelings toward the city (and the extent to which he used the death of Kirov to launch the Great Terror), vitiates much of what has been written about the siege. The depth of Stalin's feelings were not revealed until after the war, when he unleashed Zhdanov on "Old Petrograd, the Bronze Horseman as an image of that old Petrograd.... But we love Soviet Leningrad, Leningrad as the progressive center of Soviet culture." Zhdanov's horrified audi-

ence knew exactly what that entailed: "It was obvious Stalin would not rest until he had destroyed the Petrograd remnant." Zhdanov quote taken from Solomon Volkov, *St. Petersburg: A Cultural History*, translated by Antonina Bouis (New York: Simon & Schuster, 1995), 550, 450. It's tempting to speculate that Hitler was aware of Stalin's attitude, given his negative attitudes toward Berlin and Vienna, and his preferences for Munich.

5. Tikhvin was the most important town in the northern section of what in czarist times was the Novgorod Oblast. The only other settlements that could actually be called towns were further east and south. Mitcham opines, disapprovingly, that Hitler sent von Leeb off on this excursion to "seize the bauxite-producing area" around Tikhvin (Mitcham, *Hitler's Field Marshals*, 142), but this is geologically dubious, and Mitcham overstates the distances involved.

6. William Lubbeck, *At Leningrad's Gates: The Combat Memoirs of a Soldier with Army Group North* (Havertown, Penn.: Casemate, 2006), 88.

7. As is frequently the case when Hitler is concerned, the decision to accede to the senior command's desires to move on Moscow, although never disputed, is simply dismissed, despite being one of the more important decisions of the war. It contradicts the idea of Hitler as a greedy amateur single-handedly responsible for everything that went wrong. See the account in Mitcham, *Hitler's Field Marshals*, 40–41.

8. Simon Sebag Montefiore, *Stalin: The Court of the Red Tsar* (New York: Random House, 2005), 395.

9. As Montefiore notes (*Stalin*, 392), when Zhukov published his memoirs in 1966, this little detail was omitted; it appeared only in 1990. Yet another instance of the dubious reliability of Soviet writings on the war.

10. Nikolai Ivanovich Obryn'ba, *Red Partisan*, translated by Vladimir Krupnik (Washington, D.C.: Potomac, 2007), 28. I have some doubts as to the authenticity of this memoir, that is, as to the extent to which it truly represents a contemporaneous account. In his brief Preface (vii), the Russian editor, Artem Drahkin, does not address this matter sufficiently. However, it seems authentic in that it does represent the account of an eyewitness, however imperfectly remembered.

11. The first serious reference to the Moscow panic came only when Solzhenitsyn's "Incident at Krechetovka Station" was published, and most readers probably missed the elliptical reference: "Some railroad men arrived from Moscow. They had been there in the middle of October, and told of monstrous, unthinkable things— of the flight of factory directors, of the destruction of banks and stores" (16). (It's not clear if this is simply rumor, and in my experience most people assumed it was, or missed it entirely; but in fact it was rather exact, to the point of being understated, as is still the case today, although the panic is no longer unreported.) See the references in Montefiore (*Stalin*, 395, and 399). Like Marshal Zhukov's candid revelation, the incident was promptly scrubbed from memory, as it contradicted a meme of increasing importance, the unity and patriotism of the Russian people in the face of the Hitlerite aggression and subsequent barbarity. For an excellent example of how the Bolsheviks dealt with unpleasant realities once they could not be denied, and how Western scholars obliged them, see (1) the treatment of the "panic" in Alexander Werth, *Russia at War* (New York: Dutton, 1964), 232–42; (2) the brief sentences in Reina Pennington, *Wings, Women, and War: Soviet Airwomen in World War Two Combat* (Lawrence: University Press of Kansas, 2001), 39, which amount to a bland dismissal of the riots.

12. No serious work was done recounting the extent of the participation of the Romanian army until after the collapse of the Ceaucescu regime; that Romanian troops were deeply involved in the offensives of Army Group South, and gave a good account of themselves was understandably not something that could be emphasized. Most accounts of the war either ignored their efforts or spoke of them dismissively, reflecting a prejudice on the part of many German officers. See the rather more balanced judgment given by Erich von Manstein in *Lost Victories*, edited and translated by Anthony G. Powell (London: Methuen, 1958), 206–8. In sheer numbers, the Romanian contribution was substantial: easily over 250,000 men. For the best account of the siege of Odessa, see the quasi-official history by Victor Nitu and Dragos Pusca, "The Battle of Odessa—1941," available at www .worldwar2.ro/operatii/?article=7.

13. The best account of the impact of Stalin's Japanese spies is in Montefiore (*Stalin*, 403).

14. Joseph Stalin, *The Great Patriotic War of the Soviet Union* (New York: International Publishers, 1945), 20.
15. Montefiore, *Stalin*, 405.
16. Stalin, *Great Patriotic War* (36–37). Compare Stalin's remarks here with the summary in the official history, which speaks of three million men lost for the same period and says that Germany had "lost its elite divisions." Stalin is gone but his legend remains (*Geschichte*, 2:714).
17. See the brief discussion of other peace feelers and Hitler's rejection of them in Franz Kurowski, *The Brandenburgers Global Mission* (Winnipeg: J. Fedorowicz, 1997), 97–98.
18. Montefiore, *Stalin*, 403, 406. As General von Kleist pointed out, 1942 was the worst year for the Red Army in terms of equipment available. Interview recorded in B. H. Liddell Hart, *The German Generals Talk* (New York: Morrow, 1953), 221–22.
19. Stalin, *Great Patriotic War*, 18.
20. See the listing of the fates of Soviet armored units in Steve Zaloga and James Grandsen, *Soviet Tanks and Combat Vehicles of World War Two* (Harrisburg, Pennsylvania: Arms & Armour, 1984), 128–29. The existence of armored units with three-digit numbers does not indicate that the Red Army had that many armored divisions. The numbering system went from 1 to 60. The twelve independent armored divisions created during the war received the three-digit numbers.
21. Together with the light tanks, the brigade in theory would have forty-six tanks. It is worth pointing out in this connection that nearly half of the armored strength of each brigade would thus consist of light tanks. Although in 1941–1942 the Wehrmacht had nothing to compare with the T-34 and KV-1, its main battle tanks were definitely not outclassed by the Soviet light tanks. Data on the strength and composition of armored brigades from Zaloga and Grandsen (*Soviet Tanks and Combat Vehicles*, 147).
22. Andrew Nagorski concludes his highly detailed account of the late fall fighting by observing that although the Battle of Moscow "was a huge defeat for the Germans, a more contentious question is how big a victory Moscow was for the Soviet side," noting with approval an assessment by Richard Overy that it "was not the turning point" of the war. That perceptive historians with impeccable research credentials are still cautiously engaging in par-

tial deconstructions is compelling testimony to Stalin's success. Quote from *The Greatest Battle* (New York: Simon & Schuster, 2008), 315.

CHAPTER VII: THE HOLLOW VICTORIES OF 1942

1. Bilíbin's letter to Prince Andrei in *War and Peace*, Book 5, Chapter 7 (406–7).
2. Stalin immediately began complaining about the Allied failure to open up a "second front" in Europe. In his speeches from November 1942 on, as well as in private conversations, he blamed the Soviet setbacks of 1942 on "the absence of a second front in Europe [that] enabled them to transfer to our war front all their available reserves and to create a big superiority of forces in the southwestern direction." This quote prefaces a surprisingly elaborate analysis of the history and necessity for a second front. See Joseph Stalin, *The Great Patriotic War of the Soviet Union* (New York: International Publishers, 1945), 61–64, quote on 61. Typically, Stalin's complaint obscured the fact that there already was a second front, thanks to Japan. This was a splendid rhetorical ploy: Stalin succeeded in defining the basis of how the war would be seen for future generations.
3. German losses for December 1941, first ten days of 1942 (and subsequently in this text), taken from archival records reprinted in Hartmut Schustereit, *Vabanque: Hitlers Angriff auf die Sowjetunion 1941 als Versuch, durch den Sieg im Osten den Westen zu bezwingen* (Selent: Pour le Merite, 2002), 147.
4. The official Soviet data for troop strength is reprinted in Keith E. Bonn, editor, *Slaughterhouse: The Handbook of the Eastern Front* (Bedford, Pennsylvania: Aberjona, 2004), Figure 2, page 6. It tracks closely a similar tabulation in David Glantz, *When Titans Clashed* (Lawrence: University Press of Kansas, 1993), 292. The error in such computations stems from confusing the number of German troops Hitler was willing to commit to the Eastern Front with the number of troops he actually had at his disposal. In reality, the German military machine was expanding, not contracting. At 8.410 million, it was nearly twice the size it had been in 1939 (4.522 million). See the data for all combat-

ants in Mark Harrison, editor, *The Economics of World War II: Six Great Powers in International Comparison* (Cambridge: Cambridge University Press, 1998), Table 1.5, page 14.

5. Tank inventory data used here and in the text that follows is compiled from the extensive tables in Thomas L. Jentz, *Panzertruppen: The Complete Guide to the Creation and Combat Employment of Germany's Tank Force* (Atglen, Pennsylvania: Schiffer, 1996).

6. Production data taken from F. M. von Senger und Etterlin, *German Tanks of World War II*, translated by J. Lucas, edited by Peter Chamberlain and Chris Ellis (New York: Galahad, 1967), Appendix 1. For an accounting of actual losses and strengths in the armored force, see Schustereit (*Vabanque*, 165).

7. Production data taken from Steve Zaloga and James Grandsen, *Soviet Tanks and Combat Vehicles of World War Two* (London: Arms & Armour, 1984), 225. As the later discussion makes clear, there is considerable question as to the reliability of these statistics; however, the official data shows that the USSR was not producing assault guns to any extent in this time period.

8. Illuminating the unreliability of Soviet statistics: the official Soviet total of 162,282 men killed and missing, as reproduced in David Glantz, *When Titans Clashed* (Lawrence: University Press of Kansas, 1993), 293–94, is less than the German total for prisoners taken alone, nor does it include any tanks. Apparently the Kerch area was held by a quarter of a million men without any armor whatsoever. The actual total of vehicles captured or destroyed was about 350. See the confirming data in Simon Sebag Montefiore, *Stalin: The Court of the Red Tsar* (New York: Random House, 2005), 413.

9. As indeed they did, but Stalin refused to listen to them. The syntax is fascinating: instinctively he shifted the blame onto others (his "military advisers"). If things turned out badly, it was their fault. Conversation quoted by Montefiore, with even more detail (*Stalin*, 415).

10. The official Soviet figures come to only 170,958 dead and missing, and no tanks (Glantz, *When Titans Clashed*, 294). Tellingly, Montefiore uses the German figures (*Stalin*, 415).

11. "He quite reasonably presumed that Hitler would again attack Moscow," is how Montefiore puts it (*Stalin*, 411). An astonishing presumption, made reasonable only if we assume that Soviet

military intelligence was completely incompetent, or that Stalin paid attention to them only when it suited him. Interestingly, Montefiore hints at this in the next sentence: "Stalin's real fault lay in his raging overconfidence." Indeed.

12. In the immediate aftermath, Stalin considered getting rid of both Timoshenko and Khrushchev as the parties responsible for the failed attack. In the event, they both got off with withering lectures, the one given to Timoshenko to the effect that he needed to start waging war by "losing less blood, as the Germans are doing. . . . Wage war not by quantity but by skill," being particularly ripe. From Stalin's lecture, together with considerably more detail, in Montefiore (*Stalin*, 415–16).

13. The best account of the surprisingly little known German advance in the Caucasus is Wilhelm Tieke, *The Caucasus and the Oil: The German-Soviet War in the Caucasus, 1942/43* (Winnipeg: J. J. Fedorowicz, 1995).

14. In local Soviet folklore, a handful of sailors held out until the city was recaptured in 1943. The port was captured by the Romanians.

15. True enough, but like many of Stalin's remarks, highly disingenuous: Hitler's oil supply was in southern Romania; at that point in the war it might as well have been on the moon as far as the Red Army was concerned. By contrast, Hitler was advancing rapidly toward the Caspian. See the details of these conversations in Montefiore, *Stalin*, 416, 425–26 (Stalin, as quoted by Baibakov, from page 426).

16. The actual figure is 1.134 million tons. Amounts (here and as follows in the text) computed from the monthly deliveries tabulated by Hubert P. van Tuyll, *Feeding the Bear* (Westport, Conn.: Greenwood, 1989), Table 20, page 166.

17. Jodl was *Chef des Wehrmachtsführungsstabes*, literally, chief of the army general staff, and thus a sort of deputy to Wilhelm Keitel, who was chief of the *Oberkommando der Wehrmacht*, or high command of the army. But by the end of 1941, these impressive-sounding titles were largely fictions: Hitler was running the war, dealing directly with his field commanders, and using men like Jodl as errand boys and Keitel as a sort of glorified secretary. Their authority, such as it was, was largely a function of their being passive-aggressive.

18. Official Soviet records admit to 92,000 dead and missing in two

obscurely titled offensive operations in this area, but no tanks (Glantz, *When Titans Clashed*, 294). Von Manstein, who directed the operation, also records that he took 12,000 prisoners and 244 tanks. See Erich von Manstein, *Lost Victories*, edited and translated by Anthony G. Powell (London: Methuen, 1958), 266. "Shock" armies and "Guards" divisions sound impressive, and in 1914, the latter term identified elite regiments of all the European armies, particularly the Russian one. But in Stalinist usage the term simply designated units that the high command in Moscow believed, or hoped, were combat-ready.

19. Stalin, *Great Patriotic War*, 61–63.

20. Compare with the following: "The cry that all Soviet sources are 'unreliable' or, as mere extravagant propaganda, devoid of value must fall flat when the sources have never even been examined; to dismiss them or to ignore them *tout court* is patently absurd and self-defeating." As is invariably the case with such statements, the Marxist-Leninist orientation can easily be identified by the piling on of extremes ("patently absurd and self-defeating"), the use of which is in itself a logical fallacy in argumentation. Quote from John Erickson's Introduction to *The USSR in World War Two: An Annotated Bibliography of Books Published in the Soviet Union, 1945–1975*, edited by Michael Parrish (New York: Garland, 1981), xviii. The issue is not whether Soviet sources are dismissed completely, the core issue is vetting the data according to the triage of distortion, fabrication, and concealment explained by Mark Harrison; the deeper issue is the refusal of military historians to recognize what economic historians, demographers, and other specialists assume as a matter of course, that Soviet data is highly suspect. (Categories from Harrison [*World War II*, 370].)

21. Quote and assessment from von Manstein (*Lost Victories*, 260).

CHAPTER VIII: THE PLANETS AND PARADOXES OF 1942–1943

1. Erich von Manstein, *Lost Victories*, edited and translated by Anthony G. Powell (London: Methuen, 1958), 439.

2. "Volunteer" units of female aviators had begun to form by October 1941, the quotation marks suggesting a certain skepticism about the use of the term. In Bolshevik parlance most words

meant the opposite of what they seemed to mean, e.g., the use of the term "stragglers" as a condemnatory identification of soldiers who had been cut off by the German advance and made their way back to the front. But there is no doubt that the Soviet air force used women in combat roles, nor that the numbers were not trivial, perhaps as many as 150 pilots and navigators. See the listings and histories in Reina Pennington, *Wings, Women, and War: Soviet Airwomen in World War II Combat* (Lawrence: University Press of Kansas, 2001), especially Appendix A. An interesting commentary on how destitute the Red Air Force was by 1942: the 46th Guards Bomber Unit, which began flying combat missions in 1942, used Soviet Po-2 aircraft: open-cockpit biplanes. As Pennington observes, "The idea of using an open-cockpit bi-plane as a combat aircraft might seem inconceivable to us today, but dozens of Soviet women (and hundreds of men) flew the Po-2 as a night bomber in the Second World War" (73).

3. See the summary in David Glantz, *Zhukov's Greatest Defeat* (Lawrence: University Press of Kansas, 1993), 26. Until this study was published, the existence of these plans was not known. As Glantz points out, Zhukov's memoirs gloss over the incident in highly disingenuous fashion (316). Nor did the supposed candor that cautiously began under Khrushchev change the situation markedly. When Glantz published his study, he remarked that "the real story of Operation Mars remains untold in Russian publications." But the story *was* told on the German side, a salutary reminder of the extent to which Stalin's legends of the war continue to live on and why for actual facts one must rely on accounts using the German material (quote on 316). But since the Germans had no idea of the ambitious scope of the planetary operations, accounts drawn from them do not allow historians to judge the extent of Stalin's failure, again an excellent example of the durability of Stalinist mythmaking.

4. Glantz cites the official data (*Zhukov's Greatest Defeat*, 24). Although the raw numbers are impressive, and every historian cites them, the numbers are curious. Glantz cites data implying that the total size of the Soviet armor available was under 7,000 vehicles (*Zhukov's Greatest Defeat*, 19). Given the enormous inventory on hand when the fighting started, and the equally gargantuan production figures, the only conclusion to be drawn is

that the statistics are wildly inflated, a subject analyzed in detail later. Tank production data from Steve Zaloga and James Grandsen, *Soviet Tanks and Combat Vehicles of World War Two* (London: Arms & Armour, 1984), 235.

5. Glantz citing records (*Zhukov's Greatest Defeat*, 304). Significantly, by this point the Red Army was able to deploy only 500 tanks, although Zhukov had started off with over 2,000.

6. A figure that by a curious coincidence is close to the official Red Army losses for the fourth quarter of the year: 455,800. However, even if we admit these wildly improbable figures, the official Soviet total for the year, 2,993,536, when compared to the German losses of 537,922 in the same categories, still reveals the Germans winning the exchange ratio by 5.5:1. Official Soviet casualty data from David Glantz, *When Titans Clashed* (Lawrence: University Press of Kansas, 1993), 297.

7. The intelligence appreciation is quoted in Glantz (*Zhukov's Greatest Defeat*, 301), without further comment. This appreciation would hold true for all future Soviet offensive actions, which goes a long way to explain why the war dragged on even when the Germans were heavily engaged in the west.

8. Most notably Earl F. Ziemke, in *Stalingrad to Berlin: The German Defeat in the East* (Washington, D.C.: Military History Office, 1968), 115–16. See also the appreciation in Glantz (*Zhukov's Greatest Defeat*, 291).

9. Data from Jean Restayn, *Tiger I on the Eastern Front* (Paris: Histoire & Collections, 2001), 14.

10. See the organizational tables in Zaloga and Grandsen (*Soviet Tanks and Combat Vehicles*, 223). A tanks corps would have slightly more (175).

11. Quote from Hans-Joachim Jung, *Panzer Soldiers for "God, Honor and Fatherland": The History of Panzerregiment Grossdeutschland* (Winnipeg: J. J. Fedorowicz, 2000), 85.

12. Luftflotte 1 had in fact supplied the six divisions surrounded at Demyansk by air for three months (February 2 to May 18, 1942), delivering food and fuel, together with 15,446 troops, and flying out 22,093 wounded. There had also been a smaller but equally successful operation at Kholm. See Cajus Bekker, *The Luftwaffe Wartime Diaries*, translated and edited by Frank Ziegler (New York: Doubleday, 1968), 275–77, for the details.

13. Initially, von Manstein's directive was simply "to bring the enemy

attacks to a standstill and recapture the positions previously occupied by us." Quote from Erich von Manstein, *Lost Victories*,
edited and translated by Anthony G. Powell (London: Methuen,
1958), 294. Although, based on his analysis of the workings of
Hitler's headquarters, Walter Warlimont would argue that this
is yet another instance of the deteriorating quality of the orders
being issued, it can also be argued that when Hitler had confidence in the abilities of his generals he gave them a surprising
amount of discretion. See *Inside Hitler's Headquarters, 1939–
1945*, translated by R. H. Barry (Novato, California: Presidio,
1964).

14. Quote from *Lost Victories*, 303. Von Manstein makes the penetrating observation that Paulus of all the generals should have realized that this request would not be granted: "the only solution
would have been to present him [Hitler] with the fait accompli
of the army's disengagement from Stalingrad" (303).

15. Three facts are often overlooked in discussions about the Stalingrad airlift. The first is that although both Richthofen (for the
Luftwaffe) and Zeitzler (for the high command) thought the airlift strategy was impossible, Göring insisted it was not, that he
could deliver 500 tons a day. Zeitzler called him a liar, there was
a shouting match, and Hitler intervened. He said coldly, "The
Reichsmarschall has made his announcement, and I am obliged
to believe him" (Bekker, *Luftwaffe Wartime Diaries*, 280–81). The
second fact is that the air force averaged 100 tons a day. In fact,
during several periods it came close to delivering the 300 tons
that was supposedly required (see the graph in Bekker, 291). But
the Germans kept losing the airfields that were vital to the supply effort, Tazinskaya being the most critical (lost on December
24, 1942). Nor is it completely clear that the supplies dropped
were so woefully insufficient. The problem is that there is no real
agreement on the numbers of men to be supplied. The most extensive analysis of the documentary evidence is Manfred Kehrig,
Stalingrad: Analyse und Dokumentation einer Schlacht (Stuttgart:
Deutsche Verlags-Anstalt, 1974), pages 671–72. We know that
at encirclement the army numbered 249,000 men, and that by
January 13 the number had supposedly dropped to 221,191,
but the latter figure hardly seems credible, since 10,225 wounds
cases had been evacuated by December 18 and another 14,272
were evacuated afterward. There were no soldiers killed in com-

bat? There is also a discrepancy between the Soviet figures for prisoners (90,000), and the supposed army strength at the time of capitulation (201,191), and in this case the Soviet figures are consistent with the official German data for the killed and missing. It is doubtful whether this puzzle will ever be completely solved, but one logical inference is that a steadily shrinking force required far less in the way of supplies than everyone assumed; the case that Paulus was unable to continue is not quite so strong as is usually made out.

16. Quote from *Lost Victories*, 360. Von Manstein seems to resist coming to general conclusions in this rather extensive section of the memoir. Finally, however, one comes away with the feeling that Hitler was correct and that while Paulus made a whole series of unfortunate decisions, the situation for Army Groups A and B was such that there was no way that the 6th Army could be rescued.

17. Orwell's idea was that the past could be almost completely reshaped; as it turned out, however, the Soviet attempts were riddled with holes. But because they were frequently passed over in silence, the new effect was virtually the same. See the discussions and photographic evidence in David King, *The Commissar Vanishes: The Falsification of Photographs and Art in Stalin's Russia* (New York: Metropolitan, 1997).

18. Information taken from the semiofficial account of Dragos Pusca and Victor Nitu, "The Battle of Stalingrad—1942," at www .worldwar2.ro/operatii/?article=11.

19. Hungarian data from Franz von Adonyi-Naredy, *Ungarns Armee im Zweiten Weltkrieg: Deutschlands letzter Verbundeter* (Neckargemund: Klaus Vowinckel, 1971), 107. The figure of 147,971 casualties for the Hungarian 2nd Army, cited (among others) by Pusca, "Stalingrad," refers to losses suffered for the entire war; see the figures in *Ungarns Armee*, 200.

20. Divisional summaries taken from Peter McCarthy and Mike Syron, *Panzerkrieg: The Rise and Fall of Hitler's Tank Divisions* (New York: Carroll & Graf, 2002), 285–91. Tiger I data from Restayn (*Tiger I on the Eastern Front*, 14).

21. Production figures for the Mark 4 tank taken from the extensive tables in Thomas L. Jentz, *Panzertruppen: The Complete Guide to the Creation and Combat Employment of Germany's Tank Force* (Atglen, Pennsylvania: Schiffer, 1996).

22. Quote from Earl F. Ziemke, *Stalingrad to Berlin: The German Defeat in the East* (Washington, D.C.: Military History Office: 1968), 79. A fact that does not apparently deter him from dutifully repeating all the Soviet claims about German losses.

23. Such computations are hardly speculative. (1) As we have already seen, German records for the number of Soviet prisoners of war at the end of 1941 exceeded the official Soviet totals for the killed, the missing, and the wounded for the same period. (2) The official figures for the dead and the missing for the entire war (10,008,434), minus the number of recorded Soviet prisoners in German hands (5,165,381), gives a total for the war dead of 4,843,053, a number wildly inconsistent with other Soviet official data, e.g., the one in which the death toll is listed as 6,829,437. (3) In Uranus, the one example where extensive research was done, Glantz tactfully observes that the current Russian "loss figures are about 120,000 fewer than mine and 260,000 fewer than those estimated in German records" (*Defeat*, Appendix E, page 379, and note the resort to the e word). From this it would appear that official Soviet casualty figures are somewhere between 40 and 68 percent of actual losses. (4) The case cited in 3 appears rather conservative when we compare the official yearly totals with the latest estimate: the official figures for each year come to 41 percent, 30 percent, 21 percent, and 18 percent of 1941 through 1944, for an average of 27 percent. So the estimate given in the text falls well within the range.

24. The directive reprinted from Glantz (*Zhukov's Greatest Defeat*, 296), who cites numerous other signs of declining morale and indiscipline on the pages that follow.

25. Data in this paragraph taken from Mark Harrison, *The Economics of World War II: Six Great Powers in International Comparison* (Cambridge: Cambridge University Press, 1998), 14.

26. The transcript of the speech reveals "Movement in the hall" at this understandably shocking revelation. Khrushchev later amplified the remark, saying the Russians had more rifles in 1914 than in 1941. See the comment in *Khrushchev Speaks*, edited by Thomas P. Whitney (Ann Arbor: University of Michigan Press, 1963), 235.

27. From the account of Nikolai Ivanovich Obryn'ba, *Red Partisan*, translated by Vladimir Krupnik (Washington, D.C.: Potomac, 2007), 9. This quotation is taken slightly out of con-

text: Obryn'ba adds in the next sentence that they were later issued rifles and ammunition (but he does not say exactly when).
But giving troops their weapons as they march to the front is a
devastating commentary of its own.

28. Geoffrey Brooks, *Sniper on the Eastern Front: The Memoirs of
Sepp Allerberger* (Barnsley, South Yorkshire: Knight's Pen &
Sword, 2006), 27. Exactly the same situation is illustrated graph-
ically in the opening sequences of Jean-Jacques Annaud's film
Enemy at the Gates (2001). An even better illustration of the
scarcity of basic weaponry is to be seen in Elem Klimov's *Come
and See* (1985), which opens with a teenaged Belorussian digging
in the debris of some battle long past trying to find a weapon: he
can join the partisans only if he brings a weapon with him, and
indeed the first question that the two disguised partisans who
come to his house ask him speaks to that point. The insights of
artists, however impressionistic and anecdotal, provide far more
striking insights into the realities of the Red Army than the
carefully screened and censored writings the Soviet public was
besieged with in the decades after the war. It is no surprise that
Klimov's film was held up by the censors, despite its highly propagandistic view of the Germans. Like *Life and Fate*, it revealed a
dark side of the war that had to be kept secret.

29. Stalin, *Great Patriotic War*, 85.

30. Von Manstein, *Lost Victories*, 435–36.

CHAPTER IX: SUMMER 1943: THE TURNING POINT

1. Carl von Clausewitz, "On Battle," Part 1, Chapter 9 of *On War*,
translated by J. J. Graham.

2. Data from Hubert P. van Tuyll, *Feeding the Bear* (Westport,
Conn.: Greenwood Press, 1989), Tables 19–20, page 166.

3. The totals as recorded by van Tuyll, *Feeding the Bear*, Table 30,
page 171.

4. Glantz argues that "left to their own devices, Stalin and his commanders might have taken 12 to 18 months longer to finish off
the Wehrmacht; the ultimate result would probably have been
the same." A dubious bit of speculation for which no proof is offered other than hindsight: since Stalin won it was therefore obvious that he would win. Technically, such conclusions are more

an example of innumeracy than anything else: when a nation of 170 million goes to war with a nation of 80 million, there is no way it can fight on indefinitely if the casualty exchange ratio exceeds 2:1. David Glantz, *When Titans Clashed* (Lawrence: University Press of Kansas, 1993), 285.

5. Erich von Manstein, *Lost Victories*, edited and translated by Anthony G. Powell (London: Methuen, 1958), 445–46.

6. Von Manstein, *Lost Victories*, 447–48.

7. The orders and directives are reprinted in David M. Glantz and Jonathan House, *The Battle of Kursk* (Lawrence: University Press of Kansas, 1999), Appendix E; the phrase quoted: page 23. Possibly by coincidence, but the cherry picking is revealing: none of the analysts who accept von Manstein's contention about the delay are willing to agree with his conclusion that victory was within the grasp of the Germans when Hitler called off the offensive. There is an extensive and detailed discussion of the second-guessing on the part of the surviving German generals in Glantz and House (*Battle of Kursk*, 255–61). Glantz and House are the only historians to point out the context of those claims. Writing after the fact, the generals sought to blame Hitler and assumed that the defeat was inevitable (260); on the contrary, "There is absolutely no basis for assuming that Citadel would have succeeded had it been launched in spring 1943" (261). True enough (Glantz and House lay out the evidence in the pages that follow). However, given von Manstein's combat record, he was certainly entitled to such an assumption, which is hardly an example of wishful thinking.

8. German data from Matthew Cooper, *The German Army* (New York: Stein & Day, 1978), 211; the Soviet figure is from the official Soviet history. Institute für Marxismus-Leninismus beim ZentralkoCenter der Kommunistischen Partei der Sowjetunion, *Geschichte des Grossen Vaterländischen Krieges der Sowjetunion* (Berlin: Deutscher Militärverlag, 1962), 1:486.

9. Glantz and House (*Battle of Kursk*, 18) are the only analysts to recognize that the new gun on the Mark 3 tank gave it the capability to destroy a T-34 if the range was close enough, a striking contrast with the first period of the war, in which its shells, like those of the standard German antitank gun, bounced off the armor of the opposing tanks. In this regard Guderian is disingenuous: German gunners had already experienced this problem

in May 1940 against the heavily armored French tanks, and any evaluation of what is usually called Hitler's amateurishness must be seen in the context of the failures of the Germans in these two areas. For a discussion of Guderian and the tank issue, see Mosier, *Cross of Iron* (New York: Holt, 2006), 90–107. For a sample of how Hitler is regarded, see Glantz and House (*Battle of Kursk*, 17).

10. Data extracted from F. M. von Senger und Etterlin, *German Tanks of World War II*, translated by J. Lucas, edited by Peter Chamberlain and Chris Ellis (New York: Galahad, 1967), 39–40, 193.

11. These were built on the Mark 3 tank chassis or the Czech 38(t) chassis, and known collectively as Marders. Tank destroyers based on the Mark 2 chassis were known as Marder 1s (Senger, *Tanks*, 27). Vehicles based on the Czech design were known as Marder 3s; production was phased out in favor of the radically new and vastly superior armored tank destroyer, the Hetzer, which went into quantity production in 1944 (Senger, *German Tanks of World War II*, 30–31).

12. For example, although Guderian's ex post facto criticism of the heavy tank destroyer based on the Tiger 1 chassis is often cited, it is without acknowledging either his prewar failure to develop tanks that were competitive with those of France and Russia, and his implacable opposition to the stopgap measures of turretless vehicles that his failures forced on the Wehrmacht. Nor, as we shall see, is his analysis supported by the combat records of these vehicles. Unfortunately, Guderian's postwar reputation was such that his unfounded remarks are taken as holy writ. See, for example, the following sentence, virtually a paraphrase of Guderian, characterizing the new tank destroyers: "the Ferdinands proved to be a terrible disappointment. Not only were they mechanically unreliable, but they had no machine guns, so they could not deal with Soviet infantrymen." Given that over the course of fighting, the 653rd Heavy Antitank Unit, equipped with Ferdinands, destroyed 320 Soviet tanks, the equivalent of two entire armored divisions, this analysis is ludicrous. But it is made by one of the best military historians. Quote from Samuel Mitcham, *Hitler's Field Marshals* (New York: Cooper Square Press, 1990), 318. Unit record in Karlheinz Munch, *The Combat*

History of German Heavy Anti-Tank Unit 653 in World War II (Mechanicsburg, Pennsylvania: Stackpole, 2005), 52.

13. By 1943 the Grossdeutschland was so big that its commander wanted it broken up into two divisions. See the discussion in Hans-Joachim Jung, *Panzer Soldiers for "God, Honor and Fatherland": The History of Panzerregiment Grossdeutschland* (Winnipeg: J. J. Fedorowicz, 2000), 23.

14. Retrospectively, the surviving Soviet commanders tried to obfuscate the issue, and were greatly aided by the Byzantine designations of "fronts." Glantz and House quote one such analysis with apparent approval: "No one had any doubts that the Central and Voronezh Fronts would play the main role in the defensive action" (*Battle of Kursk*, 30). Indeed not, but the problem was that despite all the claims made both from the start of the battle and for decades afterward, Stalin and Zhukov had guessed wrong.

15. Samuel Mitcham begins his brief account of Walter Model with a flat assertion: "A whole book should be written about his campaigns. He was the most effective of the Nazi generals" (*Hitler's Field Marshals*, 313).

16. General Gotthard Heinrici, one of the most thoughtful and perceptive of the senior generals, noted that "the infantry forces available to the army groups were too weak. . . . Above all, infantry divisions, especially in the Army Group South area of operations, were lacking to screen the flanks of the attack groups, therefore, this mission had to be taken over by panzer divisions, which were then missing from the attack in the main direction." The British and the Americans were having the same difficulty, not nearly enough infantry, in France in June 1944. Moreover, despite Heinrici's observation, it was precisely this offensive thrust that succeeded. Quote, together with much more from Heinrici, in Glantz and House (*Battle of Kursk*, 271–72).

17. "Indeed in both a defensive and offensive sense the battles of July and August 1943 were the first modern Soviet operations of the war." Glantz and House (*Battle of Kursk*, 269). Yes, but the comment is something of a red herring given the losses sustained in both.

18. This data taken from the official Soviet account cited and abstracted by Glantz and House (*Battle of Kursk*, 274–75).

The German data he cites is consistent with the broader picture: losses on all fronts for the entire month of July came to 58,700 men.

19. Although Glantz and House give an excellent summary of all these losses and are among the few historians to offer realistic estimates of the German casualties, their conclusion hardly follows: "Although the three phases of Kursk strategic operations proved costly to both sides, the Soviets could afford the losses and the Germans could not" (*Battle of Kursk*, 277). But as long as Hitler was determined to defend the entire perimeter of his empire, determined to contest every potential invasion, he couldn't afford any losses at all.

20. Thus Mitcham: "Kursk was thus largely Model's battle, and he must be given the lion's share of the responsibility for losing it" (*Hitler's Field Marshals*, 317). Like many remarks made about operations in this war, this one is misleading. The whole point of a pincer operation is to have two jaws closing in simultaneously. Moreover, von Manstein was the commander deploying the powerful armored formations, so the clear expectation was that Kursk was his battle, since he had been given more resources. And Model was only the 9th Army commander: at the key moment, von Kluge made the most crucial decision.

21. Data from Jung, *Panzer Soldiers*, 126–30. Tiger I unit records summarized in Jean Restayn, *Tiger I on the Eastern Front* (Paris: Histoire & Collections, 2001), 58, 104, 116, 160. See the confirmation of their accuracy by Glantz and House (*Battle of Kursk*, 18).

22. As recorded by Munch, *The Combat History of German Heavy Anti-Tank Unit 653*, 52–53.

23. It would appear that American vehicles were in widespread use during Kursk. The report cited in the text was for action on the northern side of the salient. Most of the heavy armor was deployed to the south, and we have a photograph of Tiger tanks on that flank advancing past the destroyed hulk of an American-built vehicle (Restayn, *Tiger I on the Eastern Front*, 42).

24. Details on the development of the dive-bomber from R. S. Hirsch, "The Junkers JU-87 Stuka," in Heinz Nowarra and Edward T, Maloney, *Junkers JU-87* (Fallbrook, California: Aero, 1966), 1. There is an account of Rudel's successes and the Kursk aerial offensive in Cajus Bekker, *The Luftwaffe War-*

time Diaries, translated and edited by Frank Ziegler (New York: Doubleday, 1968), 298–99.

25. These records are reprinted in Jung, *Panzer Soldiers*, 128.

26. Related by von Manstein (*Lost Victories*, 448).

27. In other words, von Kluge had already made the decision to leave von Manstein in the lurch, which makes Hitler's decision more explicable. That he was probably wrong does not mean that his decision was senseless or his judgment lacking. See the summaries in Mitcham (*Hitler's Field Marshals*, 295, 319). A great deal of what has been written about Kursk is not simply based on the tank myth (see note 21 above), but rather should be seen as a series of tortuous arguments designed to trump the basic facts of the case as presented by von Manstein.

28. See the account of the argument in F. W. von Mellenthin, *German Generals of World War II as I Saw Them* (Norman: University of Oklahoma Press, 1977), 149; also Mitcham (*Hitler's Field Marshals*, 315–16). One of the many strengths of Mitcham's narrative is that he emphasizes the open disagreements and arguments that took place between Hitler and one or more of his generals. Of course this is in striking contrast to the situation in Moscow (an interesting point in and of itself), but it also speaks to a much more significant point. When it came to a military matter they cared about, many of Hitler's commanders would argue their point vigorously. But one searches the record in vain to find similar arguments being made about acts that they knew very well were immoral and criminal.

29. As quoted by Alexander Werth, *Russia at War, 1941–45* (New York: Dutton, 1964), 683. Werth's attempt at analysis of these communiqués strikes to the heart of one of the great difficulties in interpretation of Soviet claims: "No doubt some of the figures were exaggerated, but even if the Germans lost 2,000 not 3,000 tanks . . . it was good enough" (684). And since the Russians refused to release any real figures for their losses, the only conclusion (which Werth draws in the next sentence) is that they must have been about equal.

30. Martin Caidin's *The Tigers Are Burning* (New York: Hawthorne, 1974) is thus perhaps the best example of a distressingly common intellectual pattern that emerges when one studies literature about any aspect of the Soviet Union: it hews entirely to the Soviet propaganda line, accepting every Soviet

claim (such as the one about the destruction of the armored force).

31. Restayn (*Tiger I on the Eastern Front*, 62).
32. See Map 65 in Institute für Marxismus-Leninismus beim Zentralkomitte der Kommunistischen Partei der Sowjetunion, *Geschichte des Grossen Vaterländischen Krieges der Sowjetunion* (Berlin: Deutscher Militärverlag, 1962). For Khrushchev's appreciation of the situation, see George M. Nipe, *Decision in the Ukraine, Summer 1943: II. SS and III. Panzerkorps* (Winnipeg: J. J. Fedorowicz, 1996), 256. And also: "In order to grasp the significance of the situation . . . one has to understand that accepted accounts of the number of tanks lost by the Germans, in particular the SS divisions, are a myth" (256).

CHAPTER X: DEADLOCK: THE GREAT RETREAT

1. Bilíbin speaking in Leo Tolstoy, *War and Peace*, translated by Constance Garnett (New York: Barnes & Noble, 2005), Book 2, Chapter 9 (174).
2. Albert Speer, *Inside the Third Reich*, translated by Richard and Clara Winston (New York: Macmillan, 1970), 246.
3. Tiger 1 data from Jean Restayn, *Tiger I on the Eastern Front* (Paris: Histoire & Collections, 2001), 3.
4. When von Kluge assumed command in France, he promptly got in a fight with Rommel. Like most of the senior German and Italian commanders, von Kluge did not share the high opinion of Rommel that was widespread among the British. Von Kluge embodied all the character defects generally attributed to Hitler's generals: he was in most respects the archetype. Enthusiastic about Barbarossa, he then changed his tune when victory remained elusive, and his high opinion of himself does not seem justified, although in fairness it is difficult to see how anyone else could have done much better. Depending on one's view regarding suicide (he killed himself on August 19, 1944), he either redeemed himself by taking the honorable way out, or remained sly and passive-aggressive to the end. The suicide note is reprinted in Samuel Mitcham, *Hitler's Field Marshals* (New York: Cooper Square Press, 1990), 312.
5. See his account of this in Erich von Manstein, *Lost Victories*, ed-

ited and translated by Anthony G. Powell (London: Methuen, 1958), 481–83; data taken from 483, confirmed by Mitcham (*Hitler's Field Marshals*, 251).

6. Joseph Stalin, *The Great Patriotic War of the Soviet Union* (New York: International Publishers, 1945), 90–91.

7. Although historians concentrate almost exclusively on documentary evidence, that evidence is almost entirely verbal, as opposed to quantitative or visual. The images reproduced in the compilations of unit records are an important body of evidence that is consequently ignored; all the more important because it is a contemporaneous record. The photographs of German armor being transported by rail right up until the end of the war to a great extent undercuts the more extravagant claims of both Soviet and partisan accounts and the arguments of the strategic bombing enthusiasts. The photographs of the soldiers themselves do the same for the dominant meme of the end of the war. See, among the many, the images reproduced in Jean Restayn, *Tiger I on the Eastern Front* (Paris: Histoire & Collections, 2001), particularly those on pages 22, 42, 74, 80, 120, and 132; Rene Spezzano, *God, Honor, Fatherland* (Southbury, Connecticut: RZM, 1997), 158–59, 186, 214.

8. Brigadier General Harbord, 2nd Infantry Division; as quoted by Robert B. Asprey, *At Belleau Wood* (New York: Putnam's, 1965), 228.

9. Gerhard Weinberg, from the Introduction, *Hitler and His Generals: Military Conferences, 1942–1945*, translated by Helmut Heiber (New York: Enigma, 2003), vi. This brief essay is a useful antidote to the uncritical acceptance of all of the generals' claims. The German documents were not published until 1962.

10. Soviet historians "assert Stalin's strategy involved concentrating the bulk of the Red Army's strength along the northwestern and southwestern strategic axis so that the army's operating fronts could achieve the missions the *Stavka* (High Command) assigned to them, while the *Stavka* economised on the expenditure of vital Soviet manpower and material resources. In reality, however, during winter and spring of 1944, Stalin pursued the same 'broad front' strategy he had employed since the beginning of the war." In other words, he had learned nothing, continued to squander the lives of millions of soldiers on operations that had never been successful. See, together with a summary of the inter-

pretations cited, David M. Glantz, *Red Storm over the Balkans: The Failed Soviet Invasion of Romania, Spring 1944* (Lawrence: University Press of Kansas, 2007), xii–xiii.

11. "Special Report to the Twentieth Congress of the Communist Party of the Soviet Union," February 24–25, 1956.

12. In *The Economics of World War II: Six Great Powers in International Comparison* (Cambridge: Cambridge University Press, 1998), Mark Harrison uses a reference base of 168.7 million people for the USSR and 84.9 million for Germany-Austria-Czechoslovakia (Table 1.1, page 3; Table 1.2, page 7). As we shall see, the Soviet census data is highly suspect. Moreover, in manpower computations, the population of Elsass-Lothringen (the portions of Alsace-Lorraine incorporated into the Reich after June 1940) must be included, as the males of this area were regarded as German nationals, roughly three million people. However, Harrison's figures are as close to the truth as we are likely to get. Assume a distribution of the age groups approximating that of a developing country, one where the distribution of the age groups in five-year intervals actually forms a pyramid. That population distribution would mean that about 30 percent of the citizenry consisted of males between the ages of fifteen and sixty-four, the ages that became the upper and lower limits for the Red Army manpower pool. That would give a potential army of 50 million men. Each year a new cohort of fourteen-year-olds would become eligible, roughly one million souls. The number of men reaching sixty-five would be a fraction of that, no more than 200,000, so over the period of the war, the pool would be increased by roughly 3.2 million men: the total pool of eligibles would eventually approximate 53 million. By the same token, the German pool of eligibles would be approximately 25 million men (assuming that Hitler declined to recruit the youngest members of the cohort), an advantage of slightly over 2:1 for the Soviets. But given the annual rate of loss, in each successive year the ratio would become less and less favorable. At the end of 1942, for example, the Soviet pool was 35 million men, while the German pool was at worst down to 24 million, so the ratio has now changed to 1.45:1. At the end of 1943, the Soviet pool was 25 million, as opposed to the German pool of roughly 23 million. At some point in 1944, the total manpower available to Hitler would actually have been greater than what was

available to Stalin. Population data from Harrison (*Economics of World War II*, Table 1.1, page 3; Table 1.2, page 7). Soviet Loss figures for 1941–1942 taken from Keith E. Bonn, editor, *Slaughterhouse: The Handbook of the Eastern Front* (Bedford, Pennsylvania: Aberjona, 2004), 10.

13. The widespread use of women in the Red Army is no secret: there are many posters and photographs of female soldiers in battle dress and in simulated combat situations; see for example http://223rdrifles.com/redwomen.htm. A good example of how, under scrutiny, the Soviet penchant for propagandizing achievements becomes quite revealing: the army had to make use of women because they were running out of men; given the gender chauvinism of Soviet society postwar, it is hardly likely that the reliance on women was done out of some sense of gender equality. Scholarly works dealing with this topic are almost nonexistent. See the opening sentence of Mary Louise O'Brien and Chris Jefferies, "Women and the Soviet Military," *Air University Review* (January–February 1982): "Examination of Soviet military manpower utilization leads to the conclusion that there is little information available about the role, status, and employment of women in the Soviet armed forces." The article deals with contemporary practices, but has an excellent historical survey of what little is known; available at www.airpower.maxwell.af.mil/airchronicles/aureview/1982/jan-feb/obrien.html.

14. The newsreel footage of an enfeebled Hitler patting the cheeks of a uniformed schoolboy is notorious. It is also misleading: the footage was taken at the very end of the war, for propaganda purposes (strange as that may seem). In striking contrast, in the literally thousands of mostly candid photographs of army and SS troops either in combat or immediately behind the front lines, examined in the course of researching this book, the absence of extremely young (or elderly) soldiers is notable.

15. In his Introduction, Weinberg makes a similar point (*Hitler and His Generals*, 12).

16. Spezzano, *God, Honor, Fatherland*, 29.

17. Data computed from Hubert P. van Tuyll, *Feeding the Bear* (Westport, Conn.: Greenwood, 1989), Table 20, page 166.

18. The official figures: 4,666 tanks, and 1,109,528 casualties out of a force of 2.4 million men. Data from David Glantz, *When Titans Clashed* (Lawrence: University Press of Kansas, 1993), 298.

19. Data from Restayn (*Tiger I on the Eastern Front*, 55). These few German tanks thus wiped out the equivalent of an entire Soviet armored corps in a few days' fighting. Hard data such as this balances the subjective portraits from the German side, as well as the endlessly trumpeted triumphs of the Red Army. By January 1944, Soviet tank commanders should have been able to do much better than this, particularly given the supposed superiority of the new JS heavy tanks. One of the many interesting revelations of the photographic evidence is the extent to which the Wehrmacht continued both its training and its routine maintenance operations through 1944. See, for example, the photographs in Restayn (*Tiger I on the Eastern Front*, pages 56, 57, 72, 102); surprising as well as revealing, given the usual description of the desperate state of the Wehrmacht in the last years of the war.

20. Summary of Soviet claims in Douglas Nash, *Hell's Gate: The Battle of the Cherkassy Pocket, January to February 1944* (Southbury, Connecticut: RZM, 2002), 374.

21. The Germans evacuated 255,970 men and 21,230 motor vehicles, and 72,809 horses across the Kerch Strait to Crimea. See the details in Mitcham (*Hitler's Field Marshals*, 101).

22. As Hitler met with each of the two marshals privately, von Manstein does not mention this interchange, but reprints his diary entry (*Lost Victories*, 545–46). Information on von Kleist's interview taken from Mitcham (*Hitler's Field Marshals*, 103); nor should Hitler's views come as a surprise. Even after the unraveling of June 1944 he was still of the opinion that he could win the war: see the comments in Weinberg (*Hitler and His Generals*, viii).

23. The basic account can be found in Mitcham (*Hitler's Field Marshals*, 344–45); predictably, Hitler is blamed for this minor disaster, with Mitcham claiming that only 30,000 men were evacuated because Hitler gave the order too late. The more detailed account by Victor Nitu raises that figure considerably, over 110,000 men, and details the difficulties of the evacuation. See Victor Nitu, "Operation 60,000," www.worldwar2.ro/operatii/?article=776.

24. From Simon Sebag Montefiore, *Stalin: The Court of the Red Tsar* (New York: Random House, 2005), 259.

25. See the succinct but absolutely to-the-point discussion in Weinberg (*Hitler and His Generals*, vii).

CHAPTER XI: DEATH OF THE PHOENIX:
THE LAST ELEVEN MONTHS OF THE WAR

1. Fayolle, *Carnets secrets de la grande guerre*, edited by Henry Contamine (Paris: Plon, 1964), 271.
2. Initially there had been seven German divisions still there after Operation 25 (the invasion of Yugoslavia) in spring 1941. By 1943 there were fifteen divisions in the Balkans, and by 1944 there were no fewer than twenty-five German divisions stationed there, a not inconsiderable force, and the main reason the commanders in the east were increasingly short of infantry. Information taken from Matthew Cooper, *The German Army* (New York: Stein & Day, 1978), 282.
3. "He was surprised at the naivete of the Americans": Simon Sebag Montefiore, account of Tehran in *Stalin: The Court of the Red Tsar* (New York: Random House, 2005), 463. For the discussion of Poland, see 471; for Overlord, 467.
4. "Here, look at you, blind men, kittens, you don't see the enemy; what will you do without me, the country will perish," is how Stalin addressed his henchmen in 1952. As quoted by Jonathan Brent, *Inside Stalin's Archives* (New York: Atlas, 2008), 71.
5. It was not until some Moscow archives were opened up in the early 1990s that the extent to which the various national parties were controlled by Moscow was understood. For decades this was stoutly denied, especially in the United States. When Yale University Press representative Jonathan Brent went to Moscow in 1992 to begin negotiations regarding the Soviet archives, a document demonstrating just how tightly controlled the various parties were was the first thing the archivist showed him (*Inside Stalin's Archives*, 89). See also his succinct summary of the revelations about the American Communist Party (90–91), which is, as he explains, a brief description of the resulting book: Harvey Klerh and John Earl Haynes, *The Secret World of American Communism* (New Haven: Yale University Press, 1995).
6. As was the case with the Rzhev disaster, the whole matter was hushed up until David Glantz published *Red Storm Over the Balkans: The Failed Soviet Invasion of Romania, Spring 1944* (Lawrence: University Press of Kansas, 2007). Force sizes computed on page 379.
7. Taken from a longer report quoted in Glantz (*Red Storm Over*

the Balkans, 377). In Glantz's words, "Hence, although their forces were numerically superior to the Germans when the two fronts attacked during April and May, their soldiers were not skilled enough to contend with the Wehrmacht's better trained veterans" (376). Such inexperience and ineptitude in an army that had been at war for nearly three years suggests that claims both about the Soviet juggernaut and the Red Army's learning curve are wishful thinking.

8. See the perceptive analysis in Samuel Mitcham, *Hitler's Field Marshals* (New York: Cooper Square Press, 1990), 274.

9. Busch is roundly criticized for letting this happen (see the summary in Mitcham, *Hitler's Field Marshals,* 275) but this seems unfair. At the time it was certainly logical to expect either an offensive into Ukraine, or more of the same battering all along the front. In either case shifting resources, and jurisdictions, to Ukraine made sense.

10. Steven Zaloga, *Bagration, 1944: The Destruction of Army Group Center* (Danbury, Connecticut: Grolier International, 1997). A more comprehensive account is Rolf Hinze, *To the Bitter End: The Final Battles of Army Groups North Ukraine, A, Centre, Eastern Front, 1944–45,* translated by Frederick Steinhardt (Solihull: Helion, 2006).

11. The extent to which this timetable was believed is often ignored in retrospect, given the embarrassments of fall–winter 1944–1945 in the west. See Ronald Andidora, *Home by Christmas: The Illusion of Victory in 1944* (Westport, Connecticut: Greenwood, 2002).

12. The whole account is in Erich von Manstein, *Lost Victories,* edited and translated by Anthony G. Powell (London: Methuen, 1958), 504–6, who of course spins it to make it seem as though he was right and Hitler was simply being . . . Hitler.

13. The contrast between the unit records of this powerful formation and the account of it given in Guy Sajer's *The Forgotten Soldier* is an excellent example of the difference between the highly subjective retelling of combat and the more distant, objective accounts of the analyst or historian. This is not to say that Sajer's account, written in the form of a novel, is in some way inferior or misleading. Rather it comes out of a French tradition of the best combat narratives, and attempts, with a great deal of suc-

cess, to recapture the emotions, the totality of the experience, as opposed to the history of the unit and its battles. However, the photographic record makes pretty clear that the Grossdeutschland was a potent and effective combat unit with all the latest German equipment, right up through its last offensive at Vikovishken in Lithuania. For an account of the last days of this division, see Hans-Joachim Jung, *Panzer Soldiers for "God, Honor and Fatherland": The History of Panzerregiment Grossdeutschland* (Winnipeg: J. J. Fedorowicz, 2000), 237–82.

14. See the account in Hinze (*To the Bitter End*, 178–85), which is a useful corrective to those accounts that emphasize the desperation and dissolution of the Wehrmacht in those final weeks.

15. Data from Tony Le Tissier, *Slaughter at Halbe: The Destruction of Hitler's 9th Army, April 1945* (Phoenix Mill: Sutton, 2005), 212; see esp. notes 8–9.

16. Using the figures given in Keith E. Bonn, editor, *Slaughterhouse: The Handbook of the Eastern Front* (Bedford, Pennsylvania: Aberjona, 2004), 6. If one makes the not unreasonable supposition that the official Soviet data can be reconciled more or less with the higher figures used by everyone else by treating the official data for all casualties (including wounds cases) as the total of the dead and missing, then the same trend is visible. See the table of the official losses in David Glantz, *When Titans Clashed* (Lawrence: University Press of Kansas, 1993), 292.

CHAPTER XII: THE WAR OF EXTERMINATION: ALLIES, PARTISANS, CRIMINALS

1. Friedrich Dürrenmatt, *Der Richter und Sein Henker* (Zurich: Benziger, 1952), 97.

2. In *The War Against the Jews, 1933–1945* (New York: Bantam, 1975), Lucy S. Dawidowicz estimates a prewar population of 6,403,000 out of a total European population of 8,861,800, with a death toll of 4,480,000 out of a total death toll of 5,933,900 (403). These figures, including those for Poland, are somewhat higher than those given by Raul Hilberg in *The Destruction of the European Jews*, revised edition (New York: Holmes & Meier, 1985), 3.1220. There is an excellent discussion in Hilberg of the

history of such calculations (3: Appendix A, pages 1201–28). It is important to note that these estimates are mostly based on inductions from census data.

3. Joseph Stalin, *The Great Patriotic War of the Soviet Union* (New York: International Publishers, 1945), 19.

4. See the analysis of the "friendship among the Soviet peoples," as one author terms it, in Lucjan Dobroszycki and Jeffrey S. Gurock, editors, *The Holocaust in the Soviet Union* (Armonk, New York: M. E. Sharpe, 1993), 14–16.

5. The entire document is printed in Matthew Cooper, *The Nazi War Against Soviet Partisans, 1941–1944* (New York: Stein & Day, 1979), Appendix 2, page 167. Cooper also has an illuminating discussion of the internal debates and criticisms on the German side regarding the treatment of the natives (23–29). Although the fact of the debate is incontrovertible, and should be recorded, it to a certain extent leaves a misleading impression: the Germans were able to debate these issues all the way up and down the line without fear of penalty, and thus did so. No one in the Soviet leadership had that luxury. Although at the policy level that hardly matters, the effect is to emphasize German crimes and minimize Soviet ones.

6. The extent of regular army involvement in clearly defined war crimes is detailed in John Mosier, *Cross of Iron* (New York: Holt, 2006), 228–43. One key example is repeated in Richard Evans, *The Third Reich at War* (New York: Penguin, 2009), 27, who has a plethora of examples of German war crimes.

7. The only detailed analysis of these events is to be found in Franz Wilhelm Seidler, *Verbrechen an der Wehrmacht: Kriegsgreuel der Roten Armee 1941/42* (Selent: Pour le Merite, 1998), 29–32; quote from documents cited on 29.

8. Visvaldis Mangulis, *Latvia in the Wars of the 20th Century* (Princeton, New Jersey: Cognition, 1983), 139. See as well the references in Cooper, *The Nazi War Against Soviet Partisans*, 14. This fairly early study is a much more balanced account than those written afterward, which are handicapped by relying on highly dubious self-evaluations of the partisans themselves. See, among the many, Leonid Grenkevich, *The Soviet Partisan Movement, 1941–1944* (London: Frank Cass, 1999); John Armstrong, editor, *Soviet Partisans in World War II* (Madison: University of Wisconsin Press, 1964); Lester Samuel Eckman, *The Jewish*

Resistance: The History of the Jewish Partisans in Lithuania and White Russia During the Nazi Occupation, 1940–1945 (New York: Shengold, 1977).

9. Examples (taken almost at random) from the reports reprinted (as photocopies) in Fritz Baade, editor, *Unsere Ehre heisst Treue; Kriegstagebuch des Kommandostabes Reichsführer SS, Tätigkeitsberichte der 1. und 2. SS-Inf.-Brigade, der 1. SS-Kav.-Brigade und von Sonderkommandos der SS* (Vienna: Europa Verlag, 1965), 35, 37, 38.

10. Alexei Tolstoy, *Stalin's Secret War* (New York: Holt, Rinehart & Winston, 1981), 282. Tolstoy's estimate is that the Germans were responsible for about four million civilian deaths. "However one assesses the proportion, it is clear that the casualties directly attributable to the Germans account for only a third, or at most half, of Soviet overall losses in manpower in the years 1939–45.... Most Russians killed at that time died in the invasion of Finland and in the subsequent wars of the NKVD against the civil and military population of the USSR" (284). Aside from Soviet secrecy, the main difficulty in assessing the number of civilian deaths is definitions: Western analysts do not include Poland or Soviet-occupied Romania in their tallies (as in the sources cited above with reference to the Holocaust), while estimates coming from émigrés and exiles usually fail to specify exactly what categories they're including. The short answer: no one has any real idea how many civilians died during the war.

11. The order, Number 0428, was signed by Stalin and Shaposhnikov (as chief of staff). As quoted by Pavel Polian, *Against Their Will: The History and Geography of Forced Migrations in the USSR* (New York: Central European University Press, 2004), 124.

12. "Die Versorgung der Städte Russlands im noch unbesetzten Gebiet," Military Archives Freiburg/Germany, Bestand RW 31/11. Translated and reproduced by Walter Sanning, "Soviet Scorched-Earth Warfare: Facts and Consequences," *The Journal for Historical Review* 6, no. 1 (Spring 1986): 91–119; available at www.ihr.org/jhr/v06/v06p-91_Sanning.html.

13. The argument that Hitler made a "grave mistake by depriving himself of a mass of people . . . who would have supplied some of the many means necessary to achieve his ultimate end," like many of the superficially clever insights made about Hitler,

founders in the face of the observation that the elimination of European Jewry was hardly an incidental objective: it was a goal. The only feature of it to change was the means. Hitler was determined to eliminate the Jews, just as the Bolsheviks were determined to eliminate the Kulaks. This despite the theoretical impossibility of the task, not to mention the extent to which it damaged the state severely in both instances. Quote (and argument) from Ronald Lewin, *Hitler's Mistakes* (London: Secker & Warburg, 1984), 52.

14. Speech of May 1, 1943, reprinted in Stalin (*Great Patriotic War*, 89).

15. The only scholarly analysis of the fighting in the Baltic at the end of the war is Dominique Venner, *Baltikum* (Paris: Editions Robert Laffont, 1975), recently reissued as *Histoire d'un fascisme allemand* (Paris: Pygmalion, 1996). There is a brief summary of the key events, together with the more important documentary sources, in John Mosier, *Cross of Iron* (New York: Holt, 2006), 28–35.

16. The entire document is reprinted in Pipes (*Unknown Lenin*, 85–88; emphasis in the original). See the analysis by Pipes in his introduction: "Lenin made no pretense in this private communication that the projected creation of Soviet Lithuania would be of indigenous origin" (8).

17. See the discussion (together with the quotation) in Milovan Djilas, *Conversations with Stalin*, translated by Michael B. Petrovich (New York: Harcourt, Brace, 1983), 156–57.

18. Data from Mangulis (*Latvia in the Wars of the 20th Century*, 91). In the minds of many Balts, Jewish Bolsheviks played an important role in these deportations and murders; the extent to which this is the case is arguable, but it was certainly believed at the time, and provoked a murderous backlash. See the discussion in Dobroszycki and Gurock (*Holocaust in the Soviet Union*, 200–201).

19. See the account in Mangulis (*Latvia in the Wars of the 20th Century*, 96). A standard practice not limited to Riga: as Stalin considered abandoning Moscow, Beria's security personnel did the same thing. Acts such as these hopelessly confuse any accounting of the civilian death toll, but Alexei Tolstoy's estimate that between two thirds and three quarters of the civilians killed dur-

ing the war were the result of Stalin's policies and orders seems about right. See his analysis in *Stalin's Secret War*, 281–84.

20. Dawidowicz (*War Against the Jews*, 398). Favorable and indeed even enthusiastic Jewish reactions to the conquest of Poland by the Red Army, although usually unremarked, have been documented. See Dobroszycki and Gurock (*Holocaust in the Soviet Union*, 5, 157).

21. Data from Simon Sebag Montefiore, *Stalin: The Court of the Red Tsar* (New York: Random House, 2005), 394–95; Dmitri Volkogonov, *Autopsy for an Empire*, translated and edited by Harold Shukman (New York: Free Press, 1998), 118. In "Incident at Kretchetovka Station," Solzhenitsyn refers to these men as "stragglers," another euphemism. The reference is a fine example of how important aspects of Soviet life were totally missed by outsiders, and how Soviet bloc artists, forced to restrict themselves to oblique references, saw key aspects of their works misunderstood. At the same time, those foreigners who knew were reluctant to make direct public comments, knowing that their remarks would inevitably filter back and harm the person in question. The "stragglers" reference by Solzhenitsyn is in *We Never Make Mistakes*, translated by Paul Blackstock (New York: Norton, 1971), 25.

22. The data in this paragraph is taken from Paul Gregory and Valery Lazarev, editors, *The Economics of Forced Labor: The Soviet Gulag* (Stanford, California: Hoover Institution Press, 2003), Table 2.1, page 29. Over the course of the war, the figures show a decline, but there should be one owing to a declining labor pool, a shift in the gender of its composition, and the effects of incarceration and punishment: those workers not imprisoned outright suffered reduced pay and forced labor in addition to their regular work.

23. Mangulis (*Latvia in the Wars of the 20th Century*, 155). There were small isolated communities in the major cities that remained until the end of 1942; but it would seem that these were the exception rather than the rule. Moreover, the point here is that a great many people were not deported to fates unknown, but were beaten to death on the streets in plain sight.

24. After the September slaughter in Kiev, the ravine continued to be an execution site as well as prison camp. But relatively few of

the subsequent victims were Jews, simply because most of them had already been murdered. Figures for the Baltic from Mangulis (*Latvia in the Wars of the 20th Century*, 155). For details of the operations of the four Operation Reinhard camps, see Yitzhak Arad, *Belzec, Sobibor, Treblinka: The Operation Reinhard Death Camps* (Bloomington: Indiana University Press, 1987).

25. Timothy Garton Ash, *The File* (New York: Random House, 1997), 84. A rough measure of the comparative inefficiency of the two systems: as Ash observes, in its heyday in the German Democratic Republic, "The HVA [*Hauptverwaltung Aufklärung*, security services] had over 90,000 full time employees, of whom less than 5,000 were in the HVA foreign intelligence wing . . . one out of every fifty adult East Germans" (84).

26. Quote from the archival record in Baade (*Unsere Ehre heisst Treue*, 117). In the German, "Bolshevik" is simply an adjective, "Jews" the actual noun and object; however, the phrase is similar to one habitual with Hitler.

27. This particular massacre, estimated at nearly 30,000 people, was carried out by the Romanians entirely on their own. See Dobroszycki and Gurock (*Holocaust in the Soviet Union*, 137). But then the Romanians initiated their own Holocaust without much prompting from the Hitlerites, and have been extremely reluctant to deal with that aspect of their history. See the extensive work in Radu Ioanid, *The Holocaust in Romania* (Chicago: Ivan R. Dee, 2000).

28. Joseph Roth, *Radetzkymarsch* (Munich: Deutscher Taschenbuch Verlag, 1984), 284–85.

29. It is significant that Guy Sajer's *The Forgotten Soldier*, one of the most widely read as well as probably the best novel of the war, was written from the point of view of a young Alsatian. Anyone who takes the trouble to visit the cemeteries of the region will find ample corroboration of the Alsatian contributions to the Wehrmacht.

30. As quoted by Brigitte Hamann, *Hitler's Vienna*, translated by Thomas Thornton (New York: Oxford University Press, 1999), 322. It's significant that she devotes an entire chapter (9) to "Czechs in Vienna," right before 10: "Jews in Vienna."

31. See the discussions in Rigg (*Hitler's Jewish Soldiers*, 67–70). The implications are still largely unremarked, and in many cases sim-

ply denied. The first serious study of the phenomenon, related to France, was not published until 2004. The authors conclude that 100,000 French children were born of liaisons between French women and German military personnel. See Jean-Paul Picaper and Ludwig Norz, *Les enfants maudits: ils sont 100 000 on les appelait les «enfants de Boches»* (Paris: Editions des syrtes, 2004), 13.

32. Stalin, *Great Patriotic War*, 23–24.
33. See the discussion in Cooper (*Nazi War Against Soviet Partisans*, 29–30). Not coincidentally, the rather obscure figure of Ponomarenko is known (insofar as he is) for intensifying the Russification of Belorussia. Cooper identifies him as being close to Stalin, which may well be true, but his name is conspicuously absent from most biographies of the dictator.
34. See Zentralkommitee, *Vaterländischen Krieges*, Map 113.
35. Helmut Heiber and David Glantz, editors, *Hitler and His Generals: Military Conferences, 1942–1945*, translated by Roland Winter, Krista Smith, and Mary Beth Friedrich (New York: Enigma, 2003), 212.
36. Although the maps accompanying the official Soviet history of the war (notably Maps 27 and 62) depict massive amounts of partisan activity and enormous areas controlled by them, the text is surprisingly reticent about the actual achievements. See, for example, the brief comments in Zentralkommitee, *Vaterländischen Krieges*, 6.234.
37. See the map and claim (apparently made by his Russian editors) in Nikolai Ivanovich Obryn'ba, *Red Partisan*, translated by Vladimir Krupnik (Washington, D.C.: Potomac, 2007), x. Although this heavily forested area was certainly a haven for guerrillas, that was the only advantage it conferred, as the main rail lines were well outside the zone, as even the official maps admit.
38. Cooper (*Nazi War Against Soviet Partisans*, 162). Although this quote is not taken out of context, it may perhaps mislead as to Cooper's main point: the partisans accomplished very little in a military sense, but the Germans were never able to eliminate them completely. That assumes of course that extermination rather than containment was the goal, an arguable assumption given the length of the war.
39. Records in Baade (*Unsere Ehre heisst Treue*, 75, 79). In one six-

week period in 1941 this one unit killed or captured nearly 600 people identified as partisans, as distinct from Russian soldiers, Bolsheviks, and Jews.

40. Obryn'ba (*Red Partisan*, 130). Significantly, this incident occurs very late in his narrative.

41. Obryn'ba (*Red Partisan*, 147). In the event, when the woman tells him that she had sex with the man for a bucket of grain, he decides not to execute her. What is telling about this incident is the contradictions inside the narrative. He starts out by saying that the villagers were afraid, and then, three paragraphs later, he's saying "We'll just have to call in on our way back, to tell the villagers not to touch her" (149).

42. Estimates taken from Marc J. Rikmenspoel, *Waffen SS: The Encyclopedia* (Garden City, New York: Military Book Club, 2002), 182–93 (for non-Germanics) and 109–79 (for Germanics). My addition of his numbers of the latter category, volunteers from France, Scandinavia, Belgium, and the Netherlands, comes to 71,700 men; for volunteers from the Baltic states, Ukraine, Russia, and related areas, I get 245,200 men, or 3.42 as many troops. Both Rikmenspoel and I exclude ethnic Germans from these totals, as in general they served in regular army units.

43. Estimate from Samuel Mitcham, *Hitler's Field Marshals* (New York: Cooper Square Press, 1990), 100. The Vlasov Army, as it is usually known (formally, the *Russkaya Osvoboditel'naya Armiya*, or Russian Liberation Army), is somewhat of a red herring in discussions of the volunteers who joined Hitler's forces. Only four divisions were authorized, and these not until 1944. Historians never tire of pointing out that these men performed very poorly in combat, which is to say that they performed pretty much like their former comrades in the Red Army, this comparison of course never being mentioned. See the account in Joachim Hoffmann, *Die Geschichte der Wlassow-Armee* (Freiburg im Breisgau: Rombach, 1984).

44. Figures from Mangulis (*Latvia in the Wars of the 20th Century*, 118 and note). Most of the men who survived the war did not survive the aftermath, one reason their story remains largely untold and their part in the war obscured; e.g., the fate of the 35,000 Cossacks who fought with the Germans and were turned over to Stalin by the Allies after 1945, the 30,000 Georgians who formed the Georgian Legion. But from the Wehrmacht records

we do know that ninety-eight battalions were formed almost exclusively from the manpower available in the occupied territories. Not counted in these figures are the Slovenes and Croats who battled Tito's partisans in the Balkans. At the end of the war the victorious partisans are said to have murdered some 11,000 Slovenes and 90,000 Croats for their part in the struggle. Data from Hendrick Verton, *In the Fire of the Eastern Front: The Experiences of a Dutch Waffen-SS Volunteer on the Eastern Front, 1941–45* (Solihull: Helion, 2006), 385.

45. "On 1 January 1948 there were 2,199,535 prisoners in camps and colonies ... on 1 January 1950 there were 2,550,275 prisoners. ... These figures, I repeat, do not include the prison population." Dmitri Volkogonov, *Stalin: Triumph and Tragedy*, translated and edited by Harold Shukman (New York: Grove Weidenfeld, 1988), 307. These figures do not include the substantial number of political prisoners in the communist-dominated states of Poland, Hungary, Czechoslovakia, and East Germany.

46. So, for example, the pioneering efforts by Romanian historians, whose work has been cited earlier in this text, are substantially handicapped by a dependence on the official Soviet data, which as we have seen is highly misleading. Stalin's legend received a good deal of inadvertent support from the accounts of the German generals themselves, who with few exceptions regarded their allies with nothing but contempt, e.g., Rommel's attitude toward the Italian units who formed the bulk of his forces in North Africa, and whom he abandoned during his retreat.

47. This brigade should not be confused with the 15th and 19th SS Divisions formed from Latvian (and other) volunteers, or the nine border guard and police units formed. See the account in Rikmenspoel (*Encyclopedia*, 189), and Mangulis (*Latvia in the Wars of the 20th Century*, 96–98). As the photographs Mangulis reproduces make clear, these police units were military formations complete with armored cars.

48. Estimate derived from Trevor Dupuy, who computed that, on the average, 100 German soldiers were the equivalent of 120 American, British, or French soldiers, or 200 Soviet soldiers. The initial work is *A Genius for War: The German Army and the General Staff, 1807–1945* (Englewood Cliffs, New Jersey: Prentice Hall, 1977). Dupuy appended an updated summary of his

work on this subject in Trevor N. Dupuy, David L. Bongard, and Richard C. Anderson, Jr., *Hitler's Last Gamble* (New York: HarperCollins, 1994), Appendix H (498–501).

49. 5.762 million in 1940 and 7.309 million by 1941; see the table of comparative strengths (Table 1.5) in Mark Harrison, *The Economics of World War II: Six Great Powers in International Comparison* (Cambridge: Cambridge University Press, 1998), 14.

50. The exact numbers are not known. But a very good estimate can be obtained by counting up the number of nationals incarcerated after 1945 by their respective governments for their volunteer activities: 5,000 Dutch, 7,000 Norwegians, 7,717 Danes, 3,193 Belgians, 1,300 Swiss, and 2,400 French. Extrapolating from the number of known French volunteers who served in the *legion voluntaires française* brings the total to roughly 100,000 men. See the data on incarcerations in Verton, *Im Feuer der Ostfront* (Coburg: Nation Europa Verlag, 2003), 385. Data on the French from Robert Forbes, *For Europe: The French Volunteers of the Waffen-SS* (Solihull, U.K.: Helion, 2006). One of the most decorated soldiers in the SS was the Belgian politician Leon Degrelle. See his account: Leon Degrelle, *Campaign in Russia: The Waffen SS on the Eastern Front* (Torrance, California: Institute for Historical Review, 1985). The most comprehensive study of the combat record of a foreign division is Gerald Kleinfeld and Lewis A. Tambs, *Hitler's Spanish Legion: The Blue Division in Russia* (Carbondale: Southern Illinois University Press, 1979). In addition there were units of Russians fighting outside of the Eastern Front, the most important being the Russkiy Korpus, an oversize division formed by the former White general Mikhail Skorodumov that fought in Yugoslavia. Little scholarly attention has been paid to these surprisingly widespread phenomena; for the Russkiy Korpus, see http://en.wikipedia.org/wiki/Russian_Corps.

51. See the calculations in Alexei Tolstoy, *Stalin's Secret War*, 281–84. He calculates that over three fifths of the Soviet prisoners of war perished, and makes a convincing case that Stalin was responsible (261–62).

52. Djilas (*Conversations with Stalin*, 9).

53. Djilas (*Conversations with Stalin*, 187); the judgment was made before the enormity of Mao's depredation was known, whose human cost dwarfed those of both European dictators.

CHAPTER XIII: CONCLUSIONS:
FALSE VICTORIES, MISTAKEN BELIEFS

1. Martin Amis, *Koba the Dread: Laughter and the Twenty Million* (New York: Hyperion, 2002), 9. As the Polish philosopher Lezek Kolkowski observed: "There is no reliable criterion of truth apart from what is the declared truth of the moment. Thus, the lie becomes the truth, or at any rate the distinction between truth and lies, in the ordinary sense of these words, disappears. This is the great triumph of socialism in the sphere of knowledge: to the extent that it succeeds in demolishing the notion of truth, it cannot be accused of lying." Quoted by Dmitri Volkogonov, *Autopsy for an Empire,* translated and edited by Harold Shukman (New York: Free Press, 1998), 393.

2. See, e.g., Associated Press stories such as Lynn Berry, "Soviet-Nazi Pact Revisited 70 Years Later," available at http://wash ingtontimes.com/news/2009/aug/23/soviet-nazi-pact-revisited -70-years-later; Mike Eckel, "Russian Military Historian Blames Poland for WWII," available at www.seattlepi.com/ national/1103ap_eu_russia_poland_wwii.html.

3. The notion that in recent years the situation has improved is highly questionable. When, within the last few years, a respected Soviet researcher and historian "wrote a sentence with which no Western scholar would disagree: that the Soviet Army occupied Lithuania . . . prior to the outbreak of the war. . . . He was officially reprimanded for what was considered slander. . . . If he ever wrote anything of that sort again, he would be kicked out of the institute and lose his pension and the subsidy for his apartment." The incident is recorded (and expanded) by Jonathan Brent, *Inside Stalin's Archives* (New York: Atlas, 2008), 320–21. Note as well the comment by David Glantz about the "new" official history in *Red Storm over the Balkans: The Failed Soviet Invasion of Romania, Spring 1944* (Lawrence: University Press of Kansas, 2007), 371. Fifty years on, it is doubtful that much of the basic information will ever be released.

4. A good example is the titles of section headings relating to Stalin at war: "The Bungling Genius" and the "Triumphant Genius" in Simon Sebag Montefiore, *Stalin: The Court of the Red Tsar* (New York: Random House, 2005), ix.

5. Milovan Djilas, *Conversations with Stalin,* translated by Michael

B. Petrovich (New York: Harcourt, Brace, 1983), 55. By indirection, this conversation gives a good sense of Zhukov's abilities and his place in the war effort.

6. As quoted by Gerhard Ritter, in *Der Schlieffenplan: Kritik eines Mythos* (München: Oldenbourg, 1956), 54.

7. British historian Anthony Beevor, in an interview in the *Telegraph*, January 24, 2002, available at www.telegraph.co.uk/news/worldnews/europe/russia/1382565.

8. Data from Alexei Tolstoy, *Stalin's Secret War* (New York: Holt, Rinehart & Winston, 1981), 269. See also his discussion of Soviet atrocities (268–70). A practical illustration of the extent to which the well-researched claims of émigré analysts were simply ignored, even though we now have ample confirmation of their basic accuracy, as the quote referenced in the note directly above establishes.

9. Data from Jean Restayn, *Tiger I on the Eastern Front* (Paris: Histoire & Collections, 2001), 83. Given the kill ratio in armored engagements during the Middle Eastern wars after 1967, one would assume that at some point the inferiority of Soviet weaponry would have become reasonably obvious. That view would be incorrect: the imbalance was explained as owing to the ineptitude and poor training of the Egyptian and Syrian tank crews, as though the Red Army of 1941–1945 (or afterward) was much different.

10. Martin Gilbert, *Churchill, a Life* (New York: Holt, 1991), 827. The quotation is from a speech made in the House of Commons during which "Churchill tried to calm the widespread unease about the future of Poland."

11. Quote from Montefiore (*Stalin*, 607), who concludes this passage by noting "his [Stalin's] subordinates were worried by his reckless challenge to America and failing powers of judgment." Of course in the highly successful Soviet wilderness of refracting mirrors, the inconvenient fact of Stalin starting the Korean War was easily hidden. See as well the revealing discussion, based on Chinese documents, in Jung Chang and Jon Halliday, *Mao: The Unknown Story* (New York: Random House, 2005), 350–53. The title of their chapter is "Why Mao and Stalin Started the Korean War."

12. The skeptical reader who wonders if this controversy is a paper tiger is referred to the detailed summaries in Hubert P. van

Tuyll, *Feeding the Bear* (Westport, Conn.: Greenwood, 1989), 1–17.

13. Joseph Stalin, *The Great Patriotic War of the Soviet Union* (New York: International Publishers, 1945), 20.

14. For German data, see the archival extractions cited in Hartmut Schustereit, *Vabanque: Hitlers Angriff auf die Sowjetunion 1941 als Versuch, durch den Sieg im Osten den Westen zu bezwingen* (Selent: Pour le Merite, 2002), 147–49. For conventional Soviet figures, see the table in Keith E. Bonn (editor) *Slaughterhouse: The Handbook of the Eastern Front* (Bedford, Pennsylvania: Aberjona, 2004), 10.

15. Most of the key works on the 1937 census are in Russian, but there is a good English language summary at http:// en.wikipedia.org/wiki/Soviet_Census_(1937). More scholarly treatments (in Russian) may be found at the following locations (increasingly Russian scholarship is available online): http://de moscope.ru/weekly/knigi/polka/gold_fund08.html and http:// demoscope.ru/weekly/2007/0271/arxivo1.php, www.polit.ru/ research/2006/01/16/demography.html. The brief discussion that follows relies on data taken from these sources. Revealingly, there is no mention of Stalin's reaction to the census in standard Western treatments of his life.

16. Stalin understood the importance of internal consistency in using numbers. When the results of the next census appeared (the 1959 census), even though there had been a twenty-year time lag, and the prewar census was probably wildly inaccurate, expert demographers were able to make some extremely important deductions about population growth from which it could easily be inferred that the shortage of manpower in European Russia was reaching the critical stage: there were not enough people to carry out the basic tasks a modernizing society needed, much less to maintain a modern army.

17. This example taken from Harry Schwartz, *The Soviet Economy Since Stalin* (New York: Lippincott, 1963), 29; see also notes 11 and 12, page 247, which cite the Russian sources. To put the 92 million ton figure in perspective: in 1913 Russia had produced 76.5 million tons for a population of 139.3 million souls, enough to make it the world's largest exporter of grain. If the 1959 census was to be believed, then the amount of grain per capita had decreased by over 10 percent. Nor is this surprising. In *Soviet*

Agriculture (New York: Norton, 1987), Zhores A. Medvedev had demonstrated a steady decline both in the yields of basic foodstuffs and in per capita availability in the years before the war. See Table 5, page 119.

18. Nikolai Shmelev and Vladimir Popov, *The Turning Point: Revitalizing the Soviet Economy*, translated by Michele Brady (New York: Doubleday, 1989), 23. The epigraph for this chapter is a quotation from Lewis Carroll's *Alice in Wonderland*. As the authors point out, "this chapter [on Soviet statistical distortions] is probably the most technical in the book, but it is absolutely essential" (23). See also Mark Harrison, "The Soviet Union: The Defeated Victor," in *The Economics of World War II: Six Great Powers in International Comparison*, edited by Mark Harrison (Cambridge: Cambridge University Press, 1998): "Compounding the conceptual discrepancies were practical problems of distortion, concealment, and fabrication" (280).

19. An interesting example: long after the fact, Beijing insisted that the total number of Chinese "volunteers" who were killed in the Korean War was 152,000, even though privately several Chinese officials in a position to know pegged the actual figure as 400,000 dead (Chang and Halliday, *Mao*, 372). The matter would be entirely inconsequential to an understanding of the USSR, except that when one takes the multiplier in the Chinese example and applies it to the official Soviet data, the result is surprisingly close to the independent and objective estimates of Soviet losses. As a point of comparison: American deaths in the conflict came to 36,918 dead from all causes.

20. Allied totals from Steve Zaloga and James Grandsen, *Soviet Tanks and Combat Vehicles of World War Two* (London: Arms & Armour, 1984), 119, 125. Soviet factories allegedly produced 78,126 vehicles during the same period. See also van Tuyll, *Feeding the Bear*, Table 10, page 157. A good instance of how the Soviet penchant for giving things misleading names (the use of "fronts" and "armies" and "mechanized corps" to denote forces that were noticeably smaller) supports the effect produced by the fabricated data.

21. 363,080 trucks, 43,728 jeeps, and 32,200 motorcycles, in addition to 7,179 personnel carriers. Data in the sentences following taken from van Tuyll, *Bear*, Table 10, page 157.

22. As quoted by Shmelev and Popov (*Turning Point*, 44). The au-

thors draw the same conclusion as here: "Stalin did not think the war was so terrible as the battle for collectivization" (44). Tellingly, in *Stalin*, Montefiore cites only a portion of Stalin's remarks, leaving out the numbers (422).

CHAPTER XIV: EPILOGUE: THE GREAT PATRIOTIC WAR AND THE COLLAPSE

1. C. V. Wedgwood, *The Thirty Years War* (London: Jonathan Cape, 1956 [1938]), the concluding paragraph, page 528.
2. The most recent authoritative study of the Thirty Years War begins its analysis of the effects of that war by noting that history, "unlike literature, unfortunately has no obvious conclusion. The significance of the Thirty Years' War has been a bone of contention for both historians and politicians ever since it came to an end," and the thirty pages that follow certainly support that contention. Everyone knows the war was significant, but historians have had great difficulty in establishing tangible measures of its impact. In the decades since Wedgwood's study we have accumulated a great deal more data, but anyone comparing her conclusions to the most recent ones will be disappointed. Quote from Geoffrey Parker, editor, *The Thirty Years' War*, 2nd edition (London: Routledge, 1997), 170. But the great historians of earlier days were willing to take a stab at "obvious conclusions," even though they realized the immense difficulty of such an enterprise.
3. John J. Pershing, *My Experiences in the World War* (New York: Stokes, 1931), 2:119.
4. "The extent and timing of this policy is confirmed by so many sources that no real difference of opinion exists in this regard: What is strange is how scantily it has been covered so far in the scholarly literature." Walter Sanning, "Soviet Scorched-Earth Warfare: Facts and Consequences," *The Journal for Historical Review* 6 no. 1 (Spring 1986): 91–119, available at www.ihr.org/jhr/vo6/vo6p-91_Sanning.html.
5. Elizabeth Pond, in *From the Yaroslavsky Station* (New York: Universe, 1981): "it seems the closest I can get to the man on the street is the woman on the train.... All my visits to collective farms ... have been meticulously planned to exclude

any risk of unplanned conversation with plain farmers.... Foreign correspondents are shielded from any spontaneous contact with proletarians" (pp. 16–17). Pond also cites this data (192).

6. Jack F. Matlock, Jr., *Autopsy on an Empire* (New York: Random House, 1995), 43. Matlock goes on to say that "Most observers of the Soviet political process, and, for that matter, virtually all the participants in it, assumed that Party control was unshakable for the foreseeable future" (44). There is a note to the nationalities quote in the text: "Some Western scholars agreed with this analysis." Matlock cites Jerry Hough, *Russia and the West* (New York: Simon & Schuster, 1987), 105–7.

7. Quote from Zhores Medvedev, *Andropov* (New York: Norton, 1983), 67. Estimate of arrests from Olga Shatunovskaya, a member of the control committee under Khrushchev, according to David Remnick, *Lenin's Tomb* (New York: Random House, 1993), 115. See the figures cited, among the many, by Alan Bullock, *Hitler and Stalin: Parallel Lives* (New York: Knopf, 1992), 507.

8. Fyodor Dostoevsky, *The Possessed*, translated by Constance Garnett (New York: Barnes & Noble Classics, 2005), 416.

9. For instance, when the Art Theater "staged a comedy on the topic" of multiple families being forced to share a common apartment, Stanislavsky, whom the regime lavished attention on, was aghast. "Stanislavsky said 'It can't be! It can't be that people don't have their own apartments. You're pulling my leg.'" Fifty years later, the carefully screened visitors who were allowed into western Europe were told that the massive sound-deadening walls bordering urban stretches of the autobahn were built to hide the wretched plight of the workers of West Germany. The Stanislavsky anecdote recorded by Shostakovich (who witnessed it) in *Testimony: The Memoirs of Dmitri Shostakovich*, as related to and edited by Solomon Volkov, translated by Antonina W. Bouis (New York: Harper & Row, 1979), 91–92.

10. The enormous "Sources and References" sections in John Erickson's massive two-volume study of the war comprise literally hundreds of pages listing (mostly) Soviet accounts. Taken together they weave a highly convincing picture of an invasion doomed to failure, which is exactly what Stalin intended and what his heirs largely ensured. Twenty years after the collapse

of the USSR, established British historians are still accepting all Soviet statistical data and eyewitness accounts at face value. See, for example, Richard Evans, *The Third Reich at War* (New York: Penguin, 2009), esp. 707, where Evans appears to accept the official Red Army casualty figures; and 330–31, where he takes Soviet armaments production figures at face value. Such bland acceptances ensure that the Stalinist myth will have a long life.

11. Gabriel Gorodetsky, *The Grand Delusion: Stalin and the German Invasion of Russia* (New Haven: Yale University Press, 1999), x.

12. The official claim, that in 1943 the USSR produced 32.3 million kilowatts of electricity, or three times what it had been generating before the war, is not believable. Figure taken from Hubert P. van Tuyll, *Feeding the Bear* (Westport, Conn.: Greenwood, 1989), Table 31, page 172.

13. See the data offered by the official Soviet history (*Vaterländischen Krieges*, 2: 593–605). Estimates such as these suggest that the Soviet wartime data for subsequent production is fanciful. In 1940 the USSR allegedly produced 165.9 million tons of coal. In 1941 the number had dropped to 142.8, and by 1942, to 75.5. The trend supports the German data in general, although the numbers don't work out, and the claimed total production for 1943 (93.1 million tons) seems highly improbable. But then who knows what the baseline figure was for 1940? It's curious that production rises in every single category by almost the same percentage. See the data presented in tabular form in van Tuyll (*Feeding the Bear*, Table 43, page 180). Van Tuyll is one in a series of extremely diligent and scrupulous researchers who labor under the assumption that Soviet statistics are accurate, and that Soviet authors should be treated as though they were French or Germans writing on similar subjects.

14. The extent to which foreigners were not allowed to wander around freely in either the USSR or East Germany cannot be emphasized enough. Even in those countries where the restrictions were by comparison nonexistent (once one secured a visa and was allowed in), very few people drove around the countryside or through small towns. Of that small number, precious few seemed to notice even the most obvious. James Oberg's account of the reactions of the American scientist who was in Sverdlovsk during the 1979 public health crisis reveals a typical case; he terms the man's experiences as "puzzling," an extremely charitable

explanation. See James Oberg, *Uncovering Soviet Disasters: Exploring the Limits of Glasnost* (New York: Random House, 1988), 20–43.

15. "Germany was our Eden," the spouse of a high-ranking Soviet officer said afterward. Given the dismal state of affairs there, this was compelling testimony to the quality of life in the Soviet Union, and one of the reasons that for Soviet citizens, a trip to Prague or Warsaw, a visit to Bulgaria, was regarded as a significant plum. From a conversation recorded by Jonathan Brent, *Inside Stalin's Archives* (New York: Atlas, 2008), 284.

16. The Belomorsko–Baltiyskiy Kanal is a fine example of this mentality. Often called the White Sea or Belomor Canal, it was an inland waterway designed to connect the Baltic with the White Sea. It was built by slave labor and opened with great fanfare in 1933 and touted as an example of what socialism was capable of building. "But the canal's capacity for transporting cargo was limited. . . . In 1940 the canal was used to 44 percent of capacity, and in 1950, to 20 percent." It largely stands "as an expensive monument to mismanagement." Conclusions quoted from Mikhail Morukov, "The White Sea–Baltic Canal," in Paul Gregory and Valery Lazarev, editors, *The Economics of Forced Labor: The Soviet Gulag* (Stanford, California: Hoover Institution Press, 2003), 161–62.

17. The lack of a "major motor road" across the country is grudgingly admitted in Roy Mellor, *The Soviet Union and Its Geographical Problems* (Atlantic Highlands, New Jersey: Humanities Press, 1982), 166; see the elliptical references to the other road problems (165–67). But the data provided by this extremely sympathetic source is still revealing: only a little over half (53 percent) of the officially classified "motor roads" were paved, and the ratio of road to rail is about a fifth of what it is in western Europe (166). The reasonably well known photographs of cars and trucks floundering in a sea of mud that are easily available online are all taken from the "highway" to Irkutsk.

18. Serge Schmemann, *Echoes of a Native Land: Two Centuries of a Russian* Village (New York: Vintage, 1997), 13. Some pages later he describes the road as a "river of mud" and invokes Gogol (39). The physical damage done to the largely ruined and sparsely inhabited village he writes about in this book occurred during the

1920s, and was not a result of any German offensive. Examples such as this make for a certain amount of skepticism regarding the drumbeat of Soviet claims as to the extent to which the physical destruction of the USSR can be charged off to the Germans. At this time the issue is incapable of resolution.

19. Soviet data from the Soviet official history (*Vaterländischen Krieges*, 1.488); note that the prewar figure given for 1913 is actually the figure for 1903. The correct figures are in J. N. Westwood, *A History of Russian Railways* (London: Allen & Unwin, 1964), Appendix 4. Although much was made of the need for modernization after the Bolsheviks took over, very little new track was constructed in the 1930s: from 1933 to 1939 less than 5,000 kilometers, roughly 5 percent of the existing track, was unusable. See the discussion in Gregory and Lazarev (*Economics of Forced Labor*, 62–63). With a few exceptions, the rail lines of 1941 were the rail lines of 1914–1918, as a surprising amount of railway construction took place during World War I: see the summary in Mellor (*Soviet Union and Its Geographical Problems*, 155).

20. In the words of an extremely sympathetic geographer: "Although strategically and politically desirable, the dispersal of industry . . . posed critical transport problems, most serious in the eastern regions where the transport structure was distinctly backward" (Mellor, *Soviet Union and Its Geographical Problems*, 149). Typically, many of the problems are blamed on the climate; Mellor speaks of "real damage by frost distortion . . . every spring long lengths of track have to be virtually relaid. . . . Temporary speed restrictions and axle-load limits" (155). But none of these issues seems to have a significant impact on rail operations in Canada or Scandinavia. The key indicator of poor maintenance and design: passenger trains on key routes such as Petrograd–Moscow were faster in 1905 than in 1955 (Westwood, *History of Russian Railways*, 150).

21. During the period 1940–1945, 2.725 million people were relocated (to use a euphemism). Another 2.66 million had suffered the same treatment in the decades before the war, and another 400,000 were moved in the years afterward, for a total of nearly six million. See the table in Pavel Polian, *Against Their Will: The History and Geography of Forced Migrations in the USSR* (New

York: Central European University Press, 2004), 319. These totals do not count foreign nationals, i.e., citizens of the Baltic States, Poland, and ethnic Germans and Finns, or prisoners of war.

22. Marx's heirs seemed to take the phrase "industrial revolution" literally, as though it was something that could bring about change in a few short years, as had been the case with the two great revolutions of the eighteenth century. In Great Britain the process went on for a very long time, at least a century, and the changes were incremental or evolutionary: there was little about them that was revolutionary. Three important factors made the British case unique. The pre-industrial Britain of 1688 was already wealthy and prosperous. The political climate after that year was, by the European standards of the time, a model of tolerance and freedom; it encouraged people with valuable skills to move there and allowed them to flourish once they did. Finally, the long slow process of modernization was preceded as well as accompanied by an agricultural shift toward greater productivity. Although the details of these shifts, as well as their causes, are still a mystery (like the effects of the Thirty Years War noted at the start of this chapter), the basic outlines are well known, at least to economic historians. See the account in Peter Mathias, *The First Industrial Revolution: An Economical History of Britain, 1700–1804* (New York: Charles Scribner's Sons, 1969). Curiously, despite its self-proclaimed categorization as a "scientific" philosophy, and its emphasis on the importance of economic factors in history, economic history in the USSR had progressed little beyond a sort of rote recapitulation of Marx, who, regardless of the brilliance of a few insights (business cycles, for instance), was in many respects fundamentally wrong, just as his predecessor, Thomas Malthus, had been wrong about population growth outstripping food production (he may ultimately prove correct, but in the context of his predictions he was wrong). But their errors had been philosophical and rational: at the time they wrote, their accounts were logical. A century later the simplistic application of outdated theories was a ticket to disaster.

23. Murray Feshbach, *The Soviet Union: Population Trend and Dilemmas*, Population Bulletin 37, no. 2 (August 1982): 15. On the basis of his analysis of the officially recorded data, Feshbach, usu-

ally regarded as one of the West's leading authorities on Soviet demographics, concluded that "Soviet demographic problems are interwoven with the country's serious economic problems" (5). His analysis, like that of Emmanuel Todd in *La chute final: essai sur la décomposition de la sphère soviétique* (Paris: Editions Robert Laffont, [1975]) and Medvedev (*Soviet Agriculture*), sidesteps the thorny issue of the extent to which Soviet statistics were falsified and/or exaggerated: there is a certain consistency even in fictionalized data.

24. Thus the declining birth rate in western Russia exacerbated the rising nationalist tensions referred to earlier. Feshbach, looking at the record of the 1980 session of the Supreme Soviet, noted the connection in 1982 (in *Soviet Union*, 18–21), cautiously concluding that "some" Western observers have also made the connection (20).

25. See the analysis in Medvedev of the shortages of drivers for tractors, trucks, and harvesters, a practical implication of the demographical problem (*Soviet Agriculture*, 286–87).

26. Todd, *La chute final*; the final pages of the revised edition (Paris: Laffont, 1990), in which Todd reproduces the scathing comments of his original critics (368–72), are a grimly amusing reminder of the frailty of the assumptions of specialists.

27. Shostakovich (*Testimony*, 136). The same paradoxical feeling is captured hauntingly in Larissa Shepitko's early film *Wings* (1966), in the alienation of the decorated female aviator who is the central character of the film.

28. As is the case with many statements that seem extreme, this one is quantitatively precise: "of the 700 writers at the first congress of the writers' union in 1934, Ilya Ehrenburg estimates that 'possibly' 50 were still alive in 1960": Ian MacDonald, *The New Shostakovich* (Boston: Northeastern University Press, 1990), 107.

29. Data and quotation from Dmitri Volkogonov, *Stalin: Triumph and Tragedy*, translated and edited by Harold Shukman (New York: Grove Weidenfeld, 1988), 307.

30. Vladimir Bukovsky, *To Build a Castle: My Life as a Dissenter*, translated by Michael Scammell (New York: Viking, 1978), 189. Educated citizens in the West, who grew up hearing about the tyranny of the czars, fail to comprehend the differences. As Bukovsky remarks, "We forget that the Bolsheviks worked in condi-

tions of relative freedom to establish tyranny, and not the other way around. . . . The entire Russian secret police was housed in a two-story building too small even for a district police station today" (119). Volkogonov's comparison is even more to the point: "At the turn of the century, the exile population of Siberia was one third of a million, of whom political exiles made up about one percent [roughly 3,300 souls], plus about 11,000 doing hard labor" (*Stalin*, 562).

INDEX